TOOLKITS,
TRANSLATION DEVICES
AND CONCEPTUAL ACCOUNTS

Alan R. Sadovnik and Susan F. Semel
General Editors

Vol. 51

PETER LANG
New York • Washington, D.C./Baltimore • Bern
Frankfurt • Berlin • Brussels • Vienna • Oxford

TOOLKITS, TRANSLATION DEVICES AND CONCEPTUAL ACCOUNTS

Essays on Basil Bernstein's Sociology of Knowledge

Edited by
**PARLO SINGH,
ALAN R. SADOVNIK,**
and **SUSAN F. SEMEL**

PETER LANG
New York • Washington, D.C./Baltimore • Bern
Frankfurt • Berlin • Brussels • Vienna • Oxford

Library of Congress Cataloging-in-Publication Data

Toolkits, translation devices and conceptual accounts: essays on Basil Bernstein's
sociology of knowledge / Edited by Parlo Singh, Alan R. Sadovnik, Susan F. Semel.
p. cm. — (History of schools and schooling; v. 51)
Includes bibliographical references and index.
1. Bernstein, Basil B.—Criticism and interpretation. 2. Educational sociology.
3. Knowledge, Sociology of. 4. Critical pedagogy. I. Singh, Parlo.
II. Sadovnik, Alan R. III. Semel, Susan F.
LB880.B462.T66   306.43—dc22   2010009682
ISBN 978-1-4331-0364-3
ISSN 1089-0678

Bibliographic information published by **Die Deutsche Nationalbibliothek**.
Die Deutsche Nationalbibliothek lists this publication in the "Deutsche
Nationalbibliografie"; detailed bibliographic data is available
on the Internet at http://dnb.d-nb.de/.

The paper in this book meets the guidelines for permanence and durability
of the Committee on Production Guidelines for Book Longevity
of the Council of Library Resources.

© 2010 Peter Lang Publishing, Inc., New York
29 Broadway, 18th floor, New York, NY 10006
www.peterlang.com

All rights reserved.
Reprint or reproduction, even partially, in all forms such as microfilm,
xerography, microfiche, microcard, and offset strictly prohibited.

Printed in the United States of America

Table of Contents

Acknowledgments ix

Chapter 1.
  Introduction. 1
  PARLO SINGH, ALAN R. SADOVNIK AND SUSAN F. SEMEL

Chapter 2.
  Basil Bernstein as an Inspiration for Educational Research:
  Specific Methodological Approaches. 11
  ANA M. MORAIS AND ISABEL P. NEVES

Chapter 3.
  Educational Policy and Social Reproduction 33
  BRIAN DAVIES, JOHN EVANS AND JOHN FITZ

Chapter 4.
  The Structure of Pedagogic Discourse as a Relay for Power:
  The Case of Competency-Based Training 47
  LEESA WHEELAHAN

Chapter 5.
   Social Class and Pedagogy 65
   URSULA HOADLEY

Chapter 6.
   Pedagogic Discourse and Sex Education:
   Myths, Science and Subversion 85
   GABRIELLE IVINSON

Chapter 7.
   Subject Position and Identity in Changing Workplaces 103
   HARRY DANIELS

Chapter 8.
   Exploring the Transmission of Moral Order as Invisible
   Semiotic Mediator of Tacit Knowledge 121
   JEANNE GAMBLE

Chapter 9.
   Towering TIMSS or Leaning PISA? Vertical and
   Horizontal Models of International Testing Regimes 143
   WILLIAM TYLER

Chapter 10.
   Pedagogy and Moral Order 161
   JOHAN MULLER AND URSULA HOADLEY

Chapter 11.
   Invisible Tribunals: Progress and Knowledge-Building
   in the Humanities 177
   KARL MATON

Chapter 12.
   The Moral Career of Intelligence, Pedagogical Practices
   and Educational Psychology 197
   KAREN BRADLEY AND JOHN G. RICHARDSON

Chapter 13.
   School Development and Leadership in
   Norwegian Demonstration Schools 217
   RITA RIKSAASEN

Chapter 14.
  Bernstein and Empirical Research 239
  SALLY POWER

Chapter 15.
  Pedagogic Translations: Dominant Pedagogic Modes
  and Teacher Professional Identity 249
  PARLO SINGH AND JESSICA HARRIS

Contributors 267

Index 273

Acknowledgments

The chapters in this book originally were presented at the Fourth Basil Bernstein Research Symposium at Rutgers-University-Newark in July 2006. The conference would not have been possible without the administrative assistance of Diane Hill, Director of Campus and Community Relations, for ensuring that the important details for housing, food and space were handled in a most effective manner; and Yanique Taylor, Research Assistant in the Ph.D. program in Urban Systems, for her outstanding assistance in the administration of the symposium and in the editing and production of this book. We thank the Chancellor's Office at Rutgers-Newark for making the university available and for their in-kind support.

We also thank the Conference Committee, who in addition to the editors included Johan Muller and Sally Power. Their contributions to the selection of the original conference papers and the chapters in this book are greatly appreciated.

Finally, we thank Christopher Myers, Director of Peter Lang Publishing, for once again supporting the publication of the fourth collection of papers from the Bernstein symposia. In publishing the first and now the fourth collection as part of our (Sadovnik and Semel) History of Schools and Schooling series, Chris has supported the history of the sociology of education in general and the history of research on the work of Basil Bernstein in particular.

CHAPTER ONE

Introduction

PARLO SINGH, ALAN R. SADOVNIK AND SUSAN F. SEMEL

Basil Bernstein's sociology of education, particularly his earlier work of the 1960s on code theory and access to and acquisition of school knowledge, became caught up in the debates about cultural and language difference versus deficit. This was despite Bernstein's adamant stance that his research project had always been about understanding the unequal distribution and acquisition of school knowledge. The misinterpretation of his earlier work meant that Basil Bernstein's theories often became associated with deficit accounts of 'Other' students—an ironic position given that Bernstein was always unwavering about his political and ideological stance—a stance which stressed that educational failure did not rest with the students, but rather with the educational institutions. Over a period of four decades, Basil Bernstein drew attention to the ways in which educational institutions failed to provide working class students with access to powerful forms of knowledge.

> I do not understand how we can talk about offering compensatory education to children who, in the first place, have as yet not been offered an adequate educational experience.... The concept of 'compensatory education' serves to direct attention away from the internal organization and the educational context of the school, and focus our attention upon the families and the children. The concept 'compensatory education' implies that something is lacking in the family and so in the child. As a result, the children are unable to benefit from schools. It follows then that the school has to 'compensate' for the something which is missing in the family and the children become little deficit systems (Bernstein, 1971: 191–192)

Bernstein's research project over four decades was on 'the internal organisation and educational context of the school' specifically, and educational systems generally. Specifically, he was interested in the powerful forms of knowledge transmitted through schooling systems, and who gained access to these forms of knowledge, how, and with what consequences. His research project started with examining differences in language and communication patterns between the institutions of the home/family and school, and extended to examining the structuring of pedagogic discourse from the level of the state to the classroom.

The collection of papers in this edited volume, by researchers from South Africa, Portugal, United Kingdom, United States, and Australia, build on the theoretical concepts developed by Basil Bernstein to explore issues of access and acquisition to school knowledge. In addition, the papers explore the strengths and limitations of Bernstein's work for understanding the structuring of educational institutions, as well as the potential of the theory for assisting educators to make a difference in the lives of students.

In what follows, we summarise the main arguments developed by the authors in this collection into three categories: toolkits, translation devices, and conceptual accounts. By the term toolkit, we refer to the ways in which Bernsteinian theory is applied to empirical data and offers strategies to practitioners to improve educational and social practices. By contrast, the term translation device is used to refer to the ways in which Bernsteinian theory is synthesised and translated into different theoretical frameworks and empirical contexts to extend the purview of the language of description. Finally, the category conceptual account refers to the way scholars take up and extend specific concepts within the Bernsteinian framework. Of course, the work of scholars is likely to variously fit within all three categories. Consequently, the distinctions that we have drawn are purely arbitrary.

Toolkit

Morais and Neves's chapter (Chapter 2) provides a discussion of the mixed-methods methodology their research group in Lisbon has used to empirically test Bernstein's theory over the past three decades. Arguing that Bernstein's theories require both qualitative and quantitative approaches to studying classroom organisation and pedagogies in the sciences and their effects on achievement, they show how their research design has attempted to capture Bernstein's concepts of classification and framing and their differential effects on students from different social class backgrounds. The chapter provides a toolkit for moving from theory to empirical testing of that theory.

Davies et al., in Chapter 3, ask what Bernstein has 'to say about educational policy and social production.' Drawing on their own work and the work of research students and scholars from Palestine, Wales, Britain, and South Africa, they argue that Bernstein's concepts of pedagogic discourse and pedagogic device provide analytic tools for conceptualising 'policy origins, processes and destinations sociologically.' Recent policy changes in Britain, they argue, are aimed at narrowing the curriculum by demarcating what constitutes core and peripheral subjects, and are also aimed at officially telling teachers how to teach. Thus, a call to skills-based teaching as opposed to whole language instruction represents a significant shift in forms of pedagogic communication, and ultimately pedagogic identities of teachers and students. The question then becomes which factions of the middle class are pressuring for a particular policy direction and for what desired ends? And how do these power struggles over the pedagogic device, that is, the rules for the production, distribution, and evaluation of school knowledge, get played out in different contexts of the educational bureaucracy, and with what consequences for teachers and students? Davies et al. conclude that Bernsteinian sociology provides a 'finer grain detail of how policy gets made, where and by whom, and how it simultaneously regulates, educates and controls; with firmer grasp of how it is recontextualised and enacted and better understanding of how knowledge, ideology and morality are embedded in the actions of teachers, pupils and schools.'

Working out of the Australian context, Leesa Wheelahan (Chapter 4) applies Bernstein's theoretical ideas to an analysis of the curriculum and pedagogic models of training packages used in the vocational education and training sector. Wheelahan argues that competency-based training packages disadvantage working class students because they only provide 'students with access to contextually specific applications of knowledge, and not the system of meaning in which it is embedded.' The higher education sector in Australia is comprised of a university and technical and further education sector (TAFE). Wheelahan argues that the curriculum and pedagogic models of competency-based training adopted by the TAFE sector fails to provide students with abstract, disciplinary knowledge, which would enable them to 'study at higher levels and participate actively in debates and controversies shaping their field of practice.' Rather than acting as a device for social inclusion, competency-based training packages continue to marginalise working class students.

Hoadley in Chapter 5 also takes up the issue of differential access and acquisition of school knowledge. The focus of empirical analysis for Hoadley is two primary school literacy classrooms, one in a middle class area ('racially integrated') and one in a working class area ('black learners and teachers') in post-apartheid South Africa. Given the wide-ranging studies of classroom communication across the globe, what is the new contribution offered by Hoadley in this study? Specifically, Hoadley offers teachers a toolkit for analysing classroom communication, and thereby understanding their own role in contributing to educational inequality. Three main concepts form the basis of Hoadley's analytic framework, namely:

1. Power and control relations of pedagogic discourse: instructional, regulative, spaces, and agents.
2. Instructional form: (a) content and (b) classroom strategies
3. Instructional strategies: (a) individual tasks and (b) pedagogic assemblies

As Hoadley argues, the differential distribution of knowledge to students produces different forms of pedagogic identity and different orientations to meaning (abstract/context-independent; particular/context-dependent). Hoadley's analytic framework provides teachers with a toolkit for moving from an analysis of the specificities of everyday classroom talk to a whole class lesson, to a unit of work, to curriculum planning.

Ivinson's chapter (Chapter 6) applies Bernstein's theory of pedagogic discourse to sex education in the schools. She demonstrates the usefulness of Bernstein's theory in understanding the content of sex education and the pedagogic practices in its implementation. In examining the implementation of sex education in the schools, Ivinson uncovers the myths surrounding it, how scientific knowledge attempts to demystify the topic, and how school practices often subvert demystified knowledge.

All five studies described in the preceding section assert the importance of giving teachers access to tools that will enable them to code their own curriculum practices (planned, enacted, reflected). Teachers also need toolkits that will assist them to systematically develop pedagogic models for ensuring that learners 'deploy the specialised knowledge' of schooling in ways that move from context dependency to context independency, across space and time, within a lesson, and across a unit of work. In order to bring about educational reform, teachers need to take up positions as informed professionals and engage in collaborative professional learning conversations (see Singh and Harris, Chapter 15, this volume). This means that they need access to and acquisition of the types of toolkits described above.

Translation Device

The studies in this section synthesise Bernstein's theoretical ideas with concepts from social psychological studies, namely, the social semiotics of pedagogic communication. The studies propose that pedagogic communication is a semiotic mediator for the generation and formation of mental dispositions, habits of the mind, typical ways of responding to situations, and the acquisition of knowledge, concepts, and skills.

Semiotic communication is not only comprised of everyday classroom talk, but also modes of conduct, character, and posture, that is, the modelling of particular behaviours, dispositions, and demeanours. The term semiotic refers to the complexity and visibility of the discursive signification system.

Writing on a research project about interagency work in the United Kingdom, Daniels (Chapter 7) uses Bernstein's theoretical work in conjunction with activity theory (Vygotsky, Wertsch, Engeström) to examine the social semiotic construction of hybrid professional identities. Specifically, Daniels asks what mediating tools (talk, maps, diagrams) position professionals to take up hybrid identities and effectively solve social problems drawing on multiagency solutions. Daniels draws on Bernstein's ideas of the formation of human consciousness, which place semiotic mediation in the foreground through an analysis of the 'principles of transmission and their embodiment in structures of social relationships.' Bernstein links semiotic tools (principles of transmission) with the structure of material activity (pedagogic relations). From this perspective, a learner's professional development occurs firstly on a social level (meditational tools of pedagogic discourse) and then on a positional level (acquisition of ideas, thoughts, habits, dispositions).

Following the work of Durkheim and Bernstein, Jeanne Gamble (Chapter 8), writing about the South African context, explores the moral order of pedagogy, arguing a link between morality and the social collectivity and 'distinguishing three elements of a social morality, namely discipline, attachment to social groups and autonomy or self-determination.' The focus of Gamble's theoretical analysis is the component of morality dealing with autonomy and self-determination. Her empirical case study is apprenticeship pedagogy for craft work. Gamble argues that the attributes of autonomy or self-determination are acquired through both the instructional and regulative discourses of schooling. She argues that a particular form of work ethic as regulative discourse is taught via modeling behaviors in apprenticeship pedagogy of craft work, and this form of work ethic enables access to abstract and general principles of craft work, which instill worker autonomy. In other words, 'an orientation to meaning that can deal with a measure of abstractness' is transmitted through 'the language of moral conduct rather than through the technical language of mathematics or science.'

Conceptual Accounts

The chapters in this section take concepts from mainly two chapters of the last book published by Bernstein before his death in 2000, *Pedagogy, Symbolic Control, and Identity:* (chapter 4—'Official Knowledge and Pedagogic Identities' and chapter 9 'Vertical and Horizontal Discourse'). A number of the papers deal specifically with the formation of pedagogic identity via pedagogic discourse. The authors also clearly point out that Bernstein was one of the few sociologists exploring the notion of pedagogic identity. Much has been written about identity construction under conditions of global, fluid capitalism. Much of this work has focussed on different modes of identity construction associated with space-time compression, and the availability of new biotechnologies. Resources for identity construction are available across time and space, and increasingly independent of the local context. What role then do schools play in identity construction? Enter the recentred state with its focus on international testing measures, league tables, and control over the 'how of teaching,' Changes in pedagogic identity formation occur when there are changes in modes of pedagogic communication. Therefore it is important to analyse the social context of policy change, and also the structuring of the pedagogic communication through which this change is enacted.

Bill Tyler (Chapter 9) from Australia uses the international testing regimes, TIMMS (Trends in International Mathematics and Science Study)and PISA (Program for International Student Assessment), as case studies to explore aspects of Bernstein's theories about the pedagogic device, pedagogic identities, and pedagogic socialisation. Specifically, Tyler argues following Bernstein that the pedagogic device is the ensemble of rules for the distribution, recontextualisation, and evaluation of knowledge. During the current period of global/liquid capitalism, knowledge is increasingly important for the generation of wealth, and to competition within and between nation states. Accordingly, there is contestation over the pedagogic device as well as the pedagogic identities constituted through this device. During a period of late capitalism, the state increasingly loses power and control over the pedagogic device, as this is appropriated by the owners of capital, and has to re-engage in exercising control. One means to do this is through the site of evaluation. Enter the international testing schemes, which enable the state to regulate what is taught in schools through measuring the output of these institutions through testing. According to Tyler, the two dominant forms of testing, TIMMS and PISA, test knowledge and skills acquired through different modes of curricula. Collection code curricula push for discipline specific pedagogic identities. By contrast, integration code curricula push for interdisciplinary pedagogic identities.

Muller and Hoadley (Chapter 10) consider the regulative component of pedagogic discourse, specifically the relation of regulative discourse to the pedagogic device. Specifically, the chapter explores the genealogy of regulative discourse, and the expression of regulative discourse in each of the hierarchical rules of the pedagogic device, namely rules of distribution, recontextualisation, and evaluation of knowledge. The authors argue that Bernsteinian scholars have focused on an analysis of regulative discourse in terms of the recontextualisation principle, that is, the principle of framing. In turn, this implies that analyses of regulative discourse have focused on control relations in terms of selection and organisation of instructional discourse, and the models of the learner, teacher, and pedagogic relation implicit in the arbitrary ordering of instructional discourse. Such a focus, however, negates the role of regulative discourse in terms of the other two dominant rules of the pedagogic device, that is the distributive rule—who gets access to what categories of knowledge, and the evaluative rule—rules for the condensation of the power relations of the distributive rule. Examining the regulative discourse in terms of the evaluative rule of the pedagogic device 'brings an expanded notion of regulative discourse into play.' The authors also explore links between the Bernsteinian concepts of regulative discourse, moral order, and expressive order 'at different levels of the pedagogic device.' Whereas the expressive order is constituted through rules and rituals and aimed at generating solidarity, collectivity, and consensus, the instrumental order works to differentiate and generate distinctions between social groups and individuals in terms of the acquisition of skills and knowledge.

Karl Maton (Chapter 11) explores recent debates in the humanities about knowledge, knowers, and criteria for evaluating the value of different forms of knowledge. In so doing, he explores and extends Bernstein's concept of knowledge structures and generative grammar for the production, distribution, and acquisition of new forms of knowledge. Maton traces Bernstein's concepts of curricular (collection and integrated) and pedagogic (visible and invisible) codes, and the types of pedagogic identities and orientations to meaning generated through socialisation in these codes. He takes Bernstein's concept of voice and message and develops this into a notion of legitimation code theory—the relation between knower and knowledge structures. Maton uses this theoretical framework to analyse forms of knowledge production and distribution in the field of cultural studies. He proposes that the aim of the new cultural studies project was to socialise working class students into the cultivated gaze of the humanities and thus give them access to powerful forms of knowledge. There was a curricular and pedagogic component to this project. The curricular component was to select knowledge and skills that would be of interest to working class students, the pedagogic component was to use forms of communication that would engage students in learning. This was the first step in the process of educational engagement to bridge the divide between the knowledge acquired in the home and local community and school knowledge. The second step was to ensure that students increasingly gained access to the abstract, context-independent knowledge of school knowledge without reliance on 'relevant' modes of curricula and pedagogy. The problem, Maton argues, is that some popularist forms of cultural studies, based on standpoint epistemology, placed greater emphasis on knower rather than knowledge structures, and thereby failed to provide working class students with access to powerful forms of knowledge.

Contestation and debate are rife amongst the scholars of Bernsteinian theory.

For example, Tyler argues that current extensions of Bernstein's thoughts about vertical and horizontal discourses and vertical and horizontal knowledge structures are 'in danger of losing the main point of Bernstein's project—namely (a) the ways knowledge, power and control interact to reproduce class-based inequalities and (b) secondly his well-documented distinction between the primary or decontextualised fields of knowledge production and its recontextualisation in the classroom or lecture theatre.' Rather than going down the path of vertical and horizontal discourses and knowledge structures, Tyler implores scholars of educational sociology to explore the social-semiotic and social-cultural aspects of Bernstein's theory of pedagogic discourse, which in turn enables an analysis of sites of knowledge production, recontextualisation and evaluation/assessment.

Bradley and Richardson (Chapter 12) apply Bernstein's theories of pedagogic practice and discourse to a historical analysis of the development of the field of educational psychology in the United States. Using a content analysis of educational psychology textbooks in the twentieth century, the authors demonstrate how the field developed in relation to social, historical, and educational forces. Through their empirical analysis, Bradley and Richardson demonstrate how the classification and framing of fields of study change over time and in relation to the social and economic fields of production and reproduction. This chapter provides an important case study of how pedagogic discourse and practices are related to a number of factors outside and inside schools.

Finally, Riksaasen's chapter (Chapter 13) examines changes in pedagogic practices in Norwegian demonstration schools, which implemented a curriculum based on an integration rather than a collection code. Riksaasen analyses how administrators and teachers struggle with these changes and their effects on student learning. The chapter raises significant questions about the appropriate pedagogic practices for students from different social classes and whether students from lower socioeconomic backgrounds need more structured curriculum and pedagogies than students from higher ones. Her study suggests that there are no easy answers to this question, but that the effective implementation of pedagogic practices is central to student achievement.

The concluding section of the book provides two perspectives on the chapters and Bernstein's theories in general.

Commenting on some of the chapters, the work of Paul Dowling and her own work, Sally Power (Chapter 14) presents a critical analysis of the work of researchers working in the Bernstein tradition. She argues that there has been little research based on Bernstein published in the top sociology of education journals, especially the *British Journal of the Sociology of Education*, and that most of the existing work does not provide empirical testing of his theories or move his work forward in significant ways. Part of the blame she places on Bernsteinian researchers and part on

Bernstein himself. She concludes by quoting Bernstein that 'we need less an allegiance to an approach and more a dedication to a problem' (1977:171).

In a different vein, Singh and Harris (Chapter 15) use Bernstein's work and apply it to the problem of teacher identity. This concluding chapter provides examples of how researchers and theorists using Bernstein's work have contributed to our understanding of dominant pedagogic structures and processes and how taken together their research, along with Bernstein's, provided the foundation for theoretical and empirical extensions of Bernstein's project.

Reference

Bernstein, B. (2000). *Pedagogy, Symbolic Control, and Identity*. Lanham MD: Rowman and Littlefield.

CHAPTER TWO

Basil Bernstein as an Inspiration for Educational Research

Specific Methodological Approaches

ANA M. MORAIS AND ISABEL P. NEVES

INTRODUCTION

This chapter clarifies and discusses the research methodology inspired by Basil Bernstein that has guided the extensive studies carried out by the ESSA Group (Sociological Studies of the Classroom) at the University of Lisbon. We discuss how we have used Bernstein's theory (1990, 2000) to develop this methodology and we highlight the characteristics of a 'mixed methodology,' which is applicable to various contexts of educational research. We will start by presenting the epistemological positioning of the research and show the contribution of the methodology to knowledge production in the fields of both education and research methodologies. We will refer to philosophical and sociological aspects of knowledge construction and to the validity and reliability criteria we have used in our research methodology.

We discuss the way we have used Bernstein's theory in developing the research through a conceptual structure that explains the relations used in the construction of models and instruments of analysis of texts and contexts. We describe the paths we have followed in that construction and explicate the theoretical assumptions and the methodological procedures that have guided their conception. Finally, we present some exemplary cases to illustrate our procedures.

Since the chapter discusses earlier research in some detail[1], it may be of more interest to those acquainted with that research. However, we believe that the text may appeal to a larger audience.

Epistemological Positioning of the Research

Quantitative and Qualitative Paradigms

The two forms of inquiry—quantitative and qualitative—are often viewed as distinct and incompatible paradigms in educational research (Shaffer and Serlin, 2004). However, it has also been recognised that distinct methods of analysis are useful for addressing distinct types of questions. For that reason, both techniques are now often used simultaneously. For example, Tashakkori and Teddlie (1998) refer to studies where quantitative and qualitative techniques are used in the same or distinct stages of the same study and assume an equal or different status when research questions are defined. These researchers explain how quantitative analysis can help in identifying subjects for a qualitative study, how qualitative interviews can provide additional elements to quantitative analysis, how qualitative analysis can generate hypotheses for quantitative studies and how quantitative and qualitative data can be obtained simultaneously. As Shaffer and Serlin (2004) state:

> Qualitative and quantitative methods are both, ultimately, methods to warrant presentation of a fair sample. They are both attempts to project from a finite set of information to some larger population: a population of like individuals in the case of typical quantitative inquiry, or a collection of like observations in qualitative analysis. [...] The goal in any analysis is to match technique to inference, claim to warrant. The questions facing a researcher are always: What questions are worth asking in this situation? What data will shed light on those questions? And what analytical methods will warrant data-based claims about those questions? Answering these questions is a task that necessarily involves a thorough understanding of the strengths and weaknesses of a range of quantitative and qualitative techniques. (p. 23)

Similarly, Flyvbjerg (2001) problematises the dichotomies created by the two approaches:

> If not meaningless, it is counterproductive to meaning to speak of 'the victory of signs over difference' or of rules over the particular. [...] To amputate one side in these pairs of phenomena into a dualistic 'either-or' is to amputate our understanding. Rather than the 'either-or,' we should develop a non-dualistic and pluralistic 'both-and.' Hence, we should not criticize rules, logic, signs, and rationality in themselves. We should criticize only the dominance of these phenomena to the exclusion of others in modern society and in social science. Conversely, it should be equally problematic if rules, logic, signs, and rationality were marginalized by the concrete, by difference, and by the particular. [...] (p. 49)

In our research we have assumed that the two forms of inquiry are not incompatible and therefore can be used sequentially or simultaneously, depending on the kind of research questions we want to address and the data we want to obtain. Our research thus departs from the dichotomy between naturalistic approaches (qualitative or ethnographic) and rationalist approaches (quantitative or experimental) and reflects an epistemological positioning that rejects, in particular, the strongly contextualised and idiosyncratic character of qualitative methodologies, guided by postmodernist perspectives in educational research.

The Research in the Framework of Research Methodologies

As we have explained (Morais and Neves, 2001; Morais, 2002), our research methodology has used an external language of description derived from an internal language of description, whereby the theoretical and empirical are viewed dialectically. We reject both the analysis of the empirical without an underlying theoretical basis and uses of theory which do not allow for its transformation on the basis of the empirical. Theories/concepts in the areas of epistemology (e.g. Popper, 1968; Ziman, 1984), psychology (Bruner, 1973; Vygotsky, 1978) and sociology (Bernstein, 1990, 2000) have constituted our main internal languages of description, with particular emphasis on Bernstein's theory of pedagogic discourse. On the basis of this theory, we have constructed an external language of description in order to originate models and instruments to guide the research.

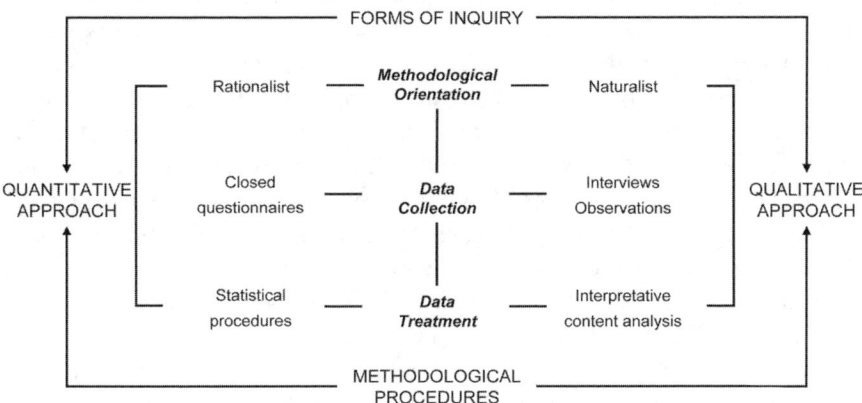

Figure 2.1 Epistemological positioning of the research.

The research methodology may be viewed as a mixed methodology, which does not integrate the two forms of inquiry but, on the contrary, uses characteristics associated with each of them. Figure 2.1 presents aspects of quantitative and qualitative approaches present in the methodological procedures of our research.

The *methodological orientation* has a fundamentally rationalist basis (a characteristic of quantitative approaches) when, for example, we construct models for data analysis on the basis of previous theoretical frameworks. This orientation has allowed us to explore hypotheses on the basis of the guiding theory (experimental hypotheses). However, we have also used a methodological orientation of a naturalistic character (a characteristic of qualitative approaches) when, for example, the indicators and descriptors used in the instruments derived from the models are fundamentally obtained from direct observation of the contexts under study. This more naturalistic approach has allowed the formulation of hypotheses on the basis of empirical data (explanatory hypotheses).

With regard to data collection, we have also used methodological procedures associated with the two forms of inquiry. In fact, for example, together with closed questionnaires (a characteristic of quantitative approaches) we have used more open modes of questioning as in the case of interviews and observations (a characteristic of qualitative approaches). Also at the level of data treatment, we have used quantitative methods (statistical procedures) and qualitative methods (interpretative content analyses).

If we consider other positionings distinct from the two traditional paradigms of educational research, the typology of educational inquiry presented by Constas (1998) can also be useful to situate the research methodology that we have developed. According to this typology, constructed on the basis of the interaction of three dimensions—*political*, *methodological* and *representational*—it is possible to consider eight research prototypes. The *political* dimension of inquiry is present when political issues are investigated and incorporated (as givens) into a particular study and when the effect that power relations may have in the research is analysed and challenged. The *methodological* dimension of inquiry refers to strategies related to the procedures of data collection (in the case of empirically based educational research) and to argumentation techniques (in the case of theoretically based educational research). The *representational* dimension refers to the nature of academic discourse (writing style, lexicon and discourse organisation).

If we take Constas's typology as the reference, we can say that our research departs from narrative and post-modernist research prototypes, which are methodologically idiosyncratic and representationally unbounded. The research we have developed corresponds, to a certain extent, to the research prototype that Constas calls *neo-Marxist inquiry*, and that is characterised by being politically *decentered*, methodologically *normative* and representationally *bounded*. In fact, when we use methodological approaches that are concerned with criteria of validity, reliability and generalisation and a writing style that intends to be objective, the research we have developed is clearly normative and bounded. On the one hand, it also represents a politically decentering variety of educational research because, although our research includes aspects of an inquiry guided by psychological assumptions, it carries a strong sociological basis where power relations are taken as a fundamental component. On the other hand, we may consider that our research has some relation to the research prototype that Constas calls *post-positivist inquiry*, which differs from the former in that it corresponds to a non-political (centering) variety of educational research. To choose one or other position depends on taking for granted power relations, without making them enter in the analyses (as in the case of *post-positivist inquiry*), or considering them as fundamental factors in problematising the study (as in the case of *neo-Marxist inquiry*).

The Research and Knowledge Production

Another fundamental aspect of our research is that its aim is the production of educational knowledge that, although being part of the area of social sciences, is embedded in the knowledge of the area of experimental sciences. In fact, most of the research is centred on science education and, therefore, its object of study is the *how* of learning (seen in terms of the social relations that characterise various pedagogic contexts) of a knowledge that is part of the experimental sciences (*the what* of learning). This means interrelating scientific areas with distinct or even opposed structures of knowledge. As Morais (2001) says:

> Experimental sciences are hierarchical structures of knowledge. Theories of instruction are horizontal structures of knowledge. That is to say that the *what* to be taught in science classes is quite distinct in its structure from the *how* to be taught. (p. 32)

Our research methodology has permitted us to reconcile the apparently irreconcilable, which has been possible because Bernstein's sociological theory, in which our research is fundamentally based, has, 'a very strong conceptual structure which places it[…]within the horizontal structures of knowledge of strong grammars and even, […] in many aspects, within a hierarchical structure of knowledge' (Morais, 2001, p. 33).

From a philosophical point of view, the research has used a fundamentally rationalist approach and, therefore, departs from the research that characterises the construction of a substantial part of knowledge in the area of social sciences, which tends to be based on descriptive and narrative methodologies by following naturalistic and ethnographic approaches. In our research, we have tried to produce educational knowledge characterised by a strong grammar rather than by a weak grammar. That is, the new knowledge is progressively more conceptualised and broader instead of being added to previous knowledge. This conceptualisation has also occurred in the production of knowledge at the level of the research methodology itself. Thus, our research has led to the production of two types of knowledge: educational knowledge (research product) and knowledge in the area of the research methodologies (research process).

When we consider the research not only with regard to the philosophical dimension of knowledge production, but also to its internal and external sociological dimension[2], some issues can be raised related to the legitimation of ideas at both the levels of research methodology and the knowledge obtained.

The research has blurred the boundaries between fields of educational knowledge that traditionally have been strongly classified, as in the case of sociology of education and science education. For this reason, it has introduced in the academic community an unusual perspective in both the area of science education and the area of sociology of education. This raises issues related to the internal sociological dimension of knowledge production. We refer to the status that the academic community can accord to the research and, consequently, the use (or not) of our research methodology to promote the development of an external language of description and, even, to some extent, of the internal language in which the former is grounded.

Although our research has gained some acceptance in the area of sociology of education, it has been less accepted by the academic community in the area of science education. The educational knowledge we have constructed is mainly in the area of science education and our research methodology corresponds to an approach closer to that followed in the experimental sciences when compared to the social sciences. On the one hand, this has led us to believe that the lesser acceptance of the research by the science education community may be related to the low status that it accords to sociological knowledge rather than to our type of research methodology. On the other hand, the sociology of education community may be inclined to accept our research more willingly because it represents one more approach (another language) in a field characterised by a horizontal structure of knowledge with multiple languages of description. However, another kind of problem arises here, which is related to the research methodology we have followed.

In terms of the external sociological dimension, our research seeks to consider the more general social contexts of education and the way in which its research findings may be used in the field of educational policy, thus establishing a relation with the world outside the academic community. However, there is still a long way to go when this dimension of research is considered. An investment is needed to make the results of the research and the knowledge constructed on the basis of those results available to people outside of the academic community, specifically in the area in which we have been working. The success of this type of dissemination requires entering a space that is dependent on the status that is given by society to this type of research and to the respective researchers. The relation between the academic community and society, which is part of the external sociological dimension of the construction of knowledge, may exert some pressure on educational policymakers but also accord more status to the research and as a consequence facilitate access to new sources of funding. To ignore or minimise the importance of the internal and external sociological dimensions of the construction of knowledge, in any of its expressions/manifestations, may constitute an obstacle to the development of research whose fundamental objective is the advancement of knowledge.

As Flyvbjerg says,

> [...]we must effectively communicate the results of our research to fellow citizens. If we do this, we may successfully transform social science from what is fast becoming a sterile academic activity, which is undertaken mostly for its own sake and in increasing isolation from a society on which it has little effect and from which it gets little appreciation. We may transform social science to an activity done in public for the public, sometimes to clarify, sometimes to intervene, sometimes to generate new perspectives, and always to serve as eyes and ears in our ongoing efforts at understanding the present and deliberating about the future. We may, in short, arrive at a social science that matters. (2001, p. 166)

These epistemological considerations about our research involve aspects that seem to be related to what Moore and Maton (2001) refer to as the epistemic relation and the social relation of knowledge. As presented by these researchers,

> The epistemic relation [of knowledge] is the relation between knowledge and that part of the world of which knowledge is claimed (its proclaimed object of study). The social relation [of knowledge] is between knowledge and its author, the subject making the claim to knowledge. Languages of legitimation are conceptualised in terms of the strength of boundaries around (classification) and control over (framing) what knowledge may be claimed and how (epistemic relation), and who may claim knowledge (social relation). (2001, p. 165)

The knowledge we have produced in the area of science education derives from conceptual models that are applicable to diverse situations/contexts: teacher education, classroom practices, family practices, scientific learning, and curriculum texts. These models have guided the construction of instruments, according to methodological procedures described below.

Validity and Reliability Criteria of the Research

When discussing the epistemological positioning of a research study, it is important to consider validity and reliability criteria. As we have mentioned, our investigative approach, although having a rationalist basis, follows a methodology that integrates qualitative features. We will now demonstrate what we have done to ensure validity and reliability in the qualitative dimension of the research.

The systematic dialectic between the theoretical and the empirical that has characterised our research methodology has allowed us to guarantee criteria of both internal validity and external validity. The fact that the research is sustained by a theoretical framework of great rigour and explanatory power is fundamental to guarantee internal validity. Internal validity has also been achieved by (a) consistency between the objectives of the research and data collection; (b) the successive reformulations of the models and instruments we have used, in order to increase the adjustment of the relation between the objectives of the research and the data to be obtained; (c) the use of a long period of observation; (d) continual personal interaction between the researcher and the subjects; (e) the comparison of data obtained from various sources (triangulation), including data from similar studies. External validity has been achieved by the transfer of results to other contexts and by making analytical generalisations when we formulate working hypotheses that will be transferred to similar contexts.

With regard to reliability, the presence of a theoretical framework to guide the research has allowed observations to be conducted in a way that is consistent to the theoretical aspects of the research. To reinforce reliability, data have been analysed by multiple researchers, all familiar with the theoretical framework. Also we have used various techniques to obtain data (triangulation). In order to guarantee one of the fundamental criteria of reliability in a qualitative approach, constancy in the application of principles (e.g., standardisation of rules of analysis, treatment and interpretation of data) has been assured, to the extent possible, by the explication of the various stages of the research.

Models and Instruments

Following this research methodology, we have constructed models and instruments for various contexts and levels of pedagogic analysis and intervention and we have focused on various objects of study. These models and instruments have been used: (a) to analyse the relations that characterise pedagogic practices in school and family contexts and the modalities of teacher education (e.g., Morais and Neves, 2001; Neves, Morais and Afonso, 2004; Neves and Morais, 2005); (b) to evaluate students' specific coding orientation and positioning, in general and specific learning contexts, and to evaluate teachers' specific coding orientation in contexts of pedagogic intervention (e.g., Morais and Neves, 2001; Morais, Neves and Afonso 2005); (c) to appreciate the ideological and pedagogical messages and their recontextualisation at the various levels of curriculum development (e.g., Neves and Morais, 2001).

In order to explicate the theoretical assumptions and the methodological procedures that we have adopted in the conception and application of the models and instruments used in the research, we will now show how those assumptions and procedures reflect the epistemological positioning of the research. To illustrate these aspects, we will refer to models related to texts and contexts that have been the object of analysis in our research (monologic text/closed text, dialogic text/open text, and contextual performance).

Theoretical Assumptions and Methodological Procedures

As mentioned earlier, the general framework of our research follows a methodological approach, fundamentally supported by a sociological matrix based on Bernstein's theory. For that reason, the concepts and ideas suggested by the theory have guided the selection and construction of categories of analysis. Furthermore, the research has been guided by theory and/or results of previous studies, which have suggested hypotheses to be tested. However, our research is also part of a qualitative paradigm, for reasons not only related to the small size of most of our samples but also by the contextual nature of most objects of study. In addition, the fact that we have selected and constructed indicators and categories based on previous readings (the case of monologic texts) and observations (the case of dialogic texts and contextual performances) of the texts and contexts under study introduces a methodological dimension characterised by content analysis, more associated with qualitative approaches. However, since the system of categories and indicators of analysis is a result of an articulation between the theoretical and the empirical, those content analyses present a less subjective character, more distanced from a process of inductive research. In summary, models and instruments are constructed on the basis of a methodological orientation that combines aspects of the two research paradigms (quantitative and qualitative) through the development of an external language of description that is the result of a constant dialectic between the concepts provided by the theory (internal language of description) and the empirical data 'observable' in the contexts under analysis.

Figure 2.2 shows the relations considered in the construction of the instruments of analysis of text and contexts

In the case of the instruments of analysis of modalities of pedagogic practice, the categories of analysis derive from theoretical propositions based on the concept of pedagogic code. According to this concept, we considered a number of categories of analysis, including the relations between subjects, the relations between discourses, and the relations between spaces. Within these categories, we constructed subcategories of analysis. For example, within the relations between subjects, we have taken as subcategories of analysis the discursive rules of selection, sequence, pacing and evaluation criteria. These categories and subcategories are operationalised

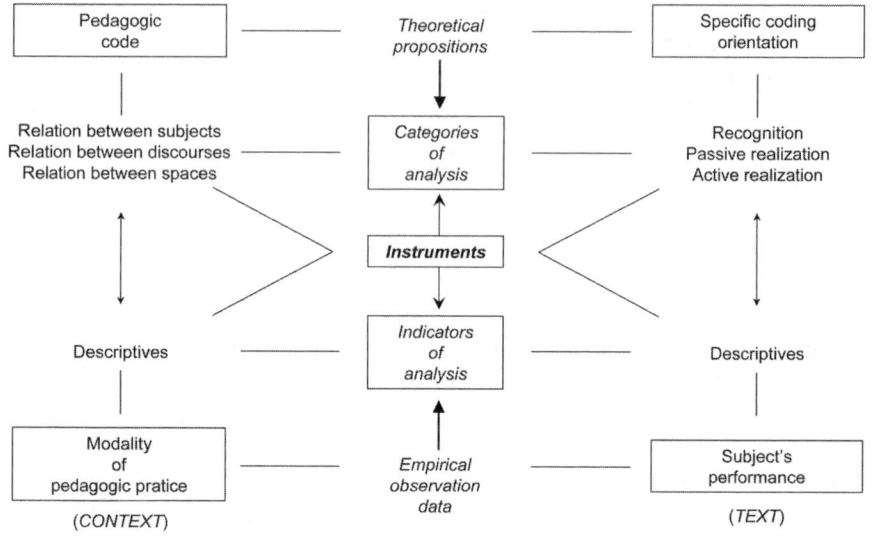

Figure 2.2 Relations used in the construction of instruments of analysis of texts and contexts.

through descriptors of the interactional contexts under study (instructional and regulative practices in schools/classrooms, family and teacher education).[3]

Instruments of analysis of subjects' performance in interactional contexts have been constructed by using categories of analysis derived from theoretical propositions based on the concept of specific coding orientation. Based on this concept, we have analysed the categories of *recognition rules* and *realisation rules*, *active* and *passive*, and their subcategories. For example, within recognition rules, we have taken as subcategories of analysis the recognition of the scientific content and the recognition of competences involved in the microcontexts of scientific learning. Each of the categories and subcategories is operationalised, in the instruments, through descriptors of the text produced by the subjects in a given context—for example, students' performance in the micro-contexts of scientific or social learning, teachers' performance in the contexts of initial and in-service education.[4]

In both cases—analysis of modalities of pedagogic practice and analysis of subjects' performances—descriptors are constructed by considering both the indicators of analysis that derive from the data from empirical observation and the categories of analysis suggested by the theory; they vary according to the texts and contexts under study. They describe the modalities of pedagogic practice or specify the performance in terms of the theoretical framework that supports the analysis, making visible the invisible and explaining and exploring the meaning of the invisible

through the visible.
The central part of the model of Figure 2.2 represents the conceptual structure of our research methodology. It may be used in other research studies provided the analyses of that research are guided by theory.

Exemplary Cases

To illustrate the procedures used in the construction of instruments, we provide a case related to the analysis of the modality of pedagogic practice and another related to the analysis of a subject's performance. The example of the modality of pedagogic practice relates to the school context in the classroom situation and the example of the subject's performance relates to a teacher's performance in the context of in-service education. We also present a case that relates to the analysis of monologic texts (curriculum texts).

Modality of pedagogic practice in the school context

In order to construct the instruments of analysis of the modalities of pedagogic practice that characterise the interactions taking place in the context of school/classroom, family and teacher education, we constructed the model seen in Figure 2.3.

The model is based on Bernstein's idea that any pedagogic interaction (as with the case of school, family and teacher education contexts) is characterised by power and control relations, which institutionalise elaborated or restricted coding orientations ($O^{E/R}$) and which can be analysed, respectively, in terms of the concepts of classification and framing. In this way, the pedagogic code present in a given context of pedagogic interaction is defined by the coding orientation and the power and control relations that characterise the contextual realisation of meanings. The pedagogic code expresses itself through the instructional (ID) and regulative (RD) discourses and through the instructional (IP) and regulative (RP) practices, therefore translating the discursive and transmission levels of the interactional context.

Using classification and framing as conceptual instruments of analysis of power and control relations that characterise the modalities of pedagogic practice in the school context, and specifying these relations in terms of the multiple aspects that constitute the relations among subjects, discourses and spaces, we constructed, on the basis of the model, a set of categories and subcategories to guide the analysis of these relations. The discursive rules of selection, sequence, pacing, and evaluation criteria and the hierarchical rules may be seen as subcategories that define the teacher–student relation, within the category relations between subjects. Interdisciplinary, intradisciplinary and academic and non-academic knowledge are subcategories that define the category relations between discourses. The relation between teacher's space and student space and the relation between the spaces of

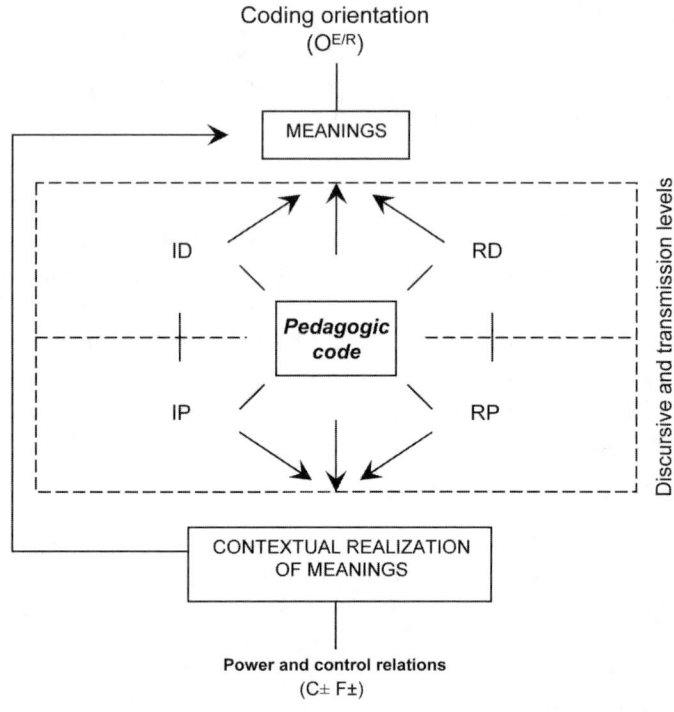

Figure 2.3 Model of analysis of modalities of pedagogic practice.

the various students are subcategories that define the category relations between spaces. The instruments constructed for the analysis of the modalities of the pedagogic practice refer to each of these categories. For the analysis to take into account the specificities of the contexts under study, the indicators which are part of those instruments were created on the basis of real situations observed in these contexts. The descriptors used to specify each of the degrees of the classification and framing scales, regarding each indicator, were also constructed on the basis of situations that could occur in the interactions under study.

Let us consider an instrument used in the analysis of the pedagogic practices implemented in the primary school, which is centred on the discursive rule *evaluation criteria* (one of the subcategories of analysis which refer to the category 'relations between subjects: teacher-student'). On the basis of data from empirical observation, we defined the following indicators to guide the analysis: *Exploring themes/problems under study; doing tasks/activities; making syntheses; discussing tasks/activities; asking questions; making records on worksheets; students' incorrect statements.* The first three indicators refer to situations more directly related to general aspects of the instructional context of the pedagogic practice (macro level of analysis); the other indicators refer to situations more directly related to specific aspects of that context (micro level of analysis). The instrument of analysis contains, for each indicator, descriptors constructed on the basis of a scale of four degrees of framing. The descriptors that refer to each degree of the scale were the result of a dialectic between data obtained from observation of classroom real situations (for each indicator) and the theoretical propositions about the meaning of evaluation criteria in terms of framing.

CATEGORY OF ANALYSIS—*Evaluation criteria*
INDICATOR—Students' incorrect statements
DESCRIPTORS

- Student's statement is reformulated/corrected/completed in detail (F^{++}).

- Student's statement is reformulated/corrected/completed, but completed only in general terms (F^{+}).

- The incorrect statement is pointed out to the student, but no reformulation is made (F^{-}).

- Student's statement is neither corrected nor reformulated (F^{--}).

To illustrate the various components of analysis, contained in the instrument, we are specifying, for one category of analysis, and for one indicator, the descriptors that refer to the various degrees of the scale of framing.

Teachers' performance in the context of in-service teacher education

Figure 2.4 shows the conceptual model we used for this analysis, which was developed to guide the construction of instruments to collect and analyse data about the specific coding orientation of subjects (teacher, student) in contexts of interaction (teacher educator–teachers, teacher–students).[5]

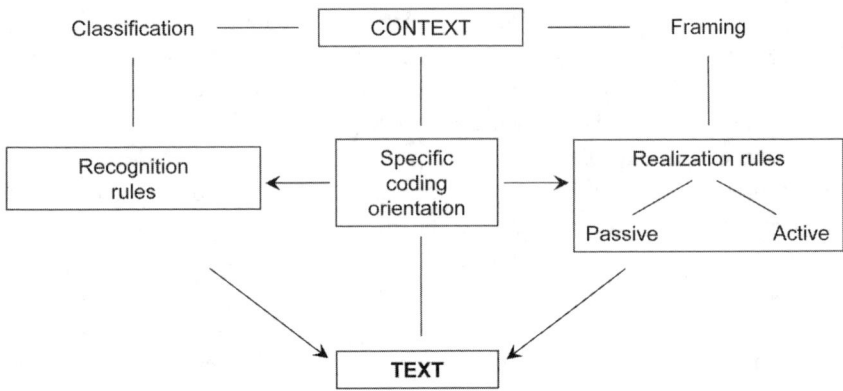

Figure 2.4 Model of the analysis of the specific coding orientation as the regulator of the production of the text in context.

According to this model, the subjects' possession of the specific coding orientation to a given context, needed to produce the text appropriate to that context, involves the possession of recognition rules and realisation rules, passive and active. Recognition rules allow recognition of the context while realisation rules allow selection of the meanings (passive realisation) and production of the text appropriate to the context (active realisation). Recognition relates to classification because to distinguish one context from other contexts means to recognise its degree of insulation. Realisation relates to framing because to select the meanings and produce a text appropriate to a context means communication adequate to specific social relations.

On the basis of this model, we constructed instruments for the analysis of teachers' performance in the context of in-service teacher education, that is, semi-structured interviews and instruments for classroom observation. Following this conceptual model, we obtained data about teachers' specific coding orientations to implement a given pedagogic practice in the classroom. The interviews were constructed to obtain data about recognition and passive realisation to the various characteristics of the pedagogic practice. We wanted to know the extent to which the teacher valued each of the characteristics (recognition). We also wanted to know the teacher's principles underlying such valuing and how s(he) would act to put the characteristics into practice in the classroom (passive realisation). The instruments were constructed to obtain data about active realisation, that is, how the teacher implemented the pedagogic practice in its various characteristics.

Let us take as an example the section of an interview related to the recognition and passive realisation rules, when these rules were analysed with reference to the characteristic of the pedagogic practice *evaluation criteria*. The teacher was asked:

When children have to do and present some work, do you think that the teacher should explicate to them what they have to do and how it should be done, or should this be left to children's own criteria? Justify. How would you act in the classroom?

The teacher's answers, not only to these questions but also to questions related to the various characteristics of the pedagogic practice, allowed the construction of the following analytical indicators: valuing of the characteristic of the practice under analysis (in the case of recognition rules); the principles that grounded the valued characteristic and the ways of acting to put into practice the valued characteristic (in the case of passive realisation rules). The descriptors indicate the nature of the answer (text) given by the teacher to each of the indicators and allow the evaluation of that text, in terms of the category under analysis (recognition or passive realisation).

To illustrate the various components of analysis, we show the indicator and respective descriptors for the recognition rules related to the characteristic of the pedagogic practice *evaluation criteria*.

> CATEGORY OF ANALYSIS—*Recognition rules*
> INDICATOR—Valuing given to the explicating of the evaluation criteria
> DESCRIPTORS
>
> • The teacher gives a high valuing to the clear explicating of the evaluation criteria, that is, s(he) values a pedagogic practice with strong framing regarding this characteristic.
>
> • The teacher gives a low valuing to the explicating of the evaluation criteria, that is, s(he) values a pedagogic practice with weak framing regarding this characteristic.

These descriptors reflect two extreme situations presented in the interview questions.[6] The situations were established on the basis of data obtained from observing teachers' practice in the classroom. Taking as the reference research results that have indicated evaluation criteria of very strong framing as a characteristic favourable to students' learning, the first descriptor shows the possession of recognition rules and the second shows absence of those rules, for that characteristic of the pedagogic practice.

Pedagogic message in curriculum texts

The relations shown in Figure 2.2, which were explicated for the case of the analysis of subjects' performance in specific contexts and the analysis of modalities of pedagogic practice, may be applied to the case of the analysis of curriculum texts (monologic texts). We used the model of analysis of modalities of pedagogic practice (Figure 2.3), as it is possible and desirable to apply to the analysis of monologic texts a conceptualisation parallel to the analysis of dialogic texts. It is possible because the conceptual and transference power of the internal language of description that characterises Bernstein's theory[7] allows the application of the concepts derived from the theory to various levels of educational analysis and various analytical contexts. It is desirable because the use of a same model allows comparisons between texts produced at various levels of the educational system to acquire a greater conceptual and methodological rigour.

The instruments constructed on the basis of this model to analyse curriculum texts, therefore, contained categories of analysis similar to the categories used in the analysis of the pedagogic practice in the classroom: (a) intradisciplinary and interdisciplinary relations and relations between academic and non-academic knowledge; and (b) teacher–students relations in terms of the theory of instruction. In this case, the instruments were used to analyse the message of curriculum texts in terms of the modality of the pedagogic practice valued by those texts. However, considering the specificity of the contexts in which the texts under study (syllabuses, textbooks) are produced, the instruments have also included, as categories of analyses of the relation between subjects, the relation between the authors of curriculum texts and the users of those texts such as, for example, the relation between the Ministry of Education, as the author of syllabuses, and the textbooks' authors and the relation between them and the teachers. In this case, the instruments have been used to analyse how texts' authors explicate both the pedagogic message contained in the texts and the foundational principles of this message. Through this analysis, it has been possible to infer the space of autonomy that is allowed to textbook authors and to teachers to reproduce/recontextualise the message present in the curriculum texts under study.

Let us take, as an example, an instrument used in the analysis of the syllabi of natural science for middle school; this analysis is centred on *intradisciplinary relations*. According to the discursive components present in the syllabus (that in this case constitute the data of empirical observation), we defined as indicators to guide the analysis the most representative components of the discourse of the syllabus: *Knowledge, aims, methodological guidelines* and *evaluation*. The instrument of analysis contained these indicators and for each indicator descriptors for a four-degree scale of classification, taking as the value of classification the degree of insulation between the various knowledges of the discipline. The descriptors that refer to each degree of the scale were the result, in this analysis, of the dialectical relation between the data obtained through the reading of the text of the syllabus, with regard to each indicator, and the theoretical propositions about the meaning of intradisciplinary relations in terms of classification.

To illustrate the various components of analysis contained in the instrument, we are specifying to the category of analysis under study, and to one indicator, the descriptors that refer to the various degrees of the scale of classification.

> CATEGORY OF ANALYSIS—*Intra-disciplinary relations*
> INDICATOR—Methodological orientation
> DESCRIPTORS
>
> • The strategies/methodologies suggested include the relation between content knowledge of a simple order[8] within the same theme *or* the absence in the strategies/methodologies suggested of the scientific knowledge necessary to the understanding of the relation between knowledges within the same theme (C^{++})
>
> • The strategies/methodologies suggested include the relation between content knowledge of a simple order of distinct themes *or* the absence in the strategies/methodologies suggested of the scientific knowledge necessary to the understanding of the relation between knowledges of distinct themes (C^{+})
>
> • The strategies/methodologies suggested include the relation between content knowledge of a complex order,[9] *or* between this and content knowledge of a simple order, within the same theme (C^{-})
>
> • The strategies/methodologies suggested include the relation between content knowledge of a complex order, *or* between this and the content knowledge of a simple order, of distinct themes (C^{--})

To reiterate, the possibility given by Bernstein's theory of constructing distinct instruments of analysis on the basis of the same concepts allows for comparisons between messages produced at distinct levels of the educational system. Taking as the object of study, for example, the pedagogic discourse present in the various fields that constitute the pedagogic device, the models and instruments, constructed according to the methodological procedures we referred to earlier, has allowed the development of comparative studies, including the relation between the family and the school. Figure 2.5 summarises the relations that have been the object of research, when we consider the recontextualisation that can occur in the whole educational system.

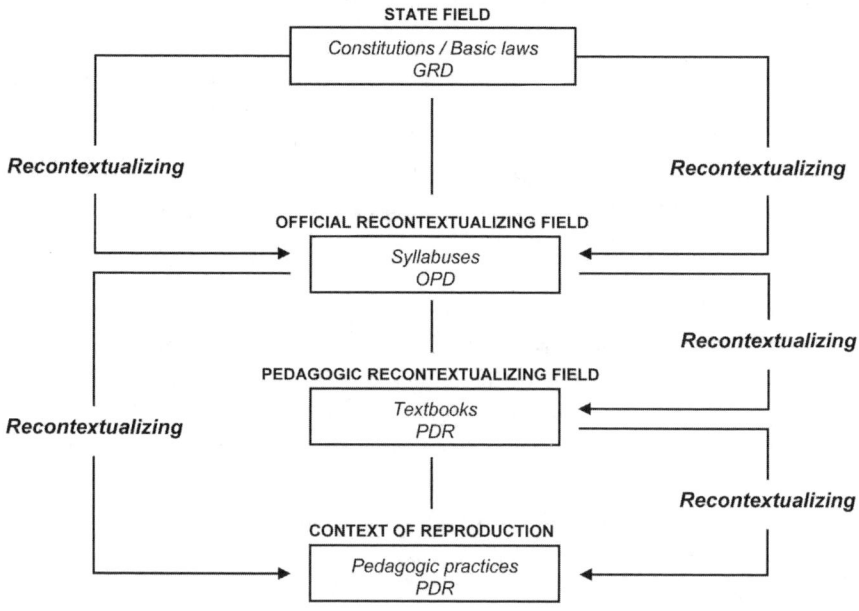

Figure 2.5 Recontextualisation of pedagogic discourse at various levels of the educational system.

Final Considerations

We have discussed the research methodology used in the studies carried out by the ESSA Group and described the theoretical assumptions and methodological procedures that have guided the construction of models and instruments of analysis to be used in various contexts of educational research. The aim of this chapter was to make evident the extent to which Bernstein's theory has inspired the progressive development of our research and consequent construction of knowledge.

The research methodology is a mixed methodology that departs from the dichotomy between naturalistic and rationalist approaches while using characteristics associated with both qualitative and quantitative forms of inquiry. The rationalist approach in the conception of models of analysis is the consequence of a methodological option of research that we believe may contribute to according greater consistency to the results obtained and therefore to allow the emergence of new knowledge. The use of qualitative procedures has improved the depth of the analyses, which is crucial to the advancement of knowledge. The qualitative character of the research associated with a general methodological orientation of a rationalist character has permitted the construction of a theoretical-empirical framework to guide our research. This methodology is possible given the conceptual rigour and transference power of the theory in which it is grounded. Bernstein's theory contains characteristics that make it closer to theories of discursive areas characterised by strong grammars, having perhaps some aspects of a hierarchical structure of knowledge. We believe that if research in the area of education is to advance in the production of knowledge it must be based on a strong conceptualisation.

These aspects are related to the philosophical dimension of the construction of educational knowledge. But it is also important to consider the sociological dimension, both internal (relative to the research community) and external (relative to relations with the external society). In fact, for a progressive increase of conceptualisation, broadness and degree of transference of educational knowledge to occur, new knowledge and methodology must be made available and accepted by the academic community, in order that new research paths are followed. The status accorded to research and knowledge by the academic community is therefore important. The acceptance of progressively more conceptualised educational knowledge, instead of a sum of facts and ideas, depends greatly on a change of the epistemological positioning within the community of educational researchers. In fact, the trend within this community has been mostly marked by descriptive and narrative studies which, we believe, have not promoted a conceptualised evolution of educational knowledge.

If we now consider the possible acceptance of research results by society, that acceptance depends greatly on the status that is given to educational researchers and their visibility at various levels, especially to the media. It is crucial that the research results are made visible and that intervention in institutions external to the academic community takes place. This principle means the need to disseminate the research, not only in contexts related to the field of knowledge production (e.g., in academic conferences), but also in contexts related to the fields of knowledge recontextualisation and reproduction. Research results may then be used to justify decisions in educational policy. Another important aspect of the external sociological dimension of knowledge construction is related to the financial support given by funding institutions, which can only be justified if the research leads to knowledge advancement and to educational improvement.

One characteristic of our research is related to the implementation of a methodology, which departs from the positioning that has mainly guided the academic community in the field of educational research and which represents a change of 'paradigm.' This raises questions related to the number of research groups that can share results within the same research 'paradigm,' a factor that may limit the advancement of knowledge in the area we have been working. Also the small investment we have made in making public to the community external to the academic community the results obtained and the research methodology developed may limit the advancement of knowledge.

However, we believe that because we have developed a research methodology with a structure that can be applied and extended to research based on theories other than Bernstein's, we may make a contribution to the construction of knowledge in the area of research methodologies. We also believe that by making the structure of that research methodology explicit we can open up possibilities of a greater interaction of ideas and studies among researchers in the area.

This chapter may provide the basis of reflection about the potentialities and limitations of the research methodology that has guided the empirical work carried out by the ESSA Group and, as a consequence, about the objectivity and value of the results. It may also contribute to a debate about methodological questions of interest to researchers doing empirical work on the basis of Bernstein's theory. The interaction of ideas in this debate may open up new paths to the development and improvement of external languages of description and, as pointed out by Bernstein, this progressive development itself may contribute to the development of the internal language of description.

Acknowledgment

A version of this article was published in Portuguese:
Fazer investigação usando uma abordagem metodológica mista.*Revista Portuguesa de Educação*, 20 (2), 75-104, 2007.

Notes

1. See, for example, Morais and Neves (2001).
2. Ziman (1984) considers various dimensions in the construction of science: philosophical, related to methods; psychological, related to the social relations in the scientific community; external sociological, related to relations between science and other parts of society.

3. See, for example, Morais and Neves (2001) and Neves, Morais and Afonso (2004) for extracts of instruments of analysis of modalities of pedagogic practice.
4. See description of instruments of analysis of subjects' performance in contexts of interaction in Morais and Neves (2001); Morais, Neves and Afonso (2005) and Morais and Neves (2006).
5. See Morais, Neves and Afonso (2005) and Morais and Neves (2006) for the application of this model in the context of teacher education, and Morais and Neves (2001) for the contexts of scientific learning.
6. Intermediate descriptors are possible.
7. See Morais and Neves (2001) for the sociological research model of methodology that illustrates the relation between the internal and external languages of description, by highlighting the characteristics of Bernstein's theory.
8. Content knowledge of a simple order refers to generalised facts or to concrete concepts which, according to Cantu and Herron (1978), 'are ones that have defining attributes and examples that are observable' (p. 135).
9. Content knowledge of a complex order refers to abstract concepts which, according to Cantu and Herron (1978), are concepts 'that do not have perceptible instances or have relevant or defining attributes that are not perceptible' (p. 135).

REFERENCES

Bernstein, B. (1990). *Class, codes and control, Vol. IV: The structuring of pedagogic discourse.* London: Routledge.
Bernstein, B. (2000). *Pedagogy, symbolic control and identity: Theory, research, critique* (rev. ed.). London: Rowman & Littlefield.
Bruner, J. (1973). *The process of education.* Oxford: Oxford University Press.
Cantu, L. L., and Herron, J. D. (1978). Concrete and formal Piagetian stages and science concept attainment. *Journal of Research in Science Teaching*, 15 (2), 135–143.
Constas, M. (1998). Deciphering postmodern educational research. *Educational Researcher*, 27(9), 36–42.
Flyvbjerg, B. (2001). *Making social science matter: Why social inquiry fails and how it can succeed again.* Cambridge: Cambridge University Press.
Moore, R., and Maton, K. (2001). Founding the sociology of knowledge: Basil Bernstein, intellectual fields, and the epistemic device. In A. Morais, I. Neves, B. Davies and H. Daniels (Eds.), *Towards a sociology of pedagogy: The contribution of Basil Bernstein to research* (chap. 7, pp. 153–182). New York: Peter Lang.
Morais, A. M. (2001). Crossing boundaries between disciplines: A perspective on Basil Bernstein's legacy. In S. Power, P. Aggleton, J. Brannen, A. Brown, L. Chisholm and J. Mace (Eds.), *A tribute to Basil Bernstein* (pp. 31–34). London: Institute of Education, University of London.
Morais, A. M. (2002). Basil Bernstein at the micro level of the classroom. *British Journal of Sociology of Education*, 23(4), 559–569.
Morais, A. M., and Neves, I. P. (2001). Pedagogic social contexts: Studies for a sociology of learning. In A. Morais, I. Neves, B. Davies and H. Daniels (Eds.), *Towards a sociology of pedagogy: The contribution of Basil Bernstein to research* (chap. 8, pp. 185–221). New York: Peter Lang.
Morais, A., Neves, I., and Afonso, M. (2005). Teacher training processes and teachers' competence: A sociological study in the primary school. *Teaching and Teacher Education*, 21, 415–437.
Morais, A. M., and Neves, I. P. (2006). Teachers as creators of social contexts for scientific learning: Discussing new approaches for teachers' development. In R. Moore, M. Arnot, J. Beck and H. Daniels (Eds.), *Knowledge, power and educational reform: Applying the sociology of Basil*

Bernstein (chap. 9). London: Routledge.

Neves, I., and Morais, A. (2001). Texts and contexts in educational systems: Studies of recontextualising spaces. In A. Morais, I. Neves, B. Davies and H. Daniels (Eds.), *Towards a sociology of pedagogy: The contribution of Basil Bernstein to research* (chap. 9, pp. 223–249). New York: Peter Lang.

Neves, I., and Morais, A. (2005). Pedagogic practices in the family socialising context and children's school achievement. *British Journal of Sociology of Education*, 26 (1), 121–137.

Neves, I., Morais, A., and Afonso, M. (2004). Teacher training contexts: Study of specific sociological characteristics. In J. Muller, B. Davies and A. Morais (Eds.), *Reading Bernstein, researching Bernstein* (chap. 12, pp. 168–186). London: Routledge & Falmer.

Popper, K. (1968). *The logic of scientific discovery*. London: Hutchinson.

Shaffer, D. W., I., and Serlin, R. C. (2004). What good are statistics that don't generalize? *Educational Researcher*, 33 (9), 14–25.

Tashakkori, A., and Teddlie, C. (1998). *Mixed methodology: Combining qualitative and quantitative approaches*. Thousand Oaks, CA: Sage Publications.

Vygotsky, L. (1978). *Mind in society: The development of higher psychological processes*. Ed. M. Cole, V. John-Steiner, S. Scribner and E. Souberman. Cambridge, MA: Harvard University Press.

Ziman, J. (1984). *An introduction to science studies: The philosophical and social aspects of science and technology*. Cambridge: Cambridge University Press.

CHAPTER THREE

Educational Policy and Social Reproduction

BRIAN DAVIES, JOHN EVANS AND JOHN FITZ

A BERNSTEINIAN FRAMEWORK

Basil Bernstein spoke quite sharply from the 1980s on about the rapid exodus of sociologists of education into curriculum and policy studies and even more exotic sub-parts of the mainly teacher education undergrowth. His worry was that, in doing so, they were more likely than ever to abandon intellectual rigour. Many reacted either by neglecting him as scrupulously as ever, or by asserting that he had nothing to say about policy anyway. But as is so often the case in our horizontally inclined knowledge structures, what goes around comes around and even those once inclined to say that Bernstein had little or nothing on policy have taken increasing interest in his views.[1] Ours, widely shared by others in this volume, has been very clearly declared in *Educational Policy and Social Reproduction* (Fitz, Davies and Evans, 2006). In the absence of a Bernsteinian turn in publicly funded empirical investigation, its leading edges have been largely shaped by our and others' doctoral students working on a variety of aspects of the formation of pedagogic discourse and competition for control of the pedagogic device. Bernstein (1996, 2000) himself noted in successive editions of *Pedagogy, Symbolic Control and Identity* that the empirical basis of the theoretical work that he was presenting had been laid, almost exclusively, by his students. Almost every one of their theses, predominantly from Latin America and southern Europe, were driven by, or strongly oriented to, providing answers to burning policy issues. Only relatively few, unusually conceptually-determined Brits and others survived the theoretical high altitude. It remains much the same, certainly in the United Kingdom, where Bernstein is still very largely the name that funded research proposals dare not speak. However, feeling neither embattled nor given to Basolatry we remain committed to tracing the usage and usefulness of his and their ideas in better understanding and researching educational policy.

Two Questions, Many Answers

Quite practically, we might ask whether Bernstein's ideas give us a handle on the character of policy process, helping in guiding us through its thickets. If they work, they will apply inside as well as outside education policy. Bernstein's work evinces consciousness that it is a long way from ministers, civil servants, advisers, lobbyists and legislatures in central government to the sites where teachers and students do the things (or not) that policymakers appear to require of them and that the loops that connect them (or not) go through a number of state-created and other agencies, as well as the 'local state' whose character differs both within and between countries. Leaving aside normatively infested versions of how 'good' people and parties conceive, initiate, detail and implement policy particulars that have haunted official and managerialist versions of processes, the broader policy analysis field is pretty much an array of conceptual cold cuts. Sociological analyses of educational policy are, for some tastes and purposes, sometimes too global or too national or too local, others insufficiently detailed, while some are immured in technical detail. Many lose individual actors in the structural wood and vice versa and 'bricolage' is everywhere, turning explanation of the apparent randomness of some policy processes into 'flailing around for anything that looks as if it might work' (Ball 1998, p. 126) While lots of honest, rational endeavour is poured in to policy making it would be a mistake to picture it, then, simply as the domain of wise people seeking clear and just goals. Partiality, ideology and self seeking are mixed with altruism and the pursuit of 'public interest.' Moreover, there is a rich and dynamic interior to processes and the sites where they take place. Many ideologically accented voices clamour for attention to their own causes. Institutions, whether departments of state, 'think tanks,' official agencies, publishers, teachers' associations, local education committees or school staffrooms all have 'lives of their own.' To borrow Lee Shulman's (1987) marvellous observation on classrooms, 'stuff happens,' everywhere there is play and contingency at the lived end of the forces of power and control.

Policy making can be regarded, then, as a multidimensional and value-laden state activity that exists in context. Evans, Rich, Davies and Allwood (2008a) seek to distinguish this as policy with a big 'P' from its more local, institutional correlates that only manage little 'p's. We all accept that policy is always more than the text and in education it interacts with those in other fields. And even if it is terribly difficult to bring it off, who would demur from the notions that adequate ways of conceptualising policy origins, processes and destinations sociologically must be ones that allow us to stay in touch with their complexity and scope, while also retaining the view that appropriate languages of description are possible that connect empirical and theoretical work? To do so would be to be a thoroughly modern Bernsteinian and would no more preclude holding strong and critical views of social arrangements and processes than it would guarantee to shape the behaviour of the powerful in directions of which we would approve. So much would lead us to assert that a Bernsteinian take on policy processes would say that they take a long time, are ideologically driven, multiply influenced and need theoretically coherent, empirical investigation.

Particular Emphases

Bernstein's ideas and their particular emphases were formed over almost 50 years of writing and researching pedagogic relations in families and schools, in interaction with others whose active work on them continues. Writing at the cusp of his shift from sociolinguistic to school focus he underlined what, for him, characterised their continuity. Like those of language and families, his analyses of schools were to be set 'against a broader canvas of changes in forms of social control,' without losing sight in the analysis of 'the grim consequences of class relationships' (Bernstein, 1975, p. 1). By 1996 (ibid., p. 12) he represented this work as having been empirically mainly about 'class inscription' and theoretically 'increasingly concerned with general questions of pedagogic communication as a crucial medium of symbolic control' and prospectively about 'understanding the social processes whereby consciousness and desire are given specific forms, evaluated, distributed, challenged and changed.'

In such quests 'policy' takes its place, in our view, as one mode of attempting control of 'pedagogic discourse,' for which Bernstein offered an encompassing framework. Viewed metaphorically, its key element is 'the pedagogic device' that 'provides the intrinsic grammar of pedagogic discourse' (ibid., p. 42) through its inter-related distributive, recontextualising and evaluative rules. A ready feature of his work and of some others has been elucidation of the way in which the extent of the scope allowed to pedagogic recontextualisers may be regarded as the measure of education's autonomy, by no means guaranteed and which, in recent decades, has been shrunk by greater incursion of governments generally invoking arguments, as if the relationship was one way, about schools,' colleges' and universities' inability to service the economy. While the latter is plainly ideological, it is also dangerously ignorant. Compulsory schooling's relative autonomy has always relied on education's systemic relation to production, attempts to increase the tightness of which have been shown to lead to paradox (Bernstein, 1977; Vlasceanu, 1976) and periods of its loosening historically somewhat transient and recent.[2] Certainly, in recent years when 'education' has become part of regular, electoral politics, as predominantly middle-class fractions, defined as critical support by converging, centrist parties in systems like the United Kingdom, have sought to tie in arrangements to their advantage, governments have been drawn toward showing that they are capable of exerting more and more control. This has been done, as often as not, on the basis of managed ignorance guaranteed by reliance on hired 'research' hands and inspection tied to policy imperatives.[3] We might expect to find an empirical world subjected to intended policy change which is rife, therefore, with revanche, revision and backsliding rather than cool implementation. After all, everything from the classroom nod and wink end of pedagogic labour to evaluation by formal examination is involved in the reproduction by 'teachers' of chosen content or text that has originated with knowledge producers and has been recontextualised, turned into its 'imaginary' school version by specialised state and educational agencies for transmission to 'acquirers' categorised in particular ways, particularly age, stage and gender. In Bernstein's language our experience of these specialisations of 'time, text and space marks us cognitively, socially and culturally' (1996, p. 49) Nothing is neutral, everything is weighed and valued, all are actual or potential policy objects, yet the adventitious, if not the serendipitous, rules.

SHAKING THE BOX: WHO'S CHANGING NOW?

Given such considerations, a wide variety of possible texts (in the old fashioned sense) might be taken. We have the greatest respect, for example, for the key judgement of the queen of U.S. policy contextualists, Theda Skocpol's (1992) insight that the best predictor of any given policy is the character and content of the one that went before. It adds that something extra to Bernstein's judgement that '(E)ducation preserves structural relations between social groups but changes structural relations between individuals and the latter is sufficient to create the impression of general and probable movement' (ibid., p. 11) to which our analyses are devoted. Patterns of educational success and failure have long been and continue to be strongly influenced by class which, in turn, mediates patterns by gender and ethnicity. It may seem paradoxical, therefore, that class has substantially disappeared from sociological discourse about educational policy until we realise how inconveniently it performs as an overt electoral banner for policymakers. For example,

Muller (2006) observes, particularly in respect of British primary and secondary school expansion from the 1940s to the early 1970s, how 'a reluctant central State exercised weak infrastructural power over the pedagogic recontextualising field, such that the teachers and the LEAs were left to take control over a expanding system without central steering.' 'New' middle class recomposition into service/symbolic and economic elements (Bernstein, 2001a,b) prefigured the former, taking initial control of the pedagogic device, ensuring uneven drift towards invisible pedagogy and competence modes and erosion of traditional, elite, performance modalities. From Thatcher on, as Muller observed:

> the State, acting in the name of an increasingly alarmed new economic middle class... attempted to re-impose two kinds of performance pedagogy from the central state level; the external form of an explicit visible form on the schools; and a market-based form— Bernstein's 'trainability'—on various forms of out-of-school and lifelong learning. (ibid., p. 404)

While the latter had all the appearance of being doomed to failure from the start, with intermediary LEAs severely disabled, school teachers:

> by and large dug in their heels...continued to favour learner centred (that is competence) modes, variable or weak framing, personal control, and other features of 'new' symbolic middle class socialisation that make 'soft skills' the preserve of their cultural capital. The upshot is twofold: the middle class continued to get by in the high-skill-demanding labour market because of their multiform resources of class subsidy, particularly in the higher reaches of the education system; the schools exercised minimal compliance in terms of the new strongly framed external pedagogic regime; and the working class continued to get the short end of the stick. (ibid., p. 405)

Or so it may appear as research evidence on policy processes, in contrast either to policy-maker sponsored evaluation or school management and improvement nostrums, rolls in.

Recent Research

A long trail a' winding...

What do we actually have? Many studies have revolved around the tribulations of introducing or sustaining competence modes. Al-Ramahi and Davies (2002), very much in the tradition of taking Bernstein's ideas to the analysis of planned change in state-dominated systems, showed how a Palestinian system with no discernible pedagogic recontextualising field was sponsored by agencies from the developed world in attempting to capitalise on informal pedagogic modalities developed while formal schooling was intermittent or prohibited during *Intifada*. Bureaucratic infighting began what generally untutored, unwilling and unconvinced teachers in relation to what was required of them finished, as traditional, Arabic rather than

Western new middle class pedagogy reasserted itself.

In a completely contrasting context, Thomas and Davies (2006) showed how contemporary change in Welsh nurse education presented an intriguing instance of where power and control actually lay in a policy process as between well-defined official and pedagogic recontextualising fields. Authoritative, officially required, new curricular formations with strong, ostensible competence orientation, in contrast with the didactic, subject focus that it replaced, were thwarted by slow staff turnover and ineffective preparation for the new, intended discourse among teacher educators fearing that the 'new nurses' to be produced were likely to be less well prepared for hands-on tasks. University autonomy allowed them effective control of continuing pedagogic forms in face of requirements of an ostensibly strong official recontextualising field to develop quite different practices.

At the Welsh secondary school level, 'performativity,' the new, beautiful, state-sponsored game in town, has imposed 'restructuring' as a series of contradictory processes of decentralisation though local management and funding and accompanying processes of centralisation, including imposition of a National Curriculum and its associated assessment, then inspection, since the eighties. James (2005) sought to locate the impact upon school target setting and performance achievement of the latter, delegated to small teams of privatised 'registered inspectors,' intended shock troops of the official recontextualising field, who relied greatly on school prepared documentation. Despite lengthy preparation and post-inspection feedback, reflection and response, disciplinary design and collegial desire left most inspectorial judgements mired in necessity, with teachers feeling stressed and only fleetingly and, in some cases, inappropriately judged by others who they felt could not do what they did. Their managers felt that some benefit arose, not least in providing them with 'levers' to realise their objectives but at a quite disproportionate cost in terms of staff time, effort and angst.[4]

Much recent policy emphasis from Britain to Taiwan has concerned (re)specifying school subject contents. In Britain, officially telling teachers how, as opposed to what, to teach has been reintroduced, though largely confined to 'the basics' in primary school in terms of literacy and numeracy initiatives. At the same time, narrowing curricular time, focus and resource in favour of 'core' subjects has created a range of policy casualties among more 'peripheral' subjects, like physical education and music.[5] These conditions have ensured, for example, that economics in United Kingdom schools has been shunned by students and parents, despite attempts backed by extraordinary amounts of corporate funding to redefine it in terms of 'economic understanding' or 'business enterprise,' cross-curricular themes to be made available to all (Jephcote and Davies, 2004, 2007). Music has also been reduced to an arcane curricular pursuit undertaken by less than 10 percent of those in state schools after the age of 14 and a curricular grace note for most others, particularly after primary school (Wright, 2006). Though its National Curriculum version aimed to combine a competence modality focussed upon skill acquisition, with emphasis on aesthetic response, nominally across 'musics' of various genres, it was tied closely to Western art music in its delivery. In an age of increasingly abundant musical 'access' among teenage students whose identities and tastes were closely bound up with 'popular music' and instruments associated with its delivery, school music tended to signify to them wrong *habitus*, wrong sounds and wrong emphasis on prolonged engagement with learning the wrong instruments for practical examination. In Wright's view, circumventing its substantially class-based unpopularity requires 'more than a little discretion over numerous aspects of regulative and instructional discourse and the classroom expression of distributive, recontextualising and evaluative rules' (p. 275).

The shaping capacity of an external world can become literally a matter of life or death among the predominantly young women aged 12 to 18 experiencing 'disordered eating' (Evans, Rich, Davies and Allwood, 2008b). Schools and other pedagogic agents ascribe values, meanings and potentials to 'the body' that have particular characteristics in time, place and space. These reflect wider, national and global, socioeconomic trends increasingly celebrating particular virtues in terms of 'flexible identities' and manifest aspects of 'performance' and 'corporeal perfection,' usually defined as 'the slender ideal.' Schools have become sites of pervasive surveillance of 'the body,' reaching into and encoding every aspect of life, in effect, making 'pedagogy' everyone's concern. Self-assessment and self-monitoring under the normalising gaze of others are routine features of their performative cultures (Burrows and Wright, 2006). Just as 'performativity works from the outside in and the inside out' (Ball, 2004, p.145) and is capable of both building a 'love of product' or belief in service provided and engendering individual feelings of pride, guilt, shame and envy that seem rational and objective, so 'trainability' entails continuous dispositions of subjects to be made ready for the requirements of their entire lives (Bonal and Rambla, 2003). The alluring call of the world outside to endless perfectibility almost literally gets under the skin of the 'eating disordered.'

Such policy studies at Cardiff and Loughborough have circled rather obsessively about what has been at stake along the trail that winds from policy production to recontextualisation and reproduction. In the main, they have been case studies which have asked how crucial social categories, particularly class and gender, form and are reformed by policy objects and processes and raise important issues as to the degree of insulation between primary, secondary and reproductive knowledge and policy contexts.

Anatomising Pedagogic Discourse

Work of highly superior quality in two other centres in particular, bears on many of the same issues. No one, for example, has yet approached the meticulous and fruitful detail with which Morais, Neves and their co-workers have anatomised pedagogic discourse, mainly in Portuguese science curriculum, working with teachers to show how intervening in pedagogic practice can alter subject understanding and achievement (see, *inter alia*, Morais, Neves and Pires, 2004). If there is a canon for empirical practice to which we might currently aspire and which has energised classroom investigation, this is it. Moreover, its relevance of their notions, such as 'mixed pedagogy,' for policy *and* to teachers' perennial 'Monday morning' question that transcends curricular sticking plaster, is extreme, as will be readily evident from their contribution to this volume.

An as yet less well publicised flow of research is coming out of Cape Town, among it a remarkably interesting investigation by Davis (2004, 2005) at UCT of pedagogic discourse in school mathematics, focussing upon notions intrinsic to 'pedagogic texts structured by a South African, constructivist-inspired teaching methodology, referred to by its proponents as the "*problem-centred approach*" (PCA) (2005, p. 17), that mathematics should be fun and 'that the student does (and must) "construct" the particular mathematics content' (p. 208). The problem that 'the everyday is not the academic' is set against the 'insistence on pleasure' in key, constructivist South African mathematics texts (*Mathematics at work*, Grades 1–4), set against the background of the boundary-dissolving propensities of contemporary utilitarianism. The issue concerns the taming of *jouissance*—how 'pedagogic discourse within competence pedagogies is obliged to engage the pedagogic subject in two ways: it must reproduce knowledge as apparently pleasurable as well as simultaneously negate the solipsistic pleasure of the pedagogic subject' (p. 79). He juxtaposes Bernstein's ideas with those of Lacan, Hegel, Freud, Althusser and Zizek as supporting cast. Among the original contributions of his investigation is detailed analysis of the relation between regulative and instructional discourse, where the former is asserted to be prior to and embedded in the latter by Bernstein but which Davis prefers to regard as 'working in the service of instructional contents, but in accord with dominant ideological imperatives.' (p. 2) He argues that Freud and Lacan's accounts of imaginary and symbolic identification appropriately supplement Bernstein's notion of the social logic of competence, serving 'to produce a more theoretically informed reading of the type of pedagogic relations produced under the conditions of a society subjected to the demands of contemporary capital.' (p. 73). It concludes that 'the PCA succeeds for the wrong reasons' its originators having 'generated a pedagogic modality that allows itself to be duped by the ideological call for the dissolution of boundaries' that 'has simultaneously attempted to maintain its fidelity to mathematics,' ending up constructing 'a world of imaginary relations structured along the lines of utilitarian moral regulation' while disrupting it 'in order to assert the Symbolic in the guise of mathematics.' (p. 208) Once again, questions are raised 'about the definition of competence pedagogies, especially around the feature of an evaluative focus on presences rather than absences in the production of the pedagogic subject.' (p. 184)

If Davis' work is a thrilling glimpse of how to close the gap between 'blue skies' research and policy imperatives, Hoadley's (2005) abiding problem is how to lay bare the mechanisms of social class differentiation that schooling appears to be all too adept at engendering. The long haul by sociologists of education to unpick the brute fact that 'stuff happens' when teachers and students interact has passed through a succession of more or less unsatisfactory periods of emphases, implicating families and their resources, cultures and attitudes, teachers and their expectations, knowledge and its class basis, teaching methods and their bearing on learning styles and, in our performative age, leaders/managers and their attachment of followers to goals. In the face of this passing parade, how the trick is induced has remained stubbornly elusive. In Hoadley's exemplary investigation, having precisely eviscerated effectiveness studies, the way out of the conceptual woods is via applications of Bernstein's theory of pedagogy by Dowling (1993, 1998) and Morais' ESSA group in Lisbon, adding a metric for setting classroom events against school and teacher characteristics. The latter are delineated in terms of social class and professional dispositions, particularly in relation to the part they play in 'the specialisation of student voice with respect to the school code' and 'the potential for teachers, as sub-relays in the process of the reproduction of school knowledge, to interrupt the community or restricted code of learners in contexts where an elaborated orientation may not have been acquired in the home' (p. 270). While elements in the design attend to specifics of the South African primary school context, concentrate on maths and literacy only and contrast very stark class extremes in her four school sample, this investigation produces results which are very striking, indeed, almost chilling.

Hoadley's work arises from a group working with Muller and Ensor whose collective contribution to our understanding of schooling has become very significant in terms of its intellectual intensity, integrity and policy relevance. Reeves (2005) sought to establish whether or not there was empirical support for the South African policy of promoting learner-centred pedagogy to improve academic outcomes in classrooms with learners from socioeconomically disadvantaged backgrounds. She concludes that teacher effectiveness in classrooms with predominantly low socioeconomic background (SES) learners relates to whether they confront principled as well as procedural knowledge adapted to their individual ability and progress, including their misconceptions and difficulties, delivered as a coherent entity underpinned by internal disciplinary principles, rather than as a series of fragmented and disconnected components within each grade. This is a finding loaded with policy implication pointing to the particularities of 'mixed pedagogy' and involving issues both of teachers' subject competency and students' opportunities to learn in Mathematics. Bolton (2005), in her study of final year secondary school achievement in the 'loosely bounded discipline' (p. 1) of school art, suggests similar issues, while Breier (2004, p. 204[D1]), in her study of postgraduate labour law students, argues that 'the recontextualization of segments of horizontal discourse (everyday knowledge) in the content of school subjects does not necessarily lead to more effective acquisition' but 'is usually confined to "less able" students and reduces vertical discourses (the hierarchical knowledge of academic disciplines) to a set of strategies to improve 'their functioning in the every day world of work and domesticity.' Gamble (2004a,b), in her study of craft apprenticeship, pursues similar concerns.

Taken together, these studies suggest that it may well be that the rhetoric flowing from both pedagogic and official recontextualising fields 'about knowledge needing to be immediately relevant to the needs of economic production (the world of work) and the individual needs of citizens' may, indeed, be 'the ideological expression in schooling of a more general political and economic demand for the dissolution of boundaries,' reconfiguring 'the pedagogic device at the level of the reproduction of knowledge,' transforming educational policy, curriculum and pedagogic practice so as to align 'the education system with the economic imperatives issuing from capital' (Davis, 2005, p. 200). While we have argued in the past that we should not underestimate the influence on the shape of our educational arrangements of 'demography's blind grope' (Davies and Evans, 1984; Davies, 1986), the injunctions of policy-makers pursuing preparative, pedagogic perfection perhaps ought to carry the ultimate health warning.

Who Wants to Know Better?

Where does all this leave us? We think with better, finer grain detail of how policy gets made, where and by whom, and how it simultaneously regulates, educates and controls; with firmer grasp of how it is recontextualised and enacted and better understanding of how knowledge, ideology and morality are embedded in the actions of teachers, pupils and schools. Sharpened global, national and local historical and contextual notions matter if our mission is to better understand the 'pedagogic device.' In the original edition of his last book, Bernstein condensed his claim, made initially in 1970 at the British Sociological Association's annual conference, that '(H)ow a society selects, classifies, distributes, transmits and evaluates the educational knowledge it considers to be public, reflects both the distribution of power and the principles of social control' (Bernstein, 1975, p. 85), to the metaphor of the school holding up a mirror in which was reflected a hierarchy of class values. Some images are negative, some positive, some excluded. Different knowledges, carrying unequal value, power and potential, are differentially distributed to social groups, greater resources going to the most prestigious, as also occurs with respect of other public and private goods and services outside the school system. Moreover, school types are not equivalent and preschool provision, along with access to other social goods, skew them in favour of 'haves.' In his very last work, he insisted on how these matters had to be seen as questions of identity formation through particular modes in increasingly pedagogised societies. It seems to us difficult to conceive of a more important conceptual seedbed for growing policy. In elaborating not only the conceptual tools but the available evidential base for doing things, rather than simply talking about them, we have aimed to be true to the Bernsteinian notions of devotion to a problem rather than perfection of specialised language. Bernstein's (1999, p. 170) awesome demand was that measures should have theoretical meaning. Moreover, our analytic 'point of departure' should reveal 'the inter-dependence between properties internal to the discourse and the social context, field/arena, in which they are enacted and constituted. Briefly, ' "relations within" and "relations to" should be integrated in the analysis.' The difficulties involved in following the procedures which he enjoined have hardly formed the basis of a mass movement. Our increasingly 'policy-driven' world and its funding implications have served to compound Bernstein's fears about the total pedagogisation of our societies and our complacency, not to say complicity, in its production. The characteristic of all big ideas, in education, as elsewhere, is their ability to bring those who receive them to the point of exclaiming 'Well, was *that* all it was *really* about?' Bernsteinian policy insights are rather like that, though where they take us is neither easy nor comfortable.

Notes

1. Moore, Arnot, Beck and Daniels (2006) faithfully reflect the work of both old and new Bernsteinian protagonists at the international symposium before this one, while Lingard (2005) shows the influence of his ideas on those attempting to intervene in Australian contexts. Perhaps most surprisingly we have Young (2008), on finding Bernstein rather late in the day, recanting an intellectual youth misspent in pursuit of 'new directions.'
2. Vlasceanu's thesis showed how, in the seventies, Romanian educational reform of an erstwhile rather Germanic secondary school system, which set out to place production in schools and schools in production contexts, foundered in spectacular fashion, not least because neither existing nor new 'worker' teachers would have it. Bernstein's (1996) position suggested that the relative educational autonomy that we had come to esteem in the United Kingdom was sandwiched somewhere between post-1944 'secondary education for all' and Thatcher's politics of envy, represented by a historically brief excrescence of the pedagogic recontextualising field.
3. The favoured sons of the school effectiveness and improvement 'movements' proved very con-

genial to 'can-do' ministers, along with those offering management and leadership solutions for 'failing' system parts (Alexander, 1997). The rest of the educational research establishment in the United Kingdom, with very few exceptions, got Tooley's (1998) official expulsion note from his governors.

4. James concluded that 'real teachers were not standing around waiting for the next well-founded piece of research or the next best way to pump up test scores but they did seem to suffer increasingly from governments fed bad research by compliant academics anxious to increase their mutual sense of control' (p. 11).

5. Bernstein (1996) noted that one of the more striking contrasts between school and post-school (further and higher) curricular formations has been the remarkable resilience of 'singulars' in school discourse, the growth of 'regional' modes in higher education and the push for 'generic' ones in further and vocational education. The former are the narcissistic, strongly bounded subjects that figure in the school curriculum that come and go only at its margins. Regions like engineering, medicine, architecture, cognitive science or communications and media recontextualise singulars, weakening their discursive and political bases. They signal a change from narcissistic, subject-based, introjected identities to more externally dependent, projected ones that schools have hitherto resisted or rejected very well. Generic modes privileging 'trainability,' the heart of Bernstein's 'totally pedagogised society,' reflect three decades of blaming state education for what neither the economic system or the state itself have been able to deliver in terms of adequate levels of employment and skill formation. They have met stout resistance in schools which have tended to provide them only for students deemed unsuited to the normal academic world of singulars.

REFERENCES

Alexander, R. J. (1997). *Policy and practice in primary education: local initiative, national agenda*, London: Routledge.

Al-Ramahi, N, and Davies, B. (2002). Changing primary education in Palestine; pulling in several directions at once, *International Studies in Sociology of Education*, 12 (1), 59–76.

Ball, S. J. (1998). Big policies/small world: an introduction to international perspectives in educational policy, *Comparative Education*, 34 (2), 119–130.

Ball, S. (2004). Performativities and fabrications in the education economy: towards the performative society, in S. Ball (Ed.) *The RoutledgeFalmer reader in sociology of education*. London: RoutledgeFalmer.

Bernstein, B. (1975). *Class, codes and control. Volume 3: Towards a theory of educational transmissions*, London: Routledge & Kegan Paul.

Bernstein, B. (1977). *Aspects of the relation between education and production, in Class, codes and control. Volume 3: Towards a theory of educational transmissions, second (revised) edition*, London: Routledge.

Bernstein, B. (1996). *Pedagogy, symbolic control and identity. Theory, research, critique*, London: Taylor & Francis.

Bernstein, B. (1999). Vertical and horizontal discourse: an essay. *British Journal of Sociology of Education*, 20 (2), 157–173.

Bernstein, B. (2000). *Pedagogy, symbolic control and identity. theory, research, critique, rev. ed*, Oxford: Rowman and Littlefield[D2].

Bernstein, B. (2001a). From pedagogies to knowledges. In A. Morais, I. Neves, B. Davies and H. Daniels (Eds.), *Towards a sociology of pedagogy: the contribution of Basil Bernstein to research*. New York: Peter Lang.

Bernstein, B. (2001b). Symbolic control: issues of empirical description of agencies and agents, *International Journal of Social Research Methodology*, 4 (1), 21–33.
Bolton, H. (2005). *Social class, pedagogy, and achievement in Art*. PhD thesis, University of Cape Town.
Bonal, X. and Rambla, X. (2003). Captured by the totally pedagogised society: teachers and teaching in the knowledge economy. *Globalisation, Societies and Education*, 1 (2), 169–184.
Breier, M. (2004). Horizontal discourse in law and labour law. In J. Muller, B. Davies and A. Morais (Eds.), *Reading Bernstein, researching Bernstein*. London: RoutledgeFalmer.
Burrows, L. and Wright, J. (2006). Prescribing practices shaping healthy children in schools. Unpublished paper, University of Otago and University of Wollongong.
Davies, B. and Evans, J. (1984). Mixed ability and the Comprehensive School, in S.J. Ball (ed.) *Comprehensive schooling: a reader*. Lewes: The Falmer Press.
Davies, B. (1986). Halting progress: some comments on recent British educational policy and practice, *Journal of Educational Policy*, 1 (4), 349–359.
Davis, Z. (2004). The debt to pleasure: the subject and knowledge in pedagogic discourse. In J. Muller, B. Davies and A. Morais (Eds.), *Reading Bernstein, researching Bernstein*. London: RoutledgeFalmer.
Davis, Z. (2005). *Pleasure and pedagogic discourse in school mathematics: a case study of a problem-centred pedagogic modality*. PhD thesis, University of Cape Town.
Dowling, P. (1993). *A language for the sociological description of pedagogic texts with particular reference to the Secondary School Mathematics Scheme SMP 11–16*. PhD thesis, University of London Institute of Education.
Dowling, P. (1998). *The sociology of mathematics education: mathematical myths/pedagogic texts*. London: Falmer Press.
Evans, J., Rich., E, Davies, B. and Allwood, R. (2008a). Body pedagogies, p/policy, health and gender. *British Educational Research Journal*, 34 (3), 1–16.
Evans, J., Rich, E., Davies, B. and Allwood, R. (2008b). *Education, disordered eating and obesity discourse*. Routledge: London.
Fitz, J. Davies, B. and Evans, J. (2006). *Education policy and social reproduction: class inscription and symbolic control*. London: RoutledgeFalmer.
Gamble, J. (2004a). *Tacit knowledge and craft pedagogy: a sociological analysis*. PhD thesis, University of Cape Town.
Gamble, J. (2004b). Retrieving the general from the particular: the structure of craft knowledge. In J. Muller, B. Davies and A. Morais (Eds.), *Reading Bernstein, researching Bernstein*. London: RoutledgeFalmer.
Hoadley, U. (2005). *Social class, pedagogy and the specialisation of voice in four South African primary schools*. PhD thesis, University of Cape Town.
James, D. (2005). *Exogenous change and institutional response: an ethnographic case study of a school inspection*. EdD thesis, Cardiff University.
Jephcote, M., and Davies, B. (2004). Recontextualsing discourse: an exploration of the workings of the meso-level. *Journal of Education Policy*, 19 (5), 547–564.
Jephcote, M., and Davies, B. (2007). Schools, subjects, and curriculum change: the social construction of economics in the school curriculum. *Cambridge Journal of Education*, 2 (37), 207–227.
Lingard, B. (2005). Socially just pedagogies in changing times. *International Studies in Sociology of Education*, 15 (2), 165–186.
Moore, R., Arnot, M., Beck, J. and Daniels, H. (Eds.) (2006). *Knowledge, power and educational reform: applying the sociology of Basil Bernstein*. London: Routledge.
Morais, A., Neves, I. and Pires, D. (2004). The what and the how of teaching and learning: going deeper into sociological analysis and intervention. In J. Muller, B. Davies and A. Morais (Eds.), *Reading Bernstein, researching Bernstein*. London: RoutledgeFalmer.

Muller, J. (2006). The other face of class. Review symposium. *British Journal of Sociology of Education*, 27 (3), 402–407.

Reeves, C. (2005). *The effect of 'Opportunity to Learn' and classroom pedagogy on Mathematics achievement in schools serving low socio-economic status communities in the Cape Peninsula.* PhD thesis, University of Cape Town.

Shulman, L. (1987). Knowledge and teaching: foundations of the new reform. *Harvard Educational Review*, 57, 1–12.

Scokpol, T. (1992). *Protecting soldiers and mothers. The political origins of social policy in the United States.* Cambridge, MA: The Belknap Press.

Thomas, E. and Davies, B. (2006). Nurse teachers' knowledge in curriculum planning and implementation. *Nursing Education Today*, 26 (7), 572–577.

Tooley, J. (1998). *Educational research: a critique.* London: OFSTED.

Vlasceanu, L. (1976). *Decision and innovation in the Romanian educational system: a theoretical exploration of teachers' orientation.* PhD thesis, University of London Institute of Education.

Wright, R. (2006). *Music as pedagogic discourse: an ethnographic case study of one Year 9 class of pupils and their music teacher in a South Wales secondary school.* PhD thesis, University of Wales Institute, Cardiff.

Young, M.F.D. (2008). *Bringing knowledge back in.* London: Routledge.

CHAPTER FOUR

The Structure of Pedagogic Discourse as a Relay for Power

The Case of Competency-Based Training

LEESA WHEELAHAN

INTRODUCTION

Basil Bernstein's key insight was that the structure of pedagogic discourse and the nature of pedagogic practices carry the message of power as much as the content of pedagogic discourse. Nowhere is this more clearly demonstrated than in the case of competency-based training (CBT) models of curriculum. CBT defines competency as the application of the specific knowledge, skills and attitudes that are needed to undertake a work role or task to the required standards in the workplace, and this is used to derive learning outcomes. CBT appears on the face of it to be progressive because of its capacity to offer a 'relevant' curriculum to students who do not find traditional academic curriculum meaningful, and because it putatively ensures that national vocational education and training (VET) systems deliver the skills and knowledge that their national industries need in an increasingly competitive international economy. Governments, particularly in Anglophone nations, have consequently been seduced by the siren call of CBT because of its seeming capacity to simultaneously meet the two government objectives of social inclusion and the development of human capital.

In contrast, this chapter uses a Bernsteinian analysis to argue that CBT acts as a mechanism for social stratification because it denies students access to the abstract theoretical knowledge they need to participate in 'society's conversation.'

Bernstein (2000) argued that democratic access to abstract theoretical knowledge is a precondition for an effective democracy because such knowledge is the means society uses to conduct a conversation about itself. This chapter argues that it is not only the *content* of CBT models of curriculum that deny students this access; the way it is *structured* is equally important. The consequence is that efforts to 'improve' the content of curriculum will not fundamentally alter the regressive character of CBT. This is because the structure of CBT ties knowledge and skill directly to workplace performances and roles, and not to systematic structured disciplinary systems of meaning. CBT thus provides students with access to contextually specific applications of disciplinary knowledge in the workplace, but not to the disciplinary system of meaning in which it is embedded.

The chapter first explains Bernstein's argument about why democratic access to theoretical knowledge is a precondition for an effective democracy. The second section analyses the way that participation in different forms of tertiary education acts as a mechanism for social stratification, using Australia as a case study. The third section assembles the Bernsteinian conceptual tools that are used to analyse the structure of CBT. It discusses the way Bernstein characterised theoretical and everyday knowledge as vertical and horizontal discourses respectively, and the way this knowledge is 'classified' and 'framed' in pedagogic practice. The fourth section draws on these Bernsteinian concepts to analyse CBT models of curriculum. It analyses a unit of competency drawn from a VET qualification in Australia to demonstrate the way in which both the structure and content of CBT act as a mechanism for social power by privileging unitary and unproblematic conceptions of work. The chapter concludes by arguing that students need access to disciplinary systems of meaning as this is the condition for not only their participation in the debates and controversies shaping their field of practice, but also for their participation in society's conversation more broadly.

Access to Knowledge as the Grounds for Democracy

Bernstein (2000, p. xx) argued that democratic access to abstract theoretical knowledge was a precondition for an effective democracy because such knowledge is the means that society uses to conduct its conversation about what it should be like and how it should change. Abstract theoretical knowledge is esoteric knowledge, while everyday knowledge is mundane knowledge; it is *'knowledge of the other*...knowledge of how it is (the knowledge of the possible)' (Bernstein, 2000, p. 29), or 'every day' commonsense knowledge (Bernstein, 2000, p. 157).

The distinction between esoteric and mundane knowledge is the means through which society navigates between the concerns of everyday life (the mundane) and a 'transcendental' realm (Bernstein, 2000, p. 29). Esoteric knowledge consists of 'collective representations' of a society that allow it 'to "*make connections*" between objects and events that are not obviously related,', and 'to "*project beyond the present*" to a future or alternative world' (Young, 2003, pp. 102–103). All societies need to connect the material and immaterial, the known and the unknown, the thinkable and the unthinkable, the here and the not here, the specific and the general, and the past, present and future. Collective representations also provide the moral 'glue' that hold society together through establishing society's values, norms and mores, and in so doing, connect the individual to the collective (Durkheim, 1960, p. 336). Esoteric knowledge has power and status precisely because it is the means that society uses to think the 'unthinkable, the impossible and the not-yet-thought' and why access to it is always regulated through a division of labour and through distributive rules that provide access to some, but not others (Bernstein, 2000, p. 31). Access to knowledge is consequently a question of distributional justice.

What does it mean to participate in society's conversation? Bernstein thought there were two conditions for an effective democracy: 'The first condition is that people must feel that they have a stake in society' (Bernstein, 2000, p. xx). People need to feel they receive something from society, but also that they can *give* to society. This is what he meant by stake—the capacity of people to draw from and contribute to society. The second ground is that 'people must have confidence that the political arrangements they create will realise this stake, or give grounds if they do not' (Bernstein, 2000, p. xx). This allows people to understand and have confidence in the reasons that explain why their stake in society is only partly realised or not realised. There have to be good reasons that explain the way in which such stakes are realised, and people need the capacity to participate in forming, evaluating and changing these reasons.

Bernstein translated these grounds into three pedagogic rights: 'The first is the right to individual enhancement' (Bernstein, 2000, p. xx). He explains that 'Enhancement is not simply the right to be *more* personally, *more* intellectually, *more* socially, *more* materially, it is the right to the means of critical understanding and to new possibilities' (Bernstein, 2000, p. xx). He explains that 'enhancement entails a discipline' (Bernstein, 2000, p. xx). Dewey makes a similar point when he argues that freedom is not the absence of external constraint, but the development of internal control. This provides the basis for the individual to make his or her own decisions and to participate in society 'in such ways that social guidance shall be a matter of his own mental attitude, and not a mere authoritative dictation of his acts' (Dewey, 1966 (1916), p. 301). The discipline that Bernstein (2000, p. xiii) refers to provides students with the critical understanding they need if they are to navigate boundaries, and they need to be able to do so because boundaries are the tension points containing the past and possible futures. A key boundary that students need to be able to navigate is the distinction between theoretical and everyday knowledge and between different types of theoretical knowledge, if they are to use knowledge effectively as participants in society's conversation. This first right operates at the level of the individual, and the condition for its realisation is confidence arising from the discipline acquired in understanding boundaries and the capacity to navigate them.

The second right Bernstein (2000, p. xx) identified 'is the right to be included, socially, intellectually, culturally and personally.' He explained that inclusion does not necessarily mean absorption, because it also includes the right to autonomy. However, inclusion is a necessary condition for the existence of the social, and it 'operates at the level of the social' (Bernstein, 2000, p. xx). The condition necessary for the realisation of this right is an inclusive community. He says that:

> The third right is the right to participate. I think one should be very clear about the word participation. Participation is not only about discourse, about discussion, it is about practice, and a practice that must have *outcomes*. The third right, then, is the right to participate in procedures whereby order is constructed, maintained and changed. It is the right to participate in the construction, maintenance and transformation of order. Participation is the condition for *civic practice* and operates at the level of politics. (Bernstein, 2000, pp. xx–xxi)

Bernstein's analysis shows us that inclusion in education is a necessary basis for realising these rights. Education is to be judged by the extent to which it contributes to the enabling conditions of confidence, communitas and civic discourse. Key to this is confidence—the extent to which individuals have developed the internal orientation (the 'discipline') to knowledge that they need to navigate its boundaries. His life work was to measure education against these rights and to find education wanting (Bourne, 2004, p. 62). Bernstein demonstrates that the issue at stake in the stratification of education is access to knowledge because of the way it endows some, but not others, with the capacity to participate in society's conversation.

The Social Stratification of Education

The way in which education mediates access to knowledge has changed over the last 30 years in the transition from elite to mass and near-universal systems of tertiary education. In Australia, as in many other Organisation for Economic Cooperation and Development (OECD) countries, most young people will finish school and go on to some form of tertiary education, whether it is in higher education or vocational education and training (VET) (OECD, 2007). The development of near-universal systems of education is a response to the economic, social and cultural changes associated with the development of the 'knowledge society' and globalisation. Arguably, the question of democratic access to knowledge and associated pedagogic rights is more important now because education is the means through which access to the knowledge society is mediated (Singh, 2002). Yet paradoxically, while access to education is emphasised in government policy and pathways between sectors of education is a cornerstone of government lifelong learning policies, relatively less emphasis is placed on *knowledge*, and on the extent to which participation in tertiary education provides democratic access to the disciplinary structures of knowledge. Instead, the emphasis in policy is on *access*.

An emphasis on access is still important because exclusion from universal systems of tertiary education has more severe consequences than in elite systems. Access to tertiary education mediates access to a much wider range of jobs than in the past, and to the lifestyle and culture associated with high levels of education (Scott, 2003, p. 74). Students who leave school early and do not participate in any form of post-school education are among the most disadvantaged and marginalised (Dusseldorp Skills Forum, 2007). The OECD (1998, p. 37) explains that 'access, therefore, is not merely to an institution but to a way of life, not for the few but for all.' This is why government policies focus on increasing school retention rates and subsequent participation in post-school education as the basis for their social inclusion strategies.

However, absence from tertiary education is not the only mechanism of social stratification; the *form* of participation in tertiary education is also important. This is illustrated in Australia, which has two sectors of tertiary education; a higher status higher education sector and a lower status VET sector. VET can only act as a mechanism for social inclusion if it opens possibilities for students rather than curtailing them. VET can do this to the extent to which it provides students with access to *knowledge* so that they can study at higher levels and participate actively in debates and controversies shaping their field of practice. The changes associated with work mean that workers need to be able to have access to and to use theoretical knowledge in different ways and in different contexts as their work grows in complexity and difficulty (Young, 2008a). This means that occupational progression is strongly related to educational progression, because education is the main way in which most people are provided with access to disciplinary knowledge.

CBT limits students' opportunities because it does not adequately provide them with access to this knowledge. Consequently, we need to understand the mechanisms that are internal to education and how they mediate access to knowledge in ways that result in unequal outcomes. Young (2008b, p. 10) explains that educational researchers (and policy makers) who emphasise the increased choices available to students through VET may have a theory of *access* but not a theory of *knowledge*, and this means that:

...there is hardly a debate about the consequences of creating such choices when many students may lack the cultural resources to make them. Without an explicit concept of knowledge acquisition, policies that give priority to widening participation and student choice could well be the basis for new, albeit less visible, inequalities.

Students' access to higher education or VET is first mediated by the different kinds of access they have to knowledge in school. Access to knowledge in school begets access to knowledge in tertiary education, or in other words, to those that have, more shall be given (Bernstein, 2000, p. xxii). 'Stronger' students are more likely to undertake academic disciplines as part of their senior school certificates and this provides entry to the elite professions and the academic disciplines in universities, particularly the elite universities. 'Weaker' students are more likely to undertake VET-in-schools subjects, which provide entry to further post-school VET qualifications in VET institutions, and to the lower status, vocationally oriented universities (Teese, Nicholas, Polesel and Helme, 2006, p. 16).

Who are the 'stronger' and 'weaker' students? Teese et al. (2006, p. 18) explain that nearly two-thirds of low achievers in the Victorian Certificate of Education in 2004 came from low socioeconomic backgrounds, while two-thirds of high achievers came from high to very high socio-economic backgrounds. This means, as Teese et al. (2006, p. 18) explain, that 'achievement differences are the means through which social disadvantage is relayed.' The apparently meritocratic basis of schooling masks the social and economic roots of under-achievement and the way this mediates access to educational pathways that are available upon completion of schooling (Young, 2006, p. 59).

Students are provided with different forms of access to knowledge once in tertiary education. This is because publicly funded VET qualifications in Australia *must* be based on national training packages, which consist of competency-based qualifications using 'industry'-specified units of competency. Training packages are the equivalent of the British National Vocational Qualifications (NVQs). In contrast, higher education qualifications are usually curriculum-driven and are therefore input focused. If CBT is structured so that students are not provided with access to theoretical knowledge, at least to the same level as those undertaking higher education qualifications, then this represents a mechanism for social stratification because VET in Australia is over-represented by students from lower socio-economic backgrounds, whereas higher education is over-represented by students from high socio-economic backgrounds (Foley, 2007).

A BERNSTEINIAN FRAMEWORK

Bernstein's analysis of the structures of knowledge, pedagogic practices and pedagogic discourses provides insights into why CBT provides less access to knowledge compared to curriculum-driven models that are characteristic of higher education. Bernstein (2000) argues that theoretical knowledge differs from everyday knowledge because each has a different structure and is embedded in a different system of meaning. Theoretical knowledge is structured as a *vertical* discourse, while everyday knowledge is structured as a *horizontal* discourse.

The academic disciplines are vertical discourses because they comprise *general, principled* knowledge. While theoretical knowledge has contextually specific applications, it is distinguished from everyday knowledge because of its decontextualised nature. This is what gives it potential to be used in ways that are not-yet-thought. It is not tied to a specific context and it can be used in other contexts. Theoretical knowledge is structured vertically because vertical discourses are 'specialised symbolic structures of explicit knowledge' in which the integration of knowledge occurs through the integration of *meanings* and not through relevance to specific contexts (Bernstein, 2000, p. 160). Bernstein distinguished between vertical discourses that are organised hierarchically such as physics or other natural sciences, and vertical discourses that are organised as 'specialised series of languages' such as the social sciences and humanities (Bernstein, 2000, p. 157). Each requires different means of access, but both require students to enter the system of meaning as the basis for acquiring this knowledge and for using its decontextualised features. In hierarchical vertical discourses, students need to understand the hierarchical structure of that body of knowledge, whereas students need to understand the different languages in disciplines that are organised as specialised series of languages (for example, the difference between functionalism and conflict theory in sociology).

In contrast, everyday knowledge is contextually specific knowledge. Bernstein (2000, p. 157) explains that everyday knowledge is 'likely to be oral, local, context dependent and specific, tacit, multi-layered, and contradictory across but not within contexts.' Its selection and usefulness is determined by the extent to which it is relevant in a particular context, and the local context is usually the site in which learning that knowledge (and how to apply it) takes place. This means that meanings, knowledge and competences acquired in one context (or segment) do not necessarily have meaning or relevance in another (Bernstein, 2000, p. 159). Rather than enter the system of meaning as in vertical discourses, it is necessary to enter the context in order to grasp meanings.

Academic disciplines are specialised bodies of knowledge. Each has its own language (as in physics) or series of languages (as in sociology) and rules that stipulate what is included as knowledge and how knowledge is to be created, with specialised texts, rules of entry, and authoritative speakers (Bernstein, 2000, p. 52). Academic disciplines are strongly *classified* bodies of knowledge because they have strongly insulated boundaries between them. Barnett (2006, p. 144) explains that

'Roughly speaking, classification refers to the way in which knowledge gets divided up and how these knowledge boundaries are sustained or challenged.' Classification refers to the 'what' of knowledge, and in pedagogic terms, the way in which knowledge is presented in curriculum. The way in which academic disciplines are structured has implications for pedagogic practices and discourses. For example, while the field of physics production is not the same as the field of physics reproduction in the curriculum, they are related by the way in which knowledge is classified within the discipline so that students who do physics at school can recognise physics at university.

However, the relationship between disciplinary structures and the way they are reproduced in curriculum can be strong or weak. Strongly classified knowledge in curriculum is knowledge that maintains the disciplinary boundaries by distinguishing each as a separate field of study. Conversely, knowledge that is weakly classified renders these boundaries opaque, as for example, in problem-based approaches to curriculum which take as the object of study a feature of the world rather than the structures of knowledge. In the latter case, students start with a problem and select appropriate knowledge to help them solve that problem. The irony of this is that students need a sophisticated understanding of disciplinary knowledge if they are to select, integrate and use appropriate knowledge (Freebody, 2006, p. 25).

As well as having implications for the 'what' of curriculum (the way in which knowledge is classified) the structure of an academic discipline also has implications for how it is translated for pedagogic transmission. Bernstein refers to the 'how' of pedagogic practice as the process of *framing*. Induction into a particular academic discipline requires induction into its system of meaning, and this may shape the way knowledge is selected, sequenced, paced and evaluated. The more hierarchical a body of knowledge (for example, physics) the more likely it is that pedagogy will need to be strongly sequenced because students need to understand what came before in order to understand what comes after (Muller, 2006). In the example of physics, the sequencing of knowledge is a product of the way in which knowledge is classified because it is related to the epistemic logic intrinsic to that particular knowledge structure. It is possible though to have some elements of pedagogic practice that are strongly framed, with others that are weakly framed. For example, students may have greater control over the pace of learning and the learning activities they engage in (weak framing), while the assessment may be clearly stipulated so that students have a clear understanding of what they are required to do (strong framing).

Bernstein (2000, p. 113) refers to the process in which knowledge is translated for curriculum and pedagogic practice as the process of *recontextualisation*. Recontextualisation entails *delocating* knowledge from the field in which it was produced and *relocating* it into pedagogic discourse. Different principles are used to construct an 'academic' curriculum and a 'vocational' curriculum. The purpose of an academic curriculum is to induct students into a field of *knowledge* (the academic disciplines) while the purpose of a vocational curriculum is to induct students into a field of *practice*. The principle of selection (the classification of knowledge) and the way knowledge is selected, sequenced, paced and evaluated (the framing of knowledge) will be different in each.

Young (2008a, p. 170) argues that vocational curriculum needs to have two purposes: the first is to provide students with access to 'the (disciplinary) knowledge that is transforming work' and the second is to assist students to acquire 'job-specific skills and knowledge.' Vocational curriculum shares this feature with curriculum that is designed to prepare students for the professions. Academic curriculum faces 'one-way' towards the academic discipline, while vocational and professional curriculum faces 'both-ways' to the knowledge base underpinning practice and the tacit and contextual knowledge of the workplace (Barnett, 2006). This means that there is continuity between the purposes of vocational and professional education and both are distinguished from education designed to prepare students for the academic disciplines. However, each must provide students with access to the knowledge that is intrinsic to the field.

Students need to be inducted into disciplinary systems of meaning as the basis of developing the 'recognition' rules they need to recognise the distinction between vertical and horizontal discourses, and between different types of vertical discourses so that they can, for example, distinguish between physics and chemistry, or microeconomics and sociology (Bernstein, 2000). In general, knowledge that is strongly classified into disciplinary frameworks provides students from disadvantaged backgrounds with more access to theoretical knowledge than weakly classified knowledge. Middle class students have had more access to the way knowledge is classified and framed throughout their pedagogic careers because of the cultural congruence between home and school and they are more able to recognise and mobilise the decontextualised features of knowledge in curriculum that is weakly classified (Bernstein, 2000). Knowledge that is strongly classified and framed provides students from disadvantaged backgrounds with more access because it explicitly signals the boundaries between different areas of knowledge and the way it is sequenced, paced and evaluated, whereas these relations are rendered opaque in knowledge that is weakly classified and framed. Bernstein (1996, p. 12) explains 'To know whose voice is speaking is the beginning of one's own voice.' Induction into the disciplines is a precondition if students are to recognise different voices and to begin to articulate their own. Muller (2000, p. 71) explains:

> to cross the line without knowing it is to be at the mercy of the power inscribed in the line. The question is *how* to cross, and that means paying detailed attention to the politics of redescription and translation and to the means required for a successful crossing.

Structure of CBT and How it Excludes from Access to Knowledge

CBT excludes students from access to disciplinary knowledge because it collapses the distinction between vertical and horizontal discourses, and because knowledge in curriculum is weakly classified and framed. Students are not provided with the 'recognition' rules they need to access different types of knowledge. CBT does not provide students with the capacity to recognise and navigate the distinction between theoretical and everyday knowledge and between different kinds of theoretical knowledge. The boundaries are rendered opaque.

As indicated earlier, VET qualifications are based on 'training packages,' which consist of qualifications made up of units of competency. Units of competency describe workplace tasks or roles. Competency is defined as the application of specified knowledge, skill and attitudes needed to undertake a work role or task to the required standard in the workplace (DEST, 2006, p. 69). The way in which units of competency are constructed is quite prescriptive. They must include, among other things, elements of competency (that break down the unit of competency into demonstrable and assessable outcomes or actions); performance criteria that specify the required level of performance; required knowledge and skills; a range statement that describes the contexts and conditions in which the performance criteria apply; and evidence guides that describe the underpinning knowledge and skills that need to be demonstrated (assessed) to prove competence (DEST, 2006, p. 117).

The *Training Package Development Handbook* (DEST, 2006, p. 114) insists that knowledge is important because students need to understand the 'why' as well as the 'how.' As a consequence, 'units of competency must detail the underpinning knowledge required for competent performance' (DEST, 2006, p. 114). However, the notion of underpinning knowledge is limited to contextually specific applications of knowledge. For example, the *Training Package Development Handbook* (DEST, 2006, p. 114) explains that:

> while knowledge must be expressed, units of competency, their elements or performance criteria should not be entirely knowledge based unless a clear and assessable workplace outcome is described. Knowledge in units of competency:
> - should be in context;
> - should only be included if it refers to knowledge actually applied at work

A bit later, the *Training Package Development Handbook* (DEST, 2006, p. 140, emphasis added) says that, 'Units of competency that integrate knowledge into the overall performance specification of the unit and the assessment process advice *should fully include all relevant knowledge as it is applied in a work role.*' This ties knowledge to the contextually specific, but also to a narrow conception of what knowledge is, and the purposes for which it can be used. As an example, the *Training Package Development Handbook* (DEST, 2006, p. 139) states that:

> Competent performance must result in a realistic expression of knowledge through problem solving, prediction of outcomes, cause and effect, or similar dynamic process specific to the unit.

This is a very fragmented, atomistic and instrumental view of knowledge. It is premised on positivist views of knowledge in which knowledge is reducible to statements about correlation and prediction. Knowledge is not and cannot be always about prediction of outcomes, unless we are limiting our statements to observation of cause and effect in closed systems, and this does not describe the world of work or any aspect of the social world (Bhaskar, 1998). Knowledge is about *understanding*.

The key problem is that students need access to the disciplinary system of meaning if they are to select and apply appropriate contextually specific applications of that knowledge. CBT translates knowledge from being general and principled knowledge to particularised knowledge, because its selection and usefulness is determined by the extent to which it is relevant in a particular context. Students thus have access to knowledge in its particularised form, but are not provided with the means to relate it to its general and principled structure and system of meaning.

This is illustrated through comparing and contrasting a unit of competency in a VET advanced diploma with a subject in a similar area from the first year of a higher education degree. Both are taken from Victoria University, which is a dual-sector university in Australia that has a higher education division and a technical and further education (TAFE) division, which is the name of public institutions in Australia that provide VET qualifications. Students who undertake advanced diplomas often get credit for the first year of their studies in a degree if the advanced diploma and degree are in the same field.

'Develop and update the legal knowledge required for business compliance' is a unit of competency in the Advanced Diploma of Hospitality Management. According to the unit descriptor, this unit 'deals with the skills and knowledge required to ensure business compliance with legislation governing the tourism and hospitality industries' (CoA, 2002, p. 477). The focus is on the specific legislation for the tourism and hospitality industries. The knowledge required is specified by the context (business compliance with the specific legislation) and not through general principles. This is quite different from the first year 'business law' subject in the Bachelor of Business (Hospitality Management). The 'business law' subject aims to 'provide students with an understanding and awareness of the basic principles of Contract Law, a familiarity with relevant case law and an introduction to the statutory provisions pertinent to the course.' It explains that the purpose is to help students 'develop an understanding of legal reasoning as it applies to the analysis of contractual relationships.'[1] In other words, students are being inducted into the system of meaning (principles of contract law and legal reasoning) as well as its contextually specific applications.

The 'underpinning' knowledge needed within the 'Develop and update the legal knowledge' unit of competency is elaborated through the elements of competency and the performance criteria, and these are presented in Table 4.1 (see page 63). Under element one, 'Research the legal information required for business compliance,' students are required to demonstrate they can do this correctly through identifying correct sources of legal information and accessing, selecting and analysing information that is relevant to the business, and not on the basis of legal reasoning or basic principles.

The evidence guide includes a long list of essential knowledge and skills that must be addressed in the assessment process, which includes the following: 'research skills in order to source and access legal information and advice' (CoA 2002, p. 480). This is addressed in element one, which requires students to research legal information required for business compliance; and in element three, which requires students to update their legal knowledge by using formal and informal methods of research. However, formal and informal research methods are rendered commensurable and not insulated from each other. Students are not given access to the particular principles and methods used to research law. The distinction between vertical and horizontal discourses is collapsed, and knowledge is weakly classified and framed. The result is that the boundaries between this form of research and everyday research are rendered opaque. For example, the range statement includes this advice:

> 'Sources of legal information and informal/formal research may include
> - reference books
> - media
> - industry and/or employer associations
> - industry journals
> - Internet
> - customers and suppliers
> - legal experts' (CoA 2002, p. 478)

The *principles* used to distinguish *different types* of knowledge in research, and to assess and evaluate their credibility, validity and reliability is not built into the structuring of the unit of competency, into the elements of competency, the performance criteria, the range statement or the required knowledge and skills.

Students undertaking 'business law' in the Bachelor of Business (Hospitality

Management) are equipped to a greater extent to begin to participate in debates and controversies in their fields of practice than are students undertaking the unit of competency 'Develop and update legal knowledge.' The unit illustrates the way in which CBT presents units of competency as unproblematic descriptions of work, rather than fields of practice characterised by debate and controversy. The voice of power speaks in defining a task and incorporating it in a unit of competency. The voice of power decides *what* is important (how knowledge is classified) and *how* it should be presented (how knowledge is framed). This shows that there is symmetry between the content and structure of pedagogic discourse in VET in which each reinforces the other to produce hegemonic and unproblematic notions of work.

In Australia, 'industry' has control over the content of VET qualifications because it has control over the outcomes of VET qualifications. The idea is that industry specifies the outcomes, which are then taught by TAFEs and other VET providers. The whole point of CBT was to reduce the power of 'educational providers' and to ensure that 'training' met the requirements of industry (Goozee, 2001). The voice of power speaks in two ways: first, through the content of VET qualifications; and second, through the structure of VET qualifications. The context in which VET qualifications are developed is within a broader policy framework underpinned by theories of human capital that takes as a given the unproblematic goal of developing a competitive economy and skilled workforce. Power relations are not problematised either within the workplace or more broadly in society, and debates and controversies are not reflected within the structuring of training package qualifications. This is illustrated in the new employability skills that must be 'front and centre' of VET qualifications as they are redeveloped (DEST, 2006, p. 170). These employability skills replace the previous broader 'key competencies' because the latter 'were too generic in their approach and no longer reflected the needs of contemporary workplaces' (Cleary, Flynn and Thomasson, 2006, p. 10). The new employability skills are designed to cultivate 'appropriate' skills and attitudes as a key objective of VET policy and are even more tightly tied to work than were the previous key competencies. They are defined as:

> Communication that contributes to productive and harmonious relations between employees and customers
>
> Teamwork that contributes to productive working relationships and outcomes
>
> Problem solving that contributes to productive outcomes
>
> Initiative and enterprise that contributes to innovative outcomes
>
> Planning and organising that contribute to long-term and short-term strategic planning
>
> Self-management that contributes to employee satisfaction and growth
>
> Learning that contributes to ongoing improvement and expansion in employee and

company operations and outcomes

Technology that contributes to effective execution of tasks (DEST, 2006, pp. 191–194)

Williams (2005, p. 45) explains that the discourse around employability skills is a normalising exercise, in which the desired attributes of 'learner-workers' are defined according to the values, beliefs and expectations of the dominant culture. The definition of employability skills here shows that this is indeed the case, if we define dominant culture as the near hegemonic dominance of *employer* interests in government policy and in the VET system.

Conclusion

Unless students understand disciplinary systems of meaning they are tied to contextual knowledge, and this limits their capacity to use that knowledge in other contexts. Hairdressers need to understand the relationship between ratios, fractions and percentages in mixing hair dyes and in other aspects of their work. Apprentice motor mechanics will have difficulty understanding when and if they should use particular mathematical formulas in other contexts if they have been taught that this *particular* formula is used in a *particular* context. They will be able to relate the specific context and the specific formula, but will not have been provided with the tools to choose, select and apply other formulas within that context or a range of other contexts. Community development workers need access to sociological understandings of cultural diversity, the nature of communities, and theories of power if they are to develop effective community development strategies.

CBT excludes students from access to disciplinary knowledge because it only provides students with access to contextually specific applications of knowledge, and not the system of meaning in which it is embedded. In doing so, it collapses the boundary between vertical and horizontal discourses, and with it, students' capacity to recognise and distinguish each. Students need access to disciplinary knowledge because this is the means through which debates are conducted within their field of practice, but it is also the means through which students can participate in society's conversation more broadly.

The structure and content of VET qualifications combine to act as a mechanism of social stratification because they deny students systematic access to disciplinary systems of meaning through tying knowledge to workplace tasks and roles, and through the content of these qualifications, which are based on unproblematic descriptions of work. So not only are VET students denied full access to the structures of knowledge that they need to participate in society's conversation, but they are also denied access to the means to participate in debates and controversies within their field of practice.

Revalorising the depth and complexity of vocational knowledge in VET qualifications would increase the status of VET qualifications by making complex, theoretical knowledge as important in VET as it is in the elite professions. There is a continuity of *purpose* between VET and professional qualifications, because both seek to prepare students for a field of practice. There is not yet a continuity of *means*. Students engaged in studying for the professions have richer access to knowledge, because higher education programs tend to be curriculum-driven. VET can open possibilities for students if it is linked to education for the professions, so that educational progression and occupational progression become linked. But to do this effectively, VET must move away from CBT as its mandated model of curriculum.

NOTE

1. Source: http://wcf.vu.edu.au/Handbook/DisplaySubjectDetails.cfm?SubjectID=32925 accessed 20 June 2008.

REFERENCES

Barnett, M. (2006). Vocational knowledge and vocational pedagogy. In M. Young and J. Gamble, *Knowledge, Curriculum and Qualifications for South African Further Education*. Cape Town: Human Sciences Research Council.

Bernstein, B. (1996). *Pedagogy, Symbolic Control and Identity: Theory, Research, Critique*. London: Taylor & Francis.

Bernstein, B. (2000). *Pedagogy, Symbolic Control and Identity* (2nd ed.). Oxford: Rowman & Littlefield Publishers.

Bhaskar, R. (1998). *The Possibility of Naturalism: A Philosophical Critique of the Contemporary Human Sciences* (3rd ed.). London: Routledge.

Bourne, J. (2004). Framing talk: towards a 'radical visible pedagogy.' In J. Muller, B. Davies and Morais (Eds.), *Reading Bernstein, Researching Bernstein*. Routledge & Falmer: London.

Cleary, M., Flynn, R. and Thomasson, S. (2006). *Employability Skills. From Framework to Practice. An Introductory Guide for Trainers and Assessors*. Canberra: Department of Education, Science and Training.

Commonwealth of Australia (2002). *THT02 Tourism Training Package Volume 2 of 5*. Canberra: Department of Education, Science and Training.

Department of Education Science and Training (2006). *Training Package Development Handbook*. Canberra: Department of Education Science and Training.

Dewey, J. (1966 [1916]). *Democracy and Education: An Introduction to the Philosophy of Education*. New York: The Free Press.

Durkheim, E. (1960). The dualism of human nature and its social conditions. In K. H. Wolff (Ed.), *Emile Durkheim, 1858–1917: A Collection of Essays*, with Translations and a Bibliography. Columbus, OH: Ohio State University Press.

Dusseldorp Skills Forum (2007). *How Young People are Faring 2007: At a Glance*. Sydney: DSF.

Foley, P. (2007). The socio-economic status of vocational education and training students in Australia. Adelaide: National Centre for Vocational Education Research.

Freebody, P. (2006). *'Obedience, Learning, Virtue, and Arithmetic': Knowledge, Skill and Disposition in the Organisation of Senior Schooling*. Brisbane: Queensland Studies Authority.

Goozee, G. (2001). *The Development of TAFE in Australia* (3rd ed.). Adelaide: National Centre for Vocational Education Research.

Muller, J. (2000). *Reclaiming Knowledge. Social Theory, Curriculum and Education Policy.* London: Routledge & Falmer.

Muller, J. (2006). Differentiation and progression in the curriculum. In M. Young and J. Gamble (Eds.), *Knowledge, Curriculum and Qualifications for South African Further Education.* Cape Town: Human Sciences Research Council.

Organisation for Economic Co-operation and Development. (1998). *Redefining Tertiary Education.* Paris: OECD.

Organisation for Economic Co-operation and Development. (2007). *Education at a Glance.* 2007 OECD Indicators. Paris: OECD.

Scott, P. (2003). 1992–2002: Where next? *Perspectives: Policy and Practice in Higher Education,* 7(3), 71–75.

Singh, P. (2002). Pedagogising knowledge: Bernstein's theory of the pedagogic device. *British Journal of Sociology of Education,* 23(4), 571–582.

Teese, R., Nicholas, T., Polesel, J. and Helme, S. (2006). *The destinations of school leavers in Victoria.* Melbourne: Communications Division for the Department of Education and Training.

Williams, C. (2005). The discursive construction of the 'competent' learner-worker: From key competencies to 'employability skills.' *Studies in Continuing Education,* 27 (1), 33–49.

Young, M. (2003). Durkheim, Vygotsky and the curriculum of the future. *London Review of Education,* 1 (2), 100–117.

Young, M. (2006). Reforming the further education and training curriculum: An international perspective. In M. Young & J. Gamble (Eds.), *Knowledge, Curriculum and Qualifications for South African Further Education.* Cape Town: Human Sciences Research Council.

Young, M. (2008a). *Bringing knowledge back in: From social constructivism to social—Realism in the sociology of education.* London: Routledge.

Young, M. (2008b). From constructivism to realism in the sociology of the curriculum. *Review of Research in Education,* 32 (1), 1–28.

Table 4.1: Unit of competency 'Develop and update the legal knowledge required for business compliance'

Elements	Performance criteria
Research the legal information required for business compliance	Identify sources of legal information and advice correctly. Access, select and analyse information for relevance to the business. Record and distribute information appropriately.
Ensure compliance with legal requirements	Assess the need for legal advice and seek assistance where appropriate. Share information with appropriate work colleagues in a timely manner. Organise information updates and training for colleagues and staff where appropriate. Establish and monitor workplace systems and procedures to ensure compliance with legal requirements. Identify aspects of operations which may infringe laws and solicit advice on how to develop and implement modifications.
Update legal knowledge	Use informal and formal research to update the legal knowledge required for business compliance. Share updated knowledge with colleagues and incorporate into workplace planning and operations.

Source: *Commonwealth of Australia (2002, p. 477)*

CHAPTER FIVE

Social Class and Pedagogy

Ursula Hoadley

Introduction

An enduring concern in the sociology of education is the persistent achievement gap between working class and middle class students. We have known for a long time, especially since Coleman et al. (1966), that schooling reproduces social class differences. In the transition from apartheid to a democratic dispensation in South Africa, class inequalities (largely welded to race) have persisted, and a highly stratified system of education in terms of social class has become entrenched. Schooling in South Africa fails the vast majority of students in enhancing their life chances. But how inequalities are reproduced has remained something of a black box, in particular in relation to how pedagogy functions. The present chapter attempts to address this problem, presenting a theoretical model based on empirical work in Grade 3 literacy classrooms in South Africa. It describes two different 'modalities' of pedagogy emerging in different contexts—a vertical modality in a middle class context, and a horizontal modality in a working class context. The study integrates analytic tools from the sociology of education in order to achieve a specificity of description of the process whereby different orders of meaning and knowledge are transmitted. The purpose is to show a model for investigating pedagogic variation in different social class contexts. The theory employed in the study allows for a linking of the micro processes of the classroom with a consideration of the macro social class set up. The chapter is located within a broader study (Hoadley, 2005) concerned with social class and pedagogy.

Apart from the macro studies of economic and cultural reproduction[1] (Bowles and Gintis, 1976; Bourdieu and Passeron, 1977), a number of studies have focused attention at the level of the classroom. In relation to the research traditions in classroom research in the 1960s, Koehler (1978) distinguishes between those that described the process and those that linked processes to desired outcomes. Cazden (1986) summarises these as positivist and interpretive in their approaches respectively. Subsequent work relating to social class was concerned more with the *effects* of social class on pedagogy, rather than the structuring of pedagogy itself, and its social class base. These include the differential distribution of knowledge to students of different social classes (Keddie, 1971; Walkerdine, 1988). Others frame the question in relation to teacher labelling (Labov, 1972; Cicourel and Kitsuse, 1963), tracking (Oakes, 1985), or teachers and students of different social classes' access to different 'ways with words' and ways of interacting (Heath, 1985).

A recent return to classroom-based research, of which this study forms part, signals a sharper focus on the mechanisms through which classroom processes reproduce or interrupt the process of class reproduction. Work in the Bernsteinian tradition, in particular, has made a notable contribution in this regard. This study contributes to this growing body of work which focuses on identifying specific aspects of pedagogic practice for working class learners favourable to the development of the school code (Morais and Neves, 2001; Morais et al. 2004; Rose 2004; Arnot and Reay, 2004; Reeves, 2005). In particular, strong framing over the evaluative criteria and variable pacing is emphasised as contributing to working class success. The work focuses on the structuring of the pedagogy—on the relay. The present study aims to extend the Bernsteinian framework to include the *relayed*, in order to achieve a greater specificity in the description of pedagogic practice and its variation. Further, whereas much of the work referred to above is experimental, the present study considers pedagogic practice in naturalistic settings and in a developing world context where conventional notions of how pedagogy and schools function cannot be taken for granted.

Theoretical Approach

How precisely do we describe pedagogic processes so that the mechanisms of social class differentiation are made explicit? Bernstein, the key theorist informing this study, allows for an analysis that links the macro and the micro, laying bare the social class base of pedagogic practice and its implications.

Bernstein makes the point that there is a differential distribution of power and control relations across different social classes, and these produce different practices and forms of consciousness. It is through Bernstein's 'codes' that we see the differential positioning of subjects of different social class groupings, dominant and dominated. He states that 'class relations generate, distribute, reproduce, and legitimate distinctive forms of communication, which transmit dominant and dominated codes, and that the subjects are differently positioned by these codes in the process of acquiring them' (1990, p. 13).

Code is concerned with the transmission of meaning, in the family and school, and how this relates to social class reproduction. Code, a mediating concept like habitus or role, refers to the principles that regulate meaning systems. The research reported here follows over 30 years of empirical and theoretical work in the Bersteinian framework that shows how working class and middle class students enter the school more or less predisposed to acquiring the specialized knowledge of schooling, and recognizing and realizing the 'school code' (Adlam et al. 1977; Cook-Gumperz, 1973; Holland, 1981; Fontinhas et al. 1995). For middle class learners, the home is a second site of acquisition; middle class family socialization is a hidden subsidy (Bernstein, 1977, p. 33), which enables them to acquire the school code more efficiently. Working class students enter the school with a 'community code'; the school code is not developed in the family prior to encountering formal pedagogy. *Orientation to meaning*, then, is taken to be the crucial background variable associated with social class which makes a difference to children's schooling experience. Orientation to meaning refers to the transmission and acquisition of more context-independent meanings (elaborated codes or a 'school code') and more context-dependent meanings (restricted codes).

The purpose of schooling is to specialize learners' voices with respect to the school code. Pedagogy inducts learners into a 'school' way of organizing experience and making meaning, in short hand, into the elaborated code of schooling or the 'school code.' *Specialization of voice* refers to the extent to which the student's educational identity, consciousness and specific school-related skills are clearly marked and bounded.

How do we identify the specialization of voice, or more precisely, whether the transmission is doing the work of specializing? Conventionally, in the Bernsteinian literature, specialization of voice is adumbrated in terms of classification and framing values. The theoretical model presented here comprises three dimensions: classification and framing of the pedagogic discourse, the instructional strategies deployed by the teacher in the pedagogy, and the instructional form that the pedagogy takes. These are discussed below. Two exemplary data texts are then presented, which show how the model was derived through interaction between theory and data. The chapter concludes with a discussion of the pedagogic modalities derived from the research, the recruitment of the theoretical resources for the study, and some of the implications of the analysis and model.

Bernstein: Classification and Framing

In order to describe how education specialises consciousness, Bernstein developed his code theory. The specialised form of communication whereby differential transmission and acquisition is effected is the pedagogic discourse (Bernstein, 1990, p. 182). Pedagogic discourse describes the *relay* of pedagogy. It consists of an instructional discourse embedded in a regulative discourse, or where a discourse of competence (the instructional, including specific skills) is embedded in a regulatory discourse (regulatory of character, conduct and manner, and of theories of pedagogy).

Bernstein provides a language for the description of pedagogic discourse through the concepts of classification and framing, referring respectively to power and control. Classification refers to the social division of labour. At the macro level classification generates categories of agents and discourses: the categories or insulations are instantiations of power. At the micro level, classification is about the organizational or structural aspects of pedagogic practice. Classification is about *relations between*, and the degree of maintenance between categories.

Classification is expressed as being strong, where boundaries are explicit and categories are insulated from one another, or weak, where there is integration, or where the boundary is blurred. These are expressed in terms of a continuum, from C^{++} through to C^{--}. In the analysis, relations between discourses, disciplines, agents and spaces are considered in terms of the strength of classification.

Where classification at the macro level is related to the social division of labour, framing refers to social relations within this social division. Framing, therefore, refers to *relations within* (within boundaries). Framing, in a sense, supports classification. It produces 'the animation of the power grid' (Hasan, 2002), but it also opens up the potential for the change of boundaries, and the contesting of power relations. It is through interaction (framing) that boundaries between discourses, spaces and subjects are defined, maintained and changed.

At the micro level of pedagogic practice, framing conventionally has to do with the way in which the relationship between the teacher and the learner is set up, where strong framing refers to a limited degree of options for students, and weak framing implies more 'apparent' control by learners. Again, framing is expressed in terms of its strength or degree of control. Strong framing would imply that students have limited control over the 'relations within' and over the sequencing, pacing, selection and evaluation of the knowledge transmitted.

In relation to framing, Bernstein asserts that 'control is double faced for it carries both the power of reproduction and the potential for its change' (Bernstein, 1996, p. 19). The distinction between power and control, unique in the discipline of sociology, thus allows for the description of the making and potential unmaking of the social reproduction of inequality. In the social reproduction script, working-class children will never make it. Bernstein's code theory opens up the possibility for talking about reproduction and its interruption.

Classification and framing describe the *structuring* of pedagogic communication. Whereas most studies of the pedagogizing of knowledge, and what makes pedagogic communication possible, have focused on what is carried or *relayed*, he is interested in the *relay*.

Dowling: Domains and Strategies

Dowling (1998) too is concerned with the operation of the relay, but in the course of deriving his categories of strategies and domains he also enables an analysis of the relayed. Dowling (1999) dispenses with framing. He does this because he does not operate with a notion of boundary. Classification for him refers to degrees of specialization rather than strength of insularities. Further, his project is different—he wants to analyze the contents of the classification as well as elucidate its structure. He presents a set of dichotomous concepts at a somewhat lower level of abstraction than classification and framing. Bernstein describes the forms of consciousness (essentially elaborated and restricted), and Dowling translates these as forms of knowledge. Forms of consciousness can only be seen in the materiality of what teachers and learners do at the level of the classroom. Dowling is interested in how knowledge types are distributed. These types are contained in domains and distributed through strategies, and it is through the differential distribution of these knowledge forms that social inequalities are reproduced.

Simply put, strategies in the present study are used to consider how the tasks set by the teachers in the classroom are related to the specialized discourse of literacy. The use of the concepts of domains and strategies differ in significant ways from Dowling's use, and have been simplified and delocated from Dowling's more general activity theory. The analysis presented later will consider 'localising' strategies, referring to the public domain (or non-specialised knowledge), and 'specialising' strategies, which refer to the esoteric domain of specialized literacy knowledge. The latter is broadly defined as addressing the phonetic, semantic and syntactic aspects of language entailed in the teaching of literacy.

In considering the tasks across time (as 'pedagogic assemblies'), generalising strategies describe an assembly constituted by an esoteric domain message (for example, the presentation and rehearsal of a concept across a number of tasks), or by fragmenting strategies, which realise the assembly as segmental, or unarticulated. As will become clearer in the analysis, Dowling thus provides a language to speak about the relation between the general and the particular, the concrete and the abstract, by relating particular strategies to domains.

Pedro (1981): Instructional Form

Instructional and regulative discourses are two of the structural components of pedagogy. The third element is the instructional form, which is theorized by Pedro (1981), who was concerned with social class and linguistic realisations in pedagogy. Instructional form allows for a consideration of the way in which learners are organised in pedagogic practice, and, in particular, the question of whether students are individualised or communalised in the pedagogy. Because Bernstein's theory of pedagogic discourse does not consider *what* is classified, instructional form cannot be expressed in terms of classification and framing.

Table 5.1 summarises the theoretical dimensions used in analysing how pedagogy functions in different social class settings, and its potential to specialize student voice with respect to the school code.

Table 5.1 Model for the consideration of pedagogic variation

1. Classification and framing of pedagogic discourse	Sequence and selection		$F^{+/-}$
	Pacing		$F^{+/-}$
	Evaluative rules		$F^{+/-}$
	Hierarchical rules		$F^{+/-}$
	Discourses	Inter-disc (subjects)	$C^{+/-}$
		Inter-disc (school/everyday)	$C^{+/-}$
	Spaces	Internal	$C^{+/-}$
		External	$C^{+/-}$
	Agents		$C^{+/-}$
2. Instructional form	Content		Differentiated/uniform
	Classroom organization		Communalised -homogenous individualised-specialized
3. Instructional strategies	Individual tasks		Localizing/ specialising
	Pedagogic assemblies		Fragmenting/ generalising

The purpose of recruiting these theories is to achieve greater precision in the description of the variation in pedagogic practice across different settings that privileges social class in the analysis.

Methodology

The study employed a particular sampling strategy in order to put differences in different social class contexts starkly on display. Four Grade 3 teachers, teaching in an upper middle class Cape Town suburban setting were selected, where students came from affluent homes, and the teachers had middle class backgrounds and livelihoods. In contrast, four teachers were selected from lower working class township schools in Cape Town, where the students came from very poor homes (largely shack dwellings), and the teachers themselves came from working class backgrounds. Each teacher was observed and video-taped for three full consecutive days. Literacy lessons were extracted from the data, and a total of 60 lessons and 103 tasks in literacy across the eight teachers comprised the data set for the analysis.

Although located in very different settings, the basic resource levels of the classrooms were uniform. All classrooms fell within the national pupil:teacher norm of 40:1, all classrooms had sufficient tables, chairs and books (though the books varied in quality). The middle class classrooms were racially integrated; the working class classrooms consisted solely of black learners and teachers.

An 'external language of description' (Bernstein, 1996) consisting of a set of coding schemes, networks and categories, was developed through interaction between the theory and the data. Concepts drawn from Bernstein, Dowling and Pedro provided the initial categories at a high level of abstraction, and the data suggested empirical indicators for the concepts, and more delicate and specific categories for analysis.[2] This external language of description was then used to code the lessons and tasks as shown below. Two examples are given to illustrate the analytic procedure.

Analysing the Data—The Working Class Context

The first example is taken from the classroom of one of the working class teachers. In this lesson the teacher stands in front of the class, paging through a textbook. The teacher begins discussing colours. What the teacher has encountered in the textbook is the end of a previous section on colours, which precedes a section on trees. A picture of leaves has led her to select this page as this relates to the more general theme in use, trees. She draws ten leaves on the board and the learners chant the numbers as she writes. The teacher then moves directly onto the next section in the book on trees.

> *Teacher*: So here are the parts of the tree. He [the textbook author] says write them in their order from the biggest to the smallest. Read these as I write them on the board.
>
> The teacher writes on the board: tree, leaf, branch, bush.

Teacher: Which are found at the bottom of a tree?

Learner: Roots

Teacher: No no. Don't tell me things you haven't seen. I'm not asking for what you've thought about, I'm asking for what you've seen. Okay, from the tree, bush, leaf and branch, which one do you get from the bottom of the tree? Things that you get at the bottom. Bottom, bottom.'

She underlines 'bottom' on the board. Another learner says roots. After a while the teacher looks back at the textbook and realises that she has made a mistake, reading 'tree, bush, branches, leaf,' instead of 'stem, roots, branches, leaves.' She moves directly on to the next question, which requires writing from biggest to smallest, tree, branch, leaf, bush. The teacher writes each word on the board, as she writes, learners repeat the words over and over again.

Learners: Leaves, leaves, leaves, leaves, leaves, leaves leaves, leaves, leaves leaves, leaves, leaves, leaves, leaves, leaves

Teacher: Hey stop. The reason why we are repeating this is because you do your own thing when I turn my back on you. Now the writer says the same words rhyme at the end. Now we've done a tree. Haven't we done a tree?

Learners: Yes Miss. Yes we've done it.

Teacher: Now we know how a tree is formed. Now the writer says there are certain words that rhyme at the end. This is what I like. And he also says write those that rhyme in the box. Ja, here's work. Close your books. I'll give you work on the board. Don't talk Grade 3. Don't talk, don't talk. Sleep on your desks. Lower your heads.

The teacher writes 6 words on the board: tree, fruits, home, flowers, smoke, bushes, roots.

Teacher: Listen, listen. I did not say shout on the top of the roof. Now write the rhyming words. He says some words are rhyming at the end so he wants you to write those that rhyme at the end. Here's the correct date, the thirty-first. Let's write. Let's work. No talking. I want rhyming words. I want rhyming words. I want rhyming words.

Later the teacher bangs on her table with a ruler and shouts at the learners to be quiet.

Teacher: Write, write, even though you don't know.

The teacher sits at her desk for the remaining 23 minutes of the lesson. At no point does she see what learners are writing. The bell rings for break and learners close their books and go out.

The coding of this lesson with respect to classification and framing (Bernstein, 1990), instructional strategies (drawing on Dowling, 1998) and instructional form (Pedro, 1981) is presented below. This will be illustrative of the coding procedure in general.

Classification and Framing

The selection and sequence in the extract above would both be coded F^{++}, as it is the teacher who decides what knowledge will be transmitted and in what order. Learners are not given opportunities to alter the selection and the sequence of the knowledge, even where at one point their interjections potentially are a corrective to the teacher's misreading of the text.³ Likewise, it is the teacher who asserts the pacing or expected rate of transmission. She decides that the lesson will continue until the bell rings, and learners' interjections and disruptions do not disturb the pace. Pacing is therefore also coded F^{++}.

The coding of the evaluative criteria is more complex. The required performance of learners ultimately is to copy down words that rhyme, but no concept of rhyming is transmitted, and its recognition is potentially opaque to the learners. Because the evaluative criteria have not been transmitted, the teacher can only elicit the legitimate text from the learners on the basis of assertion: 'Write, write, even though you don't know,' and that legitimate text appears devoid of instructional content. The learners are required to write; *what* they write does not seem to matter.

The framing of the evaluative criteria is difficult to categorise as either weak or strong. Thus the category F^0 in the coding scheme was developed in order to capture such instances of transmission, which appear devoid of evaluative criteria relating to the instructional discourse, or where these are obscured by regulative criteria. An example from the coding schema is given in Table 5.2.

Table 5.2 Extract from the coding instrument for framing of the evaluative rules

4. In the introduction / explanation / exposition to a topic/task	F^{++}	F^+	F^-	F^{--}	F^0
	Evaluative criteria very clear and explicit	Evaluative criteria quite clear and explicit	Evaluative criteria quite unclear and implicit	Evaluative criteria very unclear and implicit	Transmission of evaluative criteria not observable
	Teacher always or almost always makes the evaluative rules available through exposition. Explicitly defines and explains the meaning of concepts, addresses key aspects of the knowledge or operation under discussion through questioning and explication. She makes it clear exactly how a task should be completed.	Most of the time the teacher makes the evaluative rules available in an explicit and clear manner through explication and discussion. The requirements for the successful completion of a task are generally clear, although there may be some aspects that remain implicit.	The concepts and principles being addressed in the exposition are sometimes unclear. Attempts are made to make the requirements for the successful production of a text available to learners, but these are often unclear or not articulated. Some ambiguity as to what should be done and how it should be done exists.	Generally the teacher does not draw out the knowledge principles in her exposition. Very little or no attempt is made to make the requirements for the successful production of a text available to learners. Learners are unclear as to how to proceed, or proceed in any manner they choose.	It appears as if no attempt is made to transmit the concepts and principles in the instructional practice. It is unclear what counts as a successful production in terms of instructional knowledge. The purpose of the activity is unclear; learners are unclear as to how to proceed; or they are only given criteria relating to how they should *behave*.

Discursive rule EVALUATION RULES (F^{+-}) The extent to which teacher and learner have control over the evaluative rules of the instructional knowledge pertaining to the meaning of concepts and principles and their appropriate realisation

F^0 represents an inability to observe the code. It may also point to a breakdown in pedagogic discourse, the absence of (a particular dimension of) pedagogy, or a collapse of the instructional into the regulative (F^0 and its implications are elaborated in Hoadley [2006, 2007]). F^0 is not on the continuum, but represents a rupture. It is also evident from the example concerning rhyme that the coding of the data can at times be derived only in conjunction with an assessment of the texts that learners produce. It is necessary to establish (using this instance as an example) that the learners have not spent several prior lessons focusing on rhyme, making an explicit articulation of the evaluative rules redundant. In such cases, reference was made to learner productions and learner notebooks.

In terms of the regulative discourse, the hierarchical rules in this lesson would be coded F^{++}. The control relation is generally about constraint and is based on the teacher/pupil hierarchy, rather than an explication of rules or principles underlying the control. In this imperative form (F^{++}) the acquirer is given no options in responding to the control of the teacher, apart from an explicit challenge to authority. Three tasks were identified in this lesson for the coding of the instructional form and the instructional strategies. One was the discussion of colours and the drawing of ten leaves on the board. The second was the discussion of the parts of a tree, and the third was the writing down of rhyming words.

Instructional Form

For the coding of the instructional form, three options regarding the classroom organization were identified: *homogenous*, where the teacher worked with the class as a whole; *integrated*, where students worked with each other in groups; and *specialized*, where the teacher worked with groups of students or individual students. In this instance, the interest was in the grouping of agents in the instructional form.

In relation to the treatment of content, each task was also coded as to whether it differentiated between different members of the class or groups—and was coded *uniform* or *differentiated*. In all cases where a task was coded 'differentiated' there was differentiation on the basis of ability (although the category potentially could also refer to sex, language, religion, etc.). These are shown in the coding network in Figure 5.1.

In the given lesson, all three tasks were coded homogenous (the teacher worked with the whole class, not with individuals or groups) and uniform (all learners were required to do the same tasks). In other words, the pedagogy was characterized as communalising.

Instructional Strategies

Drawing on Dowling's concept of strategies, the first distinction for literacy is made between localising and specializing strategies. In order to recognize whether a task represents a localising or specializing strategy, the question is asked as to whether the task can be completed with or without access to specialized knowledge. Localizing tasks are those which the learners are able to perform without deploying the specialized knowledge of literacy. The 'literacy element' or concept is absent. These tasks incorporate knowledge that is familiar and local, and meanings that are generally particularistic, concrete and context-dependent. Specializing tasks, on the other hand, refer to a particular literacy element or concept, to an esoteric domain message.

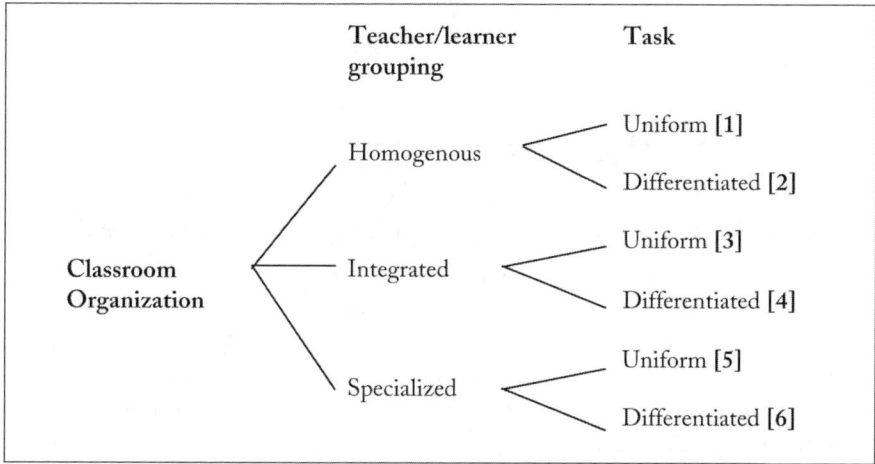

Figure 5.1 Network for the analysis of instructional form.

At the Grade 3 level, tasks which incorporated localising strategies often resembled 'play' or games. They generally required learners to do things that they enjoyed, and which they knew how to do (recite a well-known verse, colour in a picture). They did not incorporate new knowledge.

The initial categories, localizing and specializing strategies, were disaggregated to take account of different forms of these strategies. The network used in the coding is shown in Figure 5.2. I give examples of the different types of strategies in relation to the tasks identified from the lesson shown above.

The first task relating to colour, where learners chant numbers, was coded as localizing-ritual. In this instance, the exercise did not require the exercise of any particular rule relating to literacy. The task entailed mimicry, a common strategy deployed by the teachers in the working class classrooms, where learners repeated words and phrases after the teacher, and were not required to produce texts of their own. The second task consists of the naming of parts of a tree, and was categorized localising-nominal. This strategy consisted of the teacher and learners naming things—usually in relation to a theme. A clear pedagogic trajectory from these kinds

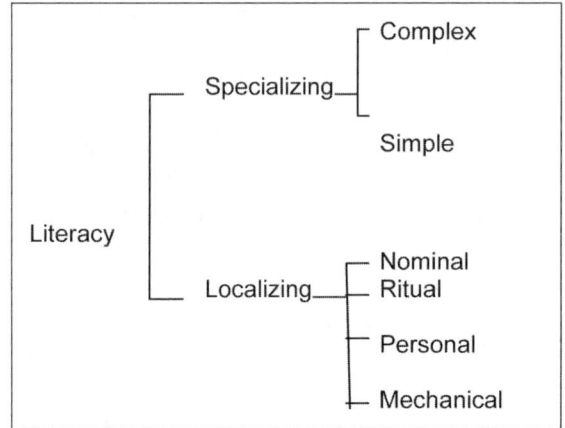

Figure 5.2 Network for the analysis of the instructional strategies for literacy tasks

exchanges was not retrievable; rather the pedagogic process consisted of building up a series of words and images in relation to a theme.

The third task, pertaining to rhyming words, was categorized as localising-mechanical. Localising-mechanical strategies were apparent when learners were required to reproduce, imitate or copy the exact text of the teacher or other resource. In these instances, the evaluative rules were implicit or absent, and very little or no application of specialized knowledge to the particular task was required. In several of the literacy lessons, learners were required to copy off the board, colour in and draw or copy from the textbook without doing any kind of operation beyond this.

Overall, the localising strategies presented here approximate what mothers do with their children in early pedagogic and socialization activities, for example, read to the child, help the child name things, recite rhymes. They are not empty of pedagogic content or potential but, in relation to Grade 3 learning, they do not specialize voice, they do not explicitly appeal to the esoteric domain and they do not require specialized performances on the part of the learner. Rather, they represent a form of initial, segmental pedagogy, aspects of which one may find in the home.

ANALYSING THE DATA—THE MIDDLE CLASS CONTEXT

A second extract is given from the middle class context. Small groups of learners sit in turn with the teacher on a mat in the front of the class, with each learner having with them a box of words and a reader. The learners read out their words, and provide some definitions, and then take turns reading from the reader.

> *Teacher:* Well done Candi, you can begin as soon as you've finished putting them out.
> *Learner:* Start, market, startle, spark, chart, sharpener, sparkle

Teacher: Sorry, I need a sentence for startle.

Learner: Brandon startled me, like scared, surprised or scared.

Teacher: 'Brandon startled me' doesn't actually tell me what it means. I walked down the passage and Brandon came into the room and startled me. Something you weren't expecting. That's what startled means. Read.

Two more students read lists and offer definitions for words. A fourth student follows.

Learner: Short, porter, reporter, order, report, perform, shorten

Teacher: Shorten. I need a sentence for shorten.

Learner: Last night we had to shorten my tracksuit pants

Teacher: Because

Learner: Because it was too long

Teacher: They were too long. Yes.

Learner: Mouth, Loud, about, trout, south, ground.

Teacher: Well done. Shoo. Give me a sentence for trout.

Learner: Me and my brother went trout fishing at the river.

Teacher: Mmm. Why didn't you go to the sea for trout fishing?

Learner: Because trout don't swim in the sea.

Teacher: You say my brother and I went trout fishing at the river. Well done

Learner: Purchase, curtain, disturb, survive, sur*face*

Teacher: Sur*face*. Did you practice these words?

Learner: Yes

Teacher: But with whom? Mmm? Alone?

Learner: No with my big brother.

Teacher: With your big brother, with your mother or father next time, hey. Read this one again.

Learner: Surface

Teacher: Sur*face*. Purpose. Now give me a sentence for surface

Learner: I surf in the sea

Teacher: You surf in the sea. Okay. You surf in the sea. That's good. That means you ride along the waves. Do you swim right under the sea or do you swim on top of the water?

Learner: On top

Teacher: You swim on the…

Learners: Surface

Teacher: Okay. You swim on the *sur*face, on the top. *Sur*face. You must do homework with your mom or your dad please.

Teacher: Good. Put your cards away.

Teacher: And what are we reading?

Learner: Atlantis' race

Teacher: Okay. Move into me. Right in. So what was the story about yesterday?

Learner: The day they found out that the worm is used for cloth.

Teacher: Yes, and what's it called? What kind of cloth do they make from those worms? It starts with a 'ssss.'

Learner: Silk

The students each take a turn in reading with similar exchanges occurring intermittently. The next reading group is then called, and a similar process is followed.

Classification and framing

Framing of sequencing and selection in this lesson was characterised as strong. The teacher decides what will comprise the lesson and the ordering of the transmission. Framing over pacing is weaker. At times, the pace of transmission is relaxed in order to address learner productions, or give learners the opportunity to respond to questions. Although generally weaker in the middle class settings, pace is coded F^+ in this instance. Classification of discourses is strong—literacy as a subject is strongly bounded from other activities through the emphasis on particular phonemes, reading and definition and interpretation activities. Framing over the evaluative criteria, or what constitutes a legitimate production/text, is also strong. The evaluative rules are explicitly transmitted by the teacher, in particular in her reformulation of students' responses. The hierarchical rules in this lesson are coded F^+ (a positional form of control). Positional control is realised when control actions/utterances are based on simple rules.

Instructional form

Two tasks were identified in the lesson. The first required that learners read out a list of words containing a particular phoneme and provide definitions for some of those words. The second entailed learners reading from a prescribed reader. Both tasks were coded as specialized (learners were organized into graded groups according to reading ability) and in terms of content, differentiated (readers and spelling lists were ability graded for different groups). The instructional form thus individualized learners through allocating them to different groups, and distributing different content to different learners.

Instructional strategies

Both tasks were also coded as specializing-complex. Specializing-complex requires that learners engage in the novel applications of rules, or that learners display their reasoning, synthesis and/or evaluation of knowledge. In specializing strategies the knowledge distributed to learners refers to the esoteric domain of the subject. In the lesson extract we see that the tasks refer to the phonological, semantic and syntactic aspects of literacy. The sounds of words are emphasized, as in

    T: Read this one again.
    L: Sur*face*
    T: *Sur*face. Purpose. Now give me a sentence for surface

The meanings of words and passages are emphasised, as in

T: I need a sentence for trowel.

L: Trowel

T: We spoke a lot about it at the beginning of the year. We even watched the builders with their trowels

L: Oh. They use trowels to put the cement on the walls.

T: A trowel is a tool.

And the correct grammatical ordering of words in order to make sentences is addressed:

T: Shorten. I need a sentence for shorten.

L: Last night we had to shorten my tracksuit pants

T: Because

L: Because it was too long

T: They were too long. Yes.

Pedagogic Assemblies: Rules for Combination

In categorising the classification and framing of lessons, individual lessons were considered. In categorizing the instructional form and localizing and specializing strategies, each of the 103 individual tasks were considered as discrete units. The analysis of instructional strategies also involved analysing the tasks *across* the three days of observation, and considering the relations between these tasks. The interest was in whether the pedagogic assemblies (a series of tasks across a number of days) represented generalising or fragmenting strategies. Thus, what *connected* the tasks to each other, and what was foregrounded in the pedagogy, was considered. The question posed to the data was whether the pedagogic assembly was generated by an esoteric domain message (generalizing), or a public domain message (fragmenting). The unit of analysis here, then, was the pedagogic assembly.

In general, the analysis showed that in the middle-class context activities and concepts were carried from one day to the next. In the foregrounding of the conceptual in the pedagogic assemblies of the middle-class teachers, it is possible to conclude that the pedagogic assembly was generated by esoteric domain principles. In the working class school setting the pedagogic assembly was characterised as fragmented because the series of tasks was generated by a theme rather than by programmatic conceptual learning. There was very little or no reference to what was learned before, or what would be learned in future, apart from the fact that the thematic emphasis was the same. The actual learning trajectory was implicit or fragmented.

The rules for combination were accordingly very different in the two different social class contexts. In literacy, the learning tasks in the working-class context required that learners collectively reproduce a sequence of naming and labelling tasks. They did not engage in the reflexive deployment of meanings in any other way. There was little space for developing meta-awareness of how words sound, mean, and are put together, or, how rules can repeatedly produce predictable results. Learning tasks in the middle-class context required learners to apply operations, procedures and concepts in a way that was highly visible to the teacher and peers, and was very repetitive. *In the working-class context learners were learning to name the world, and the middle-class context learners were learning to categorize the world.*

Pedagogic Modalities

All 60 lessons were coded in the same way. Partly due to the sampling, which sought similarity within contexts, there was remarkable consistency in the pedagogy across classrooms within the same social class contexts. Two pedagogic modalities are derived from the analyses, which represent the different orientations to classifying experience and creating meaning that are privileged in the classrooms in the different social class contexts. A *horizontal modality* emerges from the working-class context and a *vertical modality* from the middle-class context. The vertical modality presents greater opportunity than the horizontal modality for the transmission of context-independent meanings and the specialization of learners' voice with respect to the school code. The two modalities are summarised below.

The Horizontal Modality

The horizontal pedagogic modality is characterised by strong framing over sequence, selection and pace, and very weak framing over the evaluative rules. The transmission generally does not draw out the knowledge principles in exposition, and very little (sometimes no) attempt is made to make the requirements for the legitimate production of a text available to acquirers. In this modality, the hierarchical rules are strongly framed, learners are communalized, and instructional knowledge is undifferentiated. All pupils are treated as the same.

The predominant instructional strategy in the horizontal modality is that of localising, as the tasks refer to public domain principles and/or knowledge. The tasks incorporate knowledge that is familiar and particularistic, and meanings that are concrete and context-bound. The rules for combination of the pedagogic assemblies are characterised as fragmented. The rules for combination are generated by a public domain message (often in theme-based learning).

In the working-class context, through the horizontal modality, there is a weak potential for the specialization of learners' voice with respect to the reproduction of school knowledge. The knowledge introduced is local and familiar, and the evaluative rules are weak or absent.

The Vertical Modality

The vertical modality is constituted by strong framing over sequence and selection. Framing over pacing is weaker, and there is strong framing over the evaluative rules. The hierarchical rules are weaker, and the classification of agents is strong.

In the instructional form, learners are individualised in the instructional practice of the teacher. Learners are treated as different, with different learning competences and requirements. With respect to the instructional strategies for individual tasks specializing strategies predominate, where the tasks are generated by esoteric domain principles and/or knowledge. The rules for combination of the 'pedagogic assemblies' are characterised as generalising: the assembly is constituted by the elaboration of particular concepts or procedures. The model, derived from the research, is shown in Table 5.3.

Table 5.3 Pedagogic Modalities

			Horizontal modality	Vertical modality
1. Classification and framing of pedagogic discourse	Sequence and selection		F^{++}	F^{++}
	Pacing		F^{++}	F
	Evaluative rules		F^{+}	F^{+}
	Hierarchical rules		F^{+}	F
	Discourses	Inter-disc (subjects)	C^{-}	C^{++}
		Inter-disc (school/every day)	C^{-}	C^{+}
	Spaces	Internal	C^{+}	C^{-}
		External	C^{-}	C^{++}
	Agents		C^{-}	C^{++}
2. Instructional form	Content		Undifferentiated (uniform)	Differentiated and uniform
	Classroom organization		Communalized / homogenous	Communalized / homogenous and individualized/specialized
3. Instructional strategies	Individual tasks		Localizing	Specializing
	Pedagogic assemblies		Fragmenting	Generalising
	Selection		Public domain (C^{-})	Esoteric domain (C^{++})

In the middle-class context, the potential for the specializing of voice with respect to the reproduction of knowledge is facilitated largely through the extensive rehearsal of procedures and operations which refer to the esoteric domain, or specialized knowledge of literacy.

The model was derived from the aggregation of coding values assigned across the 60 lessons and 103 tasks. If the fit appears neat, that is because it was part of the intention of the research to put certain differences in expected pedagogic practices on display. The sample represents the two ends of the social class continuum: lower working class and upper middle class. The purpose of the research was not to make empirical generalisations about working class and middle class classrooms. In the study a very definite picture of the contrasts emerges, whereas, in reality, classrooms are likely to exhibit hybrid forms of the two modalities defined, as well as more complex and nuanced interplay between social class actors. What the research allows is the establishment of the lineaments of a theoretical model for the analysis of pedagogic variation across different contexts.

Discussion

To return to the theory, there is a limit with respect to classification and framing in its potential to address the question of pedagogic variation and the reproduction of difference. As argued above, Bernstein is concerned with the *relay*: here, an analysis of the reproduction of the specialized knowledge of schooling also concerns the *relayed*. In other words, the analysis shows not only the structure of the specializing of voice, but also the semantic content of what is classified. Further, through instructional form it is possible to describe the organization of the classroom independently of its semantic focus. The distinction between individualising and collectivising pedagogies enables further consideration of the regulative features of the classroom and their social class base. This is particularly relevant in light of the dominance of progressive discourses of pedagogy, which assert the importance of individualizing, privileging a pedagogic form not unlike how middle class mothers interact with their children. The possibility of this discourse being a reality in working class classrooms, where students are treated as the same, is thus questioned. The theoretical model allows us to consider each dimension of the pedagogy, the interaction between these dimensions, and the possible implications.

In this study, orientation to meaning was taken as the crucial variable associated with social class in considering the reproduction of inequality through pedagogy. It offers a model for the consideration of pedagogic variation across different social class school settings. Drawing on the theory of Bernstein, and given greater specificity through the recruitment of Dowling and Pedro, the analysis allows for a consideration of the micro processes of classroom practice and their relation to the macro social arrangements of social class.

The aim was to elucidate in stark relief, in naturalistic settings, how learners of different social class backgrounds are subjected to very different pedagogies and their voice is specialized in different ways. In this way the precise mechanisms through which inequalities are reproduced come into sharper focus. The establishment of the theoretical lineaments in the model make an exploration of the reproduction of difference in a broader and more varied sample possible.

Notes

1. Recently overviewed and critiqued in Gerwitz and Cribb (2003) and Morrow and Torres (1994).
2. The general methodology for operationalising the concepts of classification and framing broadly follows the work of Morais et al. (2004) and Morais and Neves (2001).
3. However, it could be argued that, in this case, the teacher in fact substitutes the textbook for herself; or she recruits a proxy voice—the sequence and selection of the textbook—because her voice isn't able to do the pedagogic work. Neither student nor teacher here appears to be controlling the knowledge but rather the textbook is followed to the word, strongly dictating the sequence and selection. So an initial (iconic) selection in terms of the theme 'trees' is made, but from there the sequencing follows that of the textbook from the top of the page to the bottom.

References

Adlam, D. J., Turner, G. J. and Lineker, L. (1977). *Code in context.* London: Routledge and Kegan Paul.

Arnot, M. and Reay, D. (2004). The framing of pedagogic encounters: Regulating the social order in classroom learning. In J. Muller, B. Davies and A. Morais (Eds.), *Reading Bernstein, researching Bernstein.* London: RoutledgeFalmer.

Bernstein, B. (1977). *Class, codes and control volume 3: Towards a theory of educational transmissions* (2nd ed.). London: Routledge and Kegan Paul.

Bernstein, B. (1990). *Class, codes and control, volume 4: The structuring of pedagogic discourse.* London: Routledge.

Bernstein, B. (1996). *Pedagogy symbolic control and identity: Theory, research, critique.* London: Taylor & Francis.

Bourdieu, P. and Passeron, J. C. (1977). *Reproduction in education, society and culture.* London: Sage Publications.

Bowles, S. and Gintis, H. (1976). *Schooling in capitalist America.* New York: Basic Books.

Cazden, C. B. (1986). Classroom discourse. In M. C. Wittrock (Ed.), *Handbook of research on teaching* (3rd ed.), (pp. 162–213). New York: Macmillan.

Cicourel, A. V. and Kitsuse, J. I. (1963). *The educational decision makers.* Indianapolis, IN: BobbsMerrill.

Coleman, J. S., Campbell, E. Q., Hobson, C. J., McPartland, J., Mood, A. M., Weinfeld, F. D. and R. York. (1966). *Equality of educational opportunity.* Washington, D.C.: Government Printing Office.

Cook-Gumperz, J. (1973). *Social control and socialization: A study of class differences in the language of maternal control.* London: Boston Routledge and Kegan Paul.

Dowling, P. (1998). *The sociology of mathematics education: Mathematical myths/pedagogic texts.* London: Falmer.

Dowling, P. (1999). Basil Bernstein in frame: 'Oh dear, is this a structuralist analysis?' Available at: http://www.ioe.ac.uk/ccs/dowling/kings1999/index.html. Accessed April, 20, 2006.

Fontinhas, F., Morais, A. M. and Neves, I. P. (1995). Students' coding orientation and school socializing context in their relation with students' scientific achievement. *Journal of Research in Science Teaching, 32* (5), 445–462.

Gerwitz, S. and Cribb, A. (2003). Recent readings of social reproduction: Four fundamental problematics. *International Studies in Sociology of Education, 13* (2), 243–259.

Hasan, R. (2002). Semiotic mediation, language and society: Three exotropic theories—Vygotsky, Halliday and Bernstein. Presentation to the Second International Basil Bernstein Symposium: Knowledges, pedagogy and society. Cape Town, July.

Heath, S. B. (1985). *Ways with words.* Cambridge: Cambridge University Press.

Hoadley, U. (2006). Analysing pedagogy: the problem of framing. *Journal of Education, 40,* 15–34.

Hoadley, U. (2007). The reproduction of social class inequalities through mathematics pedagogies in South African primary schools. *Journal of Curriculum Studies, 39,* 679–706.

Hoadley, U. K. (2005). Social class, pedagogy and the specialization of voice in four South African primary schools. Unpublished PhD thesis, Cape Town, University of Cape Town.

Holland, J. (1981). Social class and changes in orientations to meaning. *Sociology, 15,* 1–18.

Keddie, N. (1971). Classroom knowledge. In M. F. D. Young (Ed.), *Knowledge and control: New directions of the sociology of education.* London: Collier-MacMillan.

Koehler, V. (1978). Classroom process research: Present and future. *Journal of Classroom Interaction, 13*(2), 3–11.

Labov, W. (1972). The logic of non-standard English. In P. P. Giglioni (Ed.), *Language and social context.* Harmondsworth: Penguin.

Morais, A. and Neves, I. (2001). Pedagogical social contexts: Studies for a sociology of learning. In A. Morais, I. Neves, B. Davies and H. Daniels (Eds.), *Towards a sociology of pedagogy: The contribution of Basil Bernstein to research.* New York: Peter Lang.

Morais, A., Neves, I. and Pires, D. (2004). The *what* and the *how* of teaching and learning. In J. Muller, B. Davies and A. Morais (Eds.), *Reading Bernstein, Researching Bernstein.* London: RoutledgeFalmer.

Morrow, R. and Torres, C. (1994). Education and the reproduction of class, gender, and race: Responding to the postmodern challenge. *Educational Theory, 44,* 43–61.

Oakes, J. (1985). The distribution of knowledge. In R. Arum and I. R. Beattie (Eds.), *The structure of schooling: Readings in the sociology of education.* California: Mayfield Publishing Company.

Pedro, E. R. (1981). *Social stratification and classroom discourse: A sociolinguistic analysis of classroom practice.* Stockholm, Stockholm Institute of Education: Department of Educational Research.

Reeves, C. (2005). The effect of opportunity-to-learn and classroom pedagogy on mathematics achievement in schools serving low socio-economic status communities in the Cape Peninsula, unpublished PhD thesis, University of Cape Town.

Rose, D. (2004). Sequencing and pacing of the hidden curriculum: How indigenous children are left out of the chain. In J. Muller, B. Davies and A. Morais (Eds.), *Reading Bernstein, Researching Bernstein.* London: RoutledgeFalmer.

Walkerdine, V. (1988). *The mastery of reason.* London: Routledge.

CHAPTER SIX

Pedagogic Discourse and Sex Education

Myths, Science and Subversion

GABRIELLE IVINSON

INTRODUCTION

The topic 'sex' can be associated with birth and death, separation and union, and masculinity and femininity. The term 'sex' carries an almost limitless symbolic potential yet, once framed within a discourse, the network of meanings associated with it is brought into alignment. Therefore the structure of the discourse within which the term 'sex' is framed provides the key to how it is understood. This paper focuses on the structure of discourses as a key to investigate the potential for sex education within elements of the curriculum. Insights from Moscovici's work on common-sense knowledge and Bernstein's work on pedagogic discourse are used to argue that one potential source of sex *education* lies in juxtaposing discourses that frame 'sex' in different ways.

The term 'sex' can be seen to cover at least the following five strands:
- the sex act performed between people or auto-erotic sex acts;
- the anatomy and physiology of reproduction;
- forms of social identification and recognition such as heterosexual, les, bi, gay;
- eroticism; and
- aspects of morality such as family values and gender relations.

Schools are modernist institutions (Epstein et al., 2003) that privilege scientific knowledge above common-sense knowledge. The curriculum can be viewed as a collection of scientific or specialist discourses (cf. Bernstein, 1990, 1996, 1999) and therefore, within schools, teachers frame the topic 'sex' within scientific discourses. Sex education often aims to limit and curtail young people's sexual thoughts, practices and desires rather than expand their imaginative repertoires. Yet, the term 'sex' has its own subversive potential. It is an unruly topic because it invokes the body. As Grosz (1995, p. 214, cited in Gard, 2003, p. 107) states:

> There is an instability at the very heart of sex and bodies, the fact that the body is what it is capable of doing, and what any body is capable of doing is well beyond the tolerance of any culture.

The topic 'sex' represents the ever-present 'irrational' that teachers fear can erupt into disorder and chaos. Understanding how this subversive potential can be exploited for the purposes of sex education requires a detailed consideration of the structure of discourses.

Science and Myths

One requirement of sex *education* is to provide young people with information about biological and social functions. Such education is crucial to help prevent sexually transmitted disease, sexual oppression and social injustice experienced by minority, non-heterosexual groups. The need to reduce risk-taking in the sexual behaviour of adolescents (for example, Cleland & McKay, 1992; Warwick et al., 2003) is acute. The problem that sex educators face is that young people often fail to see the relevance of information provided in school to their own lives and find it difficult to apply it to their sexual practices. We confront issues in our lives through common-sense rather than scientific discourses.

As modernist institutions, schools privilege the movement of ideas from the common-sense realm to the scientific realm, and not a movement in the opposite direction. Yet, sex education requires two-way traffic between scientific and common-sense discourses so that students can be encouraged to bring knowledge from the scientific realm to bear on everyday situations (Whitty et al., 1994a, b). First, schools need to understand and legitimate common-sense knowledge and, second, they have to find ways to encourage two-way traffic between common-sense and scientific discourses.

Researchers within the field of sex education recognise that students come to school already equipped with social representations of sex as part of their local cultures (Renold, 2000, 2001; Duveen, 2001; Elliot, 2003; Epstein et al., 2003). Common sense involves myths, beliefs and superstitions. Myths about sex circulate in peer groups as hearsay, rumour and bravado. One of the roles of sex education is to disrupt these commonly held myths in order to make alternative ways of thinking available. One way to challenge sexual myths is to confront common sense with scientific discourses. But schools can only do this if they understand more about the structure of common-sense discourse and its role in everyday life. Moscovici's work provides considerable insight by characterising common-sense and scientific knowledge as two universes each obeying a different logic.

Two Universes: Two Systems of Thought

Distinctions between realms such as the sacred and the profane, the public and the private, the moral and the amoral have a long history. Scientific and common-sense knowledge are often viewed as an opposition between abstract and concrete thinking (cf. Dowling, 1998). This distinction implies a hierarchy in which abstract thinking is privileged above concrete thinking. Moscovici's (1961 [1976], 1981, 2001) theory of social representations is a study of common-sense knowledge that seeks to reverse this hierarchy. According to this approach, the scientific realm provides a reservoir of terms, vocabulary and resources that people appropriated when they need to make sense of new or unfamiliar situations in everyday life. Moscovici argues that, in this respect, science has replaced religion as the realm in which ideas are invented or reinvented.

Moscovici based the division between common-sense and scientific knowledge on Lvy-Bruhl's (1925/1926) distinction between pre-logical and logic thought, and conceptualised this as two universes: a 'consensual' universe and a 'reified' universe, which he explained in the following way:

> In the consensual universe society is a visible, continuous, creation, permeated with meaning and purpose, possessing a human voice, in accord with human existence and both acting and reacting like a human being. In other words, man [sic] is, here, the measure of all things. In the reified universe, society is transformed into a system of solid, basic unvarying entities which are indifferent to individuality and lack identity. The society ignores itself and its creations which it sees only as isolated objects, such as persons, ideas, environments and activities. The various sciences that are concerned with such objects, can, as it were, impose their authority on the thought and experience of each individual and decide, in each case, what is true and what is not. All things are the measure of man. (Moscovici, 1984, p. 20)

In the reified universe, the scientific method, including the law of non-contradiction, and its 'truths' dominate. People are reduced to reified objects or data and human desires and meanings are killed off (cf. Devereux, 1967). Therefore, we cannot recognise ourselves in and through scientific discourses, because within these discourses 'society ignores itself and its creations.' This is precisely what research examining sex education has found. Young people do not recognise themselves in or through the scientific discourses of the curriculum and view such knowledge as 'irrelevant' to their lives.

Within the consensual universe, society has a 'human voice.' People recognise and anchor themselves in the world as they comment, make judgements and gossip in pubs, cafs and homes. In schools this takes place within peer groups at leisure times, between lessons and within lessons when the framing of scientific discourses is loosened. In this process of making sense, we appropriate terms, ideas and concepts from scientific discourses for our own everyday purposes. Moscovici's seminal text, *La Psychoanalyse son image et son publique* (1961 [1976]) described how groups in contemporary society appropriated terms from the scientific realm of psychoanalysis to differentiate types of anxiety. For example, terms such as 'neurosis,' 'phobia' and 'panic attack' entered common-sense use only within the past 50 years. Moscovici demonstrated how different social groups such as Catholics and Marxists selectively excluded aspects of psychoanalytical discourse (such as libido) that did not fit with their dominant system of thought. This means that as scientific terms are drawn into common-sense discourses they are transformed and moulded to fit the everyday needs of specific groups. In relation to sex education, we can see that young people express commonly held ideas about sex, its social significance and symbolic meanings within peer-group conversations in ways that make sense to them and that allow them to be recognised, validated and to achieve social status. If one way of being validated is through stories of sexual exploits or through not using condoms, then these stories will continue to be used as a way to achieve social recognition.

It is a feature of common-sense discourses that they do not obey the law of non-contradiction. Ideas align, attract and repel each other according to a different logic. Mauss (1950) characterised this as somewhere between magic and religion, and Durkheim said it involved 'negative acts' with 'the function of preventing mixture and unwanted contact' (Durkheim, 1976, cited in Jodelet, 1991, p. 265). Many of the ways in which ideas are kept apart within common-sense discourse relate to societies' fears and anxieties about contagion, prohibition and impurity. This patterning of ideas constitutes the moral order of society. The initial reasons for the ritualistic maintenance of boundaries between pure and impure, good and evil, masculine and feminine have become lost in the mists of time. Yet such boundaries are continuously re-invoked when fears and uncertainties arise. We use disease, for example, as a common metaphor for social disorder. 'Feelings about evil are projected onto a disease. And the disease (so enriched with meaning) is projected onto the world' (Sontag, 1978, p. 63). The fear that AIDS can be transmitted through saliva or sweat can be traced back to 'the nightmare belief in the transmission of syphilis through bodily fluids' that accompanied fears surrounding sexual liberation in the nineteenth century (Jodelet, 1991, p. 301). The patterning and alignment of ideas within common sense can be partially mapped through historical or genealogical research (cf. Foucault, 1972). Yet, such research is not easy because associations between ideas get hidden and condensed (Heider, 1958). Unlike scientific ideas, the norms, beliefs and myths that make up common sense are not shaped by the relatively visible structures of institutions. Yet, it is common sense and not scientific discourse that provides people with resources to make sense, to reflect on their lives and to be recognised by others. Without common-sense discourses, people would be alienated from their own societies.

Ideas from the reified universe become absorbed into the consensual universe and vice versa through dynamic processes that take place in everyday conversations. Ideas from one realm are appropriated and used in the other. It has been recognised that science is not free from the influence of common sense (cf. Latour, 1993). However, common-sense discourses are structured differently to scientific discourses and pedagogic discourse operates at the boundary between them. Teachers aim to induct learners into scientific discourses. The skill of teaching is to start from a topic that students can meaningfully connect with and reframe it within a scientific discourse. This process of recontextualisation shifts thinking into a different symbolic realm. Bernstein described the distinction between common-sense and scientific discourse as one between horizontal and vertical discourses (Bernstein, 1996, 1999). Within the next section the structure of scientific discourse is considered in more detail.

Vertical and horizontal discourses

The curriculum is composed of a collection of scientific discourses. In Bernstein's earlier work, subjects such as science and art were conceptualised as 'contents.' Later, influenced by Foucault, he re-conceptualised subjects as discourses. This shift emphasised that subjects are dynamic: active constructions and reconstructions that are formed between teachers and students in every day practice. Therefore the slippage and movement of ideas as they are framed within different discourses becomes central to the process of learning. In his last essay, 'Vertical and Horizontal Discourse,' Bernstein (1999) clarified his position on the relation between concrete and abstract thinking. He linked concrete thinking with horizontal discourses, which he described as:

> ... likely to be oral, local, context dependent and specific, tacit, multi-layered, and contradictory across but not within contexts ... the crucial feature is that it is segmentally organised. (Bernstein, 1999, p. 159)

Horizontal discourses are context specific and therefore 'contradictory across but not within contexts' (Bernstein, 1999, p. 159). He also made a distinction between discourses and the knowledge structures that underlie discourse. Bernstein referred to the knowledge structures that underlie horizontal discourse as:

> contextually specific and context depended, embedded in on-going practices, usually with strong affective loading and directed towards specific immediate goals, highly relevant to the acquirer in the context of his/her life. (1999, p. 161)

Although Bernstein's aim was to characterise what Jean Lave and others have called situated knowledge, it is also possible to recognise features such as 'relevance' and 'the context of his/her life' that apply to common-sense discourses.

In contrast, the curriculum can be viewed as a collection of vertical discourses that relate, although not directly, to disciplines such as science, art and the humanities. Bernstein's work on vertical discourse provides a way to differentiate between scientific discourses. He defined two forms of knowledge underlying vertical discourses: hierarchical knowledge structures and horizontal knowledge structures. Horizontal knowledge structures consist of a series of segments that:

> form a series of specialist languages with specialised modes of interrogation, specialist criteria for the production and circulation of texts e.g. in humanities and social sciences. (Bernstein, 1999, p. 159)

The humanities and social sciences have horizontal knowledge structures, and in English literature the segments are the languages of criticism. In sociology the segments are 'functionalism, post-structuralism, post-modernism, Marxism, etc' (Bernstein, 1999, p. 162). In contrast, science is a vertical discourse with a hierarchical knowledge structure because it:

> attempts to create very general propositions and theories, which integrate knowledge at lower levels, and in this way shows underlying uniformities across an expanding range of apparently different phenomena. (Bernstein, 1999, p. 162)

Acquiring vertical discourses involves learning principles. Principles are 'procedures . . . linked to other procedures hierarchically—it is an ongoing process in extended time' (Bernstein, 1999, p. 161). Bernstein differentiated horizontal knowledge structures further into those with strong and weak grammars. Those with strong grammars make the rules for acquiring the languages of the discipline relatively explicit. An example of this is mathematics, which is a vertical discourse with a horizontal knowledge structure and which consists of a series of segments, such as algebra, arithmetic and calculus. Disciplines with weak grammars, such as sociology and English, have less explicit rules for acquiring its various languages. Overall, the rules by which ideas are aligned within vertical discourses are relatively explicit and publicly available. The rules reside in communities of scholars in universities and colleges, in academic journals and other texts. Because the knowledge related to vertical discourse is institutionalised, there are more signposts available for tracking structure and content in comparison with horizontal discourses.

Bringing together insights from Bernstein and Moscovici, it could be argued that social representations underlie horizontal discourses just as hierarchical and horizontal knowledge structures underlie vertical discourses. Although common-sense beliefs are not strictly speaking irrational, they align through association, condensation and sedimentation. Social representations have deep historical roots and their fused structures endow them with a force that makes them seem *natural*. Ideas that circulate in the consensual universe obey a *different logic* to ideas that circulate in the reified universe. Understanding the structure of the ideas that underlie common sense makes it easier to see why rumours, myths and superstitions about sex are ubiquitous and resistant to rational argument. However, education is dependent on there being discourses that are differently structured and that can disrupt and challenge each other. The following section considers the potential of a range of scientific discourses for sex education.

SEX EDUCATION AND SCIENTIFIC DISCOURSES

Sex *education* lies in the potential for disrupting the inner logic of common-sense discourses in order to challenge sexual myths in the interest of sexual health, social justice and sexual equality. One way to achieve this is to juxtapose scientific with common-sense discourses about sex. Given that lessons in school are usually framed within scientific discourses, it ought to be possible to introduce aspects of the topic 'sex' in most subjects. The argument presented so far emphasises that people cannot recognised themselves in and through scientific discourses because they are structured in ways that expel personal meanings. People do not make sense of their lives using the laws of scientific rationality. This does not mean that people are irrational. It means that in everyday life we employ a different logic: the logic of the moral order or of the consensual universe. Therefore successful sex education requires that personal as well as scientific meanings are recognised. The following section considers the possibilities and limitation of achieving this in a range of subjects starting with science. Examples given in the next section are drawn from classroom observations carried out in a range of secondary schools, mainly in year nine classes (students aged 13/14). The incidents arose in lessons observed while tracking cohorts of students across a range of curriculum subjects. The observational focus was on students undertaking activities set by teachers with specific attention paid to how teachers introduced activities to classes.[1]

Science

Scientific discourses are arguable the furthest removed from common-sense discourses. Sex as a topic can be framed within discourses of biology, physiology, chemistry and anatomy. Science is governed by an internal logic that privileges objectivity, distance and linearity, which *destroy* (cf. Bernstein, 1999, p. 158) subjective views, personal experiences and individual expression. This appears to be a most unlikely discourse for introducing aspects of sex that might be useful to students in their everyday lives. Yet scientific discourses carry information that can directly challenge common sense myths about sex.

Common-sense ideas, for example, about how AIDS/HIV can be transmitted are caught up with ideas about moral purity and fears about sexual practices that break with the moral order maintained for example by patriarchy. Yet, disease is impersonal; it ignores people and their subjective experiences. Scientific discourses can deal, for example, with the mechanics of a condom as a barrier to the spread of disease. The juxtaposition of scientific discourse with common-sense discourse can be used to disrupt and disturb chains of associations that form the inner logic of commonly held myths about the spread of sexually transmitted disease, contamination and beliefs about *who* is prone and not prone to such disease. In this case, scientific discourses can usefully be used to *destroy* such myths.

However, the limitation of teaching about sex using scientific discourses is that students are highly likely to view this knowledge as irrelevant in their personal lives. For example, Elliot (2003) recently discussed how the vagina was presented within school textbooks. She argued that 'when exclusively examined as part of the reproductive process' the vagina was disconnected from any notions about sexual experiences either pleasurable or painful. Thus girls are not able to recognise themselves within textbook discourses, and in addition male/female penetrative copulation is restricted to 'a narrow non-pleasurable heterosexist conception of sexuality' (Diorio & Munro, 2000, cited in Elliott, 2003). Elliott (2003, p. 135) suggests that this 'misleading universal representations separates the body from the rest of the person, their emotions their intellect, their spirit' and, in doing so, it denies young women the opportunity to explore and understand their bodies in any way other than reproductive and heterosexual. However, opportunities do arise to integrate horizontal and vertical discourse in the science lesson.

In lessons there are moments when students inject anecdotes from their own experiences into classroom discourse. For example, in one biology lesson as part of the national curriculum science syllabus entitled 'Life processes and the organisation of livening things,' a male teacher in a year nine (students aged 13/14 years) lesson was using a worksheet entitled' Keeping the Body in a Steady State.' The syllabus stated that 'They [students] should consider how hormones can be used to control and promote fertility.' A girl interrupted by calling out:

> What are hormone tablets? My aunt May said you get things growing in and out that you don't want. (Year nine girl, co-education class)

The class collapsed into laughter and the male teacher was thrown off course as the pedagogic discourse dissolved. In this case, the teacher failed to recognise the pedagogic potential of the girl's intervention and interpreted it as a subversive act, which in part it was. Even so, he could have followed up her funny comment to make a point about subjective experiences of drugs, hormones and bodily regulation. Instead, he disciplined the girl for interrupting as a bid to regain control.

English

English can be described as a vertical discourse with a horizontal knowledge structure and a weak grammar. Discourses in literature connect to personal quests for meaning and therefore can be used to *expand* available ways of imagining sexual life without necessarily challenging beliefs and myths about sex. Romance, love, passion, sexual intrigue, marriage, jealousy and sexual betrayal are found within both contemporary and classical texts. Literature can be used to signal historical changes in social norms relating to, for example, marriage, non-heterosexual sexual identities and lifestyles, and to address social and political aspects of human relationships. Reading authors such as D.H. Lawrence can open up sexual landscapes that take young people beyond their local cultures. Thus, literature has the potential to subvert and challenge contemporary sexual norms.

However, the subversive power of literature is often not realised within the classroom. One reason for this may relate to its weak grammar, which means it can be colonised by conservative influences (cf. Peim, 2004). Peim argues that in schools in England and Wales, English is 'structured around a normative model of language privileging standard English while failing to define it' (2004, p. 7). The texts that make up English literature in the United Kingdom are tightly controlled and any radical intrusions from post-structuralism or critical literacy have been successfully fended off (cf. Peim, 2004). English constitutes a 'narrow concept of textuality referred to as literature and gives nodding recognition to literature from other cultures' (Peim, 2004, p. 7). Peim suggests that success in English requires 'an already acquired cultural capital' that fulfils the demand for a 'personal response.' Thus, 'getting it right' in English can be both a class and a gender issue. The following example is taken from Ivinson and Murphy (2003).

In a year nine lesson on creative writing, Adam and Tom started to experiment with the romance genre after listening to extracts that girls had read out in the

English lesson. Adam said that his story started off as a way of taking the 'mickey' out of Tom, who during the lesson had tried writing an 'erotic type thing.'

> Yeah cause I—it started out with me hearing Tom Bank's I think and he was trying to write an erotic type thing you know, one of those, and I started taking the mickey out of him and I just thought I came up with like a sort of comedy/romance type thing, with him getting ready for his girlfriend to come round 'cos he was baby-sitting at his home and his girlfriend was coming round and it was about him and checking himself in the mirror and making himself look smart and buttoning up his top buttons. He said he was going to play scrabble with her, she walked through the door, he could not find the scrabble set. She asked where the scrabble set was—he was like, 'What scrabble set?' and stuff like that so it was me basically really just taking the mickey out of Tom. (Year nine boy, co-educational class)

Normally, Adam did not enjoy writing, yet in this lesson he said that he was 'actually getting into it.' While he was writing the teacher came and read what he had written. Adam confided to us that his writing was 'starting to get a bit rough.' Instead of pursuing his interest and helping Adam to employ appropriate writing techniques that would have allowed him to explore emotion and desire, the teacher said 'Make sure it doesn't get into an X-rated sort of thing.' The scenario described by Adam related to his experience of dating and had great pedagogic potential, yet, after his teacher's comment, Adam abandoned his exploration of romance and started writing a war story.

Art

Art is also a vertical discourse with a horizontal knowledge structure and a weak grammar. Art comprises segments such as classical art, fine art, modern art, abstract art, cubism, expressionism, and so forth. The mode of transmission is tacit as with other craft pedagogies (cf. Lave, 1988; Gamble, 2002) and knowledge is acquired through showing and modelling followed by repeated practice. Creativity in the curriculum is associated with individuality and autonomous meaning-making and requires the expression of feelings through images and artefacts. Students learn to interpret images and artefacts, their own and others, as expressions of human emotion and meaning. Art objects can be used as mediating tools to facilitate discussion about love, romance, eroticism and beauty as well as fear, violence, oppression and destruction. In this way, art discourses allow students to recognise and reflect upon personal emotions and desires.

The limitations of teaching about emotions, and specifically sexual emotions, through art derive from its weak grammar and tacit mode of instruction. The art that students encounter in lessons is often governed by the school of art that was privileged in the teacher training college attended by the teacher. In the United Kingdom, this is often modern, abstract art. The required cultural capital needed to recognise the weak grammar of modern art is likely to be available to only a minority of students. School art is in danger of mis-recognising students' experiences and therefore limiting potential for self-expression and autonomous meaning making. The following example is taken from an art lesson in all boys' class with a male teacher (Ivinson & Murphy, forthcoming).

> In one all-boys art class the male teacher had instructed boys to imitate the style of a famous artist who specialised in jazz scenes depicting male figures. The focus of the lesson was on the use of tones. Students were required to mix flesh colours and to restrict paintings to the use of yellow, grey and black. On inspecting the boys' paintings we noticed that hardly any boys had used pink paint for flesh and instead had chosen black or dark brown. Throughout the lesson an undercurrent of homophobic discourse was audible. Boys regularly accused each other of being 'queer.' This talk rose to a crescendo at the point when the teacher demonstrated how to mix flesh-coloured paint, which in effect was pink. Probably to avoid trouble, the teacher did not insist that the boys mix pink paint. He let them off the hook. Mixing pink paint and drawing male figures challenged the maintenance of masculine identities. In order to defend themselves the boys indulged in 'negative acts' that involved othering: accusing other boys of being queer. The boys at this point needed some support to break with the common-sense myths about masculinity being carried by the peer group. Yet, instead of providing this, the teacher colluded with the boys in their football banter, referring a number of times to shared football trips.

Tales of football activities were appropriated to support the teacher's masculine as opposed to art identity. Although it would have been challenging, the teacher could have confront the boys with their anxieties about drawing male figures and 'pink' flesh by invoking male artists and drawing attention to the diverse subjects and colours legitimated by art discourses. Instead, the teacher colluded in the collapse of the art discourse, and joined the boys in maintaining a narrow, hegemonic version of masculinity that was being use as a defence within the uncertain gender territory of the art activity. The male art teacher was responding to a threat to his gender identity. The example demonstrates the power of common-sense ideas to take hold of a situation and the difficulty teachers can experience in maintaining a scientific discourse when they perceive that they too are being judged by the norms of the consensual universe.

PHYSICAL EDUCATION

In contrast to art and literature, physical education (PE) is a vertical discourse with a horizontal knowledge structure that has a strong grammar. The rules for taking part in sport are explicit, yet the mode of transmission is tacit. Teaching about sex in PE revolves around the body, in terms of movement, exercise, health and hygiene. There is a growing *rapprochement* between the scientific discourses of physiology, health psychology and sport. In the United Kingdom a GCSE in PE that integrates personal, practical and scientific knowledge has been available since the early 1990s. Unlike English, school PE has absorbed the vertical discourse of sport science. Sport is about disciplining the body, yet a body connected to the mind. Sex education potentially involves exploring of the connection between physical and mental life. Yet, a limitation to teaching about sex through PE is furnished by the tacit mode of transmission that makes it difficult to *articulate* relations between mind and body.

PE purports to expand the recreational options of children and young people, yet it has become a discipline restricted to sport. There is no such thing as *raw* physical experience: experiences are mediated by available discourses. Therefore, in schools students' experiences of their bodies are framed by the discourse of sport, which excludes other discourses such as those that describe erotic pleasure and displeasure. Kirk argues that the emphasis on sport in PE is a hangover from the games ethic of the late-nineteenth-century English private schools (Kirk, 1998, 1999). Therefore a wide range of bodily possibilities are neglected in schools. Kirk argues that sport draws on a discursive association with institutional (male) heterosexuality for its legitimacy and that this excludes or marginalises female forms. Gard (2003, p. 105) points out that 'contemporary theories of the body and embodiment are yet to make a substantial impact on educational research and particularly PE,' which remains an overtly rational and scientist vision of physical activity (McKay et al., 1990; Macdonald, 1993; Pronger, 1995).

In a co-educational school in which girls and boys were taught in separate classes we spoke to girls about PE (Ivinson & Murphy, forthcoming). They said they had requested and won the case for football to be included in the year nine curriculum. Their motivation was that they did not want to be excluded from a sport that they knew was held in high esteem by boys. Boys and girls took PE in separate classes. When we accompanied the girls onto the field one wet and windy morning they were unenthusiastic and had to be cajoled by the female teacher to take part. Their teacher said that few of them went on to play football after year nine. In the school, the high status attached to masculine activities dominated, leaving the girls with few discursive resources to value and so request activities that would have allowed them to celebrate movement in ways that they genuinely enjoyed such as dance. Schools can develop local cultures that do not support hegemonic masculinity and a narrow range of sport, yet to do so PE departments need to create structures that legitimate, value and celebrate a wider range of physical activities.

Personal, Social and Health Education

Personal, social and health education (PSHE) can be categorised as a horizontal discourse because it has no agreed disciplinary base and as such there is no recognisable boundary between PSHE and common-sense discourse. PSHE lessons provide a space in which students can potentially voice anxieties, curiosities and commonly held ideas about sex. Potentially, teachers can gain insights into the sexual myths that circulate in peer group culture and challenge them, yet this rarely happens in schools.

The following vignette is from a co-educational school that taught boys and girls in separate classes (Ivinson & Murphy, forthcoming). A sex education lesson was taking place within a PSHE class. The female teacher described a pub scenario to the boys. She asked them to imagine going to the bar with a new girlfriend.

> You both get up to pay for drinks. Imagine that as she goes to pay, the girl's handbag falls open and you see that she has a packet of condoms with her. Would you feel pressurised to have sex with her? (Female teacher, year nine boys' class)

Her intention was to make the boys think about this scenario from a personal perspective and to encourage them to be assertive. As she continued, her pedagogic discourse painted a picture of adolescent girls as marauding and predatory. She positioned boys as victims, using comments such as 'do you really want to do it' and 'what would happen if you started and then found you could not get it up.' By drawing on an inappropriate discourse of male impotence, she used shock tactics to scare the boys. Had it been available, boys could have countered her description using a scientific discourse to point out that male impotence is predominantly found in older and not younger men. In PSHE, common-sense discourses can be used to invoke fear because they are the discourses that we use to recognise ourselves and to make sense. In PSHE, teachers are free to impose moral positions without any check from scientific discourses that might prompt them to reflect on common-sense views.

SUMMARY: SCIENTIFIC DISCOURSES AND SEX EDUCATION

The degree of insulation between scientific discourses and common-sense discourses provides opportunities for sex education. The further the structure of the scientific discourse is from the structure of the common-sense discourse, the greater the power it has to disrupt, challenge and upset myths and beliefs about sex. However, this very distance also creates limitations. The greater the difference between scientific and common-sense discourse, the less likely it is that students will connect knowledge gained in lessons to everyday life. On the other hand, teaching about sex through literature and art has the potential to expand students' sexual repertories and encourage them to imaging alternative sexual futures and practices to those encountered in local cultures. The boundary between PSHE and common sense is weak, creating a pressing need for PSHE teachers to examine their own social representations of sex to avoid imposing unexamined moral views on students.

Tipping Points and Slippage

Vertical discourses suppress embodied knowledge, evacuate subjectivity and deny emotions. They limit, in different ways, the horizons for students' subjective re-signification. However, the more a scientific discourse suppresses emotion, embodied knowledge and subjective experiences, the greater the potential for subversion. All discourses, even scientific discourses, shift and change, are inherently unstable and contain contradictory as well as coherent elements (Moscovici, 1981; Latour, 1993). Classrooms are sites where 'play,' contestation and resistance as well as compliance are visibly at work (Luke et al., 1995; Singh, 2002). The potential for subverting scientific discourses is ever present. Tipping points can be defined as moments when students introduce unruly topics such as bodies or sex into classroom discourse. Teachers often fear these moments because they puncture the vertical discourse and threaten chaos. In these moments, teachers can feel personally under attack. As the pedagogic discourse is subverted, as in the example for the science lesson given above, teachers have a choice; they can either abandon the pedagogic role and join students in a shared moment of hilarity, or retain their distance and show disapproval. Such interjections from students are a common feature of everyday classroom life and teachers can either exploit them for their pedagogic potential or over-ride them. Recovery from such situations depends greatly on the teacher's skill, authority and relationship with the class. If managed with expertise, tipping points can provide cathartic moments because they are based on an unspoken recognition of sexual taboo. Students become aware of their teacher's vulnerability and are often relieved to have a moment of shared humanity with them. Skilled teachers are able to abandon the pedagogic role momentarily and as they recover they can juxtapose a vertical discourse alongside common-sense discourse, allowing the topic of sex to be recognised in a new way. However, it takes confidence to exploit these moments and teachers need to be supported by a tolerant school culture and a strong sense of professional autonomy.

Concluding Remarks

Bernstein's analysis of the pedagogic device describes instructional discourse as embedded within regulative discourse, where regulative discourse relates to the moral order of the school. Vertical discourses have the potential to disrupt common-sense myths about sex and make them available for critical inspection. Teachers do not teach the principles of vertical discourses maintained by communities of scholars; rather they change and adapt them for the purposes of schooling. Schools are positioned to fulfil political and social functions that become manifest in the moral order to the school. Bernstein (1974) has spoken about the importance of analysing the degree of insulation between schools and other social contexts. This becomes particularly important when thinking about sex education. If there is no insulation between the institution and the social world beyond the school, then instructional discourse collapses back into regulative discourse. In such cases the moral order of the school comes to mirror the moral order of society in general. It has been argued that effective sex education relies on the juxtaposition of discourses with different structures. In this sense the boundary between schools and everyday life is essential for education. Modernist institutions have a role to play; they disrupt the spread of archaic beliefs.

This raises the question about what kind of internal cultures schools need to foster in order to make sex education possible. By staying close to the grammar of scientific discourses, teachers can confront issues arising in the lesson that relate to sex; for example, aesthetics including eroticism in art, alternative ways of living and relating such as Romanticism encountered in literature, bodily pleasure and pain in PE and physiological knowledge of the vagina in science. These possibilities rely on teachers knowing their subjects in depth and on school cultures that privilege instructional discourse above regulative discourse (i.e. where the primary intention is not to control but to educate). Such culture can be fostered if there is a shared understanding that the *raison d'tre* for regulative rituals and discourses is the pursuit of knowledge.

In the United Kingdom, teachers have experienced a loss of autonomy through increasingly centralised government control over education. Loss of autonomy decreases the possibility that teachers will choose to exploiting the subversive potential of scientific discourses. Teachers have become susceptible to, for example, common-sense discourses about the feminising of the curriculum that some say has led to boys' underachievement. Pedagogic interventions to alleviate such perceived problems are often based on deeply entrenched myths about gender and sexuality. Teachers need autonomy and a strong sense of the subversive potential of disciplinary knowledge to challenge such myths. As Kehily (2002) points out, the present climate of increasing regulation and surveillance through national testing is making students' sexual cultures even more resistant to the intervention of adults and the curriculum. While scientific discourses do not fulfil all the requirements of sex education, they are usually a better resource than common-sense discourses that collude with and perpetuate myths about sexuality as with the art and PSHE teachers described above. In an ideal world sex would cease to be a taboo topic, and education about sex would be truly cross-curricula. Yet, as we pointed out when health education was introduced as a cross-curricular theme in the national curriculum (Whitty, Rowe and Aggleton, 1994a, b), the strong framing of scientific discourses prevented teachers and students from recognising health issues within subject lessons. Within the present political climate in the United Kingdom, sex is even less likely to be a topic that teachers will be willing to address. There is an urgent need to re-examine the role of education within society.

Acknowledgements

The author thanks Katie Featherstone and William Housley for comments on earlier versions of this paper.

This article was originally published in *Sex Education* Vol. 7, No. 2, May 2007, pp. 203-218. Reprinted here with the permission of Taylor and Francis Publishers.

Note

1. Examples are drawn from classroom observations undertaken as part of two funded research projects: 'Assessing Quality in Cross Curricular Contexts,' ESRC Project Directors Prof. G.J. Whitty and Prof. P. Aggleton (1991–1993) (example from science lesson), and 'Investigating Teaching and Learning in Single Sex Classes,' Open University Project Directors Patricia Murphy and Gabrielle Ivinson (1998–2000) (examples from English, art, PE and PSHE lessons).

References

Bernstein, B. (1974) *Class, codes and control 1, theoretical studies towards a sociology of language* Routledge, London—(2nd rev edn)
Bernstein, B. (1990) *The structuring of pedagogic discourse* Routledge, London & New York
Bernstein, B. (1996) *Pedagogy symbolic control and identity theory, research, critique* Taylor & Francis, London & Bristol
Bernstein, B. (1999) Vertical and horizontal discourse: an essay,. *British Journal of Sociology of Education* 20:(2), pp. 157–173. [informaworld]
Cleland, A. and McKay, L. (1992) *Studying the effectiveness of sexuality education programmes* University of Auckland, New Zealand—Research report
Devereux, G. (1967) *From anxiety to method in the social sciences* Mouton & Co., The Hague & Paris
Diorio, J. and Munro, J. (2000) Doing harm in the name of protection: Menstruation as a topic for sex education,. *Gender and Education* 12:(3), pp. 347–365. [informaworld]
Dowling, P. (1998) *The sociology of mathematics education: mathematical myths, pedagogic texts* Falmer Press, London & Washington, DC
Duveen, G. Deaux, K. and Philgne, G. (eds) (2001) Representations, identities, resistance. *Representations of the Social* Blackwell, Oxford
Elliott, K. J. (2003) The hostile vaginal: reading vaginal discourse in school health texts,. *Sex Education* 3:(2), pp. 133–144. [informaworld]
Epstein, D., O'Flynn, S. and Telford, D. (2003) *Silenced sexualities in schools and universities* Trentham, Stoke on Trent
Foucault, M. (1972) *The archaeology of knowledge* Pantheon Books, New York—(A. M. Sheridan Smith, Trans.)
Gamble, J. (2002) Teaching without words: tacit knowledge in apprenticeship,. paper presented

at the *2nd International Bernstein Symposium*, Cape Town
Gard, M. (2003) Moving and belonging: dance, sport and sexuality,. *Sex Education* 3:(2), pp. 105–118. [informaworld]
Heider, F. (1958) *The psychology of interpersonal relations* Wiley, New York [crossref]
Ivinson, G. and Murphy, P. (2003) Boys don't write romance: the construction of knowledge and social gender identities in English classrooms,. *Pedagogy, Culture and Society* 11:(1), pp. 89–111. [informaworld]
Ivinson, G. and Murphy, P. *Working with gender: sex groupings and subject teaching* Open University Press, Buckingham
Jodelet, D. (1991) *Madness and social representation* Wheatsheaf, London & New York
Kehily, J. M. (2002) *Sexuality, gender and schooling: shifting agendas in social learning* Routledge Falmer, London [informaworld]
Kirk, D. (1998) *Schooling bodies: school practice and public discourse 1880–1950* Leicester University Press, London
Kirk, D. (1999) Physical culture, physical education and relational analysis,. *Sport, Education and Society* 4:(1), pp. 63–73. [informaworld]
Latour, B. (1993) *We have never been modern* Harvester Wheatsheaf, Hemel Hempstead
Lave, J. (1988) *Cognition in practice* Cambridge University Press, Cambridge
Luke, A. Luke, C. and Gore, J. (eds) (1995) Getting our hands dirty: Provisional politics in postmodern conditions. *Feminisms and critical pedagogy* Routledge, London
Lvy-Bruhl, L. (1925/1926) *How natives think* George Allen & Unwin, London—(Lillian Clare, Trans.)
Macdonald, D. (1993) Knowledge, gender and power in physical education teacher education,. *Australian Journal of Education* 37:(3), pp. 259–278.
Mauss, M. (1950) *Sociologie et anthropologie* Presses Universitaires de France, Paris
McKay, J., Gore, J. M. and Kirk, D. (1990) Beyond the limits of technocratic physical education,. *Quest* 42:(1), pp. 52–76.
Moscovici, S. (1961 [rev edn 1976]) *La Psychoanalyse, son image et son public* Presses Universitaires de France, Paris
Moscovici, S. Forgas, J. (ed) (1981) On social representation. *Social cognition* Academic Press, London
Moscovici, S. Farr, R. M. and Moscovici, S. (eds) (1984) The phenomena of social representations. *Social representations* pp. 3–69. Cambridge University Press, Cambridge
Moscovici, S. (2001) *Social representations: exploration in social psychology* New York University Press, New York—(G. Duveen, Ed.)
Peim, N. (2004) Bernstein and curriculum politics: rethinking theory, English and English teaching,.' paper presented at the *Third International Bernstein Symposium*, Cambridge
Pronger, B. (1995) Rendering the body: The implicit lessons of gross anatomy,. *Quest* 47:(4), pp. 427–446.
Renold, E. (2000) 'Coming out': Gender, (hetro)sexuality and the primary school,. *Gender and Education* 12:(3), pp. 309–326.
Renold, E. (2001) Presumed innocence: sexualised bullying and harassment in primary school. paper presented at the *5th Conference of the European Sociological Association*, Helsinki, Finland
Singh, P. (2002) Pedagogising knowledge: Bernstein's theory of the pedagogic device,. *British Journal of Sociology of Education* 23:(4), pp. 571–582. [informaworld]
Sontag, S. (1978) *Illness as metaphor: and AIDS and its metaphors* Penguin Modern Classics, London

Warwick, I., Douglas, N., Aggleton, P. and Boyce, P. (2003) Young gay men and HIV/AIDS: towards a contextual understanding of sexual risk,. *Sex Education* 3:(3), pp. 215–229. [informaworld]

Whitty, G., Rowe, G. and Aggleton, P. (1994a) Discourse in cross-curricular contexts: Limits to empowerment,. *International Studies in the Sociology of Education* 4:(1), pp. 25–41.

Whitty, G., Rowe, G. and Aggleton, P. (1994b) Subjects and themes in secondary school curriculum,. *Research Papers in Education* 9:(2), pp. 159–181. [informaworld]

CHAPTER SEVEN

Subject Position and Identity in Changing Workplaces

HARRY DANIELS

OVERVIEW

In the course of a workshop, which forms part of a large-scale research project entitled 'Learning in and for interagency work,' a community paediatrician remarked that her biggest learning challenge was 'to learn to *be and talk* like a multi-agency person when I am not in multi-agency meetings.' The theoretical challenge implicit in this short statement is how to understand the relations between the social organisation of work, discursive practice and social position. Empirical research in this field requires a theoretical account that provides a descriptive and analytical purchase on the principles of regulation of the social figured world, the possibilities for social position and the voice of participants. This is the challenge that I will try and address in this paper. I have opted to initiate the discussion with an exploration of a rapidly developing branch of social theory, which is primarily concerned with psychological functioning and yet seeks to locate its development in the social world.

VYGOTSKY, ACTIVITY THEORY AND THE SOCIAL WORLD

The Russian social theorist L.S. Vygotsky presents a dialectical conception of the relations between personal and social life. He provides a socio-genetic model of development:

> Every function in the child's cultural development appears twice: first, on the social level, and later, on the individual level; first between people (interpsychological), and then inside the child (intrapsychological). This applies equally to voluntary attention, to logical memory, and to the formation of concepts. All the higher functions originate as actual relations between human individuals. (Vygotsky, 1978, p. 57)

He developed the concept of 'mediation,' which opens the way to a non-deterministic account in which 'psychological tools' serve as the means by which the individual "acts upon and is acted upon by social, cultural and historical factors." Human behaviour is shaped by and through the use of psychological tools, such as speech, which are in turn shaped through human action. This account of mediated engagement with the world brings social, cultural and historical features into a theory of the formation of mind.

As Ratner (1997) notes, Vygotsky did not consider the ways in which concrete social systems bear on psychological functions. He discussed the general importance of language and schooling for psychological functioning, however he failed to examine the real social systems in which these activities occur and reflect. Vygotsky never indicated the social basis for this new use of words. The social analysis is thus reduced to a semiotic analysis, which overlooks the real world of social praxis.

> The feature that can be viewed as the proximal cause of the maturation of concepts, *is a specific way of using the word*, specifically the functional application of the sign as a means of forming concepts. (Vygotsky, 1987, p. 131)

While it is quite possible to interpret 'a specific way of using the word' to be an exhortation to analyse the activities in which the word is used and meaning negotiated, this was not elaborated by Vygotsky himself. The analysis of the structure and function of semiotic psychological tools in specific activity contexts is not explored.

Recent developments in activity theory have attempted to respond to the challenge that the absences in Vygotsky's work present. The first generation model of activity theory drew heavily from Vygotsky's concept of mediation and included in a triangular model notions of subject, object and mediational tools (Engeström, 1999). Engeström (1999) sees joint activity or practice as the unit of analysis for activity theory, not individual activity. He is interested in the processes of social transformation and includes the structure of the social world in his analysis while taking into account the conflicting nature of social practice. He sees instability (internal tensions) and contradiction as the 'motive force of change and development,' (Engeström, 1999, p. 9) and the transitions and reorganisations within and between activity systems as part of development. It is not only the subject, but the environment, that is modified through mediated activity. He views the 'reflective appropriation of advanced models and tools' as 'ways out of internal contradictions' that result in new activity systems (Cole and Engeström, 1993, p. 40).

The 'third generation' of activity theory as proposed by Engeström intends to develop conceptual tools to understand dialogues, multiple perspectives and networks of interacting activity systems. The idea of networks of activity within which contradictions and struggles take place in the definition of the motives and object of the activity, calls for an analysis of power and control within developing activity systems. In this chapter, I will draw on Bernstein's (2000) ideas about the formation of human consciousness, which also place semiotic mediation in the foreground, albeit driven by profoundly sociological concerns. As Atkinson (1985) notes, Bernstein's approach epitomizes an essentially macrosociological point of view.

> It is undoubtedly true that in Bernstein's general approach there is little or no concern for the perspectives, strategy and actions of individual social actors in actual social settings. (Atkinson, 1985, p. 32)

In the same way psychological studies of learning which ignore contextual constraints will confound and confuse the interpretation of results, Vygotsky's approach lacks that which Bernstein explicitly has set out to provide—a theoretical framework for the description and analysis of the changing forms of cultural transmissions:

> I wanted to develop a different approach which placed at the centre of the analysis the principles of transmission and their embodiment in structures of social relationships. (Bernstein, 1977, p.3)

Bernstein seeks to link semiotic tools with the structure of material activity. Crucially he draws attention to the processes that regulate the structure of the mediating tool rather than just its function.

> Once attention is given to the regulation of the structure of pedagogic discourse, the social relations of its production and the various modes of its recontextualising as a practice, then perhaps we may be a little nearer to understanding the Vygotskian tool as a social and historical construction. (Bernstein, 1993)

He also argues that much of the work that has followed in the wake of Vygotsky 'does not include in its description how the discourse itself is constituted and recontextualised':

> The socio-historical level of the theory is, in fact, the history of the biases of the culture with respect to its production, reproduction, modes of acquisition and their social relations. (Bernstein, 1993, p. xviii)

Hasan (1992a,b; 1995) and Wertsch (1985; 1991) note the irony that while Vygotsky developed a theory of semiotic mediation in which the mediational means of language was privileged, he provides very little if anything by way of a theory of language use. In an account of the social formation of mind, there is a requirement for theory, which relates meanings to interpersonal relations. The absence of an account of the ways language both serves to regulate interpersonal relations and its specificity, which is in turn produced through specific patterns of interpersonal relations and thus social regulation constitutes a serious weakness. This absence has carried through in the development of activity theory. As Engeström and Miettinen (1999) note, it has yet to develop a sophisticated account of discursive practice, which is fully commensurate with the assumptions of activity theory itself. At the same time, Engestrom acknowledges the methodological difficulty of capturing evidence about community, rules and division of labour within the activity system (Engeström, 1999). The theoretically powerful move would be to understand the discursive regulation of interpersonal relations in terms of processes of social, cultural and historical regulation as witnessed in activity theory by the notions of rules and division of labour. I have used the term 'witnessed' because I argue that there is theoretical work to be done here. As Pirkkalainen et al. (2005, p. 7) note at the end of their paper, the study of hybridisation raises key questions such as "how do we understand division of labour—how do we understand rule in any given activity system?" They also suggest that there is a need to differentiate/unify concepts of agency, subject and actor. In the rest of this chapter, I will attempt to address some aspects of these questions.

Engeström (1999) offers the suggestion that the division of labour in an activity creates different positions for the participants and that the participants carry their own diverse histories with them into the activity. This echoes the earlier assertion from Leont'ev:

> Activity is the minimal meaningful context for understanding individual actions.... In all its varied forms, the activity of the human individual is a system set within a system of social relations....The activity of individual people thus *depends on their social position*, the conditions that fall to their lot, and an accumulation of idiosyncratic, individual factors. Human activity is not a relation between a person and a society that confronts him...in a society a person does not simply find external conditions to which he must adapt his activity, but, rather, these very social conditions bear within themselves the motives and goals of his activity, its means and modes. (Leont'ev, 1978, p.10)

In activity, the possibilities for the use of artefacts depends on the social position occupied by an individual. Sociologists and sociolinguists have produced empirical verification of this suggestion (e.g., Bernstein, 2000; Hasan, 2001a; Hasan and Cloran, 1990). The notion of 'subject' within activity theory requires expansion and clarification. In many studies, the term 'subject perspective' is used, which arguably infers subject position but does little to illuminate the roots or formative processes that gave rise to this perspective.

LIMITATIONS EXPOSED THROUGH RESEARCH

In our study of learning for and in interagency working (LIW), we drew on the third generation of activity theory as we modelled networks of interacting activity

(Daniels et al., 2005). The project was concerned with the learning of professionals in the creation of new forms of practice, which require joined up solutions to meet complex and diverse client needs. We were studying professional learning in services that aim to promote social inclusion through interagency working. Working with other professionals involves engaging with configurations of several, diverse social practices and the development of new forms of hybrid practice, which, as Hakkarainen et al. (2004, p. 17), point out challenge dominant understandings of professional expertise:

> Expertise in a certain domain may also be represented in a hybrid expert who is able to translate one expert culture's knowledge into form that participants of another expert culture can understand…innovation emerges in networks of these kinds of communities. Creation of innovations supports gradually developing division of labour and increased specialization as well as combination of existing dispersed resources for novel purposes.

Pirkkalainen et al. (2005) have argued that such hybrid practice is different from collaboration, cooperation or networking in which the constituent activities remain distinct. They suggest that hybridization involves change in positional relations *between* the agents of different activity systems and positional change of agents *within* some activity system. Such changes involve shifts in relations of power (in the division of labour) and control (within the categories established by the division of labour) within and between activity systems. The work of these shifts in the division of labour may well be discursive work. The notion of hybridisation carries with it a focus on positional relations instead of object formation, and historically generated forms of social relations instead of historical forms of work and organisations as is the case in activity theory in its current state.

IDENTITY AND AGENCY IN CULTURAL WORLDS

Holland et al. (1998) have studied the development of identities and agency specific to historically situated, socially enacted, culturally constructed worlds. They draw on Bakhtin and Vygotsky to develop a theory of identity as constantly forming and a theory of person as a composite of many often contradictory, self-understandings and identities, which are distributed across the material and social environment, which are rarely durable (p. 8). They draw on Leont'ev in the development of the concept of socially organised and reproduced *figured worlds*, which shape and are shaped by participants, and in which social position establishes possibilities for engagement. They also argue that figured worlds:

> distribute 'us' not only by relating actors to landscapes of action (as personae) and spreading our senses of self across many different fields of activity, but also by giving the landscape human voice and tone. Cultural worlds are populated by familiar social

> types and even identifiable persons, not simply differentiated by some abstract division of labour. The identities we gain within figured worlds are thus specifically historical developments, grown through continued participation in the positions defined by the social organisation of those world's activity. (Holland et al., 1998, p. 41)

Thus, this approach to a theory of identity in practice is grounded in the notion of a figured world in which positions are taken up, constructed and resisted. The Bakhtinian concept of the 'space of authoring' is deployed to capture an understanding of the mutual shaping of figured worlds *and* identities in social practice. They refer to Bourdieu (cf. 1977) in their attempt to show how social position becomes disposition. They argue for the development of social position into a positional identity, into disposition and the formation of what Bourdieu refers to as 'habitus.' However, the origins of a specific habitus are, as Bernstein (2000, p.133) points out, somewhat elusive:

> ...if we take a popular concept *habitus*, whilst it may solve certain epistemological problems of agency and structure, it is only known or recognised by its apparent outcomes. Habitus is described in terms of what it gives rise to, and brings, or does not bring about....But it is not described with reference to the particular ordering principles or strategies, which give rise to the formation of a particular habitus. The formation of the internal structure of the particular habitus, the mode of its specific acquisition, which gives it its specificity, is not described. How it comes to be is not part of the description, only what it does. There is no description of its specific formation....Habitus is known by its output not its input.

Thus the study of processes of hybridisation would be left without a means of distinguishing between key aspects of the activity systems in play. The challenge is then to develop a theoretical account of the discursive regulation of interpersonal relations, which is compatible with the assumptions of post-Vygotskian theory, and thus retains an account of the mediated social formation of mind, and yet avoids the problems of the lack of analytic discrimination between social contexts.

BASIL BERNSTEIN

Hasan (2005, p. 41) believes that attention to social structure and social positioning marks the main point of departure between Bernstein and Vygotsky's ideas of social formation of mind based on semiotic mediation. As Bernstein (2000) points out, 'what is missing from theories of cultural reproduction is any internal analysis of the structure of the discourse itself, and it is the structure of the discourse, the logic of the discourse, which provides the means whereby external power relations can be carried by it' (p. 4).

Bernstein (1990, p.13) used the concept of social positioning to refer to the establishing of a specific relation to other subjects and to the creating of specific relationships within subjects. This seems to me to concur with the analysis outlined by Holland et al. (1998). He relates social positioning to the formation of mental dispositions in terms of the identity's relation to the distribution of labour in society.

> We have seen how these classifications disguise the arbitrary nature of power relations, create imaginary identities, replace the contingent by the necessary, and construct psychic systems of defence, I do not simply mean at the conscious level. (Bernstein, 2000, p. 12)

It is through the deployment of his concepts of voice and message that Bernstein forges the link between division of labour, social position and discourse and opens up the possibilities for a language of description that will serve empirical as well as analytical purposes. In what follows, I will provide a very brief presentation of the essence of this argument. Full details may be found in Bernstein (2000).

Bernstein (2000) provides a generative model of modalities of pedagogic discourse and practice and subject position in those contexts. This model allows research to proceed on the basis of analyses and descriptions of pedagogic practice, which carry with them implications for practices of communication and social positioning. He proposes a dialectical approach to determining and analysing subject position as well as a model which can generate a range of modalities of pedagogic discourse and practice. He is concerned both with the 'translation of...power relations, and...the translation of control relations' (p. 5). The translation of power relations into principles of classification and how these principles establish social divisions of labour—and therefore identities and voices—is called 'classification.' This is the structural level. The translation of control relations into forms of realisation of discourses—and therefore messages—is called 'framing.' This is the interactional level. Pedagogic codes are the result of differences in strong or weak classification and framing.

Bernstein used classification and framing to analyse pedagogic contexts. Classification (C) refers to the degree of maintenance between categories (subjects, spaces/agencies, discourses), and framing (F) to the communicative outcomes of the relations between categories in the context of the pedagogic relation. Framing between subjects refers to the control they have over selection, sequence, pacing, and evaluation criteria, that is the discursive rules, which regulate instructional pedagogic practice. It also refers to the hierarchical rules that regulate norms of social conduct, or regulative pedagogic practice (Morais & Neves, 2001)

He defines modalities of pedagogic practice in terms of principles for distinguishing between contexts (recognition rules) and for the creation and production of specialized communication within contexts (realization rules). Modalities of pedagogic practice and their discourses may then be described in terms directly referenced to the theory. Features of cultural artefacts may be described in terms of the cultural context of their production. Bernstein (1993, p. xi) argues that much of the work that has followed in the wake of Vygotsky 'does not include in its description how the discourse itself is constituted and recontextualised.'

Thus for Bernstein power relations regulate the degree of insulation between categories. Boundaries are established and challenged in relationships of power. For him, power establishes 'voice' in that it demarcates that which is legitimate within categories and thus establishes the rules by which voice may be recognised. The distinction between what can be recognised as belonging to a voice and a particular message is formulated in terms of distinction between relations of power and relations of control. Bernstein (1990) adapted the concept of voice from his reading of *The Material Word* by Silverman and Torode (1980). He grounds the concept in the material division of labour. In this way he allows for the move between the analysis and description of the social order and that of the practices of communication.

> From this perspective, classificatory relations establish 'voice.' 'Voice' is regarded somewhat like a cultural larynx which sets the limits on what can be legitimately put together (communicated). Framing relations regulate the acquisition of this voice and create the 'message' (what is made manifest, what can be realised). (Bernstein, 1990, p. 260)

In his last book he continues:

> Voice refers to the limits on what could be realised if the identity was to be recognised as legitimate. The classificatory relation established the voice. In this way power relations, through the classificatory relation, regulated voice. However voice, although a necessary condition for establishing what could and could not be said and its context, could not determine what was said and the form of its contextual realisation; the message. The message was a function of framing. The stronger the framing the smaller the space accorded for potential variation in the message. (Bernstein, 2000, p. 204)

Thus social categories constitute voices and control over practices constitutes message. Identity becomes the outcome of the voice—message relation. Production and reproduction have their social basis in categories and practices; that categories are constituted by the social division of labour and that practices are constituted by social relations within production/reproduction; these categories constitute 'voices' and that practices constitute their 'messages'; message is dependant upon 'voice,' and the subject is a dialectical relation between 'voice' and message (Bernstein, 1990, p. 27).

One may speak with the 'voice' of psychology but the particular identity as a psychologist is revealed in the actual messages produced/spoken. Change occurs when 'new' messages are produced and give rise to changes in voice/classification/power relations. Identity may be studied in terms of utterance and the principles of social regulation through which it is generated and transformed. The rules of activity theory include what Bernstein refers to as framing and the division of labour (hierarchical and vertical) refers to classification. Hasan (2002) argues that Bernstein paid very close attention to invisible semiotic mediation—how the unself-conscious everyday discourse mediates mental dispositions, tendencies to respond to situations in certain ways and how it puts in place beliefs about the world one lives in, including both about phenomena that are supposedly in nature and those which are said to be in our culture. She asserts that discourse is not treated as simply the regulator of cognitive functions; it is, as Bernstein (1990, p. 3) states, also central to the shaping of 'dispositions, identities and practices.'

Hasan (2001b, p. 8) suggests that Bernstein's analysis of how subjects are positioned and how they position themselves in relation to the social context of their discourse offers an explanation of hybridity, in terms of the classification and framing practices of the speaking subjects. The invisible semiotic mediation is to be found in the relations of power and control, which give rise to voice message relation in which identities are formed and social positions are bequeathed, taken up and transformed. In Hasan's empirical work, she has evidenced this effect: "What the mothers speak, their selection and organization of meanings is a realisation of their social positioning" (Hasan, 2002 p. 546).

Empirical Work

This LIW project is concerned with the learning of professionals in the creation of new forms of practice, which require multiagency solutions to meet complex and diverse client needs. It is a study of professional learning in services that aim to promote social inclusion through interagency working. Working with other professionals involves engaging with configurations of several, diverse social practices. The necessary learning in, and for this work, is often inhibited by a variety of constraints. The project involves a consideration of the learning that takes place in professional trajectories of participation in activity, which aims to support young people at risk. Our specific focus is on professional learning in and across professional boundaries.

In one of three study sites, a multiprofessional team (MPT) has been formed by the local authority. It is one of four which have been established in this large rural/suburban authority near London. At present, the MPT is comprised of individuals who were formerly members of professional teams within education, which were centrally managed within the authority (Special Need Support, Educational Psychology, Language Support, Attendance Officers, etc). Each MPT is now managed locally. In the case of the MPT to which reference is made here, the local manager is a former attendance officer. Patterns of 'line management' have transgressed well-established and powerful professional categories. For example, the educational psychologists are now managed by an attendance officer. The data extract below suggests that major changes such as these take considerable time and effort.

> It's early in some ways stages of development. I mean we're still going through a process of development and there's a lot more work to be done in order to achieve if you like the ultimate government aim which is a totally holistic approach for children in delivering the out-…on the outcomes of the you know, Every Child Matters outcomes….The multi-professional team has come together and that works in an integrated way because formerly all those different Education professional groups worked separately. And now we're working much more closely together. Erm…but there…there's a way to go before we're all working together, and also we have our partner agencies such as Health partners and police. But we're only at the very early stages of making those links. So there's quite a lot of…still a lot work to be done.

The MPT is a rapidly changing workplace for these professionals, although as they all share a professional root in education, there is some coherence in the regulative practice and its discourse across members of the team. The extract below shows how an educational psychologist is motivated by a goal, which she believes is common to all members of the team.

> It's to really, to try and direct service at that child who he may have a bit of an attendance problem, his family circumstances may not be wonderful, there may be a minor learning difficulty, but none of those individually triggers, hits if you like, the criteria for triggering a response or an intervention from our services. But collectively he has a need that is unmet. If we offer a holistic service to him he will then hit our criteria in some way because we can offer a collective response that actually targets that child. So it's really to achieve better outcomes for children. It was some visionary thinking I think in those days.

The old patterns of classification have been disrupted and the framing over practice has weakened. Participants recognise that they are in a rapidly changing situation and that the expansion of the team through the incorporation of social services and health professionals whose regulative practice does not necessarily cohere with that of education constitutes a challenge. As the following extract from a language support worker reveals:

> That you were signing up to be (pause) a senior manager in this service and you believed in the idea of a Children's Service. But the key difference, which we have tried to broadcast is that basically everyone is a Children's Service worker. People are responsible for the whole child; you're not responsible for this bit of a problem that is presented in relation to this child or this family. And so there is an overarching responsibility. Erm…and that's…that's taken a while for people to really get to internalise, and I'm not sure we've completely achieved that yet. But there's certainly (pause) certainly within the leadership team there has…it has taken time for people to stop thinking of themselves as Education or Social Care people. And there is now, you know, if someone (pause) if I say something and say from the Education perspective, people might say well you know we're not supposed to say that anymore. And you know, we're…we're supposed say things from the Children's Service perspective. However there's still…there is still erm…a…a kind of split of perspective between Education and Social Care his-

tories with individuals. So and…and sort of completely integrated philosophy is tempered by that I think.

MPT members discuss a period of getting to know what and how their colleagues with education worked and understand that a next step may be to adopt more flexible patterns of working.

> So that (pause) first of all they needed to…to get to know each other and the next…and now they are actually beginning to use each other to actually help with children. And from my point of view the next stage is to actually being able to…to recognise their shared skills and to be able to er…erm…(pause) be happy to do some of the things that somebody else would do. (Behaviour Support Worker)

In the early days of the MPT, there was some evidence of local forward planning at the level of the MPT itself.

> So that if you're actually wanting to get a change in working practice it tends still to be an agreement amongst (pause) the EPs or behavioural and pupil support staff meeting together and agreeing that they as a body will accept and move onto the new thing rather than a multi-professional group then saying something [inaudible—00:41:13]. In a sense the decision [inaudible—00:41:19] the decision is made first and then the multi-professionals will get together and agree that they will implement the decision that has been made before they go into it. (Attendance Officer)

In our most recent workshop, a new form of working was discussed. Old lines of control were being disrupted as new forms of 'personalised' collaborative patterns of working emerged. For example, an attendance officer made direct (mobile phone mediated) contact with a psychologist in order to ensure that a child who was not attending school could get access to support for the bullying she experienced and her difficulties in learning. The traditional pattern of communication would have been for the attendance officer to ensure the child returned to school (which she did not) and that her difficulties with bullying and learning were reported to the school. The attendance officer 'broke the rule' of instituting attendance procedures and also subverted the traditional pattern of reporting. When the psychologist engaged with the child, she also made enquiries at the school, which reported that her needs were not a priority and that the school's allocation of psychological support should not be expended on this pupil. The psychologist maintained engagement with the child. The emergent and strengthening regulative discourse of the MPT, which is cast in terms of the moral and ideological commitment to the needs of the whole child rather than the services that have existed, subverted the former patterns of classification and framing of the professional practices.

The messages of the local services are being transformed. The study is gathering data on new forms of voice/message relation that emerges in this rapidly changing circumstance. However, the patterns of professional voice outside the MPT remain the same and very strongly classified, particularly in the case of educational psychology and welfare work. The external framing of this MPT is strengthening in response to the contradictions between local and national patterns of classification and framing. As the MPT becomes more insulated from the practices, the possibilities of the emergence of new forms of professional identity are enhanced. This situation carries with it significant dangers for those involved. If the national message systems are brought into conflict with the emergent local patterns, as could happen in an appeal, then these new voices will be very vulnerable.

The data presented above provide a brief glimpse of a rapidly changing dynamic, which will be studied across three modalities of MPT practice. These are one in which workers remain within their established professional domains and yet are directed by strategy to participate in multiprofessional work, one in which a school becomes the site for multiprofessional engagement as well as the MPT already described. Changes in patterns of classification and framing regulating instructional and regulative practice will be described and data that permits the analysis of changes in discursive practice will be collected. In this way, we will be able to make an empirical contribution to the theoretical framework outlined above.

Hybridity

In order to refine an understanding of organisational, discursive and transmission practices in such situations, new theories of concept formation, which emphasise the complex nature of concepts, will need to be deployed. An important part of the challenge is to show how written and spoken hybrid discourse arises and to investigate the consequences of its deployment. This feature has been noted by Engeström et al. (1995).

> In their work, experts operate in and move between multiple parallel activity contexts. These multiple contexts demand and afford different, complementary but also conflicting cognitive tools, rules, and patterns of social interaction. Criteria of expert knowledge and skill are different in the various contexts. Experts face the challenge of negotiating and combining ingredients from different contexts to achieve hybrid solutions."(Engeström, Engeström & Kärkkäinen, 1995, p. 320)

In response to the challenge of studying new and emergent expert practices, an understanding of discursive hybridity (Sarangi and Roberts, 1999) may provide an important opening for the development of an understanding of changes in discursive practice as different activity systems are brought into different forms of relation with each other. Figure 7.1[1] shows an outline model of modalities of hybrid formation that arise from different combinations of classification and framing.

	Weak control over professional behaviour (F --)	Strong control over professional behaviour (F++)
Strong categories of professional (C++)	Switching between specialists	Collection of distinct specialists
Weak categories of professional (C--)	Generalists 'melting pot' Which may be given coherence through a strong regulative practice	Succession of generalists (people)

Fig. 7.1 Tentative Typology of Hybridities

Our data witness strong boundaries around the professional categories and the strong control over professional behaviour, which maintained the practices of individual specialists. Whereas there were weak boundaries around the professional categories in which professionals were situated and they were more in control, but in which operational professional practice witnessed strong boundaries between services and their professional values coordinated by strategy, a coordinated collection of specialists in the field resulted. In a case of weakened professional boundaries and relations of control, which had been weakened through rule breaking and bending hybridisation, this gave rise to a collection of workers who drew on the primary strengths of their colleagues when they recognised the need for their expertise. The following statement made by an educational psychologist attests to the recognition of the need to retain in depth skills, knowledge and understanding.

> We might not see our colleagues from one month to the next, so we don't have their support but we have the support of the multi-professional team. So I, to be honest, since I've been part of the multi-professional team I haven't really taken too much notice of the other educational welfare officers because I see myself I suppose more a part of the multi-professional team. And they're all in…I mean my educational welfare officer colleagues are all in their teams as well. I mean we all got together yesterday because we had a training day and that's quite unusual. You know it's nice to catch up because obviously we can talk about our particular discipline which we can't do so much in the team.

This recognition of the need to retain professional strengths is set alongside the emergent attributes of relational agency by the same psychologist.

> I mean I've found it's a learning curve because I've found out more about other members of the team and what they do, which has actually helped me as a professional. […] So that has actually helped me in my professional development and it's helped me to feel more confidence as well because I can say to a family, well I think perhaps, you know, you need support from such and such and, you know, I can follow that through and get that support for you. And then when that all works I think, yes!

The development of this way of working also helps organizations' need to destabilize their categorical knowledge. This is knowledge that constrains action to possibilities afforded in gaze of the single professional acting alone. We saw many examples where new ways of working gave rise to shifts from what Engeström (2007) has called stabilization knowledge to possibility knowledge.

> Stabilization knowledge is constructed to freeze and simplify a constantly shifting or otherwise bewildering reality. It is used to turn the problematic into a closed phenomenon that can be registered and pushed around rather than transformed. It commonly takes the shape of fixed and bounded categories, but also narratives may be used to stabilize. Stabilizing categories often become stigmatic stamps on objects, both human beings and things….Possibility knowledge, on the other hand, emerges when objects are represented in fields with the help of which one can depict meanings in movement and transformation. One traces transitions of positions in a field, which destabilizes knowledge, puts it in movement and opens up possibilities. In this sense, possibility knowledge is agentive knowledge, the instrumentality of agency at work. (p. 271)

The emergence of this agentic collaboration between actors is a form of what Engeström (2004) has called collaborative intentionality, which he argues constitutes a new form of capital and is a central feature of organizations which are successful in developing multiagency workers. The agentic collaboration between the practitioners involved in the sites we studied provided valuable assets for the organizations involved.

> They perform a dual job in that they solve very complex problems and also contribute to the reshaping of the entire way of working in their given fields. They are very cost-efficient in that they do not require the establishment of new positions or new organizational centers. Indeed, these formations tend to reject such attempts. Rejection and deviation from standard procedures and scripted norms are foundational to the success of such amoeba-like formations. Their efficacy and value lie in their distributed agency, their collective intentionality. In this sense, I suggest the notion of collaborative intentionality capital as an emerging form of organizational assets. (p. 28)

Conclusion

Research in this field requires a unified theory that can give rise to a coherent and internally consistent methodology rather than a collection of compartmentalised accounts of activity, discourse and social positioning, which have disparate and often contradictory assumptions. Subject–subject and within subject relations are under theorised in activity theory. These relations require a theoretical account of social relations and positioning. Holland et al. bring Bakhtin's notion of the 'space of authoring' into play as they outline the processes of mutual shaping of figured worlds and identities in social practice. They also argue that multiple identities are developed within figured worlds and that these are 'historical developments, grown through continued participation in the positions defined by the social organisation of those world's activity' (Holland et al., 1998, p. 41). This body of work represents a significant development in our understanding of the concept of the 'subject' in activity theory. For my point of view, there remains a need to develop the notion of 'figured world' in such a way that we can theorise, analyse and describe the processes by which that world is 'figured.' However, the theoretical move which Bernstein makes in relating positioning to the distribution of power and principles of control opens up the possibility of grounding the analysis of social positioning and mental dispositions in relation to the distribution of labour in an activity. Through the notions of 'voice' and 'message,' he brings the division of labour and principles of control (rules) into relation with social position in practice. This theoretical stance suggests that activity theory should also develop a language of description, which allows for the parameters of power and control to be considered at structural and interactional levels of analysis. A systematic approach to the analysis and description of the formation of categories through the maintenance and shifting of boundaries and principles of control as exercised within categories would bring a powerful tool to the undoubted strengths of activity theory. This would then allow the analysis to move from one level to another in the same terms rather than treat division of labour and discourse as analytically independent items. Given that, in Bernstein's terms, positioning is in a systematic relation to the distribution of power and principles of control, it is argued that this approach leads to an understanding of the notion of social positioning as the underlying, invisible component, which 'figures' practices of communication.

> [A] specific text is but a transformation of the specialized transactional practice; the text is the form of the social relationship made visible, palpable, material....Further the selection, creation, production, and changing of texts are the means whereby the positioning of the subjects is revealed, reproduced and changed. (Bernstein, 1990, p. 17)

Such theoretical work would, hopefully, provide tools for engaging in the empirical study of the processes of hybridisation which abound in the cultures of our everyday worlds.

NOTE

1. Thanks are due to William Tyler for an informal conversation on this topic.

References

Atkinson, P. (1985). *Structure and reproduction: an introduction to the sociology of Basil Bernstein.* London: Methuen.
Bernstein, B. (1977). *Class codes and control.* Volume 3. *Towards a theory of educational transmissions* (2nd revised ed.). London: Routledge & Kegan Paul.
Bernstein, B. (1990). *The Structuring of pedagogic discourse.* Volume IV: Class, Codes and Control. London: Routledge.
Bernstein, B. (1993). Foreword in H. Daniels (ed.) (1993). *Charting the agenda: Educational activity after Vygotsky,* London: Routledge.
Bernstein, B. (2000). *Pedagogy, symbolic control and identity: Theory research critique.* (revised edition). Oxford: Rowman and Littlefield.
Bourdieu, P. (1977). *Outline of a theory of practice.* Cambridge: Cambridge University Press.
Cole, M., and Engeström, Y. (1993). 'A cultural-historical approach to distributed cognition.' In G. Salomon (ed.), *Distributed cognitions: Psychological and educational considerations*, New York: Cambridge University Press.
Daniels, H., Edwards, A., Martin, D., Leadbetter, J., Warmington, P., Popova, A., Middleton, D., & Brown, S. (2005). Learning in and for Interagency Working. ESRC & TLRP.
Engeström, Y. (1999). Innovative learning in work teams: analysing cycles of knowledge creation in practice. In Y. Engeström, R. Miettinen, and R.L. Punamaki (eds.), *Perspectives on activity theory*, Cambridge University Press.
Engeström, Y. (2004). New forms of learning in co-configuration work. *Journal of Workplace Learning*, 16(1/2), 11–21.
Engeström, Y. (2007). Putting Vygotsky to work. The change laboratory as an application of double stimulation. In H. Daniels, M. Cole & J. V. Wertsch (Eds.), *The Cambridge companion to Vygotsky.* Cambridge: Cambridge University Press, pp. 363–382.
Engeström, Y., Engeström, R. & Kärkkäinen, M. (1995). Polycontextuality and boundary crossing in expert cognition: Learning and problem solving in complex work activities. *Learning and Instruction*, 5, 319–336.
Engstrom, Y. and Miettinen, R. (1999). Introduction. In Y. Engstrom, R. Miettinen, & R-L Punamaki (Eds.), *Perspectives on activity theory.* Cambridge: Cambridge University Press, pp. 1–18.
Hakkarainen, K., Lonka, K., & Paavola, S. (2004). Networked intelligence: How can human intelligence be augmented through artifacts, communities, and networks? http://www.lime.ki.se/uploads/images/517/Hakkarainen_Lonka_Paavola.pdf (downloaded June 2005).
Hasan, R. (1992a). Speech genre, semiotic mediation and the development of higher mental functions. *Language Science*, 14(4), 489–528.
Hasan, R. (1992b). Meaning in Sociolinguistic theory. In *Sociolinguistics today: International perspectives*, In K. Bolton and H. Kwok (eds.),. London: Routledge.
Hasan, R. (1995). On social conditions for semiotic mediation: the genesis of mind in society. *Knowledge and pedagogy: The sociology of Basil Bernstein*, Alan R. Sadovnik (eds.). Norwood, NJ: Ablex.
Hasan, R. (2001a). Understanding talk: directions from Bernstein's sociology. *International Journal of Social Research Methodology*, 4 (1), 5–9.
Hasan, R. (2001b). The ontogenesis of decontextualised language: some achievements of classification and framing. In A. Morais, I. Neves, B. Davies & H. Daniels (Eds.), *Towards a sociology of pedagogy: the contribution of Basil Bernstein to research.* New York: Peter Lang.
Hasan, R. (2002). Ways of Meaning, Ways of Learning: code as an explanatory concept. *British Journal of Sociology of Education*, 23 (4): 537–548.

Hasan, R. (2005). Semiotic Mediation, Language And Society: Three Exotripic Theories—Vygotsky, Halliday And Bernstein. In J. J. Webster (Ed.), *Language, society and consciousness: Ruqaiya Hasan*. London: Equinox.

Hasan, R. and Cloran, C. (1990). A sociolinguistic study of everyday talk between mothers and children. In M.A.K. Halliday, J. Gibbons, & H. Nicholas (Eds.), *Learning keeping and using language*, Volume 1. Amsterdam: John Benjamins.

Holland, D., Lachiotte, L., Skinner, D., & Cain, C., (1998). Identity and agency in cultural worlds. Cambridge, MA: Harvard University Press.

Leont'ev, A. N. (1978). *Activity, consciousness, and personality*. Englewood Cliffs, NJ: Prentice-Hall.

Morais, A. M., and Neves, I. P. (2001). Pedagogic social contexts: Studies for a sociology of learning. In A. Morais, I.Neves, B. Davies and H. Daniels (Eds.), *Towards a sociology of pedagogy: The contribution of Basil Bernstein to research* (chap. 8, pp. 185-221). New York: Peter Lang.

Pirkkalainen, J., Kaatrakoski, H. & Engestrom, Y. (2005). Hybrid agency as hybrid practices—Mimeo [author]

Ratner, C (1997*). Cultural psychology and qualitative methodology. Theoretical and empirical considerations*. London: Plenum Press.

Sarangi, S. and Roberts, C. (1999). Introduction: Discursive hybridity in medical work. In S. Sarangi and C. Roberts (Eds), *Talk, work and institutional order: Discourse in medical, mediation and management settings*. Berlin: Mouton de Gruyter.

Silverman, D. and Torode, B. (1980). The *material word: Some theories of language and its limits*. Routledge, London.

Vygotsky, L. S. (1987). Thinking and speech. In R. Rieber and A. Carton (Eds.), *L. S. Vygotsky, collected works, Vol. 1*, trans. N. Minick. New York: Plenum, pp. 39–285.

Vygotsky, L.S. (1978). *Mind in society: the development of higher psychological processes*, M. Cole, V. John-Steiner, S. Scribner and E. Souberman, (Eds. and trans.). Boston, MA: Harvard University Press.

Wertsch, J. V. (1991). *Voices of the mind: A socio-cultural approach to mediated action*. Cambridge, MA: Harvard University Press.

Wertsch, J.V. (1985). *Vygotsky and the social formation of mind*. Cambridge, MA: Harvard University Press.

CHAPTER EIGHT

Exploring the Transmission of Moral Order as Invisible Semiotic Mediator of Tacit Knowledge

JEANNE GAMBLE

> Made to regulate social relationships in societies as complex as ours, morality itself is very complex. (Durkheim, 2002, p. 173)

INTRODUCTION

Basil Bernstein's characterisation of his later theoretical work as an attempt towards 'a sociology for the transmission of knowledges' (Bernstein, 2001, pp. 367–368), has stimulated researchers working within a Bernsteinian framework to establish a relation between knowledge and pedagogy and to interpret the classification and framing values of code modalities as realisations of forms of discourse (for example, Breier, 2003; Gamble, 2004a; Bolton, 2005). There has simultaneously been a move to research studies that not only investigate the effect of students' social background on educational achievement but that use research findings to develop models of pedagogic practice that lead to the success of *all* students (for example, Morais and Neves, 2001; Morais, Neves and Pires, 2004; Rose, 2004).

Similar trends are discernable in the field of systemic-functional linguistics, whose dialogue with Bernstein's work dates back to the late 1950s and 1960s (Christie, 1999). Disciplinary fields and subjects have been investigated as linguistic/semiotic practices (for example, Halliday and Martin, 1993; Veel, 1999; Christie 2002); as multimodal discourses (O'Halloran, 2005) and through exploration of the question 'what enables the move into vertical discourse?' (Christie and Martin, 2007).

Influenced by the above trends, this chapter turns to craft apprenticeship to examine the link between its knowledge base and its pedagogy. The interest in this relation is prompted by the way in which three different 'knowledge maps' locate craft or trade on different sides of the boundary between empirical and non-empirical domains of meaning generation. Given this boundary status, the question arises as to whether an apprenticing pedagogy provides pointers towards a pedagogic prescription for a route from common sense or everyday understanding into specialised, context-independent forms of meaning, which Bernstein calls vertical discourse. This is an important question for all forms of educational provisioning and especially so for young people who are 'cooled out' (Hopper, 1973) of academic schooling at a fairly early stage and encouraged to pursue a more practical route. In exploring this question, I draw on both the literature of sociology of education and of systemic-functional linguistics (SFL).

Craft's Ambiguous Position in Knowledge Terms

Somewhat anomalously, Bernstein (1996, p. 175) positions craft as a modality of vertical discourse, characterised by a horizontal knowledge structure with a weak grammar and tacit transmission. Elaborating on this position, he describes craft as a 'horizontal knowledge structure nearest to horizontal discourse, emerging as a specialised practice to satisfy the material requirements of its segments' (Bernstein, 1999, p. 168). This positioning of craft in vertical discourse has perplexed the systemic-functional linguists. Noting the early affinity between research done by what he calls the Sydney School of systemic-functional linguistics and Bernstein's work on knowledge structure, Martin (2007, p. 38) explains how, in 1992, he attempted to map fields of discourse (a specialised term in systemic functional linguistics), in terms of the way in which he imagined they were learned, as well as according to their degree of lexical specialisation. Following Bernstein (1975, p. 99), Martin sets up a cline (a continuum with a number of gradations) from 'common sense' to 'uncommon sense,' which is represented in Figure 8.1.

In this model, trades, with apprenticing as mode of acquisition, are positioned closer to the 'common sense' end of the cline, as specialised participation under oral transmission (doing). Martin argues that, from a social semiotic perspective, specialised discourses such as trades do not rely on grammatical metaphor for construal, as is the case with fields that are positioned on the written transmission (studying) end of the cline. Since, from a functional linguistic perspective, grammatical metaphor whereby a process first construed as a verb is reconstrued in the form of a noun—thus a transformation in the grammar from one class to another (Halliday and Martin, 1993, p. 13), is the defining feature of verticality he thus questions Bernstein's positioning of trades in vertical discourse and suggests that they may be better treated as horizontal discourses of a specialised kind (Christie, Martin et al. 2007, p. 241).

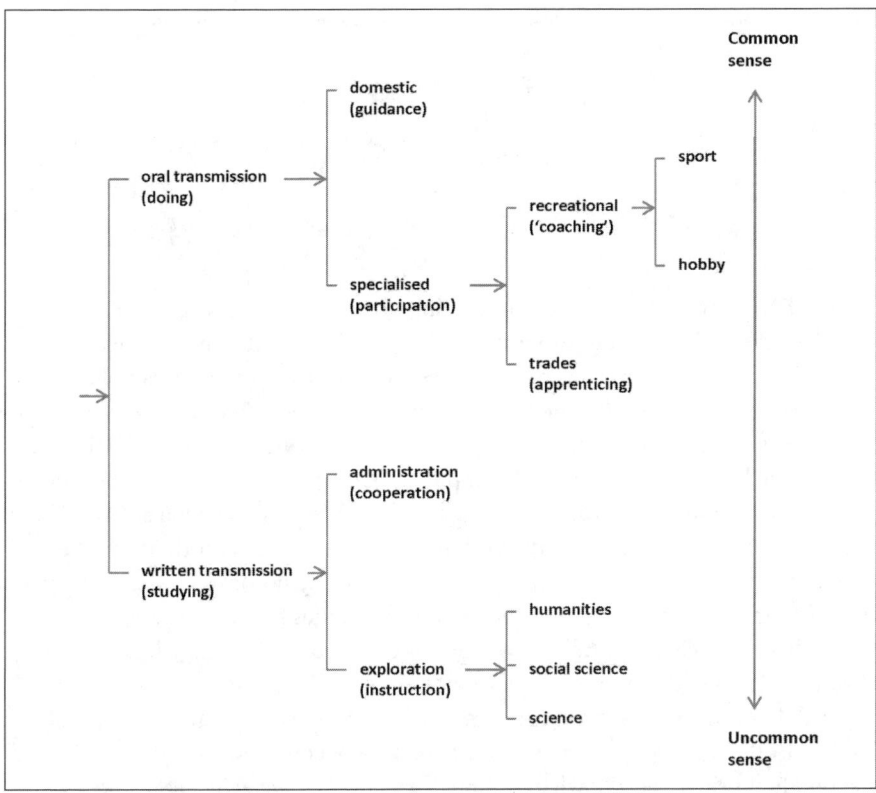

Figure 8.1 Common and uncommon sense fields
(Martin, 1992, p. 544, as reproduced in Martin, 2007, p. 37).

The difference between the two positions lies in Bernstein's assertion that crafts are '*tacit* horizontal knowledge structures' (1996, p. 181, Note 5; original emphasis), which is transmitted tacitly (that is, mainly through modelling). Since a position on the oral transmission side of a common sense-uncommon sense continuum obviously does not entertain the tacit, or what Polanyi (1958, p. 88) calls the 'ineffable,' these two positions must, of necessity, be at odds.

Gamble (2001, 2002, 2004a, 2004b) developed a conceptual model that agrees with both Bernstein's positioning of craft in vertical discourse and Martin's positioning of craft in the field of common sense. This model is presented in Figure 8.2.

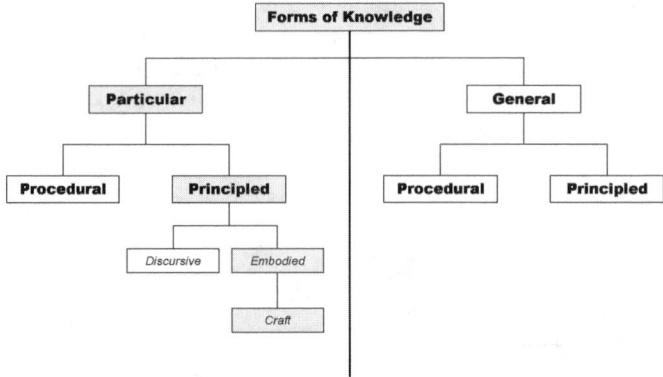

Figure 8.2 A conceptual model of general and particular forms of knowledge (adapted from Gamble 2004a & 2004b).

Rather than viewing Martin and Bernstein's positioning of craft or trades as contradictory, the model employs Abbott's (2001) principle of self-similarity in the fractal division of cultural and social structures. Abbott argues that at each level of a fractal chain of division, one finds the original fractal repeated so that 'the relation of the general terms is recapitulated in the specific ones' (Abbott, 2001, p. 9). Moore and Muller (2002) similarly employ Abbott's logic when they interrogate Bernstein's horizontal–vertical distinction at different levels of a fractal chain to show how downward elaboration avoids rigid dichotomisation or what they call 'the distorting simplicities of a two-column fractionating dichotomy' (p. 632). Hegel's dialectic logic that synthesis sheds elements of both thesis and antithesis but simultaneously retains elements of both (Hegel, as discussed in Honderich (Ed.), 1995) is latent in both of the above explanations.

Although the model's theoretical lineage is discussed elsewhere (Gamble 2004a, 2004b), I offer a truncated explanation here of why craft knowledge is positioned as embodied principled knowledge. The distinction between 'general' and 'particular' is based on Sohn-Rethel's (1978) argument that the division between intellectual and manual labour is a fundamental epistemological division between non-empirical meanings, generated through deductive reasoning, and empirical meanings generated in an experiential context of human action. The second level of the fractal chain is made possible by Pye's explanation that an 'essential principle of arrangement' (Pye, 1978, p. 21) is embodied in every invention and in every design. In diagrammatic form, which is the way in which craft apprentices would encounter a design, a principle of arrangement is visualised rather than described. Given that the maker grasps the principle in visual form, the abstract nature of the principle is not manifest. However, whether visualised or rendered in discursive form, the principle operates at the level of class and not at the level of token or instance. The designer prescribes a particular embodiment of that principle and when the maker gives realisation to the principle in the construction of the particular item, the interpretation required is one at the level of generalised class or type. For Pye, this is not 'seeing' in the ordinary sense of the word; it is an act of interpretation that is wholly different from what he calls 'the utilitarian perception of everyday life' (Pye, 1978, p. 117). What is 'seen' is not only the formal features of an object but also the relations of order between parts and the whole. Craft workers do not have access to particular principles of arrangement in discursive form, yet, they recognize such principles through visualisation.

By acknowledging that one side of a binary divide always contains elements of the other side at a lower fractal level, it is thus possible to place craft on the particular side of the knowledge divide but as an embodied principled knowledge form, without this necessarily being a contradiction. This positioning is consistent with Bernstein's discussion of the resemblance between horizontal knowledge structures and horizontal discourse.

Acquisition of *Horizontal discourse* is a tacit acquisition of a particular view of cultural realities, or rather of a way of realising these realities. The 'way' itself is embedded in the unity latent in the contextual segmentation of this discourse. The 'way' may be likened to the 'gaze' as it becomes active in the experience and ongoing practices of the speakers. This is similar to the 'gaze' embedded in the acquisition of the specialised languages of a *Horizontal Knowledge Structure* with a weak grammar (Bernstein, 2000, p. 165; original emphasis).

Visualisation, as it has been used above, is analogous to 'gaze' as it is more specialised than a 'way' of realising cultural realities, which Bernstein attributes to horizontal discourse. However, in craft one cannot really speak of a grammar because the relation between subsidiary segments cannot be articulated. The relational whole is constituted through and by the ability to visualise—as a kind of non-articulable compensation for the lack of a clear syntax.

From the above, it is evident that both Bernstein and Gamble ascribe to craft the capacity to cross the horizontal-vertical (Bernstein) or particular-general (Gamble) boundary to display features of both forms of knowledge. This is the unity of head and hand described by Marx (1867/1976, pp. 283–284) and later by Braverman (1974, p. 109). However, being able to characterise craft as a knowledge form rather than as skill does not yet tell us anything about the pedagogy that transmits this form of knowledge. While pointing to its tacit transmission (Bernstein, 2000, p. 169), Bernstein is also adamant that modelling of a principle without verbal elaboration ultimately produces a restricted code (Bernstein, 1996, p. 191). In this, he clearly follows the systemic-functional linguists in posing access to educational knowledge as a process of grammatical construction (Halliday, 1993a). The implication that follows is that the boundary between horizontal and vertical cannot be crossed without language being present in the pedagogy.

In my study of a master–apprentice pedagogy in cabinet making (Gamble, 2004a), technical instruction proceeded mainly through modelling, with verbal elaboration most markedly present in the transmission of rules of character, identity and social order, or what Bernstein calls the 'regulative discourse'—in fact, this was almost the only time when the apprentice master could be observed to be 'teaching' a group of students at the same time. The possibility that must thus be explored is whether explicit instruction in rules of moral order has the potential to provide access to a meaning orientation that goes beyond the immediate, experiential moment. Put in another way: Are there modalities of restricted code just as there are modalities of elaborated code? This question is explored through a brief discussion of how Emile Durkheim—and later, Basil Bernstein—pose the relation between instructional and moral orders in pedagogy and how this relation has been taken up in empirical studies. Thereafter I present extracts from my own study of craft pedagogy (Gamble, 2004a) and analyse these via a lens provided by the work of several systemic-functional linguists.

The Relation between Instructional and Moral Orders in Pedagogy: Theoretical Antecedents and their Impact on Research Practices

At a time when state-supported schools in France were moving to secular moral education, Durkheim (1961/2002) links morality to the social collectivity and distinguishes three elements of a social morality, namely discipline, attachment to social groups and autonomy or self-determination (which he defines as the requirement for as complete an understanding as is possible of the reasons for our conduct). He argues that human conduct is influenced by the way in which we conceive of action and our conception of social reality is thus theoretically built. From this perspective, school subjects that transmit theoretical concepts play an important role in determining the way in which we see things. For Durkheim, issues of morality are not compressed into special lessons (Durkheim, 1961/2002, p. 125); both the content (the 'what') of instruction and the mode of instruction (the 'how') are relays for the moral order. History and science are cited as particularly important contributors, in the sense that history builds a sense of impersonal continuity that transcends any one individual and science builds a sense of the complexity of the world.

> Suppose we are discussing a given discovery, say the laws governing light. Instead of merely summarizing the results, we must tell the child how we arrived at these laws after long and patient experiments, gropings and failures of all sorts. We must indicate the hypotheses that successively followed and displaced one another, the investment in thought and labour that they entailed. We must explain to him [*sic*] that the knowledge we now have is itself provisional and that tomorrow, perhaps, a new fact may be discovered that may put everything into question again, or may require us to modify these conclusions, at least in part. We are far from being able to discover truth at a single stroke, far from shaping it to fit our abstract understanding. In short, we must convey the need for experimentation, for observation, and the necessity of getting out of ourselves and submitting to the teaching of experience, if we really want to know and to understand (Durkheim, 1961/2002, p. 262).

In his seminal paper, 'On the Classification and Framing of Educational Knowledge' (1973), Bernstein also refers to the relation between the subject discipline and the moral order. He explains the specialised consciousness that results from strong classification of the curriculum as an educational identity created through socialisation into a subject loyalty (for example, science or arts), through which the student acquires the cognitive and social style particular to the sociological identity. Initially the subject is what he calls the 'linchpin of identity' (Bernstein, 1973, p. 373). Later this leads to an occupational identity (for example, as a physicist, economist and so forth). There thus seems to be an early indication that, like Durkheim, Bernstein views the knowledge discipline as a carrier of moral regulation. Indeed, by 1996 both the 'what' and the 'how' of the theory of instruction are included as elements of regulative discourse.

> Finally, the recontextualizing principle not only recontextualizes the *what* of pedagogic discourse, what discourse is to become subject and content of pedagogic practice, but it also recontextualizes the *how*; that is *the theory of instruction*. This is crucial, because the selection of the theory of instruction is not entirely instrumental. The theory of instruction also belongs to the regulative discourse, and contains within itself a model of the learner and of the teacher and of the relation. The model of the learner is never wholly utilitarian; it contains ideological elements. The recontextualizing principle not only selects the *what* but also the *how* of the theory of instruction. Both are elements of regulative discourse (Bernstein, 1996, p. 49; original emphasis).

In this depiction of a pedagogic discourse as one discourse constituted by an instructional discourse embedded in a regulative discourse, the regulative discourse is viewed as dominant (Bernstein, 1996, p. 49) to signal the ideological nature of the choices that construct curriculum (Bernstein, 2000, p. 32).

It is, however, when the explanation that 'in one sense this is obvious, because it is the *moral* discourse that creates the criteria which give rise to character, manner, conduct, posture etc.' (Bernstein,1996, p. 48; original emphasis) is linked to his earlier assertion that hierarchical rules 'establish the conditions for order, character and manner' (Bernstein, 1990, pp. 65–66), that we find researchers working within a Bernsteinian framework, for example Neves, Morais and Alfonso (2004); Reeves (2005); Hoadley (2005), operationalising the regulative order in terms of communication relations in the classroom between teachers and students and communications relations between peers, with varying degrees of delicacy in terms of the coding categories used. Apart from Bolton (2005), who, in her study of the relation between social class, pedagogy and achievement in art, distinguishes between 'art-conduct norms' and 'social-conduct norms' (Bolton, 2005, p. 139), there is little empirical evidence to date that the content of the normative order has been considered in terms of its pedagogic role.

The study (Gamble, 2004a), on which this analysis draws, similarly characterises the strength of framing over the hierarchical rules but the analysis offered here veers from the established analytical track, as described above, in that it sets out to explore, after Durkheim, whether there could possibly be a connection between a knowledge base that remains largely opaque as a result of its tacit nature and the structure of the content of the moral regulation present in the pedagogic transmission. It is to this characterisation that I now turn.

Regulative Discourse in Craft Transmission: A Case Study

The Pedagogic Outcome

The case presented here refers to a research study (Gamble, 2004a) in which the master–pedagogy relation between a master–artisan in cabinet making and various groups of apprentices was observed over a period of about 18 months. A systematic description of the apprenticeship pedagogy observed was achieved through the employment of Basil Bernstein's theoretical concepts of classification and framing, which focuses on a pedagogic practice's structuring relations in space and time in order to illuminate issues of power and control.

In synopsis (as shown below), craft pedagogy in this case study is characterised by two modalities of selection, sequencing and pacing, two modalities of criterial rules and two modalities of regulative discourse. These are empirically intertwined but, when analytically separated, the two modalities link consistently to the two knowledge forms found to be present in the pedagogy (Table 8.1).

Table 8.1 Relation between knowledge form, instructional discourse and regulative discourse (condensed from Gamble 2004a)

Knowledge form	Principled (tacit)	Procedural (explicit)
Instructional discourse		
Selection, sequencing and pacing	Very weak framing	Strong framing
Evaluative criteria	Strongly framed criterion rule of 'readiness'	Strongly framed criteria of material and tool usage, precision and accuracy
Regulative discourse		
Strongly framed hierarchical rule transmits:	Relations of autonomy (rules of moral conduct)	Relations of subordination (rules of procedural conduct)

The outcome of this pedagogy is neither 'performance' nor 'competence' (Bernstein, 2000, pp. 44–50), but both, as characterised in Figure 8.3.

Externally visible performance
—————————————————
Internally held competence

Figure 8.3 Pedagogic outcome of craft pedagogy (Gamble, 2004a, p. 135).

The term 'competence' as used here, shares with Bernstein's use of the term the idea that competence is tacitly acquired. However, it does not carry the emancipatory meaning of intrinsic creative potential and in-built virtuous and benign self-regulation as described by Bernstein (2000, pp. 31–44). It is also not the 'competence' or 'competency' used in formulations such as competency-based modular training, to refer to narrow behavioural specifications of a procedural kind—in fact, exactly the opposite! It is competence in the form of an internally held sense of space and time that allows the formal principle of arrangement, inherent in the design of any artifact, to be visualised as a relation between part and whole and realised as a specific instantiation of craft performance. This is the capacity to which the criterial rule of 'readiness' refers, without it ever being put into words or explicitly taught. One could rather say it is 'caught' through sustained work in the presence of the 'privileged repertoire' (Ensor, 2004, p. 155) transmitted by the master. Such competence should, however, not be seen as the inevitable outcome of craft pedagogy, as there are many apprentices who can perform all the individual operations and yet would not be judged ready in terms of having attained the craft mastery required for passing the trade test.

WORK ETHIC AS REGULATIVE DISCOURSE

While Durkheim and Bernstein provide us with the essential tenets of transmission of a secular moral order, both are concerned with moral education as it is transmitted in schools. However, in education directly concerned with preparation for work it is work itself that is deemed to be at the centre of the construction of an occupational identity, accompanied by an emphasis on work ethic as the carrier of moral value. The notion of work ethic depends on what counts as work for its meaning. In this regard, Marx's depiction of the three phases of the transformation of the labour process under capitalist production is instructive. For Marx, the phases of cooperation, manufacture and machinofacture (Marx, 1867/1976, pp. 438–639) are abstractions. They are not meant to sum up any particular historical period but are part of a model of capitalist development with pre-industrial craft as the starting point of his analysis

Marx sees cooperation, or the rise of the factory system, as an enlargement of the workshop of the master craftsman during the time of the guilds. Under relations of cooperation, a number of craft workers belonging to the same craft work together under one roof and are involved in the same or in different but connected processes. Each of these craft workers (with the assistance of one or more apprentices) still makes the entire commodity and performs in succession all the operations necessary to produce it (Marx, 1867/1976, pp. 439–443; also discussed in Webster, 1985, pp. 2–4).

At the other end of the spectrum, we find machinofacture as an 'an entirely objective organisation of production…[which] confronts the worker as a pre-existing material condition of production' (Marx, 1867/1976, p. 508). Labour under the machine becomes repetitious and unvaryingly uniform even though craft does not disappear altogether. The machine trades found in engineering fields originate at this time and many parts of machinery continue to be produced by handicraft or by manufacture.

When Zygmunt Bauman (1998) traces the shift from what he calls a society of producers guided by a work ethic to a society of consumers ruled by an aesthetic of consumption he shows how, in many modernising industrial societies, the notion of 'work ethic' served to instill the discipline and obedience necessary for work in the new mass production factories. He also points out that this sense of work ethic, as subordination, was a re-formulation of an earlier work ethic of work autonomy.

The moral crusade recorded as the battle for the *introduction* of the work ethic (or as the training in the application of the 'performance principle') was in fact an attempt to *resuscitate* basically pre-industrial work attitudes under new conditions which no longer made them meaningful. The moral crusade aimed at the re-creation, inside the factory under owner-controlled discipline, of the commitment to the whole hearted, dedicated workmanship and the 'state of the art' task performance which once upon a time came to the craftsman naturally when he himself *[sic]* was in control of his work (Bauman, 1998, p. 7; original emphasis).

The case study shows that both forms of work ethic, as described by Bauman, are present in the regulative discourse transmitted through a master–apprentice trade pedagogy where rules of hierarchy are strongly framed (F^{i+}). As it is in the transmission of these two regulative discourses that language is explicitly used, extracts that relate to each variable are presented in order to show their substance.

Rules of Hierarchy

In master–apprentice relations, an asymmetrical relation of hierarchy is inherent in the very nature of such a relationship. What the extract in Table 8.2 shows, however, is that the master-trainer in the trade school assumes the role of 'master' in surrogate kinship terms. The social relations of the family, reminiscent of the domestic mode of production, are strongly in evidence, with the focus on general attributes of those subject to control (common age, master–apprentice relation, older–younger relation), or what Bernstein calls 'control of the positional type' (Bernstein, 2000, p. 136).

Table 8.2 Framing of the hierarchical rule in master-apprentice pedagogy

Relations of hierarchy between master-trainer and apprentices (F^{i+})
[One of the younger master-trainers introduced a written Disciplinary Code, with 20 'do's' and 'don'ts' of the trade school. The decision was made that the Code should be distributed and discussed with apprentices at the start of each block of training. This incident occurred at the start of the Stage 3-block, in a class taught by the most experienced of the master-trainers.]
The master-trainer in cabinet making [identified as MT1] hands out the Disciplinary Code and goes on talking. The apprentices scan the form and also say nothing. MT1 then tells them that if they are late he will report them to their companies. His next sentence is: 'If you have problems you must tell me. We must talk about these things.'
A short while later he returns to the issue of discipline. 'You're not small children and I'm not a police officer. I'm not going to tell you all the time. If I'm out then find something to do. Don't wait for me to say: "do this" or "do that". It's that extra bit that you do that counts. What I hate is when people never do anything extra. They start cramping a carcass at 5.25 but at 5.30 they leave and it's not squared up.
I don't keep anything back. If there's a good apprentice and there's a position the right person gets it—not the favourite. I've also got a son. He's 28. You've got to be taught, like I taught him. I'm teaching you discipline. It's good. One day you'll teach your children' (Field Notes, 14/08/2000).

This relation of hierarchy provides the basis for the transmission of a set of intertwined regulative norms that each has a distinctive character (as represented in Figure 8.4).

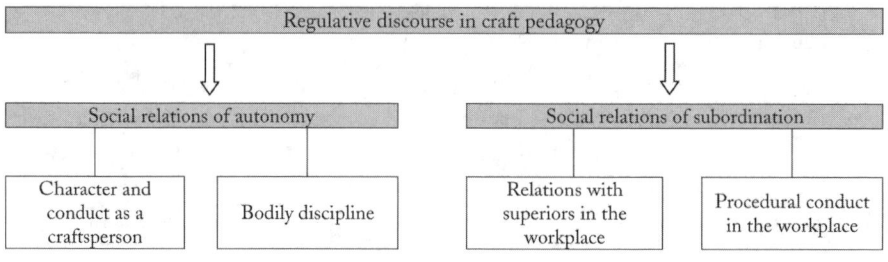

Figure 8.4 Regulative discourse in craft pedagogy.

Relations of Autonomy

This strand of the regulative discourse is marked by an emphasis on the kind of person that a cabinet maker must be, with moral self-regulation and bodily self-regulation interwoven (Table 8.3).

Table 8.3 Character and conduct as a craftsperson

Character and conduct as a craftsperson (F^{i+})

[Master-trainer speaking to apprentices]
(1) MT1: 'If you see somebody taking something, please tell him it's wrong.'
    Appr: 'We must report him. What's the reward?'
    MT1: 'No, you tell him yourself.'

(2) MT1: 'If something is wrong, do something or say something. Don't just stand there.'
(3)   'You complain about the bosses. But maybe the bosses also complain about you.' (The apprentices mumble amongst themselves.) 'Boys must have some fire. A boy mustn't just sit there, accepting everything.' (They all laugh.)
(4)   'I don't give you bad advice. Yes, you can say: "Oh he just talks—he's in with the boss." But I'm not saying this for the boss. It's for you.'
(5)   'Don't just do it my way. You must find your own way'.
(Comments 1, 2, 3, 4 from Field Notes, 14/08/2000. Comment 5 from Field Notes, 11/02/01)

Even injunctions about bodily self-regulation convey a strong sense of moral order and are often used as markers of 'character' (Table 8.4).

Table 8.4 Bodily discipline

Bodily discipline (F⁺)
(1) MT1: 'Come, come you're late. You're six minutes late. This is no good.' (Field Notes, 16/09/99).
(2) *[In an aside to the researcher]* 'Those two over there—in their factories they have "boys" to clean up. But here they must learn to clean up for themselves' (Field Notes, 07/09/99).
(3) The prize for Apprentice of the Year should have gone to ….. (names an apprentice). His work is excellent, but how can I give the prize to someone who comes late all the time? What kind of a tradesman is he going to be? *[Comment made during a conversation with MT1, conversation undated]*

Relations of subordination

The extracts in Table 8.5 show that injunctions to be compliant and obedient have a strong procedural base, which, while not removing the craftsperson's right to autonomous judgement in workmanship, nevertheless acknowledges management's right of control and require that the prerogative of management be respected.

Table 8.5: Relations with superiors

Relations with superiors in the workplace (Fi+)
[First session with Stage 1- apprentices, conducted on the premises of a craft factory.]   MT1: 'You're young. You don't know how they're running their business. Always check with your supervisor. Work as closely with management as you can. Don't just do your own thing. The job might be a "special" and the customer wants it in a particular way. Always ask management what they want. If he says it must be like that, then you're safe. Then it is management's fault' (Field Notes, 11/02/01).
[A discussion that takes places in a theory session for Stage 2-apprentices.]   MT1: 'A foreman is not picked as the guy who's got his arm around everyone. The foreman is an individual. He sits alone and reads his paper. He can't be everyone's friend. He must give instructions.'
An apprentice: 'Nobody wants to listen to a Coloured foreman. It must be a "boer" [local term used to refer to a White, Afrikaans-speaking man: JG]. Then they sit up.'
MT1: 'I became foreman in the heart of Apartheid. I had guys who were in the trade thirty to forty years ahead of me. Why did they give me the job? Because I do my work well. I'm always on time. I do extra things. So nobody must come and tell me it's about Apartheid. It's about you and who you are. Do as you are told and somebody will see it. If someone steals your idea as their own, it's okay. In the end it comes out' (Field Notes, 14/08/99).
Note [JG]: Both master-trainer and apprentices belong to the population group known as Coloured in South Africa. Here the apprentices are being mischievous and trying to rile the master-trainer by implying that race would be a legitimate excuse for not always obeying the foreman.

Compliance and obedience are, however, not unconditional. While trade unions are never mentioned directly a sense of legal rights and adherence to correct industrial relations procedure is emphasised (as illustrated in Table 8.6).

Table 8.6: Procedural conduct in the workplace

Procedural conduct in the workplace (F^{i+})
[This comment was made during a conversation with the master-trainer in cabinet making.]
MT1: 'I tell the apprentices always to write down what they are doing. Sometimes they're busy with a job and then they get interrupted and told: "Just do this." Then they don't write it down and at the end of the day the foreman says: "Why did you do so little work today?" And then if you're E ... ([referring to a particular apprentice: JG], you say nothing. You just leave when you can't take it any longer' (Field Notes, 15/02/01).
[During a discussion in a session with Stage 1-apprentices an apprentice gives an example of a mistake by his 'boss' [the artisan under whose supervision he works]. The apprentice explains how the artisan was careless and put a staple through his finger. The master-trainer ignores the implied criticism of the artisan and uses the opportunity to issue a procedural admonition.]
MT1: 'If this happens to you, you must make a note and you must go to the doctor. Otherwise you go to the doctor and the boss says, no, you did not get hurt at work. So you must pay the doctor yourself and you don't get 'time off' to go to the doctor (Field Notes, 11/02/01)

The Intertwining of Normative Relations

The autonomous strand of the moral order transmitted in the trade school can be interpreted as a backward recontextualisation to the work ethic of craft control, or semi-control over the organisation of work and production under early industrial capitalism. By reverting to surrogate relations of kinship, the rules of social hierarchy in the trade school enables the transmission of a social order that govern craft or trade membership, while at the same time inducting apprentices into relations of subordination that regulate factory practices. Should any of the intertwined components of the regulative discourse be dropped the normative order would shift to one of collective craft protectionism and resistance to changes in production, or to mindless compliance and obedience. It is the capacity of the regulative order in craft transmission to relay complex social relations that is undoubtedly its strongest feature, with a strong occupational identity as the anchor around which the other strands are woven. We also find Ray's (1986, pp. 292–293) two strategies for responding to forms of control, namely *acting as if* and *believing* condensed into one. While apprentices start off by being required to *act as if* they have autonomy over their work it is through the building of a strong occupational identity that they start *believing* in their own sense of 'being a cabinet maker.' It is this belief that provides the normative basis for acquiring a craft ethic.

The Regulative Order as Semiotic Mediator of Meaning

What we have so far is an exemplification of how language features in the transmission of moral order in craft pedagogy and a question about whether explicit instruction in rules of moral order has the potential to provide access to a meaning orientation that goes beyond the immediate or experiential. In other words, can a claim be sustained that there is a link between the nature of the regulative order (that is, whether it is of a principled or procedural nature) and the form of knowledge transmitted? In order to explore this question we turn to the work of theorists in systemic-functional linguistics, notably the work of Ruqaiya Hasan and Michael Halliday.

Hasan's analysis of the concept of 'semiotic mediation' is based on the premise that 'mediation is, in one sense, different from pedagogy: things get mediated whether or not they are generated with mediation in mind' (Hasan, 2004, p. 39). With reference to the work of both Vygotsky and Bernstein, she goes on to distinguish between two forms of semiotic mediation:

> ...one mode that mediates mental dispositions, habits of the mind or typical ways of responding to situations, and one that targets some specific concept, some element of some vertical knowledge structure. The latter I would refer to as *visible semiotic mediation*, the former as *invisible semiotic mediation*. Visible semiotic mediation is pedagogically generated, whereas invisible semiotic mediation occurs without either party's awareness of what is being or has been mediated. For example, the component of pedagogic discourse that Bernstein refers to as *regulative* is normally invisibly mediated (Hasan, 2004, p. 39; original emphasis).

For Hasan, 'wherever there is language in use, there is semiotic mediation' (Hasan, 2004, p. 33). If regulative discourse is invisibly mediated, it follows that regulative discourse itself may also mediate something else invisibly. To get to what this 'something else' may be we need to return to the concept of grammatical metaphor that was briefly discussed earlier in the chapter and remind ourselves of the link between a systemic-functional linguistic perspective and Bernstein's later work on vertical and horizontal discourses. Martin makes the link succinctly when he argues that '…if no grammatical metaphor, then no verticality. This means that from a functional linguistic perspective access to vertical discourse is bound up with control of grammatical metaphor, which in Western societies students are expected to master in secondary school. Failure to access this resource entails exclusion from hierarchical and horizontal knowledge structures' (Martin, 2007, p. 55).

But, the route to grammatical metaphor does not start in secondary school. Halliday (1993a) traces a developmental path to grammatical metaphor that brings connecting points at a lower developmental level into view. Referring to various studies of children's language development, Halliday draws a distinction between the opposition of general and specific and the opposition of abstract and concrete to postulate a three-step model of human semiotic development, with a three to five year gap between the three post-infancy stages

(protolanguage →) generalisation → abstractness → metaphor

Figure 8.5 A model of human semiotic development (Halliday, 1993a, p. 111).

Halliday argues that, while grammatical generalisation is the key for entering into language and into systematic commonsense knowledge, grammatical abstractness is the key for entering into literacy and primary educational knowledge. Grammatical metaphor (which, through nominalisation, turns reality into an object instead of a process) is the key to secondary education and to knowledge that is discipline-based and technical. In this regard, Halliday (1993b) and Martin (1993) show, for instance, that specialised scientific and technical language cannot be created without recourse to grammatical metaphor. With regard to the prior notion of 'abstractness,' Halliday cites studies that show that it seems likely that children first come into contact with abstract conceptualisation of experience through interpersonally oriented expressions of 'right and wrong,' 'fair and not fair' (Halliday, 1993a, p. 104). He goes on to argue that until children learn to exchange abstract meanings they cannot get access to education 'because without this one cannot become literate' (1993a, p. 109). Regression in semiotic age is what often happens in the first years of schooling when children struggle to present their knowledge in written form. They may talk about a topic with fluency and commonsense understanding, but semiotic regression is necessary to allow them to reconstrue their experience in the form of systematic knowledge (Halliday, 1993a, p. 110).

If we interpret the findings of the case study through the lenses offered by Hasan and Halliday, it allows us to pose the regulative discourse relating to tacit principled knowledge as an invisible semiotic mediator of abstractedness. While both master and apprentices shy away from what they call 'book learning' or 'theory,' when talking about moral conduct in everyday terms the master uses words of which the referents are abstract entities. Even though neither master nor apprentices intend this or are aware of the invisible semiotic mediation that is taking place, the regulative discourse of moral conduct may in fact provide a lexical conduit for the relay of an orientation to meaning that can deal with a measure of abstractedness. This orientation exists in the mind and not in language. It is transmitted through the language of moral conduct rather than through the technical language of mathematics or science.

The relation suggested here is not intended to imply that there is an easy bridge between the everyday and the symbolic or that, being able to visualise an abstract principle of arrangement, apprentices are well on their way to achieving a grasp of grammatical metaphor which will lead them to technicality (creating systematic taxonomies of technical terms) and consequentiality (constructing ongoing sequences of logical argument) (Halliday, 1995, p. 139), in other words to the technical and scientific discourses that characterise knowledge required in technologically advanced workplaces. The point though is that some children are exposed to abstractedness and to meanings 'detached' from the immediate situational context well before they go to school (Painter, 1999). It is thus not implausible to suggest that the regulative discourse transmitted in the cabinet making apprenticing relation, as described in the case study, may be the invisible mediator of acts of semiosis that impart at least a modicum of the preparation that middle class children often receive in the home through semiotic interactions within the family. If this is so, it follows that tacit transmission of a tacit knowledge structure is able to fit into a developmental continuum at a point prior to grammatical metaphor. This removes its 'special status' to show the capacity but also the ultimate constraint of craft apprenticeship as boundary pedagogy.

So, What Pedagogic Prescription?

A consideration of the tacit knowledge base of craft pedagogy has indicated that explicit regulative discourse may play a crucial role in providing the language that mediates the semiotic formation of meanings that go beyond the experiential. While this tentative conclusion is inferred rather than being empirically provable, it tells us something about the function of moral transmission in pedagogy more generally. With reference to academic education, Durkheim argued that it is the content of the disciplinary subject (the *what*), as well as the mode of transmission (the *how*) that transmits abstractions crucial to mediating attachment to the impersonal rule outside of the self (Durkheim 1961/2002, p. 207, 230). The conclusion drawn from an interrogation of craft pedagogy suggests the reverse side of the same coin, namely that the content of moral transmission (that is, a sense of 'right' and 'wrong' as abstract entities) similarly mediates a move towards an abstract orientation to meaning that can entertain a measure of distance and objectivity beyond the immediate moment.

So what pedagogic prescriptions can provisionally be put forward on the basis of the case examined in this chapter? The first is a warning against the tendency described by Martin (2007, p. 241) when he argues that 'radical progressive and constructivist educators seem to believe that all vertical discourses have to be reconstructed as crafts in order for students, especially younger or less successful students, to really learn them.' Craft apprenticeship, per se, does not make it possible for people to move from horizontal to vertical discourse. It depends entirely on the knowledge base on which such apprenticeship pedagogy rests. When Kvale (1997, pp. 188–189) describes, for instance, the apprenticing process between promising scientists, who work next to Nobel laureates to acquire the 'feel' for putting parts together into new wholes—a process which is at the heart of scientific innovation—he is describing an apprenticing process where the substantive knowledge and techniques that constitute 'parts' have been acquired through years of undergraduate and post-graduate study. This is a long way from craft as conventionally understood. To term all apprenticing relations as craft apprenticeship with a potential for gaining access to vertical discourse is to misrecognise both what craft apprenticeship can and cannot do. The systemic-functional linguists have shown conclusively that language is the prototypical resource for making meaning and that the semiotic developmental trajectory cannot be short-circuited. To ascribe to craft apprenticeship a capacity that it does not possess, is either a romanticisation of craft that does violence to a pedagogic tradition with a proud heritage or, at best, misplaced optimism.

At the same time, the tentative conclusions drawn here serve the function of illuminating our understanding of restricted codes. Davies (1995, p. 48) argues that in the development of code theory 'restricted codes got left behind and Bernstein focussed almost entirely on elaborated codes.' Halliday asserts that, although Bernstein labelled codes 'in terms of two poles, restricted and elaborated, he was well aware that a number of different dimensions of meaning were involved and that the overall pattern was one of gradience, not discrete categories' (Halliday, 1995, p. 140). The argument offered in this chapter goes some way towards beginning to explore restricted codes in a more nuanced way than has been possible up to now. It does so by opening up the notion of tacit knowledge and its transmission beyond conventional progressivist or constructivist interpretations of tacit knowledge as transmitted though 'shared or situated practice' and therefore always in the service of the particular. While such interpretations fit with 'post-modern versions of heterogeneous local knowledges not transferable to context-independent meaning' (Christie et al. 2007, p. 242), it undermines the generative potential of tacit knowledge to take students beyond the immediacy of local meaning. Not all students move beyond a restricted orientation to the specialised language of technology and science, but why should this mean that all students should not achieve the exhilaration of mastery that rests on tacit principled knowledge that resides *in* the everyday but is not *of* the everyday? Herein lies the challenge to pedagogy in general. Without fetishising craft there is much to learn from the master–apprentice relation and the invisible semiotic mediation effected by transmission of principled moral discourse—not least about the crucial role that the knowledgeable teacher plays in pedagogic transmission.

References

Abbott, A. (2001). *Chaos of disciplines*. Chicago and London: The University of Chicago Press.
Bauman, Z. (1998). *Work, consumerism and the new poor*. Buckingham: Open University Press.
Bernstein, B. (1973). On the classification and framing of educational knowledge. In R. Brown (Ed.), *Knowledge, education and cultural change: Papers in the sociology of education*. London: Tavistock Publications Limited, pp. 363–392.
Bernstein, B. (1975). *Class, codes and control, Volume 3: Towards a theory of educational transmissions* (2nd ed.). London: Routledge & Kegan Paul.
Bernstein, B. (1990). *The structuring of pedagogic discourse, Volume 1V, Class codes and control*. London: Routledge.
Bernstein, B. (1996). *Pedagogy, symbolic control and identity: Theory, research, critique*. London: Taylor and Francis Ltd.
Bernstein, B. (1999). Vertical and horizontal discourse: An essay. *British Journal of Sociology of Education*, 20 (2), 157–173.
Bernstein, B. (2000). *Pedagogy, symbolic control and identity* (rev. ed.). Lanham: Rowman & Littlefield Publishers Inc.
Bernstein, B. (2001). From pedagogies to knowledges. In A. Morais, I. Neves, B. Davies and H. Daniels (Eds.), *Towards a sociology of pedagogy: The contribution of Basil Bernstein to research*. New York: Peter Lang. 363–368.
Bolton, H. (2005). Social class, pedagogy, and achievement in art. Unpublished PhD dissertation, University of Cape Town.
Braverman, H. (1974). *Labor and monopoly capital: The degradation of work in the twentieth century*. New York: Monthly Review Press.
Breier, M. (2003). The recruitment and recognition of prior informal experience in the pedagogy of two university courses labour law. Unpublished PhD dissertation, University of Cape Town.
Christie, F. (Ed.) (1999). *Pedagogy and the shaping of consciousness: Linguistic and social processes*. London and New York: Continuum.
Christie, F. (2002). *Classroom Discourse Analysis: A Functional Perspective*. London and New York: Continuum.
Christie, F. and Martin, M. (Eds.) (2007). *Language, knowledge and pedagogy: Functional linguistics and sociological perspectives*. London and New York: Continuum.
Christie, F., Martin, J. R., Maton, K. and Muller, J. (2007). Taking stock: Future directions in research in knowledge structure. In F. Christie and J.R. Martin (Eds.), *Language, knowledge and pedagogy: Functional linguistic and sociological perspectives*. London and New York: Continuum, pp. 239–257.
Davies, B. (1995) Bernstein, Durkheim and the British sociology of education. In A.R. Sadovnik (Ed.), *Pedagogy and knowledge: The sociology of Basil Bernstein*. Norwood, NJ: Ablex, pp. 39–57.
Durkheim, E. (1961/2002). *Moral education* (Everett K. Wilson and Herman Schnurer, Trans.). New York: Dover Publications Inc.
Ensor, P. (2004). Towards a sociology of teacher education. In J. Muller, B. Davies and A. Morais (Eds.), *Reading Bernstein, researching Bernstein*. London: RoutledgeFalmer, pp. 153–167.
Gamble, J. (2001). Modelling the invisible: The pedagogy of craft apprenticeship. *Studies in Continuing Education*, 23 (2), 181–196.
Gamble, J. (2002). Teaching without words: Tacit knowledge in apprenticeship. *Journal of Education*, 28, 63–82.
Gamble, J. (2004a). Tacit knowledge in craft pedagogy: A sociological analysis. Unpublished PhD

dissertation, University of Cape Town.
Gamble, J. (2004b). Retrieving the general from the particular: The structure of craft knowledge. In J. Muller, B. Davies and A. Morais (Eds.), *Reading Bernstein, researching Bernstein*. London: RoutledgeFalmer, pp. 189–203.
Halliday, M. A. K. (1993a). Towards a language-based theory of learning. *Linguistics and Education, 5*, 93–116.
Halliday, M. A. K. (1993b). Some grammatical problems in scientific English. In M. A, K, Halliday and J. R. Martin, *Writing science: Literacy and discursive power*. London: Falmer, pp. 69–85.
Halliday, M. A. K. (1995). Language and the theory of codes. In A.R. Sadovnik (Ed.), *Pedagogy and knowledge: The sociology of Basil Bernstein*. Norwood, NJ: Ablex, pp. 127–143.
Halliday, M. A. K. and Martin, J. R. (1993). *Writing science: Literacy and discursive power*. London: Falmer.
Hasan, R. (2004). The concept of semiotic mediation: Perspectives from Bernstein's sociology. In J. Muller, B. Davies and A. Morais (Eds.), *Reading Bernstein, researching Bernstein*. London: RoutledgeFalmer, pp. 30–43.
Hoadley, U. K (2005). Social class, pedagogy and the specialization of voice in four South African primary schools. Unpublished PhD dissertation, University of Cape Town.
Honderich, T. (Ed.) (1995). *The Oxford companion to philosophy*. Oxford: Oxford University Press.
Hopper, E. (1973). Educational systems and selected consequences of patterns of mobility and non-mobility in industrial societies: A theoretical discussion. In R. Brown (Ed.), *Knowledge, education and cultural change: Papers in the sociology of education*. London: Tavistock Publications Limited, pp. 17–69.
Kvale, S. (1997). Research apprenticeship. *Nordisk Pedagogik, 17* (3), 186–194.
Martin, J. R. (1992). English text: system & structure. Amsterdam: Benjamins.
Martin, J. R. (1993). Technicality and abstraction: Language for the creation of specialized texts. In M. A. K. Halliday and J. R. Martin (Eds.), *Writing science: Literacy and discursive power*. London: Falmer, pp. 203–220.
Martin, J. R. (2007). Construing knowledge: a functional linguistic perspective. In F. Christie and J.R. Martin (Eds.), *Language, knowledge and pedagogy: Functional linguistic and sociological perspectives*. London and New York: Continuum, pp. 34–64.
Marx, K. (1867/1976). *Capital: Volume 1* (paperback ed.). London: Penguin Books.
Moore, R. and Muller J. (2002). The growth of knowledge and the discursive gap. *British Journal of Sociology of Education, 23* (4), 627–637.
Morais, A. and Neves, I. (2001). Pedagogical social contexts: Studies for a sociology of learning. In A. Morais, I. Neves, B. Davies and H. Daniels (Eds.), *Towards a sociology of pedagogy: The contribution of Basil Bernstein to research*. New York: Peter Lang, pp. 185–221.
Morais, M., Neves, I. and Pires (2004). The *what* and *how* of teaching and learning: Going deeper into sociological analysis and intervention. In J. Muller, B. Davies and A. Morais (Eds.), *Reading Bernstein, researching Bernstein*. London: RoutledgeFalmer, pp. 75–90.
Neves, I., Morais, A. and Afonso, M. (2004). Teacher training contexts: Study of specific sociological characteristics. In J. Muller, B. Davies and A. Morais (Eds.), *Reading Bernstein, researching Bernstein*. London: RoutledgeFalmer, pp. 168–186.
O'Halloran, K. L. (2005). *Mathematical discourse: Language, symbolism and visual images*. London and New York: Continuum.
Painter, C. (1999). Preparing for school: developing a semantic style for educational knowledge. In F. Christie (Ed.), *Pedagogy and the shaping of consciousness: Linguistic and social processes*. London and New York: Continuum, pp. 66–87.
Polanyi, M. (1958). *Personal knowledge: Towards a post-critical philosophy*. London: Routledge and

Kegan Paul.
Pye, D. (1978). *The nature and aesthetics of design*. London: Barrie & Jenkins.
Ray, C. A. (1986). Corporate culture: The last frontier of control? *Journal of Management Studies, 20* (3), 287–297.
Reeves, C. A. (2005). The effect of 'opportunity-to-learn' and classroom pedagogy on mathematics achievement in schools serving low socio-economic status communities in the Cape peninsula. Unpublished PhD dissertation, University of Cape Town.
Rose, D. (2004). Sequencing and pacing of the hidden curriculum: How indigenous children are left out of the chain. In J. Muller, B. Davies and A. Morais (Eds.), *Reading Bernstein, researching Bernstein*. London: RoutledgeFalmer, pp. 91–107.
Sohn-Rethel, A. (1978). *Intellectual and manual labour: A critique of epistemology*. London and Basingstoke: The MacMillan Press Ltd.
Veel, R. (1999). Language, knowledge and authority in school mathematics. In F. Christie (Ed.), *Pedagogy and the Shaping of Consciousness: Linguistic and Social Processes*. London and New York: Continuum, pp. 185–216.
Webster, E. (1985). *Cast in a racial mould: Labour process and trade unionism in the foundries*. Johannesburg: Ravan Press.

CHAPTER NINE

Towering TIMSS or Leaning PISA?

Vertical and Horizontal Models of International Testing Regimes

WILLIAM TYLER

INTRODUCTION: THE SOCIOLOGY OF KNOWLEDGE AND THE BERNSTEINIAN PROJECT

The origins of this chapter can be found in a response to the dominant themes of the *Reclaiming Knowledge* conference, which combined themes from systemic linguistics and social and cultural reproduction at the University of Sydney (2004). The sociological framework for this conference was based around the issues of official knowledge arising from Bernstein's models of horizontal and vertical discourse. This framework appeared to me at the time, while raising important questions of philosophical enquiry into the epistemological basis of disciplinary knowledge, in danger of losing the main points of Bernstein's project—namely (a) the ways knowledge, power and control interact to reproduce class-based inequalities and (b) his well-documented distinction between the primary or decontextualised fields of knowledge production and its recontextualisation in the classroom or lecture theatre. This emphasis on the sociology of knowledge forms (and their associated structures and grammars) produced some bizarre offshoots such as an interest in the importance of Isaac Newton's class origins and the unexplicated conflation of knowledge structures and their modalities of transmission. Whatever Bernstein's project has taught us, it is clear that curricula forms cannot be readily equated with knowledge structures, cultural transmission with epistemic process, nor can the discursive 'gaze' of educational assessment be effectively described in terms more suitable to the social constitution of disciplinary fields.

While interesting, the defensive positioning of Bernsteinian models of vertical forms of knowledge production strikes a discordant note in the totality of Bernstein's egalitarian project, given the well-established links between the greater power of these more abstract and 'vertical' forms of knowledge to reproduce inequalities through private schooling, university selection processes and the processes of early childhood socialisation. Were the directions of pedagogic discourse becoming merely a reflex of the wider culture wars that raged in the 1990s in all fields of cultural production and reproduction? Was pedagogy to be reduced to a debate about the principles of knowledge production, selection and distribution? Was the implicit conflation of discourses of knowledge production, their structures and grammars with modalities of reproduction just one more example of what Bernstein called in his final paper (2001), in which he presages the rise of the Totally Pedagogised Society (TPS)?

In this emerging vision of late-capitalist society, the internal logics of pedagogic discourse are subsumed by, and merge with, those of the general systems of social stratification: the labour market, the politics of symbolic control and the commodification of knowledge driven by the globalised processes of the information age (Bernstein, 2001; Tyler 2004a). In such a setting, it is perhaps not surprising that the relationship between Bernstein's initial project and educational policy and practice seems to have changed tack. What was originally a critical sociological analysis of the role of decontextualised meanings and their forms of transmission has now been subsumed into a defense of those very forms of knowledge production, which have historically been associated with elitist forms of selective schooling whose strongest adherents are to be found in the private and most selective of schools and universities (Teese, 2000).

With these latter uses of Bernstein's project as a background, I shall treat the results and debates surrounding international testing regimes as an example of the way the politics of school knowledge has become unnecessarily polarised around what appears to be the horizontal/vertical axis rather than its deeper structures of social and semiotic context. By inference, I shall show that this typology or dichotomy is far too limiting and fails to exploit the full complexity of the Bernsteinian approach to pedagogic discourse. This will lead to a detailed model of the socio-semiotic basis of educational measurement technologies, rather than the surface features represented by the horizontal/vertical model and its attendant debates between curricula constructivism and its opponents.

INTERNATIONAL TESTING REGIMES: RESULTS AND REACTIONS IN CONTEMPORARY DEBATES

The contestation over what constitutes official knowledge should be closely linked with the debate about national standards expressed as concerns about the relative standing of national levels or means of performance in basic skills. In this area, there are two main players, going under the acronyms of TIMSS (Trends in International Mathematics and Science Study) and PISA (Program for International Student Assessment), each with its own aims and genealogy. The more established of the two, TIMSS grew from the International Association for the Evaluation of Educational Achievement (IEA) group, based in the International Study Center, Boston College (TIMSS, 2000; Smithers, 2004). This first cross-national survey of mathematics and science achievement under the IEA auspices was carried out over several elementary and middle school grades, with a first sweep of 12 countries in 1964 and the second sweep in the 1980. The next sweep became the Third International Mathematics and Science Study in 1994–95, repeated to include 35 countries in 1998–99. The acronym was then changed to refer to a four-year cycle of studies in 2003 and then in 2007 in which over 60 countries participated. The more recently inaugurated program of PISA was a collaboration of the members of the Organisation for Economic Policy and Development (OECD) based in Paris. Its main aim is to measure how well 15-year-olds perform across member countries on a range of 'literacies,' not only reading and writing, but also mathematical and scientific. The PISA group has performed three of these cross-national surveys across 32 member countries in 2000, 2003 and 2006. Initially, its board which determined priorities was led by the Australian Council for Educational Research, with Director Barry McGaw.

The aims, testing, sampling methods and pedagogical emphases of these two testing regimes could not appear more different (Smithers, 2004, p. 10). While TIMSS is age-graded and aimed at testing mastery of science and mathematical curricula, PISA aims to capture the students' abilities to use their knowledge and skills in the challenges of real-life situations at the end of their primary schooling. As Barry McGaw stated in evidence to the House of Education and Skills Committee: 'TIMSS is interested to discover "what science you have been taught and how much you have learned",' while for PISA the aim was to discover 'what you can do with the science that you have been taught' (2002, quoted by Smithers, 2004). The styles of questioning, particularly in mathematics, emphasise different approaches (textbook knowledge vs. context), and a different balance and coverage in each area (TIMSS with 308 items completed in one ninety minute booklet, PISA assessing math and science literacy in a total of 32 items to a maximum of 30 minutes each). Their marking schemes also differed widely, with PISA awarding marks for appropriate method in mathematics, even if the answer was incorrect, and for reading and writing, no correction of faulty grammar, punctuation and spelling.

One of the most systematic comparisons of the results of the ranking of participating countries in each of these programs was carried out by Smithers (2004) at the Centre for Education and Employment Research at the University of Liverpool. Given the age and sampling differences, he was limited to a comparison of the mathematics and science results from two closely related cohorts—those born in 1984, sampled by both the first or 2000 PISA survey and TIMSS-R 1999 (the Third International Mathematics and Science Study Repeat). Both, he claims, came up with 'very different pictures' of the relative standing of the countries that participated in both surveys (2004, p. 6). While the mathematics rankings for these scores do correlate significantly (at about +.6) at the 5 per cent level, explaining about a third of the variation in each others scores, and the same countries appear at the top (Korea, Japan and Flemish-speaking Belgium) and the bottom (Italy), there are claimed to be 'major discrepancies' (p. 8). New Zealand and England tend to do well in PISA tests but poorly in those for TIMSS, while the opposite holds for Hungary and Russia.

Trends over different sweeps also show swings in relative position. England/United Kingdom scored 40 or so points behind a group of European countries in the IEA surveys of 1995/9, while in the PISA 2000 studies, it appeared to be some 20 points ahead of those countries on the average (Smithers, 2004, p. 15). Comparison with other studies such as the PIRLS (Progress in International Reading Literacy Survey, 2001) and the IALS (International Literacy Survey) conducted by Statistics Canada show similar variations, with England/United Kingdom scoring very well in PISA and PIRLS, but falling to 14th out of 17 countries for the IALS, while the results for France indicated that 65 per cent of its population were functionally illiterate—a finding that led to a European-commission funded enquiry (Blum, Goldstein and Gerin-Pace, 2001), which reduced this figure to about 5 per cent. Major differences were also found between regions, countries with differing proportions of immigrant and Indigenous-native populations and between private and public schools, as well as in the spread of scores. Measures of the social gradient or equity were also fairly inconclusive according to Smithers (2004, p. 23), depending on which measure of a student's social background is employed (material possessions or wealth vs. social status, whose scores were found not to correlate).

While these discrepancies have been explained in terms of the differing aims, test and item construction, cultural and educational system differences, and covariate measurement in the target populations (Adams, 2003), this has not prevented politicians, officials and public commentators from interpreting the findings to suit particular agendas. Public dissemination of the league tables for both surveys for 2003 has been widespread and well debated in most media (OECD Newsletter 18, Assessment Activities) with fairly predictable and often confusing results, often due to the proximity of their release. On the one hand, OECD spokespersons tend to promote the success of comprehensive systems such as the Scandinavian and to denigrate those with selection or high levels of differentiation such as the German, Swiss or the United Kingdom. TIMSS supporters, on the other hand, concentrate on the poor performance of the Anglophone countries—Australia, the United Kingdom and the United States—in their tests and tend to deprecate their higher placing in PISA rankings, particularly in mathematics and science (Naylor, 2004; Donnelly, 2004, pp. 120–121).

The debates around the performance of selective and hierarchically differentiated systems are mirrored in preferences for testing, which privileges traditional curricula of TIMSS over everyday situational applications of the PISA tests. The political preference for knowledge-based, norm-referenced systems of TIMSS has been reflected in the reforms of national curricula and their accompanying national testing systems, which have had such an impact on educational practice in the United Kingdom and other Anglophone countries from the mid-1980s (Tyler, 1999). In the United States, the movement towards age-graded achievement rather than individual assessment has contributed to 'No Child left Behind' policies of the George W. Bush administration (U.S. Department of Education, 2008), and may even find resonances in the phonic/whole language debate and in school reporting practices (Department of Education, Employment and Workplace Relations, 2005). In the Australian case, the debates about the constructivist and exploratory foundations of the proposed West Australian Outcomes Based Education curriculum running through the national and local press may also be positioned along a TIMSS vs. PISA type model of evaluation.

VERTICAL OR HORIZONTAL? FIRST POSITIONINGS OF TIMSS AND PISA

From an academic viewpoint, it is remarkable that these programs should be so influential in political circles in the absence of a theory of educational evaluation, whether theoretical or methodological. The absence of such a framework can no doubt explain the tendencies of commentators to become absorbed in the technical minutiae of educational measurement, or inspired by the political and economic ideologies such as social democracy or neo-liberalism. The very opaqueness of the questions, which may lead to any definite conclusions about the validity of any one international ranking scheme, have tended to deter serious academic comment, although some of the universals or constants found in the cross-national results, such as the superior literacy of female over male students in the case of the PISA findings, has spawned some positive and important academic investigations (Rowe, 2005).

However, the polarisation between the two positions occupied by TIMSS and PISA in public policy appears to parallel very closely those underlying Bernstein's distinction between vertical and horizontal discourses of knowledge (2000), with clear implications for the generation of the 'discursive gap' between the everyday and the disciplinary forms of knowledge that frames the 'Reclaiming Knowledge' debate (Moore and Muller, 2002).

Tyler (2004b, p. 12) explicates this model in these terms:

> Bernstein first distinguishes between two fundamental forms of discourse, the horizontal and the vertical. Horizontal discourse is typified as everyday or common-sense knowledge which is 'likely to be oral, local, context dependent and specific, tacit, multi-layered and contradictory across but not within contexts.' These contexts are restricted to 'maximizing encounters with persons and habitats' (2000, p. 158). Vertical discourses by contrast, take the form of a 'coherent, explicit and systematically principled structure, hierarchically organized as in the sciences, or…in the form of specialised languages with specialised modes of interrogation and specialised criteria for the production and circulation of texts as in the sciences and humanities' (p. 158). The ways in which units or contexts are realised are also contrasted. In the case of horizontal discourse, the units are segmented and integrated only at the level of context. By contrast, the relationship between the elements of vertical discourse is achieved through integration at the level of meanings which are communicated through specialised symbolic structures and procedures.

The surface features of the different emphases of the PISA and the TIMSS testing regimes therefore appear to resonate with Bernstein's distinction between the common sense knowledge of everyday life and experience and that of the school text or the lecture theatre. This chapter will therefore attempt to test the hypothesis that the vertical/horizontal models of discourse can supply an adequate critical space for describing and positioning the social and cultural processes represented by these two types of international testing regimes within the context of Bernstein's latest writings on symbolic control and identity. A model is then proposed, which brings together the 'profane' aspects of testing regimes and the 'sacred' aspects of their social and cultural meanings, a distinction which Bernstein owed to the Durkheimian tradition (cf. Beck, 2002). Finally, the chapter will derive a socio-semiotic framework for the 'profane' techniques of statistical analysis used to interpret the multitude of data that are produced by these surveys that goes well beyond the vertical/ horizontal typology as a framework for positioning these two assessment regimes.

This exploration will proceed in two stages, by:

1. Identifying the place of evaluation or assessment, as a component of the pedagogic device in a globalised culture. This will mark the redefinition of the relationships between education, the state and society in poststructuralist terms, which positioned the palette of pedagogic identities within what Bernstein called the 're-centred state.'
2. Relocating the methodological and technical issues arising from this analysis in terms of the socio-semiotic structures underlying Bernstein's theories of the changing relationships between education and society.

Evaluation, Globalisation and the 'Re-centred State'

Bernstein's account of the social context of education in the twenty-first century, which he terms 'reorganised capitalism' (1990, pp. 157–160), bears remarkable similarities to several other analyses of post-industrial and later capitalist societies (Tyler, 2004a). Here the destabilising effects of communication control systems have profound effects on the social division of labour and the expansion of the field of symbolic control through the commodification of knowledge, which is rendered more efficient by the concentration and movement of capital on a global scale. This revolution in the field of production and control repositions the agencies of social and cultural reproduction by decentralising the sites of acquisition and transmission while privileging what he calls the 'pedagogic device' as the principal producer of symbolic control as well as of social destinies. This device has three main principles or sets of rules: the distributive, which 'mark and distribute who may transmit what to whom, and under what conditions' (1990, p. 183); the recontexualising, which determine the 'constitution of specific pedagogic discourse'; and the evaluative, which 'are constituted in pedagogic practice' embedded in the rules by which 'the text is transformed into age-related content' (1990, p. 180). The internal ordering of the relationships among these three sets of rules is itself hierarchical, with the distributive at the top and the evaluative at the bottom. Together, the device sets the conditions for 'the production, reproduction and transformation of culture' (1990, p. 180).

Evaluation (broadly equivalent to 'assessment' in this context), although perhaps lowest on the hierarchy of the regulative ordering of the pedagogic device, has a separate dimension or voice and cannot be reduced to either knowledge or teaching styles. In a sense, it is the possibility (or threat) of being formally asked to validate one's interpretation and retention and recall of a transmission, which distinguishes education from other cultural forms. However, it has tended to be neglected in the face of the 'reclaiming knowledge' debate, which seems to be most concerned with the distributive aspects of the device, to the relative neglect or conflation with, the other two sets of rules. This is unfortunate, since it sets limits on the full examination of the device as an entity that shapes and reproduces consciousness.

How, then, did Bernstein see the interaction between the pedagogic device and the emerging information-based society? There appear to be two main stages, the first in the paper on the production of official knowledge, which was concerned with the specialised discourse of the educational institution (Bernstein, 1999). This positioned the new national strategies towards educational systems as a function of what he called the 're-centred state', defined as the centralised forms of state control through the setting and assessing standards in a de-centred environment. The second, a more radical vision, was expressed in his final paper on the Totally Pedagogised Society (2001), where the pedagogic device has become more central to, if not constitutive of, the distribution of life chances (see also Bernstein, 2001; Tyler, 2004a).

These two models for locating the pedagogic device, whose internal ordering regulates pedagogic discourse as a whole, each provide particular emphases and roles for the stabilising functions of the evaluative principle (Figure 9.1). In this model, a synthesis of Bernstein and other social realist thinking, educational systems are pulled between the fissile and decentring tendencies of pedagogic identity formation, whether towards the market, therapeutic intervention, or their counter-tendencies in retrospective, elitist or traditional practice, each with a particular social correlate within the emerging TPS. The three axes of the pedagogic device, which underpins these formations, is seen to find a source of stability in the 'objective' performativities of a testing regime, which can operate at all levels of the classroom, the school, the regions and, as we have seen, that of the nation state.

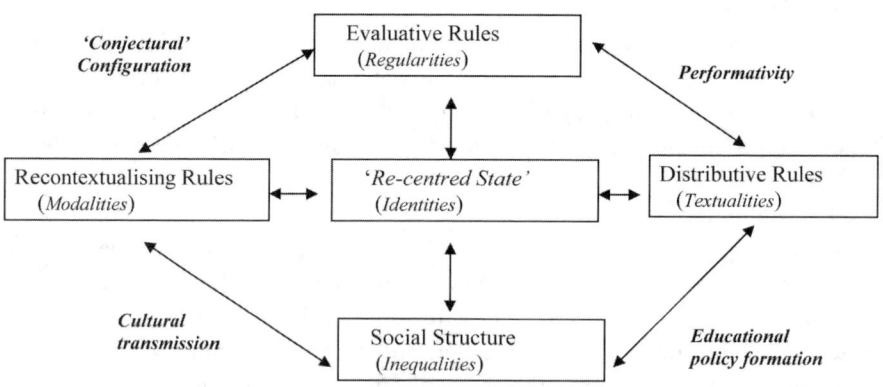

Figure 9.1 Device, identity and discourse: pedagogy and the 're-centred state

The evaluative aspects of Bernstein's account of the role of the state in a globalised environment therefore invites further consideration of Lyotard's (1984) notion of performativity as a central mechanism of social control, defined in pragmatic terms such as the generation of wealth within Bernstein's programmatic model of the Totally Pedagogised Society. In Lyotard's seminal analysis of the 'postmodern condition,' nation states, as well as corporations and individuals, are continually subject to the evaluative gaze. There are many parallels between Bernstein's model of the re-centred state in the phase of 'reorganized capitalism' and the postmodern condition as described by Lyotard—the commodificaton of knowledge, the importance of the new communication technologies and the centrality of education and scientific research to the emerging social order. A more curious and potentially important parallel is the position of performativity in resolving the tensions between the decline of the meta-narratives of state systems of education (narrative knowledge) and the growing importance of 'little narratives,' which regulate the production of scientific knowledge (1984, p. 26).

This tension between the 'little narratives' of educational testing and a declining 'grand narrative' of social and material progress reformulates in rather different terms the basis of the 'discursive gap' between the legitimation of each discursive order that underpins the knowledge debates, that is, between the everyday motivations of the narratives of identity politics of horizontal discourse and the distinctive rules of scientific knowledge embedded in other forms of vertical discourse. This unexpected parallel (or indeed intersection) of the readings of educational assessment invites some inclusion of performativity within Bernstein's model of the re-centred state, centred to a large part around the evaluative rules of the pedagogic device. By implication, the notion of performativity has particular relevance to the sociological understanding of the position of the international testing regimes such as TIMSS and PISA, as the nation state searches for every improved measurement of efficiency.

Important as these insights into the dynamics of the postmodern condition may be, they ignore the political dimension, which underlies the overt/covert paradox of late modernity and which also helps to explain the polarisations and ideological divide that inheres in public debate. Why should, for example, the pragmatic emphases of the PISA regime be sponsored but the economic concerns of the OECD be espoused by the proponents of a more 'horizontal' and context-relevant rhetoric? Why, conversely, are the more disciplinary and market-conscious versions of the so-called 'postmodern' pedagogic positions fixated with the non-economic concerns of national history, the preservation of canonical literature and traditional morality? In other words, how adequate is the alignment of the surface features of rhetorics of the politics of official knowledge with a horizontal/vertical dimension? What kind of model can take into account the inherent complexities and paradoxes of globalised society, which generate the collection codes of identities (Tyler, 1999), whether market or retrospective in orientation, within fields characterised by a complex specialised division of labour and highly technicised forms of knowledge and skill? In other words, how may the contradictions or anomalies be better explained by a more elaborate discursive positioning of the entire strategy of international testing than that offered by the sociology of knowledge polarities of vertical/horizontal discourse?

While Lyotard suggests that non-traditional scientific approaches, such as chaos theory, fractal mathematics and quantum mechanics may be important theoretical and methodological resources for capturing some of the paradoxes and anomalies of contemporary culture, these directions have been insufficiently exploited by sociologists and psychologists in educational measurement. It remains to be seen how a more complex reading of the interaction between Bernstein's formulation of the pedagogic device and the dynamics of global cultures may generate a more theoretically informed basis to evaluation than that which typifies the crude positivism of the rankings of the international testing surveys.

THE SOCIO-SEMIOTICS OF PERFORMATIVITY: TOWARDS A TYPOLOGY OF EDUCATIONAL ASSESSMENT

The development of a more elaborate and sensitive model of the products of international testing than that captured by the vertical/horizontal axis has two aspects. At one level is a methodological task of testing the validity of the PISA and TIMSS method of basing evaluation of entire national systems on unidimensional measures in individual performance. Second, at a deeper, more theoretical level is grounding the logic of evaluation itself in a framework, which is consistent with the social realist foundations of the Bernsteinian notions of pedagogic discourse as articulated in his socio-semiotic analyses of the changing relations between education and society. Is it possible, in other words, to interrogate the data generated by these international regimes in such a way as to render their sociological foundations more transparent and at the same time alert the task of empirical investigation to the theoretical implications of operational procedures? Behind this too is the task of opening up public debate to the more complex and pedagogically informed reading of the results of these surveys than those provided by the rhetorical positions of educational politics.

The first problem has been addressed by Goldstein's (2004) critique of data modeling of the PISA surveys, which have equal substantive import for the TIMSS methodologies. While acknowledging that the PISA represents an advance on previous international comparisons, he sees some severe methodological and technical flaws in its research design, data analysis techniques and the validity of inferences drawn for inter-country comparison. His main criticism focuses on the item response modelling (IRM), which absorbs or marginalises the existence of second or further factors in a set of scores (and the possible relationship among them), in order to produce a single unidimensional scale. His second criticism is that the comparison of mean scores of individual students without regard to the contexts in which they are located can be misleading. Although there was some recognition of between-school differences, these become lost in the ranking procedures and did not take into account the specific effects of school context.

These contextual effects can be estimated by multilevel modeling methods as random coefficient effects, which do not assume the uniform distribution of the between-school variance allowed for in the PISA design, by the introduction of covariates such as the gender or class composition of the school specific to that or higher levels of analysis. Goldstein also makes an important point that the correct design for drawing trend inferences would be longitudinal rather than cross-sectional. Goldstein demonstrates the effect that the first two of these considerations can have on test scores by applying a two-dimensional multilevel binary factor model to a comparison of PISA Mathematics scores for England/ United Kingdom and France. The results of this analysis showed up a different ordering of loadings for each item, and hence of the interpretation of mean differences from those of the PISA results, demanded by policy-makers. In other words, because the first pattern of item responses revealed by the two-factor model differs across the two countries and second because the covariates of between-school differences are also subject to variability across cultures, the validity of a single, unidimensional comparison based on the mean of a set of scores is placed in doubt.

These methodological observations in Goldstein's critique are of considerable sociological relevance, and indeed may provide the basis for a more broadly based theoretical model of the discursive features, which are concealed within data modeling procedures. An examination of these deeper, less visible features go well beyond the rejection of the ideological and empiricist critiques of public debate and point towards the possibility of a reconstruction of the methodologies along the lines suggested by Goldstein. The first step towards this exercise is to look for a social realist epistemology that could underpin such a task, resonant with Bernstein's own project as identified by other commentators. The development of such a theory of the logic of evaluation has already been well advanced by Pawson and Tilley's (1997) critique of classical experimental and quasi-experimental methods of evaluation, which neglect to take into account their highly contingent nature. In addition to the apparent rigours of the classical experiment or survey design, they postulate the necessity to consider any regularities that these may discover as 'contingent and conditional, and thus only fired in particular local, historical or institutional contexts' (1997, p. 71). The realist philosophy of evaluation, which would subsume the comparison of the performance of educational systems, is to find the features of the context that links cause to effect.

What then are the specific features of the contexts of international educational evaluation that may be identified by Bernstein's models of pedagogic discourse and how might these frame the methodological approaches and analytical techniques? To begin with, it is possible to isolate in Bernstein's models of the historical instances of the relationships between education and society at least four stages, from the medieval or pre-capitalist case, to that of the Totally Pedagogised Society, with which it shares some important characteristics in its central positioning of pedagogic discourse for social and cultural reproduction. These and intervening stages, those of competitive and transitional capitalism, have been shown by Tyler (2004a, Table 1) to be typified by a particular discursive modality (visibility and vocality) framed by two axes—the social as defined by level of institutional autonomy, and semiotic, defined by the determinacy or indeterminacy of the semiotic field of the surrounding culture.

These axes would seem to be closely related to the dimensions of the analytical field. On the one hand, there is the social and economic, which generates the autonomy of the local site as measured by the size of the between-school component. This axis would contrast the pre-bureaucratic school with those of the large, centralised systems of the mature nation state and which reappears in the self-governing and market-oriented institutions so beloved by neo-liberal policies. The semiotic level field, on the other hand, is defined by the complexity and visibility of the signification system, as demonstrated in the number, latency and inter-relationships of the instruments of evaluation themselves. In this latter case, the historical shift from simple, visible testing as in the memorisation exercises of the pre-bureaucratic era can be contrasted with the interpretation of latent (not directly observed) dimensions discovered by factorial techniques.

It would seem that the international testing regimes are torn between two fields of evaluative practice, the visible pedagogies of the stage of competitive capitalism which demands simple, interpretable comparisons and the rather less determinate complexities of multivariate and multilevel modeling (Table 9.1). In this transition, we move from ordinal scales through to the complex factorial scores generated by the kind of modeling suggested by Goldstein, while at the same time, discursive autonomy of the mid-twentieth century of pedagogic discourse is gradually eroded by the intrusions of the performative, re-centred state.

In this typology, evaluative modalities are seen as stages of the changing interdependencies between the social and semiotic dimensions of pedagogic discourse. They are just as much a resource for the conjectural models of evaluation as they are an integrative and heuristic framework for exploring and predicting the changing effects of context. Across the columns of the figure, the hierarchical components (variance and coefficients represent intercepts and regression gradients) and the degree of contextual variations across differing levels of nested design (marks within students, students within schools, schools within regions, regions within national systems or subsystems) represent levels of localised autonomy or centralised conformity that accompany a certain stage of institutional autonomy. Down the rows, the methodological sophistication represents the increasing levels of complexity and inter-relationships among the measured outcomes and their predictors, both observed and latent or 'invisible.'

Table 9.1: A socio-semiotic typology of models of educational assessment*

Contextual Dependency (Socio-economic Axis)

Complexity of Instrumentation (semiotic axis)	High	Low
Low	Tradition-centred (voiced/ visible)	Content-centred (unvoiced/visible)
High	Information-centred (unvoiced/ invisible)	Student-centred (voiced/ invisible)

Based on Tyler, 2004a, Table 1. A socio-semiotic typology of pedagogic discourse

Here there is increasing importance of operational design and theoretical depth that goes well beyond the crude polarities of positivism and constructivism by drawing on the power of the social realist models of evaluation. If there is a degree of indeterminacy in the information-centred stage of reorganised capitalism, this is not attributable to the ideological predilections of the teachers' cultures any more than it is to the demands of the simplicities demanded by the political exigencies of funding bodies. In the realist positioning of Table 9.1, both testing regimes—TIMSS and PISA—despite their different approaches, origins and emphases, can be seen to be sociologically and discursively very similar, rather than easily situated within one or the other side of the 'culture wars' divide. The rankings, which each produce, can be seen to be an emergent feature of an information-generated discursivity, and an attempt to introduce a 'transparency' and determinacy into a field whose constructive substrates and contextual dependencies are inherently both complex and indeterminate. However, it would appear that the closures of contemporary political debates impose on these indeterminacies the surface rigidities of a collection code that finds its home in the comforts of the league table.

Do the parallels between stabilities of the league table and the verticalities of knowledge structures suggest similar strategies of retreat from the complexities and indeterminacies of the present erosion of the autonomy, however relative and partial, of pedagogic discourse? Both responses, in different senses, are extra-discursive, since they deny the internal intricacies of the pedagogic device in favour of either the securities of political rankings or the construction of disciplinary fields within the sociology of knowledge. From a Bernsteinian perspective, the socio-semiotic origins of both strategies are readily explicated in terms of their socio-semiotic resources—whether by the erosion of the boundaries of institutionalised schooling under an emerging TPS, or by the internal indeterminacies of the integrated code that generates the discursive conditions for verticality. The socio-semiotic processes of assessment can be shown therefore to provide important insights into the machinery of legitimation that surrounds the contemporary penchant for testing regimes, by grounding the sociology of pedagogy in its discursive origins.

Conclusion

It is clear from this analysis that the vertical/horizontal model of knowledge discourse captures only a part of the sociological problematics generated by the experience of international testing. The emphasis on evaluation, its principles, its logics and its methodologies, on the other hand, has opened up possibilities for not only relating these attempts to the socio-semiotics of the changing context of pedagogic discourse, but also of expanding the repertoire of technical analysis that are consonant with the exigencies of a practical object. In a sense, these two international testing regimes have served principally as an illustrative study in the intrusions of reductionist tendencies in both policy and sociological debate, whose superficialities are exposed within the context of the insights of Bernstein into the dynamics of the 're-centred state,' the 'Totally Pedagogised Society' and the centrality of pedagogic identity within its reproduction. The intersections of the political and the epistemological in each case have positioned the role of the assessment regime, whose outcomes are embodied in the league tables of schools or of nations, as both a re-integrative device of the re-centred state and as complex socio-semiotic closures of an emergent collection code, reconstituted at the level of ideological positionings. Neither of these central sociological processes, it would appear, can be captured by the terms of the present debates.

While this chapter has focused on the reactions to the international testing regimes in public debate, it has also attempted to throw light on the paradoxes of embedded aspects of Bernstein's writings on pedagogic discourse. One of these paradoxes might be the emergence of collection codes of pedagogic identity within a decentred, culturally fracturally fragmented, social system. Another might be the anomaly of Bernstein's invocation of the integrated code as the regulative principle of vertical discourse, ironically identified by disciplinary insulations of the collection code. However, Bernstein's writings do show a thematic unity, just as they explore in increasing detail and depth the ambiguities and complexities of the relationships between society and a specialised educational discourse. The application of Bernstein's writings to the rather nebulous yet contested field of international testing regimes has also demonstrated that the pedagogic device cannot be reduced to the sociology of knowledge and its seemingly endless philosophical conundrums. All three dimensions of the pedagogic device in its synchronic and diachronic dimensions must be treated as having their own regulative principles and autonomies, which reinforce one another in often unexpected ways.

The involutions and elisions of power and knowledge have been shown to produce strange eruptions, extreme positionings around content rather than context, and form rather than process. This analysis has attempted to draw the debates within educational policy back to a pedagogical centre that finds some depth and communality within the 'wars' of policy, practice and interpretation. At a programmatic level, such an analysis opens up possibilities for the sociology of education on a global scale by integrating into policy debates with a richer theoretical framework (socio-semiotic) than those which inform contemporary debate. It is hoped that the social realist models of evaluation are expounded and contextualised through Bernstein's insights into the nature of pedagogic discourse by unifying the theoretical and the methodological in ways that expose the limitations of the rhetorical positioning, which threatens to overwhelm sociological, as well as political, analysis of educational policy. Above all, the case study of international testing aims to take Bernstein's project back to its roots as a sociological project with political implications rather than what at times can look like a political project with sociological underpinnings.

REFERENCES

Adams, R.J. (2003). Response to 'Cautions of OECD's recent educational survey (PISA).' *Oxford Review of Education, 29*(3), 378–189.
Blum, A. Goldstein, H. and Guerin-Pace, F. (2001). International Adult Literacy Survey (IALS);

an analysis of international comparisons of adult literacy. *Assessment in Education, 8*, 225–246.

Beck, J. (2002). The sacred and the profane in recent struggles to promote official pedagogic identities. *British Journal of the Sociology of Education, 23*(4), 617–626.

Bernstein, B. (1990). *Class, codes and control, Vol. 4: The structuring of pedagogic discourse.* London: Routledge.

Bernstein, B. (1999). Official knowledge and pedagogic identities. In F. Christie (Ed.), *Pedagogy and the shaping of consciousness: Linguistic and social processes.* London and New York: Cassell, pp. 246–261.

Bernstein, B. (2000). Vertical and horizontal discourse: An essay. In *Pedagogy, symbolic control and identity: theory, research, critique (revised edition).* Oxford: Rowman & Littlefield, pp. 155–217.

Bernstein, B. (2001). From pedagogies to knowledges. In A. Morais, I. Neves, B. Davies, H. Daniels (Eds.), *Towards a sociology of pedagogy: The contribution of Basil Bernstein to research.* New York: Peter Lang.

Department of Education, Employment and Workplace Relations. (2005). *Australian Government Programmes for Quadrennial Administrative Guidelines 2005–8.* Commonwealth of Australia, Government Printing Office, Canberra.

Donnelly, K. (2004). *Why our schools are failing: What parents need to know about Australian education.* Sydney: Duffy and Snelgrove.

Goldstein, H. (2004). International comparisons of student attainment: Some issues arising from the PISA study. *Assessment in Education: Principles, Policy and Practice, 11*(3), 319–330.

Lyotard, J-F. (1984). *The postmodern condition.* Minneapolis: University of Minneapolis Press.

Moore, R. and Muller, J. (2002). The growth of knowledge and the discursive gap. *British Journal of Sociology of Education, 23*(4), 627–637.

McGaw, B. (2002). Paragraph 1, Examination of Witnesses, Select Committee on Education and Skill, House of Commons, United Kingdom, 20th March. Retrieved from www.publications.parliament.uk.[a/c,200102/cmselect.

Naylor, F. (2004). 'OECD: The Trojan horse within: Short history of the OECD and its PISA activities,' *Current Concerns,* No. 1.

Pawson, R. and Tilley, N. (1997). *Realistic evaluation.* London: Sage.

Rowe, K. (2005). *Teaching reading: Report of the National Enquiry into the Teaching of Literacy.* Commonwealth Department of Education, Science and Training, Canberra: Australian Government Printer.

Smithers, A. (2004). *England's education: What can be learned by comparing countries?* Centre for Education, Employment and Research, University of Liverpool.

Teese, R. (2000). *Academic success and social power: Examinations and inequality.* Melbourne: Melbourne University Press.

Trends in International Mathematics and Science Study (TIMSS) (2000). *International Reports.* International Study Center, Lynch School of Education, Boston College, Boston, MA.

Tyler, W. (1999). Pedagogic identities and educational reform in the 1990s: The cultural dynamics of national curricula. In F. Christie (Ed.), *Pedagogy and the shaping of consciousness: Linguistic and social processes.* London and New York: Cassell, pp. 262–289.

Tyler, W. (2004a). Silent, invisible, total: Pedagogic discourse in the age of information. In Muller, J., Davies, B., Morais, A., *Reading Bernstein, researching Bernstein.* London: RoutledgeFalmer.

Tyler, W. (2004b). Multiple fractures: Disciplinary knowledge and pedagogic discourse. Plenary session paper presented at *Reclaiming knowledge: Registers of discourse in the community and school,* Conference held at the University of Sydney, Faculty of Education and Social Work (with the Australian Systemic Linguistics Association), 13–15 December.

United States Department of Education. (2008). *Overview: No Child Left Behind.* Office of Elementary and Secondary Education. Available at http: www.ed.gov/ about/offices/listoese/legislation.html.

CHAPTER TEN

Pedagogy and Moral Order

JOHAN MULLER AND URSULA HOADLEY

INTRODUCTION

> We can see that the key to pedagogic practice is
> continuous evaluation (Bernstein, 1996, P. 50).

This chapter considers the concepts of instructional and regulative discourse specifically in relation to the pedagogic device. In doing this, two issues are drawn out. We argue for a consideration of two forms of regulative discourse in operation in the theory—a regulative modality operating at the macro level, and an 'expressive order,' which is concerned with classification at the level of the distributive rules. Tracking Durkheim's influence on Bernstein, this leads us to consider how the 'what' is constituted at the level of the distributive rules. At the level of the recontextualising rules, we identify a second regulative modality operating in terms of framing. This is generally expressed as control over the hierarchical rules, but it also regulates the instructional discourse. According to the theory, the regulative discourse at this level regulates the instructional discourse—both in terms of what is selected and how it is to be transmitted. Bernstein is emphatic when considering the recontextualising rules that the regulative discourse is dominant.

Thinking about the regulative discourse in terms of two levels, we argue that current classroom based empirical work has focused attention on regulative discourse solely at the level of the recontextualising rules. Instructional discourse in these studies is really a regulative outcome. Moving the focus to the third level of the device, the level of the evaluative rules, where the pedagogic device is 'condensed,' we argue that a more complete description of regulative discourse, as well as its relation to instructional discourse, is made possible. Two challenges arise from this move. The first concerns the assertion in the theory that the regulative discourse is dominant. We identify the need to free the instructional discourse from under the yoke of the regulative discourse. Secondly, considering pedagogic practice at this third level—that of the evaluative rules—brings an expanded notion of regulative discourse into play. It also opens up the space for the development of the theory in terms of acquisition, as opposed to the more narrow analysis of transmission at the level of the recontextualising rules only.

Although we focus specifically on regulative and instructional discourse in relation to the pedagogic device, we recognize that this was Bernstein's final expression of this aspect of the theory. By way of introducing the argument, then, we present an overview of the development of the concepts from the 1970s.

A Brief Genealogy of the Regulative and the Instructional Couplet

By Bernstein's own admission (in Appendix 5.1: 'The concepts of instructional and regulative discourse,' Bernstein, 1990, pp. 210–212), the notion of 'the moral,' essentially Durkheim's, enters his (Bernstein's) work first via his appropriation of the distinction Parsons makes between expressive and instrumental roles and actions. Although Parsons claims to have derived 'instrumentalities' from economic theory, especially from Adam Smith, faithful Durkheimian that he is he assigns goal-directed action of the ego to the profane world, as we will see Durkheim did. For Parsons, socialisation can be into either an expressive role or an instrumental role. Expressive denotes integration at the level of collective values (intra-systemic), while instrumental denotes the axis of achievement (inter-systemic). This distinction is explicitly linked by Bernstein (ibid., p. 212) to Durkheim's mechanical (similar-to) and organic (different-from) forms of solidarity, and more confusingly, to the Trivium and the Quadrivium. Why this is confusing is that the latter distinctions—between forms of solidarity and types of mediaeval curriculum—are both evolutionary couplets, while the expressive/instrumental couplet is designed to characterise any kind of society, especially modern society. Bernstein means us to concentrate on the relational aspect (similar to/different from) rather than their substantive meanings.

Bernstein's first use of this relational couplet is to distinguish between expressive and instrumental 'cultures' or 'orders' of the school. The expressive order is enacted through ritual, the instrumental through bureaucracy. Already in these early formulations (see Bernstein, 1977, first published in 1966), Bernstein is asserting the dominance of the expressive order:

> The expressive order can be considered as a source of the school's shared values and is therefore potentially cohesive in function, whilst the instrumental order, on the other hand, is potentially divisive. It is the expressive order which is the major mechanism of social consensus…(Bernstein, ibid., p. 55).

Although Durkheim does not make this kind of distinction, the assertion of the dominance of the expressive or moral order in this context is recognisably Durkheimian.

In Bernstein (1971), we find him discovering an analogous typology in Halliday (1971), and he switches to the new language. Halliday had originally distinguished between four socialising *contexts*:

regulative—contexts which position subjects in the moral system;
instructional—contexts which afford access to competencies for managing objects and persons;

The last two contexts, *interpersonal* and *imaginative*, are not taken up by Bernstein, and henceforth the terms 'regulative' and 'instructional' become canonical.

It may be interesting to note that contemporary Hallidayans like Frances Christie continue to use the Bernsteinian terms, but in a seemingly idiosyncratic manner. For example, her gloss on the 'regulative' below would without doubt be called 'instructional' by most contemporary Bernsteinian sociologists:

> Adapting Bernstein's terms, I shall argue that the pedagogic discourse found in the curriculum genres of schooling functions in such way that it is realized primarily in first order or regulative register, to do with the overall pedagogic direction taken, their goals, pacing and sequencing, and a second order or instructional register to do with the 'content' and its specialized skills at issue. (Christie, 2002, p. 25).

After what follows below, this usage may not be so idiosyncratic after all.

In the next iteration of the theory, Bernstein, under the prompting of the work of Pedro (1981)—who is apparently the first to recruit Foucault to the Bernsteinian oeuvre—changes the designation from *contexts* to *discourses*. Instructional discourse is now defined, Bernstein says quoting Pedro, in terms of 'the principles of the specific discourse to be transmitted and acquired' (Bernstein, 1990, p. 211). There is a brief moment of wobble, where the roles are reversed: 'Rules of social order, relation, and identity are embedded in rules of discursive order (selection, sequence, pace, and criteria). The first we have called *regulative* and the second *instructional* discourse' (Bernstein, 1990, p. 108; see also Bernstein, 1986). Taken literally this would mean that the regulative discourse is embedded in (or subordinated to) the instructional discourse. In all subsequent formulations, the regulative and the instructional are treated as discourses, with the instructional embedded in the regulative and the regulative discourse dominant.

As the classification and framing schema becomes more formalised (Bernstein, 1996), the relation between instructional and regulative discourse stabilizes, and in the pedagogic device the domination of the regulative discourse over the instructional discourse becomes the algebra that expresses framing:

$$\text{framing} = \frac{\text{instructional discourse}}{\text{regulative discourse}} \quad \frac{ID}{RD}$$

Bernstein, 1996, pp. 27–28; italics in the original.

Davis (2005a) notes the rather unexpected emergence in this iteration of the theory of the notion of evaluative rule, as a third and culminating category of rule to accompany classification (the distributive rule) and framing (the recontextualising rule). What is the significance of this development? Davis (2005b) reasons that we should understand the odd couple—ID/RD with RD dominant—as pedagogy's alibi for why pedagogy in normal modern capitalist societies has to fail a large number of the children of the working class who have misrecognised the criteria of the elaborated code required for schooling success. The regulative discourse in effect acts as an agent of consensual smoothing. The failure of the miscast, unavoidably visible only at the point that the evaluation rule confirms that they are unable to provide a legitimate text, has to be assuaged. As Davis explains it:

> the distinction drawn between the instructional and the regulative tells us that the criteria of the instructional, as it pertains to the reproduction of specialised knowledge, is different from the criteria demanded by social solidarity; the dominance of the regulative tells us that the mode of social solidarity…facilitates recognition/misrecognition of the criteria demanded by specialised knowledge (that is, of the elaborated code of schooling). (op. cit., p. 68).

In other words, for Davis, the distinction serves to explain differential attainment in society, and to mask (trigger misrecognition of) its legitimating criteria. Regulative discourse, we may say, has in this formulation a purely negative control function. It operates solely to mask the operation of knowledge and its class bias, as cultural arbitrary. With this formulation, the possibility for justifying curricular knowledge as 'real' knowledge is rendered extremely difficult, since it is but a small step from making the seemingly ineluctable class bias of knowledge the central point of the theory to saying that *therefore* the knowledge itself must be intrinsically arbitrary.

In what follows, we consider the moral order at different levels of the pedagogic device. We identify a Durkheimian regulative discourse at the level of distributive rules (classification), and a more micro contextual notion of regulative discourse at the level of the recontextualising rules (framing), which subordinates instructional discourse to the dictates of regulative discourse.

REGULATIVE DISCOURSE AT THE LEVEL OF THE DISTRIBUTIVE RULES: THE REGULATIVE AS SACRED ORDER

The jury is still out as to whether Durkheim's work is internally coherent and conceptually all of a piece, as Bellah and others would have it, or whether we can discern a fundamental discontinuity between the early materialist/positivist Durkheim of the *Division of Labour* and the *Rules*, and the more idealist mid and late-period Durkheim of *Moral Education*, *The Evolution of Educational Thought* and *The Elementary Forms*, as Parsons and Alexander would have it. In what follows below, we will follow Alexander (1982), a text Bernstein himself cites in telling us that 'We can trace the conceptualising of pedagogic discourse back to Durkheim' (Bernstein, 1990, p. 212). What is beyond dispute is that this period of Durkheim can only be grasped in the light of his uncompromising anti-utilitarianism and his religious/sacred model of society.

The great flaw in all utilitarian theories, according to Durkheim, is that they have a unitary view of humanity: 'man is one' (Alexander, 1982, p. 233). In this view, moral sentiment is reduced to self-interest.[1] On the contrary, for Durkheim human nature is fundamentally dual, with an earthy, sensuous, egoistic side that governs action in the profane world of economic transactions and personal self interest; and a socialised, disinterested, universalised side that governs the pursuit of impersonal ends: 'morality begins with disinterest, with attachment to something other than ourselves' (ibid: see also Moore's [2004, pp. 127–129] illuminating discussion). The prime aim of education is to 'socialise' us, to lead us to internalise the moral order, which is the collective order of society.

In order for modern specialised society to exist and persist, for organic solidarity to reproduce itself, cooperation is required, and in order to internalise the ideal of cooperation it is necessary to learn how voluntarily to subordinate particular desires to the greater good. This greater good, in modern society, is refracted into multiple forms of association: 'the sacred has become differentiated into a set of specialised spheres' (Alexander, 1982, p. 263). The prototypical model of non-utilitarian association is religious ritual. But in modern society, the sacred has become secularised. Its principal properties however remain, and other social institutions now carry the energies of abstract collective life. Education mediates thus not as it does for Marx between the class-based family and the class-based labour market, but between the context-bound particularities of family and local community, and the universalistic culture of modern society, which is the moral order.

In his writings on schooling, it is noteworthy that Durkheim never speaks about the moral realm in terms of the social relations of the classroom. Regulative discourse is not a feature *of* the classroom; it is produced *by* the classroom. This is apparent throughout the book dedicated to delineating the operation of regulative discourse in schooling, *Moral Education*. There is no characterisation of the communicative modality. Durkheim is clearly not well disposed towards weak framing over classroom relations, the mark of all learner-centred or progressive pedagogies (…'nothing is more contrary to the spirit of discipline than to disguise it with a sugary façade. We distort it by presenting it as…something easy and pleasant. Everything in life is not beer and skittles. Consequently it would be a calamity to believe that everything can be done as though it were play') (Durkheim, 2002, pp. 159–160). While we shall return to the 'spirit of discipline' below, note here that there is really no sense that pedagogic modality might be of the slightest importance. The teacher's sole purpose is to represent the necessary instrument for the tutoring of consciousness, for the internalisation of the moral order of society, from egotism to altruism, to beneficial associations outside of the ego and the family.

All of this can be overstated. It is hard to think of the purpose of today's school as being solely to 'instil in him (the pupil) the inclination for collective life' (ibid., p. 239). In like manner, society as The Sacred smacks of a kind of mystical holism. Nor is it as plausible to us as it might have been in Durkheim's republican France that we have an 'innate desire to live together' and that the 'more profoundly men are socialised, that is to say, civilised—for the two are synonymous—the more those joys are prized (Durkheim, 1996, p. 25). Fortunately there is more to the sacredness of society than the literal sense of joy in 'joining.' This is brought out with peculiar force in Durkheim's extended discussion of punishment.

The 'moral function' of school discipline is to 'inculcate respect for the abstract and impersonal rule, training the child in self-control and self restraint' (Durkheim, 2002, p. 158). Teachers can only do this if they themselves embody the rule, if they enact it with moral authority. This brings to the fore the function of punishment: to mark out the line between legitimate and illegitimate texts, between the sacred and the profane. Crucially, 'a sacred thing profaned no longer seems sacred if nothing develops to restore its original nature' (ibid., p. 165). It falls to the teacher to mark the boundary, positively or negatively, because by definition, the pupils have not yet internalised it (learnt to produce legitimate texts). To mark out the lineaments of the rule is exemplary, for the other learners too, in order to inculcate respect for the rule. This is done by 'putting the guilty on the *index*, holding him at a distance…making a void around him…' (ibid., p. 175). This is what punishment is:

'To punish is not to make others suffer in body or soul; it is to affirm, in the face of an offence, the rule that the offence would deny' (ibid., p. 176). The punishment is thus 'only the palpable symbol through which an inner state is represented; it is a notation, a language...' (ibid).

Even from these brief excerpts it should be clear that at least part of what Durkheim called punishment Bernstein called 'evaluation.' What we see in Durkheim's meticulous explanation of punishment are the procedures for establishing the evaluative rule. It is noteworthy that there is very little discussion of pedagogy. What teachers do, or should do, is make knowledge available and then mark out the degree of legitimacy of the produced text. This is underlined in a remarkable passage discussing corporal punishment. Durkheim the anthropologist has surveyed a wide range of primitive cultures and come to the conclusion that mechanical solidarity societies have a child-centred modality of rearing. They coddle their young and rarely if ever hit them. Violence as punishment, 'corporal punishment was only established once man had outrun his early barbarism, once the school had made its appearance' (ibid., p. 192). Corporal punishment thus, pace his student Foucault, was a product of organic solidarity, of modernity. Nevertheless, in one of the surprising swerves, which makes him such a pleasure to read, Durkheim declares himself to be absolutely opposed to corporal punishment. Why? Because it is too difficult to *grade it to the infraction*. All punishments should be graded to the infraction: 'A glance, a gesture, silence...' (ibid., p. 199), these are all in the arsenal of the good teacher. It is now quite plain that we are talking about evaluation.

For Durkheim crucially, then, the regulative is contained in the instructional order—he does not effect a separation. His notion of instructional knowledge, what should be included and excluded, are focused on the development of a sense of the sacred, of the impersonal rule that inheres in symbolic forms, and respect for that rule. It should also be clear from the foregoing that the Durkheimian moral order is about classification—about the instantiation of the 'what,' and marking the boundaries between the sacred and profane.

In *Evolution*, Durkheim is also concerned to chart the institutional evolution of schooling from the outer sacred (classical) to the inner sacred (Christianity, scholasticism, humanism and heyday of the Trivium) to the dawn of modernity, and the ascendancy of the sciences forming the new outer sacred. On account of this history, he confirms the choice he made rather schematically in *Moral Education*, namely that children should first be taught language. By this he does not mean literature, but what he calls 'stylistics' (what the structural-functional neo-Hallidayans would call 'genre-based language teaching'), teaching a propensity to logical thought, the ability to make distinctions. After the basis is laid for distinction-making thinking, then children should be taught the sciences, principally physics and biology, and history. These disciplines depict reality/nature, which is the residence of the sacred, and hence the provenance of society; not so literature, art or aesthetics, which hark back for Durkheim to a superseded inner sacred, as does mathematics, which tends towards a simplicity that is untrue to reality. Particularly the sciences are favoured because they embody the ever-evolving fruits of social cooperation over time (Durkheim, 1977, p. 346). It is in the *Forms* that Durkheim discovers the true modern location of the sacred in symbolic formations of a certain sort, namely the sciences (Durkheim, 1995).

At the level of the distributive rules, then, the regulative discourse can be seen to constitute the 'what' of moral order. It is not separated from the instructional order, but the regulative is *in* the instructional order, in marking out symbolic forms, legitimate from illegitimate texts, the sacred from the profane.

REGULATIVE DISCOURSE AT THE LEVEL OF THE RECONTEXTUALISING RULES: THE REGULATIVE AS DOMINANT

If at the level of the distributive rules we find, via Durkheim, regulative discourse *in* instructional discourse, then at the level of the recontextualising rules, we find instructional discourse embedded in regulative discourse. Both what is recontextualised and how knowledge is organized for transmission is determined by the regulative discourse. At this level of the device, Bernstein is particularly concerned with the ideological contestation over curricular knowledge and control over the device.

The recontextualising rules are also concerned with framing, and we recall that framing is defined as pedagogic discourse at this level:

Regulative discourse in this late formulation, as in earlier ones, is summarily asserted to be dominant:

> However, I also want to argue that regulative discourse produces the order in the instructional discourse. There is no instructional discourse which is not regulated by the regulative discourse. If this is so, the whole order within pedagogic discourse is constituted by the regulative discourse (Bernstein, 1996, p. 48).

At this level the consideration of how knowledge is transformed into pedagogic communication is concerned with the *how*, and with relations of control.

$$\text{framing} = \frac{\text{instructional discourse}}{\text{regulative discourse}} \quad \frac{ID}{RD}$$

Bernstein, 1996, pp. 27–28; italics in the original.

This is so, Bernstein goes on to say, because activities in the field of production (he takes the case of physics) are fundamentally different to activities in the field of physics textbook writing. Because the fields, activities, and agents are different, curricular physics 'cannot formally be derived from the logic of that discourse' (ibid). Why not? 'There is selection' (but from what exactly is unclear at this point: ibid). Further, 'these sections (sic) (probably selections) cannot be derived from the logic of the discourse of physics' (ibid., p. 49). And for good measure: 'Pedagogic discourse can never be identified with any of the discourse it has recontextualised' (ibid., p. 47). The insistence is clear enough, but what can it mean? First of all, as Dowling (1999) points out, quite a few textbook writers are practicing researchers. Does this vitiate the conclusion? Apparently not. The difference must then lie in the process of recontextualisation: hence we get curricula that can be weakly stipulated or strongly stipulated, weakly paced or strongly paced, and so forth (Muller, 2006a). This clearly will be aligned to the pedagogical ideology in force, and the results will have determinate effects on the differential attainments of different groups, as contemporary Bernsteinian work on pedagogy makes plain. But *what knowledge have the learners gained?*

Bernstein may well have replied that what learners learn is not 'real physics,' insofar as they don't know how to investigate and produce new knowledge. This is true. For that they need a further fairly lengthy apprenticeship. Nevertheless, a condition for entry into that tertiary apprenticeship is some prior grounding in physics. Why would this be a condition for entry if there was no elective affinity between what students learn at school and what they will become apprenticed to at university?

In what follows we suggest that Bernstein overstates the disjuncture between 'real knowledge' and 'school knowledge,' at least insofar as hierarchical knowledge structure disciplines are concerned, where there are subsumptive (vertical) and grammatical (corroborative) checks and balances to keep most scholars everywhere on the same page, as he himself might have said (Bernstein, 1996; see also Muller, 2006b). We will suggest below, furthermore, that when it comes to empirical classroom-based work, instructional discourse all but disappears in the presented results of these studies. The theoretical priority of regulative discourse at the level of the recontextualising rules seems to have rendered invisible the ways in which instructional knowledge directs the logic of curriculum and pedagogy. While Durkheim had them conjoined, regulative discourse and the play of ideology obscures from view the independent status of knowledge in their separation in the recontextualising rules, which we showed above, contains within it a moral injunction. For Bernstein the rules of one level of the device are hierarchically derived from those above it. So the 'what' of the distributive rules should be visible in the operation of the recontextualising rules.

The Evaluative Rules: Condensation and a Turn to Acquisition

When Bernstein states that the whole of the device is condensed in the evaluative rules, he means that at this level it is possible to see, through the lens of the recognition and realization rules, what the work of the device has been; in other words, in terms of the distribution of what knowledge to which social groups, and how that knowledge has been transformed into pedagogic communication and transmitted. In terms of regulative discourse, the 'what' of the distributive rules and the control over the process of transmission (through the recontextualising rules) result in differential specialisation of consciousness through acquisition (at the level of the evaluative rules). It is at the moment of evaluation that we see the extent to which the regulative patterning of the distributive rules has been realized. The evaluative rules bring the what (classification) and the how (framing) into a final relation to each other. It condenses the device. It is only at the point of evaluation that we can see the mutual operation of the distributive rules and the recontextualising rules.

With this in mind, we turn now to classroom-based research, and ask the question as to why recent Bernsteinian classroom-based research has focused so much attention on transmission, on pedagogic discourse. We suggest that a consideration of acquisition at the level of the evaluative rules (in the recognition and realization rules), with respect to different social groups and the (differential) specialization of consciousness, can be read back through the device from the vantage point of the evaluative rules. These make clear how the specialization of consciousness is produced—in Bernstein's phrasing, 'Pedagogic practice is, in fact, the level which produces a ruler for consciousness' (2000, p. 28). We may then come to a more delicate description of why or how specialization does or doesn't occur, one that incorporates both instructional and regulative dimensions of pedagogic practice, both classification and framing.

Empirical Studies

In the highly significant recent classroom-based work in the Bernstein tradition, there are two noteworthy aspects, uncanny in their commonality.[2] The first is that, without exception, they foreground the importance of *explicit evaluation*. Here is an emblematic statement from the major source for many of these studies:

> When there is a good pedagogic practice at the level of the *what* (defined here as good teacher competence, JM and UH) and it is characterised at the level of the *how* by strong framing of evaluative criteria...there is a high level of scientific learning and low differential achievement among children (Morais, Neves and Pires, 2004, p. 84).

The same is found for mathematics learning—'explicit evaluation criteria improves achievement gain for the sample, particularly teachers' use of error to provide explicit feedback on incorrect answers' (Reeves, 2005; see also Lubienski, 2004 and Hoadley, 2007) and also for pedagogic disciplines where the criteria are traditionally tacit, like cabinet making—'criterial rules are very strongly framed throughout' (Gamble, forthcoming)—and school art—'criteria need to be agreed upon, specified and made explicit' (Bolton, 2006, p. 73). Indeed, the demonstration of the *centrality of explicit evaluative criteria* is perhaps one of the most, if not the most, significant aspect of the recent classroom-based studies.

The second noteworthy feature of these studies is that, without exception, they treat evaluation as part of the recontextualising rule, that is, as *part of framing*, and explicitness of evaluation is treated as strong framing. As Bernstein has himself commented (Bernstein, 1996, p. 104), one great benefit of distinguishing between instructional and regulative discourse is that one can entertain the possibility of a variation in framing values between them. So, for example, nearly all the studies cited show that weak framing of the hierarchical rules, variable/responsive framing over instructional discourse (ability to modulate control over pacing and sequence), and strong framing over the evaluative criteria makes a benign and effective hybrid (Gamble develops an alternative argument in this volume).

But there are two uncomfortable questions that cannot be ducked. The first is what a focus on evaluative criteria at the level of recontextualising rules can tell us; the second is how the 'condensation' of the pedagogic device can be demonstrated if evaluation is embedded within pedagogic discourse.

In relation to the first question, in the focus on the level of recontextualising rules, both the instructional and the regulative discourse are narrowed. What in fact occurs in the studies is a focus on evaluative *criteria* rather than evaluative *rules*. On closer inspection, in analyzing whether the criteria are explicit or implicit, and who has control over them, the research in fact presents an account of the regulative discourse—of teaching *styles*, rather than an analysis of the operation of instructional discourse or the meeting of knowledge criteria. In these accounts, then, the regulative order truly is dominant, and the instructional discourse is lost from view. The macro regulative order, at the level of the distributive rules, is also lost, and the analysis focuses on control over the social relations of the classroom only, or 'hierarchical rules.' Thus, in the analysis of framing at the level of recontextualising rules, in much of this empirical work, regulative discourse is operationalised only as the hierarchical rules, and control over the social relations of the classroom, and instructional discourse, the pedagogised knowledge, is parcelled into dimensions of pedagogy—selection, sequencing, pacing and evaluation. A particular understanding of the relation between the instructional and regulative discourses then emerges, one which places an emphasis on the social relation as the basis of the form of transmission. The notion of the moral order within instructional discourse, or the regulative discourse in the knowledge, is lost. In other words, the moral social-formative dimension of knowledge eludes analysis.

In relation to the second question, the research does not consider the distinctiveness of the evaluative rule and its evoking context, or how the evaluative rule condenses the entire device (Davis, 2005b may be an exception). The discussion of Durkheim has at least suggested that evaluation partakes of both cognitive and moral regulation, but also, through its reliance on 'reality,' both social and natural, as an external check on the teacher's authority, evaluation partakes also of both classification and framing. To treat evaluation as solely part of the 'how,' as an extension of the control relations of regulative discourse, is, we would argue, not only to miss the explanatory power of the evaluative rule, but also to miss the crucial passage that both Bernstein and Durkheim make to the realm of sacred symbolic relations, that is, the realm of knowledge proper and the modes of its social distribution. What is it that children learn at school? They learn a cognitive orientation to knowledge in the process of learning some of its amassed truths. But also, and thereby: 'To think conceptually is not merely to isolate and group the features common to a certain number of objects. It is also to subsume the variable under the permanent and the individual under the social' (Durkheim, 1995, p. 440). To understand generative abstraction is not only to understand type token relations, but individual social relationships. Symbolic relations are social relations; induction into symbolic relations—discursive or knowledge forms and their internal articulations—is to be socialised into complex modern society. *The instructional and the moral orders are one.* They are joined, or rather re-joined, in the consecration of realisation by evaluation, and acquisition occurs in this reconnection.

Conclusion

The methodological advances and sophistication, especially with regard to developing external languages of description to describe *transmission*, have been significant. Perhaps a next stage of research might be to shift the focus to the evaluative rules, in order to develop similar methodologies for describing acquisition. It is at this level, we argue, that an expanded notion of both instructional and regulative discourse, which can take proper account of the permeation of the device by the distributive rules, can be considered. As opposed to regulative discourse being considered solely in terms of framing, we argue that both instructional and regulative discourse partake of both classification and framing. In recouping a sense of the Durkheimian moral order, we may also thereby relieve the overall dominance of the regulative discourse, and lay stress on the privileged connection between curricular knowledge's connection to 'real knowledge,' to resuscitate the effectivity of symbolic forms in determining 'what counts' as knowledge. This is the only way to sustain a claim that the knowledge enshrined in the curriculum is not wholly arbitrary, but at least in part, perhaps in its most important part, necessary (Nash, 2004). This is essential, in turn, to be able to sustain a strong claim for social justice, for the inalienable right of disadvantaged children to be given unfettered access to 'real knowledge,' not simply the deformed forms of the 'relevant' curriculum deplored by Durkheim.

The restriction of analysis to the context of recontextualisation, and consequently to the dominance of the regulative discourse, has played its part in keeping the structural effectivity of discursive forms underplayed in Bernstein's theory. While it was Durkheim who initially led him to place this large valuation on the moral order at the expense of the discursive, it was finally with the help of Durkheim that he came to see that the moral order is carried by symbolic order, as he had it in Bernstein (1986), and not vice versa. This is at least part of Bernstein's programme signaled in his call for a change of analytic focus 'from pedagogies to knowledges' (Bernstein, 2001) and the need for an 'analysis of the discourses subject to pedagogic transformation,' which we suggest would help to revivify instructional discourse. This would also take seriously the notion of condensation of the device in the evaluative rules, and the much neglected area of acquisition in the theory. Developing ways of working with this part of the theory empirically would open up room for its development in relation to Bernstein's enduring question: 'How does the outside become the inside, and how does the inside reveal itself and shape the outside?' (Bernstein, 1987, p. 563).

Acknowledgement

Thanks to Parlo Singh for helpful comments on an earlier draft of the paper.

Notes

1. Or 'judgment' to 'preferences,' in Rob Moore's (2007) neat skewering of Oxford literary scholar Carey's utilitarian aesthetic theory.
2. There are of course numerous earlier empirical studies of the classroom. Singh (2002) provides a succinct overview of these studies in relation to the pedagogic device.

References

Alexander, J.C. (1982). *Theoretical logic in sociology, Vol. 2. The antinomies of classical thought: Marx and Durkheim*. London: RKP.
Bernstein, B. (1971). *Class, codes and control, Vol. 1: Theoretical studies towards a sociology of language*. London: Routledge & Kegan Paul.
Bernstein, B. (1977). Sources of consensus and disaffection in education. In *Class, codes and con-*

trol. Vol. III. London: RKP.

Bernstein, B. (1986). On pedagogic discourse. In J.G. Richardson (Ed.), *Handbook of theory and research for a sociology of education*. New York: Greenwood.

Bernstein, B. (1987). Class, codes and communication. *Sociolinguistics: An international handbook of the science of language and society, 1.* Berlin: Walter de Gruyter.

Bernstein, B. (1990). *The structuring of pedagogic discourse. Vol. IV.* London: Routledge.

Bernstein, B. (1996). *Pedagogy, symbolic control, and identity: Theory, research, critique.* London: Taylor & Francis.

Bernstein, B. (2000). *Pedagogy, symbolic control and identity: Theory, research, critique. Revised edition.* Oxford: Rowman & Littlefield.

Bernstein, B. (2001). From pedagogies to knowledges. In A. Morais, I. Neves, B. Davies and H. Daniels (Eds.), *Towards a sociology of pedagogy: The contribution of Basil Bernstein to research.* New York: Peter Lang.

Bolton, H. (2006). Pedagogy, subjectivity and mapping judgement in art, a weakly structured field of knowledge. *Journal of Education, 40*, 59–78.

Christie, F. (2002). *Classroom discourse: A functional perspective.* New York: Continuum.

Davis, Z. (2005a). On the notions of the instructional and regulative discourse in the work of Basil Bernstein. Cape Town, unpublished mimeo.

Davis, Z. (2005b). Pleasure and pedagogic discourse in school mathematics: a case study of a problem-centred pedagogic modality. Unpublished Ph.D. thesis, University of Cape Town.

Dowling, P. (1999). *Basil Bernstein in frame: 'Oh dear, is this a structuralist analysis?* Retrieved March 13, 2006 from *http://www.ioe.ac.uk/ccs/dowling/kings1999*.

Durkheim, E. 1977 (1938). *The evolution of educational thought: Lectures on the formation and development of secondary education in France.* Trans. Peter Collins. London: Routledge.

Durkheim, E. 1995 (1912). *The elementary forms of religious life.* Trans. Karen Fields. New York: The Free Press.

Durkheim, E. 1996 (1957). *Professional ethics and civic morals.* Trans. Cornelia Brookfield. London: Routledge.

Durkheim, E. 2002 (1961). *Moral education: A study of the theory and application of the sociology of education.* Trans. Everett Wilson and Herman Schnurer. New York: Dover Publications.

Gamble, J. (2010). 'The relation between tacit knowledge and moral order in the vocational curriculum.' This volume.

Halliday, M.A.K. (1971). 'The functional basis of language,' in B. Bernstein (Ed.), *Class, codes and control. Vol. II.* London: RKP.

Hoadley, U. (2007). The reproduction of social class inequalities through mathematics pedagogies in South African primary schools. *Journal of Curriculum Studies, 39*, 679–706.

Lubienski, S. (2004). 'Decoding mathematics instruction: A critical examination of an invisible pedagogy. In J. Muller, B. Davies and A. Morais (Eds.), *Reading Bernstein, researching Bernstein.* London: RoutledgeFalmer.

Moore, R. (2004). *Education and Society: Issues and explanations in the sociology of education.* Cambridge: Polity Press.

Moore, R. (2007). Hierarchical knowledge structures and the canon: A preference for judgments. In F. Christie and J.R. Martin (Eds.), *Language, knowledge and pedagogy: Functional linguistic and sociological perspectives.* London: Continuum.

Morais, A., Neves, I. and Pires, D. (2004). The *what* and the *how* of teaching and learning. In J. Muller, B. Davies and A. Morais (Eds.), *Reading Bernstein, researching Bernstein.* London: RoutledgeFalmer.

Muller, J. (2006a). Differentiation and progression in the curriculum. In M. Young and J. Gamble (Eds.), *Knowledge, curriculum and qualifications for South African further education.* Cape Town: HSRC Press.

Muller, J. (2006b). On the shoulders of giants: Verticality of knowledge and the school curriculum. In R. Moore et al. (Eds.), *Knowledge, power and educational reform: Applying the sociology of Basil Bernstein*. London: RoutledgeFalmer.
Nash, R. (2004). 'Can the arbitrary and the necessary be reconciled? Scientific realism and the school curriculum.' *Journal of Curriculum Studies, 36* (5), 605–623.
Pedro, E. R. (1981). *Social stratification and classroom discourse: A sociolinguistic analysis of classroom practice*. Stockholm: Stockholm Institute of Education, Department of Educational Research.
Reeves, C. (2005). The effect of opportunity-to-learn and classroom pedagogy on mathematics achievement in schools serving low socio-economic status communities in the Cape Peninsula, unpublished PhD thesis, University of Cape Town.
Singh, P. (2002). Pedagogising knowledge: Bernstein's theory of the pedagogic device. *British Journal of Sociology of Education, 23* (4), 571–582.

CHAPTER ELEVEN

Invisible Tribunals

Progress and Knowledge-Building in the Humanities

KARL MATON

> Every writer carries in his or her mind an invisible tribunal of dead writers, whose appointment is an imaginative act and not merely a browbeaten response to some notion of authority. This tribunal sits in judgement on our own work. We intuit standards from it....If the tribunal weren't there, every first draft would be a final manuscript. You can't fool Mother Culture. (Robert Hughes [1993]. Culture of complaint. Oxford: Oxford University Press, p. 111).

INTRODUCTION

Over recent decades, few academic debates have been as intense, wide-ranging and bitter as that over the rationale, role and form of the humanities. The 'culture wars' have extended well beyond the academy, with such interventions as Allan Bloom's *The Closing of the American Mind* (1987), E.D. Hirsch's *Cultural Literacy* (1987), Harold Bloom's *The Western Canon* (1996) and David Denby's *The Great Books* (1996) becoming international best-sellers. The war still rages. Recently, John Carey's *What Good are the Arts?* (2005) attracted widespread attention in Britain and beyond. This ongoing debate has raised questions of progress, originality and innovation in the humanities. Can we speak of progress in these fields? What is the basis of humanist 'knowledge,' and who can be said to 'know'?

These questions have also been raised by Basil Bernstein's later work. Analysing the form taken by knowledge in intellectual fields, Bernstein (1999) distinguishes first between 'horizontal discourse' (everyday knowledge) and 'vertical discourse' (scholarly or professional knowledge), and secondly within vertical discourse between hierarchical and horizontal knowledge structures. A 'hierarchical knowledge structure,' illustrated by the sciences, is 'an explicit, coherent, systematically principled and hierarchical organisation of knowledge,' which develops through the integration of knowledge at lower levels and across an expanding range of phenomena (1999, pp. 161–162). In contrast, a horizontal knowledge structure, illustrated by the humanities, is 'a series of specialised languages with specialised modes of interrogation and criteria for the construction and circulation of texts' (1999, p. 162). Bernstein's model highlights two key features of knowledge structures: first, the way knowledge develops over time or 'verticality' (Muller, 2007). Hierarchical structures develop through new knowledge integrating and subsuming previous knowledge, whereas horizontal structures develop by adding another segmented approach or topic area and exhibit weaker verticality. Secondly, knowledge structures are distinguished by the strength of their 'grammar' or the ability of their conceptual languages to generate unambiguous referents. In this model, the humanities are characterised by a weaker grammar, which removes a crucial resource for cumulative knowledge-building: the capacity to compare competing explanations to consensually agreed upon evidence.

Bernstein's model offers fresh tools for addressing questions raised in debates over the humanities. At the same time, the model itself raises questions. First, do horizontal knowledge structures progress and grow vertically or are they confined to only segmental development? Are the humanities simply characterised by weaker verticality and weaker grammar or does their 'strength' lie elsewhere? Put another way, are they merely failures relative to hierarchical knowledge structures or are they achieving something different, and if so what? Secondly, are all horizontal knowledge structures the same or are some more capable of knowledge-building than others, and how might their particular kind of progress shape this capacity for knowledge-building? In this chapter, I explore these questions. I argue that to understand how the humanities progress requires seeing educational and intellectual fields differently: we need to build on Bernstein's model to explore not only their knowledge structures but also their *knower structures*, and specifically how they define a legitimate 'gaze.' To describe this new perspective requires first an excursion into theory: I begin by outlining the concept of 'knower structures' and describe different forms of 'gaze.' I then explore what light this perspective can shed on knowledge-building in the humanities by focusing on debates over canons and specifically different kinds of 'gaze' characterising the history of cultural studies.

KNOWER STRUCTURES: A SECOND DIMENSION OF FIELDS

In distinguishing different 'discourses' and 'knowledge structures,' Bernstein focuses on one dimension of social fields: their discursive or ideational formation. This reflects a longstanding focus of the theory. For example, Bernstein's analysis of the sociology of education (1977, chap. 7) explores the ideological stances of intellectual approaches within the field. Similarly, fields of intellectual production are conceptualised in terms of their structurings of knowledge (1999). This focus on the knowledge formation of social fields is one of Bernstein's key contributions—his approach enables us to see knowledge as an object. However, at the same time, this focus makes it difficult to fully understand fields where knowledge is less explicit. For example, in Bernstein's analysis of educational knowledge codes (1977), the identities of actors are said either to reside in the possession of subject knowledge (collection code) or to be less certain and require constant negotiation (integrated code). Similarly, markers enabling actors to know they are operating within a hierarchical knowledge structure are explicit:

> the acquirer does not have the problem of knowing whether she/he is speaking physics or writing physics, only the problem of correct usage. The strong grammar visibly announces what it is. (1999, p. 164).

However, in horizontal knowledge structures (especially with weaker grammars) where knowledge-based markers are less visible, the recognition and construction of legitimate texts is said to be more problematic. Wherever knowledge is explicit (collection codes, hierarchical knowledge structures), Bernstein's analysis is explicit: identity, insight, etc. flow from this knowledge formation. Wherever knowledge is less explicit (integrated codes, horizontal knowledge structures), Bernstein's analysis becomes less explicit. For fields like the humanities, the basis of insight, recontextualisation and pedagogy is unclear. The question becomes: if they are not based on explicit structures of knowledge specialised to objects of study, then what are they based on?

Bernstein's model provides clues. He argues that for such fields:

> The *social basis* of the principle of this recontextualising indicates *whose 'social'* is speaking. The *social basis* of the principle of the recontextualising constructs the perspective of the horizontal knowledge structure. *Whose perspective* is it? How is it generated and legitimated? (1999, p. 164; emphases added).

As this suggests, the basis of these fields resides in something other than the formation of knowledge. However, to see what this might be requires a change of focus: one needs to see there are two analytically distinct structures that *together* shape educational and intellectual fields. In other words, fields comprise more than a formation of knowledge, they also comprise a formation of knowers. This represents a shift of perspective because the existing framework explores knowers only indirectly—one analyses the knowledge formation and then reads off implications for knowers. Thus where knowledge is less explicit (as in the humanities or crafts), the basis of the field becomes harder to see. I am arguing that for such fields this basis resides in a formation of knowers, and that this *knower structure* is not an epiphenomenon of the knowledge structure but rather has structuring significance of its own.

Fields as Knowledge-Knower Structures

Building on Bernstein's approach, a series of papers in Legitimation Code Theory (LCT) has progressively conceptualised these two dimensions of social fields.[1] This approach argues that for every knowledge structure there is also a knower structure; i.e. fields are *knowledge-knower structures*. These structures are empirically inseparable (as a social field of practice) but analytically distinguishable. Where 'knowledge structures' conceptualises the arrangement of knowledge within fields, 'knower structures' conceptualises the arrangement of knowers. Crucially, the forms they take are not necessarily the same: each may be independently arranged hierarchically or horizontally.[2] For example, Maton (2007) illustrates how science can be characterised as possessing not only a hierarchical knowledge structure but also a *horizontal knower structure*: a series of strongly bounded knowers, each with specialised modes of being and acting, with non-comparable habituses or embodied dispositions based on different social trajectories and experiences. The social profile of scientists is often held to be irrelevant for scientific insight—anyone can ostensibly claim legitimate knowledge so long as they follow scientific procedures. So, in terms of their non-scientific dispositions, scientists can represent a segmented series of knowers strongly bounded in terms of their non-scientific gaze. This can be visually represented as follows, where each segment represents a different primary habitus (Kr1, Kr2, etc):

| Kr1 | Kr2 | Kr3 | Kr4 |

In contrast, the humanities can be characterised as possessing not only a horizontal knowledge structure but also a *hierarchical knower structure*: a systematically principled and hierarchical organisation of knowers based on the construction of an ideal knower and which develops through the integration of new knowers at lower levels and across an expanding range of different dispositions. The position and trajectory of knowers within the field's hierarchies are arranged in relation to the ideal knower. This can be represented as a triangle of knowers:

(There may be more than one ideal knower and triangle of knowers.) Here specific procedures for accessing a delimited object of study are less significant than possessing the legitimate dispositions.

Alongside hierarchical and horizontal knowledge structures, one can thus speak of hierarchical and horizontal knower structures. These can vary independently, giving four modalities of fields as knowledge-knower structures. This describes the form taken by intellectual and education fields. The principles underlying these forms can be analysed in terms of *legitimation codes of specialisation*, where each form is generated by a different code modality (see Figure 11.1). The code is given by the epistemic relation to the knowledge structure (ER) and social relation to the knower structure (SR). Each may be more strongly or weakly classified and framed; or more briefly, each may be more or less emphasised (±) as the basis of claims to legitimate insight, identity and status. This gives four principal code modalities (ER±, SR±). Typically, a stronger relation ('+') indicates a hierarchical structure; e.g. a stronger epistemic relation (ER+) is associated with a hierarchical knowledge structure. So, if the sciences exhibit a hierarchical knowledge structure and a horizontal knower structure, these are underpinned by emphasising knowledge, skills and procedures and downplaying the dispositions of knowers—a *knowledge code* field (ER+, SR−). Conversely, if the humanities embody a horizontal knowledge structure and hierarchical knower structure, these are underpinned by placing less emphasis on procedures and more on aptitudes, attitudes and dispositions—a *knower code* field (ER−, SR+). In addition, one can describe an *elite code*, where both possessing specialist knowledge and being the right kind of knower are emphasised (both structures are hierarchical; ER+, SR+), and a *relativist code*, where neither is significant (both structures are horizontal; ER−, SR−).

This necessarily brief summary highlights that LCT brings together knowledge structures and knower structures. I should emphasise that in intellectual and educational fields there are always knowledges and always knowers: *knowledge-knower* structures. For example, scientists do not merely follow procedures, they also develop a specialised gaze, 'a developed sense of the potential of a phenomenon aris-

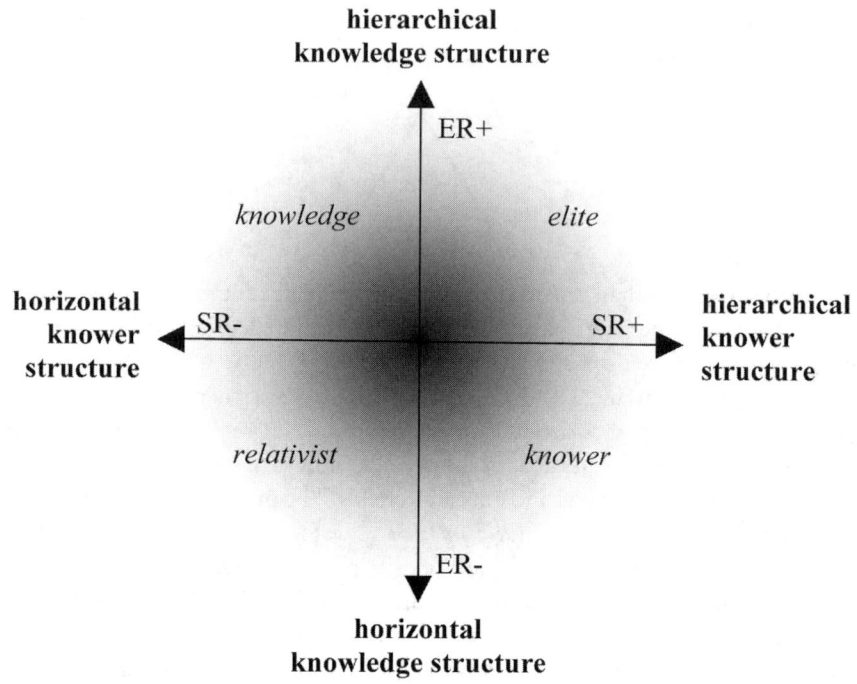

Figure 11.1: Knowledge-knower structures and legitimation codes.

ing out of practice' (Bernstein 1999, p. 165). Conversely, the humanities are not knowledge-free; they have their own theories, methodologies and so on. The key distinction between these kinds of fields is how knowledge and knowers are articulated. For knowledge-code fields the principal motivation is developing knowledge and training specialised knowers is a means to this end. For knower-code fields the principal motivation is developing knowers, and creating specialist knowledge is secondary. Thus, adding 'knower structures' to the framework builds on rather than displaces 'knowledge structures.' The approach thereby enables fields to be seen along two dimensions, revealing issues that were previously obscured. For one thing, it shows that a field's hierarchy may not reside in its knowledge structure (Maton, 2007). Put another way, Bernstein's model raises the question of what is 'vertical' in a horizontal knowledge structure. By conceptualising fields as knowledge-knower structures, we can see that *in vertical discourse there is always a hierarchy somewhere*—something is serving as the principle of production, recontextualisation and evaluation. In distinguishing between fields the question becomes: where is the 'vertical' in different forms of vertical discourse? Or more accurately: what is hierarchical? Where is the '+' in the legitimation code (ER±-, SR±)? Is it in the knowledge structure (knowledge code), knower structure (knower code) or both (elite code)? (If neither, a relativist code, the field has no vertical discourse).

A second issue this approach reveals returns us to the issue of progress in the humanities. These concepts suggest the 'hierarchical' may reside in the knowledge structure for the sciences but in the knower structure for the humanities. Bernstein states that hierarchical knowledge structures develop through the subsumption and integration of knowledge: 'verticality.' We can now add that fields with horizontal knowledge structures may develop through the subsumption and integration of habituses: 'sociality.' In other words, where one kind of field develops through knowledge-building, another kind develops through knower-building. Knower structures can thus be distinguished by the degree to which they integrate and subsume new knowers, their *sociality*, highlighting whether they develop through integration or accumulation of habituses.[3] So, while the knowledge structure of the humanities might exhibit lower levels of verticality, progress and growth of a different kind may be found in their knower structures.[4] This is not to argue that fields like the humanities must *necessarily* develop in this way or cannot build knowledge (different issues entirely), but rather to provide a way of seeing how actually existing progress may be occurring within such fields.

Gazes and Knower-Grammars

The issues brought into view by thinking in terms of knowledge-knower structures—that the primary basis and locus of growth of fields may reside in their knower structure—in turn raise two further questions. First, what is the basis of insight, recontextualisation and evaluation in these fields? As mentioned earlier, for hierarchical knowledge structures this resides in their strong grammar; for example, truth claims can be judged against available evidence using shared criteria. In contrast, Bernstein argues:

> In the case of horizontal knowledge structures, especially those with weak grammars, 'truth' is a matter of acquired 'gaze' (1999, p. 165).[5]

I defined knower structures as based on constructed knowers; each of these ideal knowers possesses a privileged 'gaze.' As Bernstein puts it, a '"gaze" has to be acquired, i.e. a particular mode of recognising and realising what counts as an "authentic"…reality' (1999, p. 165). For knower-code fields, this gaze embodies the principle underlying production, recontextualisation and evaluation in the field— 'to know is to "gaze"' (Bernstein, 1999, p. 165). One can, I suggest, analyse this 'mode of recognizing and realising' in terms of its strength of *knower-grammar* (Maton,

2007, 2008). Analogous to Bernstein's 'grammar' of knowledge structures, knower-grammar refers to the degree to which this gaze is related to a specific base. We can redescribe Bernstein's concept as 'knowledge-grammar,' the strengths of classification and framing of objects of study and their specialised procedures (or, using LCT, the epistemic relation). Knower-grammar refers to the strengths of classification and framing of privileged knowers and their dispositions (or social relation).

One can then conceptualise different kinds of gaze underlying fields in terms of their strengths of knower-grammar (or social relation). Here I shall identify born, social, cultivated and trained gazes (Figure 11.2). (I have used 'gaze,' but one could also talk of 'ear' in music and 'taste,' 'smell,' 'touch' or 'feel' and 'voice' in various arts). The relatively strongest knower-grammar is illustrated by notions of 'natural talent' and 'genius' (for example, in debates over musical ability), or genetic inheritance and biological explanations of practice, where the privileged knower is held to possess a *born gaze*. Less fixed but still relatively strong is where ideal knowers possess a *social gaze* determined by their social category, such as standpoint theories based on social class or on race, gender and sexuality when constructed as social categories. Weaker is the *cultivated gaze*, where insight is held to arise from the socialised dispositions of the knower but these legitimate ways of thinking and being can be inculcated through education; for example, in literary or art criticism insight has often been held to result from prolonged immersion in great cultural works. Relatively weakest is the *trained gaze*, where legitimate insight is gained through prolonged training in specialised methods and procedures. For example, in the sciences the source of the privileged gaze is less the knower than the knowledge they possess, and in principle anyone can be trained into the legitimate gaze.[6]

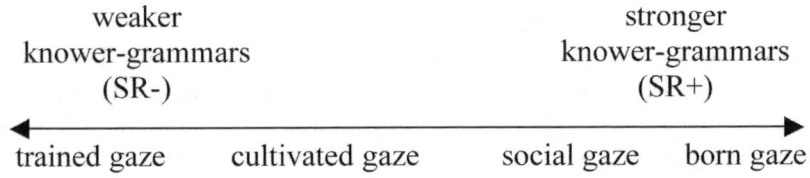

Figure 11.2 Knower-grammars and gazes.

This brings us to a second question: why might some kinds of fields have greater capacity for progress and growth than others? The different kinds of gaze outlined here trace a continuum from fixity of knower categories towards increasingly changeable features, and from knowers towards knowledge. They also trace a continuum of increasing openness to potential knowers. Strengths of knower-grammars help shape the conditions for entry, position and trajectory within a field's hierarchies. The stronger the knower-grammar, the more tightly restrictions are placed on membership of and ascension through a knower structure hierarchy. The born gaze is the most difficult to attain for those not already a member of the privileged knower group; the social gaze restricts potential knowers to social categories that may be difficult to join; the cultivated gaze holds out the possibility of attainment of legitimacy through prolonged immersion in a way of being, seeing or acting; and the trained gaze proclaims openness to anyone willing to be trained in specialised procedures. (They thus also trace a continuum of strengthening ER and weakening SR: a movement from knower-code to knowledge-code fields). The kind of gaze underlying the knower structure of fields may thus be crucial to the degree of extension of its epistemic community through time and space (Moore and Maton, 2001): gaze may shape sociality and capacity for growth of the knower structure. Moreover, sociality may in turn affect verticality, the capacity for knowledge-building in a field; that is, knower structures may affect knowledge structures. It is to these issues that I now turn, using the concepts to explore the effects of different gazes on progress in the humanities.

Gazes, Canons and Critiques

Central to debates over insight and progress in the humanities has been a 'canon brawl' (Morrissey, 2005) over what and how cultural works should be valued and whether canons should exist (e.g. von Hallberg, 1984b). Critiques of canons often portray the traditional belief in Western cultural understanding, following Kant's *Critique of Judgement*, as maintaining that if someone judges something as, for example, beautiful 'he [sic] supposes in others the same satisfaction, he judges not merely for himself, but for everyone, and speaks of beauty as if it were a property of things' (1790/1951, pp. 46–47). This position views the canonical status of a cultural work as immutable, universal and transhistorical and portrays the reader or viewer as enjoying an unmediated, immediate relationship with its intrinsic value (Kermode, 1983). Challenges to this view have been made by a variety of positions, including feminist, postcolonial, Marxist, Foucauldian, deconstructive, post-structuralist and post-modernist approaches. These highlight its asocial and ahistorical nature and argue there is no universal measure of 'Beauty' (or 'Truth' in epistemology or 'the Good' in ethics) but rather different beauties or truths. Such critiques relate cultural values to their temporal and social contexts and shift emphasis from the intrinsic form of culture to its extrinsic function. Particularly vocal in the 'canon brawl' have been standpoint critiques which emphasise the contingent, subjective and arbitrary nature of cultural valuations and view canonical status as reflecting the needs and interests of dominant social groups, so that:

> A canon is commonly seen as what other people, once powerful, have made and what should now be opened up, demystified, or eliminated altogether. (von Hallberg, 1984a, p. 1)

These two positions—conservative defences of an essentialist canon and radical critiques of the possibility of such canons—have often been portrayed as defining the terrain of the 'culture wars' (Graff, 1992). Significantly, both impose limitations on the ability of the humanities to build knowledge over time. For essentialism, cultural meaning is independent of context and its value transhistorical and self-evident—there is little to add; for reductionist critiques, meaning and value are reflections of specific socio-historical contexts—there is little that can transfer across space and time. However, if critiques of canons are redescribed in terms of their knower-grammars and gazes, one can distinguish between those based on either a cultivated or a social gaze and explore the different effects these have for a field's capacity to embrace new knowers and build cumulative knowledge.

The Cultivated Gaze

An example of a critique of a canon based on a cultivated gaze can be found in the early history of British cultural studies. Faced with the rise of new commercial forms of mass media, many educators argued during the early 1960s for teaching young people how to 'look critically and discriminate between what is good and bad in what they see' (Newsom Report, 1963, p. 156). The founding figures of cultural studies— Richard Hoggart, Raymond Williams, E.P. Thompson and Stuart Hall—argued that such calls for discrimination were often accompanied by a devaluing of working-class interests and made cases for the cultural value of the 'popular arts' (Hall and Whannel, 1964, pp. 23–37). They agreed with the need to cultivate critical discrimination and retained a conviction that much 'high' culture was of value, but highlighted that existing canons excluded the experiences of many people and the basis of choosing such canons could be extended to include new forms of culture. Through their work in adult education and the first New Left movement, they aimed to enable working-class learners to critically appreciate both new media and 'high' culture and so bring them into a cultural conversation from which they had been excluded. This was an 'attempt at a majority democratic education' (Williams, 1989, p. 154) where the aim was to democratise access to a means of 'discrimination': a cultivated gaze.

At the same time, the founders of cultural studies argued that the means of ascending towards the critical literary gaze needed overhauling. New forms of media needed new forms of pedagogy and a new 'critical method for handling these problems of value and evaluation' (Hall and Whannel, 1964, p. 15). In particular, they emphasised the need to build on the experiences of students; as Williams stated:

> I believe that communication cannot be effective if it is thought of as simply transmission. It depends, if it is to be real…on real community of experience' (in Hoggart and Williams 1960, p. 30).

However, though early cultural studies began from and engaged with learners' experiences, it did not end with those experiences. Williams (1968), for example, argued that 'the teacher who pretends he is not a teacher…is a pathetic and irrelevant figure' and Hoggart emphasised that it 'is a joint matter, but one in which the tutor has primary responsibility for keeping the lines braced' (1969, in 1982, p. 9). It thus aimed to integrate the interests and experiences of learners without slipping into 'that sloppy relativism which doesn't stretch *any* student because "they are all, in their own ways, doing wonderfully"' (Hoggart, 1969, in 1982, p. 12). They thereby aimed to provide an explicit and 'thoroughly-planned syllabus' to help 'fill out the sense of a coherent journey' towards the appreciation of cultural works in which neither

> the tutor nor the student should be in doubt about the overall aims of the course and its larger pattern of working over the session; nor about the place of each week in that pattern; nor about the shape of any one week in itself. (Hoggart, 1982, p. 9)

This explicit path for ascending towards legitimate insight remained focused on achieving a literary gaze and was still to be attained through engaging with exemplars of aesthetic excellence, expanded to include new forms of culture. Hoggart, for example, proclaimed:

> first, without appreciating good literature no one will really understand the nature of society; second, literary critical analysis can be applied to certain social phenomena other than 'academically respectable' literature (for example, the popular arts, mass communications)…the first is the more important and the second the less obvious (1966, p. 277).

Progress and Growth with a Cultivated Gaze

The kind of critique exemplified by early cultural studies is based on a hierarchical knower structure, one which works to integrate different habituses through cultivation into legitimate dispositions (see Figure 11.3). The tip of the triangle is the ideal knower's gaze; the base represents the range of habituses integrated through education. Progress and growth of this knower structure can be understood along two dimensions: first, the horizontal expansion of the range of habituses embraced by the field; and secondly, the vertical ascension of knowers towards the gaze through the cultivation of their dispositions. The basis of progress thereby resides in the belief that a wide range of potential knowers can be inculcated into the legitimate gaze. This represents a knower-grammar (or social relation) that is relatively weaker than those of born or social gazes (though stronger than a trained gaze). Bernstein describes hierarchical *knowledge* structures as motivated towards integrating the greatest number of empirical phenomena into the smallest number of axioms; hierarchical *knower* structures can be described as motivated towards integrating the greatest number of habituses into the smallest number of gazes.

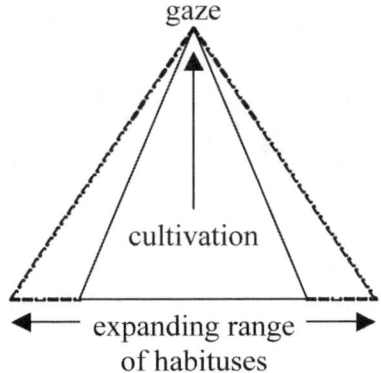

Figure 11.3: Progress and growth of knower structure under a cultivated gaze.

It is notable that the position illustrated by early cultural studies is often neglected by portrayals of the 'culture wars.' Radical critiques often present the essentialist understanding of canons as the historically dominant position. Yet this little reflects the common practice in the humanities of reinterpreting and critiquing an evolving canon rather than treating canonical works as universally transcendent (von Hallberg, 1984b). Though radical in many ways, early cultural studies were continuing a long tradition of debates over authorities and models. The first writer known to have called such choices 'classics' is Aulus Gellius of the second century, who pronounced '*Classicus…scriptor, non proletarious*': the classic writer is distinguished from the rabble (Kermode, 1983, p. 15). The genesis of canonisation in English literary criticism dates back to at least the eighteenth century and such texts as Samuel Johnson's *Lives of the English Poets*. In these debates, writers engage with the opinions of contemporary and earlier writers on the value of particular texts (Beer, 1989; Morrissey 2005). Such debates extend across time and space; they embrace other past and present thinkers. Moreover, they are capable of cumulative knowledge-building such that writers can argue 'that Dante understood more than Virgil, but Virgil was a great part of that which he understood' (Kermode, 1983, p. 25) or, as T.S. Eliot proclaimed:

> Someone said: 'The dead writers are remote from us because we *know* so much more than they did.' Precisely, and they are that which we know. (1980, p. 16)

A key to this potential sociality and knowledge-building resides in the cultivated gaze shaping the field's knower structure. This is based on the belief that knowers are not born but made through the re-formation of their habituses in prolonged exposure to great cultural works. Pedagogy thereby initiates learners into ways of knowing rather than explicit states of knowledge, instilling both 'an invisible tribunal' that sits on judgement on their work and a shared library that enables allusions, references, intertextual play and the myriad effects of what Bloom (1973) called the 'anxiety of influence,' the desire to go beyond what has come before, to be assumed and left tacit. Sociality resides in the degree to which this invisible tribunal and library is shared, for possessing the gaze represents a gateway to the public sphere of such fields. This in turn affects their potential for knowledge-building, for the definition of 'art' or 'literature' is projected by the artistic or literary gaze onto a canon which provides the Archimedean point for debate. Thus, canons and cultivated gazes may represent for the humanities the knower-based equivalents of the objects of study and specialised procedures of the sciences: they provide a focus and basis for intersubjective debate. Because the cultivated gaze is based on a canon, immersion in which helps develop what Williams called a 'community of experience,' it both enables the possibility of debate over something (a canon) and a shared means of conducting that debate (the shared sensibilities of knowers).

The Social Gaze

A second form of critique begins from a similar position to early cultural studies. It rightly highlights that dominated social groups have historically been denied access to the means of creation and circulation of symbolic products and their experiences often excluded from the shared library. However, this form is based on a social gaze. Such a form came to dominate cultural studies from the mid-1970s.

In the early 1970s, the highly influential Centre for Contemporary Cultural Studies (CCCS) engaged on a major project of trying to 'distil the field in terms of a basic set of core-texts' along with critical commentaries, with the goal of producing *A Reader in Cultural Studies* to 'prevent succeeding generations of students having to start again at first base' (Hall 1971, p. 5). This shared library aimed to provide a basis for cumulative knowledge-building and cultivating cultural studies knowers. However, this project was disrupted when the field moved to broaden its base further. Having attempted to include working-class learners among the range of knowers accessing a literary gaze, cultural studies increasingly focused on women. As Stuart Hall, director of the CCCS during the 1970s later recounted, 'we tried to buy it in, to import it, to attract good feminist scholars' (1992, p. 282). However, 'many of the women in cultural studies weren't terribly interested in this benign project' and, rather than 'good, transformed men,' scholars such as Hall were portrayed as 'fully installed patriarchal power, which believed it had disavowed itself' (1992, p. 282). The practices and beliefs of male practitioners were redefined by feminist critics as gendered and rooted in unequal relations of power. This became particularly salient when deciding the 'shared library':

There are no leaders here, we used to say; we are all graduate students and members of staff together, learning how to practice cultural studies. You can decide whatever you want to decide, etc. And yet, when it came to the question of the reading list....Now that's where I really discovered about the gendered nature of power. (1992, pp. 282–283)

The influence of standpoint theory saw feminist critiques of the emerging canon of cultural studies proclaim that not only its contents but also its basis of choice was patriarchal, denying the legitimacy of the gaze and those who possessed it. The personal nature of struggles at this time echo in Hall's proclamation: 'Talking about giving up power is a radically different experience from being silenced' (1992, p. 283). The cultivated gaze was thus redefined as socially based: a male gaze. From this perspective, integrating women into the field was attempting to inculcate them into social ways of knowing other than their own—symbolic violence. One response was thus to call for 'a literature of our own' and 'a criticism of our own' or 'gynocriticism,' a female framework for analysing literature written by women (Showalter, 1977, 1989). This set in train a series of similar debates over the imperialist, Western, racialised and sexualised nature of knowledge in the field with new, previously excluded social groups often proclaiming their own gaze and derailing the project of building a fully shared library.

Progress and Growth with Social Gazes

Critiques based on a social gaze correct the essentialist temptation to misrecognise a cultivated gaze and its canon as asocial and ahistorical. However, as early cultural studies illustrates, this can be achieved while maintaining belief in the value of canons and cultivated gazes. Contrary to many accounts of the 'culture wars,' the move to a social gaze is not necessarily integral to critiquing canons. It also has consequences for intellectual and educational fields. Where cultivated gaze critiques aim to integrate previously excluded knowers by broadening the knower structure's base (Figure 11.3), those based on social gazes create their own, new triangle. The former aim to inculcate more potential knowers into an established conversation; the latter aim to carve out a new space for already legitimate knowers to find a voice and speak to each other. While the field remains based on a knower code, this strengthens the social relation underpinning the code, affecting the nature of the field.

The social gaze restricts a field's capacity for sociality and knowledge-building along two dimensions. First, the range of potential knowers is diminished. If the knower structure begins as a single triangle (Figure 11.4, n0.1), rather than expanding this triangle a social gaze adds a second, separate triangle (no. 2). Where a cultivated gaze may be shared by knowers originating from a range of different social backgrounds, a social gaze is shared by those who possess it already, unless they successfully change gender, social class, ethnicity, etc. With such a broad social category as 'women,' this may at first appear to dramatically expand the field as a whole: a new space is carved out for a previously excluded social group. However, the new triangle can be maintained only so long as its social category remains unified, and the tendency is for it to be fragmented as more adjectives are added based on other social categories (Maton, 2000). With each successive adjective (e.g. white-female-heterosexual-Western-etc.) more separate knower structures emerge within the field, one for each new social gaze. This adds more triangles with successively smaller bases (no. 3). Though embracing more knowers, each new group has their own knower structure, fragmenting the field. The result is to move towards a horizontal knower structure (no. 4). If the field also has a horizontal knowledge structure, this diminishes the capacity of members to engage in fruitful debate and build knowledge over time. Different social groups have their own gazes and so their own objects, their own canons—each a literature or culture or art of their own. There is thus no Archimedean point, no shared object of study over which debate between segments can be engaged and no shared means of doing so.

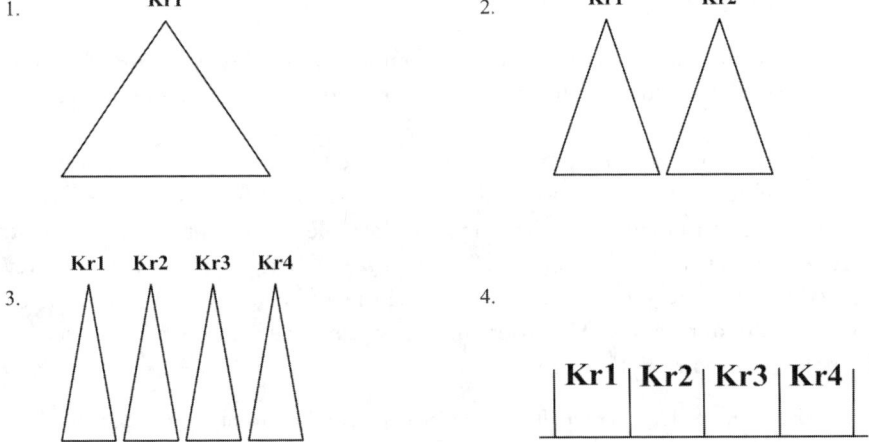

Figure 11.4 Progress of knower structure under social gazes.

A second dimension concerns the triangle's height: the distance between entry as a novice and achieving the ideal gaze may diminish. Pedagogy is less likely to focus on a prolonged apprenticeship for inculcating sensibilities and more on removing ideological obstacles (including prior cultivation) to enable the authentic social self to shine forth and so raise to consciousness one's social gaze. The gaze is still a gateway to a public sphere but now more restricted; one cannot enter or ascend the knower structure unless one is already an ideal knower. This also fragments the educational experience. For example, Richard Johnson (CCCS director 1979–88) describes the early 1980s as witnessing 'the apparent splitting up of the field of cultural theory by the often separated and even antagonistic claims of different political movements,' illustrated by a masters degree course being 'organised around the political sequence of class, gender, and "race" rather than some more synthesizing account of tensions and best options in the field' (1997, p. 65). Instead of a coherent journey towards a cultivated gaze, students may experience segmented learning as they move between approaches; indeed, a common criticism of the masters course was its lack of 'coherence' (Johnson, 1997, p. 65).

The endpoint of this process is subjectivist relativism, the notion that there is nothing beyond the different subjective knowledges of a potentially infinite number of different knowers. The social category underpinning the gaze is thus broken down and replaced by individual gazes, as illustrated by such arguments as:

> The art-world has lost its credibility. The electorate has extended, has, indeed, become universal. My answer to the question 'What is a work of art?' is 'A work of art is anything that anyone has ever considered a work of art, though it may be a work of art only for that one person.' Further, the reasons for considering anything a work of art will be as various as the variety of human beings. (Carey, 2005, p. 30)

From this perspective, discrimination is only misrecognised social power, differentially valuing art is judging personal experiences and 'such a claim is nonsense psychologically' (2005, p. 25). There is thus no hierarchy, no sequencing of achievements, and nothing to be taught or learned. There is only the horizontal addition of new lists of personal preferences (see Moore, 2007). The 'invisible tribunal' results from individual biography: 'we assemble our own literary canon, held together by personal preferences' (2005, p. 242). Though critics such as Carey believe this is democratic as it overthrows the rule of 'the art-world,' it does so by emptying 'art' of meaning. Moreover, there is no 'electorate' for there is no election. From this position, anything goes:

> If this seems to plunge us into the abyss of relativism, then I can only say that the abyss of relativism is where we have always been in reality—if it is an abyss. (2005, p. 30).

Returning to the question of finding the 'hierarchical' in vertical discourse, there is now no hierarchy, only a horizontal segment of knowledge for each segmented knower.

Conclusion

I began with questions raised by both the culture wars and Bernstein's model of knowledge structures: what is the basis of humanist knowledge, do the humanities progress and how? Bernstein's model highlights the 'horizontal' form of development taken by the knowledge structure of such fields; they have weaker verticality and weaker grammars than hierarchical knowledge structures. This, however, leaves unanswered where their basis or 'strength' might lie, how such fields might differ, and whether and how they might progress hierarchically. I argued that Bernstein's approach enables knowledge to be analysed but this focus means the basis of fields where knowledge is less explicit remains unclear. The question became: if the humanities are not based on explicit structures of knowledge specialised to clearly defined objects of study, then what are they based on? To address this I introduced the notion of knower structures based on the gaze of ideal knowers, and suggested that where knowledge structures are characterised by verticality and knowledge-grammars, knower structures are characterised by sociality and knower-grammars. The forms taken by fields can then be analysed in terms of legitimation codes, which bring these grammars together (as ER±, SR±). Intellectual and educational fields were thereby described as knowledge-knower structures. Focusing on knower structures, a range of different gazes was defined in terms of the strengths of their knower-grammars.

These concepts were used to compare two states of a field in the humanities both of which Bernstein's model would define as horizontal knowledge structures: cultural studies before and after the mid-1970s. The first was based on a cultivated gaze and characterised by a hierarchical knower structure; in the second the basis of insight, recontextualisation and evaluation was redefined as a social gaze and the knower structure increasingly horizontalised. This strengthening of knower-grammar was shown to have implications for a field's ability to extend across time and space. The cultivated gaze affords greater opportunities for cumulative knowledge-building (greater verticality) because a greater number of habituses can be integrated and subsumed (greater sociality). This verticality is, however, of a particular form: it is limited to *within* the knower-defined field, to those deemed sufficiently cultivated to judge the aesthetic or literary merits of a work in relation to other cultural works. Nonetheless, defining the ideal knower's gaze as something that can be taught and learned enables this segment to be potentially more inclusive, allowing the possibility for (though not by itself guaranteeing) cumulative knowledge-building. In contrast, the social gaze restricts sociality and verticality because access into and ascension through the field's hierarchy of knowers is restricted to a particular social group. Moreover, this may begin a process of fragmenting the field into a series of separate knower structures, moving towards subjectivist relativism. The underlying rule of the cultivated gaze is 'habituses must be brought together,' that of the social gaze is 'habituses must be kept apart.' More broadly, the trained gaze (of science, for example) reflects a hierarchy of knowledge; the cultivated gaze reflects a hierarchy of knowing; and the social gaze reflects a hierarchy of being, though positions proclaiming a social gaze typically deny hierarchies of being and so move towards horizontalism.

The capacity for a segment-limited form of verticality within fields like the humanities thereby depends on their knower structures. In short, the knower structure of a field can affect its knowledge structure. So, while Bernstein's framework allows us to see knowledge, to fully understand intellectual and educational fields we also need to see knowers. LCT embraces knowledge *and* knowers. Using LCT it becomes clear that: fields with horizontal knowledge structures may progress 'vertically' through their knower structures (if operating a knower code); their 'strength' lies within these structures; their basis of insight, recontextualisation and evaluation resides in a 'gaze'; and some fields are more capable of sociality and verticality than others, depending on the nature of this gaze.

Theorising fields in this way also brings into view a position often obscured by accounts of the culture wars: critical engagement with a canonic tradition based on a cultivated gaze. Against essentialism, this position highlights the veracity of arguments that definitions of culture are related to actors located in socio-historical contexts rather than universal and transcendent. It also highlights, against subjectivist relativism, that there can be intersubjective, rational bases for judgement that may be taught and learned. The quote opening this paper describes invisible tribunals as imaginative acts rather than simply the result of browbeaten responses to social power. Such acts are not made outside society by decontextualised knowers but rather result from articulating the personal 'inner' with the social 'outer' via cultural authority, that is, from a cultivated gaze. The key to avoiding the Scylla and Charybdis of symbolic violence and relativism is thus to discover a gaze and a means of cultivating that gaze capable of embracing knowers from a multitude of social backgrounds. This is an urgent task facing the humanities if we are to enable a culture peace, one characterised not by an unchanging, socially imposed canon, factional trench warfare or relativism, but by an enlarged cultural sphere in which everyone is able to join a living and visible tribunal.

Notes

1. See, for example, Maton (2000, 2007, 2008, 2009) and Moore & Maton (2001). For examples of research using LCT, see Carvalho & Dong (2008), Doherty (2008) and Lamont & Maton (2008); see also Shay (2008).
2. Horizontal knowledge structures are not necessarily based on knowers; mathematics is an obvious counter-example. One needs to explore the knower structure as well as the knowledge structure when describing fields.
3. Moore (2007) uses 'sociality' to highlight that knowledge claims are practices 'that people do within a special type of socio-historical context (a field or arena) that can be described in terms of its structural features' (p.109). Here I am redefining 'sociality' as the degree to which this field integrates and subsumes habituses and conceptualising the structural features of this special type of

context in terms of knower-grammars (see below).
4. Lacking the dimension of 'knower structures,' Bernstein's model can be criticised as overly focused on progress in the sciences and offering a deficit model of the humanities (e.g. Young & Muller, 2007). The approach offered here overcomes such criticisms and does so through a cumulative and integrative development of the existing theory rather than horizontally accumulating another approach.
5. 'Gaze' refers to the acquirer not to the discourse to be acquired, and to the outcome of the principles' underlying fields not to the principles themselves (cf. Bernstein, 1999, pp. 171–172). For example, I shall argue the 'cultivated gaze' shapes and is shaped by canons, rather than is the gaze of the canon itself, and is the result of a knower code with a particular strength of knower-grammar. The necessity of these distinctions becomes clear when considering the move to a 'social gaze,' which elides them both.
6. All fields are knowledge-knower structures, so all include a gaze. Where the cultivated gaze makes possession of a specialised sensibility the basis of legitimacy, the trained gaze emphasises possession of specialist knowledge as the criteria for membership of a field and the means of inculcation into its principles of organisation (cf. Moore & Maton, 2001). One emphasises knowers over knowledge; the other emphasises knowledge over knowers.

REFERENCES

Beer, G. (1989). *Arguing with the past*. London: Routledge.
Bernstein, B. (1977). *Class, codes and control, volume III*. London: Routledge & Kegan Paul.
Bernstein, B. (1999). Vertical and horizontal discourse: An essay, *British Journal of Sociology of Education*, 20(2), 157–173.
Bloom, A. (1987). *The closing of the American mind*. New York: Simon & Schuster.
Bloom, H. (1973). *Anxiety of influence*. Oxford: Oxford University Press.
Bloom, H. (1996). *The Western canon*. London: Macmillan.
Carey, J. (2005). *What good are the arts?* London: Faber.
Carvalho, L. and Dong, A. (2008). Sociology of education and the design field. *Proceedings of the fifth international Basil Bernstein symposium*. Cardiff: Cardiff University.
Denby, D. (1996). *The great books*. New York: Simon & Schuster.
Doherty, C. (2008) Student subsidy of the internationalized curriculum: Knowing, voicing and producing the Other, *Pedagogy, Culture and Society*, 16(3), 269–288.
Eliot, T.S. (1980). 'Tradition and individual talent,' *Selected essays* (2nd ed.). London: Faber.
Graff, G. (1992). *Beyond the culture wars*. London: W.W.Norton.
Hall, S. and Whannel, P. (1964). *The popular arts*. London: Hutchinson.
Hall, S. (1971). The Centre—history and intellectual development, *CCCS Sixth Report, 1969–1971*, pp. 1–6.
Hall, S. (1992). Cultural studies and its theoretical legacies. In L. Grossberg, C. Nelson and P. Treichler (Eds.), *Cultural studies*. London: Routledge.
von Hallberg, R. (1984a). 'Introduction.' In R. von Hallberg (Ed.), *Canons*. Chicago, IL: University of Chicago Press.
von Hallberg, R. (1984b). (Ed.) *Canons*. Chicago, IL: University of Chicago Press.
Hirsch, E.D. (1987). *Cultural literacy*. New York: Random House.
Hoggart, R. (1966). Literature and society, *American Scholar*, Spring, pp. 277–289.
Hoggart, R. (1982). *An English temper*. London: Chatto & Windus.
Hoggart. R. and Williams, R. (1960). Working class attitudes, *New Left Review 1* (Jan–Feb), pp.

26–30.
Hughes, R. (1993). *Culture of complaint*. Oxford: Oxford University Press.
Johnson, R. (1997). Teaching without guarantees: Cultural studies, pedagogy and identity. In J.E. Canaan and D. Epstein (Eds.), *A question of discipline*. Boulder, CO: Westview.
Kant, I. (1790/1951). *Critique of judgment*. New York: Hafner.
Kermode, F. (1983). *The classic*. London: Harvard University Press.
Lamont, A. and Maton, K. (2008). Choosing music: Exploratory studies into the low uptake of music GCSE. *British Journal of Music Education*, 25(3), 267–282.
Maton, K. (2000). Languages of legitimation: The structuring significance for intellectual fields of strategic knowledge claims, *British Journal of Sociology of Education*, 21(2), 147–167.
Maton, K. (2007). Knowledge-knower structures in intellectual and educational fields. In F. Christie, and J. Martin (Eds.), *Language, knowledge and pedagogy*. Continuum: London.
Maton, K. (2008). Grammars of sociology, Part I. *Proceedings of fifth international Bernstein Symposium*. Cardiff: University of Cardiff.
Maton, K. (2009). Cumulative and segmented learning: Exploring the role of curriculum structures in knowledge-building, *British Journal of Sociology of Education*, 30(1), 43–57.
Moore, R. and. Maton, K. (2001). Founding the sociology of knowledge: Basil Bernstein, intellectual fields and the epistemic device. In A. Morais, I. Neves, B. Davies and H. Daniels (Eds.), *Towards a sociology of pedagogy*. New York: Peter Lang.
Moore, R. (2007). Hierarchical knowledge structures and the canon: a preference for judgments. In F. Christie and J. Martin (Eds.), *Language, knowledge and pedagogy*. Continuum: London.
Morrissey, L. (2005). The canon brawl: arguments over the canon. In L. Morrissey (Ed.), *Debating the canon*. New York: Palgrave Macmillan.
Muller, J. (2007). On splitting hairs: Hierarchy, knowledge and the school curriculum. In F. Christie and J. Martin (Eds.), *Language, knowledge and pedagogy*. Continuum: London.
Newsom Report (1963). *Half our future*. London: HMSO.
Shay, S. (2008). Beyond social constructivist perspectives on assessment: the centring of knowledge, *Teaching in Higher Education*, 13(5), 595–605.
Showalter, E. (1977). *A literature of their own*. Princeton, NJ: Princeton University Press.
Showalter, E. (1989). A criticism of our own: Autonomy and assimilation in Afro-American and feminist literary theory. In R. Cohen (Ed.), *The future of literary theory*. London: Routledge.
Williams, R. (1968). Different sides of the wall, *The Guardian*, 26 September.
Williams, R. (1989). *The politics of modernism*. London: Verso.
Young, M.F.D. and Muller, J. (2007). Truth and truthfulness in the sociology of educational knowledge, *Theory and Research in Education*, 5(2), 173–201.

CHAPTER TWELVE

The Moral Career of Intelligence, Pedagogical Practices and Educational Psychology

KAREN BRADLEY AND JOHN G. RICHARDSON

INTRODUCTION

The notion of intelligence is the conceptual lynchpin of educational psychology. Following Bernstein, we argue that shifts in conceptualizations of intelligence are associated with changes in the *pedagogic discourse* surrounding learning and achievement, and will in turn prompt changes in the pedagogic *practice* of teaching (Bernstein 1990). In this chapter, we explore the changing conceptualizations and pedagogical practices associated with the concept of intelligence as expressed within educational psychology textbooks. These textual representations of the relationship between intelligence and academic success embody more than ruminations among intellectuals about the nature of intelligence. Textbooks also are written with an audience in mind: in this case, students of educational psychology, and increasingly, teachers (current and prospective). In this way, these texts also represent historical documentation of the rationalization of intelligence.

Our examination of these texts reveal three distinct periods surrounding the notion of intelligence: the period of the *individual* (1903–1939); the period of the *person* (1940–1969); and the period of the *self* (1970 to present). We investigate the factors that shift both the conceptualization of intelligence as well as its associated practices from one period to the next. A specific focus is given to links between conceptions of the moral attributes of intelligence, the student classification structure, and conceptions of teaching as pedagogic practice. As we reviewed the texts, we noted a remarkable similarity between the discourses and practices surrounding economic and educational labor. Just as pedagogic practices are manifestations of the individual, person, and self, so do the imageries of manager/worker relations develop along a similar trajectory associated with period-specific labor practices. Specifically, the aforementioned period of the *individual* is consistent with the logic and practices associated with scientific management principles; the period of the *person* corresponds to parallels an emphasis on human relations practices; and the period of the *self* corresponds to the current emphasis on team-based, process-oriented, continual-improvement labor strategies such as Total Quality Management.

We explore the parallels between industry/labor and education/learning with particular attention to the pedagogic discourse found within educational psychology texts. We explore these within each time period, and in the context of their dominant theory of work and labor.

The Structure and Dynamics of Pedagogic Discourse: Extending the Theory of Basil Bernstein

The parallels between industrial psychology and educational psychology are striking. This is especially evident when the major concepts and theories of each are juxtaposed. Schooling—its methods, goals and measures of success—is framed by macro-, meso-, and individual-level labour market concerns as they are variously defined across the 100 years of our study. The content and trajectory of *pedagogic discourse* corresponds to, but is not determined by, the prevailing imageries of work and of occupational placement. This education/labor market nexus is constituted by the 'social division of labor' in work generally, in class relations specifically, and by the 'classificatory relations' of education (Bernstein 1990, p. 43; see also Bowles and Gintis 1976).

The similarities between the two raise the problem of causality, and the alluring tendency to conceive of the economic as the determinant of the educational. Yet, as Bernstein argues, the cultural field of education is 'relatively autonomous' from the economic field, and as a consequence, 'the pedagogic text is in some sense free of external determinancy and in some important sense…is an intrinsic product of the educational process itself' (1990, p. 174). This relative autonomy creates a 'discretionary space'—a third force as it were that permits and encourages an 'appearance of neutrality' for the pedagogic discourse of education. Nonetheless, twin features of educational discourse remain: it is simultaneously neutral *and* common to the discourse of industry and work. Neither an explanation of educational discourse as autonomously produced, nor as dependent on the prior exigencies of industry and labor are adequate. It may be that Bernstein's *discretionary space* is external to both education and work, as much as it is internal to each.

We develop this proposition in the discussions that follow. The affinities between the discourse of educational psychology and the discourse of industry and work are examined for the three periods noted previously. We seek to weave an explanatory course between internal autonomy and external determinancy. To do so, however, we argue for the necessity of a third, intervening discourse that is theoretically approximate to Bernstein's notion of a *discretionary* space. This space, we propose, is the 'meta-narrative' at the societal level, external and prior to the discourses of both education and the economy. Following Somers (1995) and Alexander and Smith (1993), we explore the proposition that it is constituted by binary oppositions, distinctions that mark the prevailing issues at the time, and structure their debate and implementation. The discourses of education and the economy draw on these oppositions in a discretionary manner that approximates what Bernstein implies by *recontextualization*.

The conceptualization of a meta-narrative level as a third, intervening discourse, is incomplete without the mechanisms that link it to the discourses of education and the economy. We propose three such mechanisms that may be viewed as rhetorical devices, strategies that enable both discourses to appear relevant to broader social issues, yet relatively autonomous as well. We argue that these devices provide a means for us to examine and understand the dynamic nature of the moral career of intelligence as it unfolds within educational psychology.

One strategy is the delineation of motives that function to anticipate actions in future circumstances. The 'vocabularies of motives' as Mills phrased it (1940), are the linguistic terms with which individuals (students, employers/employees) 'discern situations' and 'anticipate consequence of conduct' (p. 906). Motives are not 'in' persons; they are, like a meta-narrative, external and prior to actions. Depictions of the advantages of higher intelligence, be it superior school and occupational achievement or greater social adjustment, are vocabularies of motive that constitute the pedagogic discourse of education. They are conceptually akin to Bernstein's *criterial rules*, for the vocabularies that link intelligence to 'moral' outcomes 'enable the acquirer to understand what counts as a legitimate or illegitimate communication, social relation, or position' (Bernstein 1990, p. 66).

A second strategy, closely related to the vocabularies that anticipate and structure future situations, is one that explains and justifies disturbances of expected behavior or outcomes. In the terms of Scott and Lyman (1968), *accounts* are statements that are intended to explain 'unanticipated or untoward behavior' (p. 46). As Mills notes, anticipated behavior and/or outcomes are sustained by delimited vocabularies of motive; as Scott and Lyman suggest, however, unanticipated behaviors or outcomes force a shift in vocabularies, from delimited motives to *excuses* and *justifications* (p. 47).

An examination of accounts may reveal disturbances and inconsistencies of previously advanced arguments. Thus, if anticipated outcomes claimed to be associated with superior intelligence become 'untoward,' such as when gifted students, once defined as scholastically involved and more sociable, are now described as bored and inclined toward maladjustment, vocabularies of motive shift to accounts to explain such discrepancies. Similarly, when evidence mounts that weaken commitments to previously held claims, vocabularies become 'defeasible' accounts. If, in Bernstein's terms, the rules that define the relation between teacher and student are strong and visible, vocabularies of motive are clearly delimited, and there is no need for accounts. If the relation becomes less visible, previously understood hierarchical rules lose their predictive and stabilizing capacity, prompting a shift from delimited motives to accounts.

A third strategy, critical as a mainstay to delimited vocabularies of motive and to the shift towards accounts, is a discourse akin to the religious sermon. Witten describes the dominant features of the sermon as *coherence, compactness, and redundancy* (1992, p. 20; see also Witten 1993a). These 'centripetal qualities' are measures of how frequently textual statements are interconnected. The more redundancy in textual statements, the more 'interpretive closure' that is achieved. In essence, more redundant sermons are immune to criticism, especially to counterinterpretation.

The pedagogic discourse of educational psychology texts exhibit similar centripetal features. One manifestation is expressed through agnosticism towards a topic, as exemplified in the following statement: 'There are many different theories concerning the structure of intelligence' (Craig et al. 1975, p. 283). Yet in apparent violation of such neutrality, a sermon discourse could stress the need for new evidence about an issue, as a base upon which a practical recommendation could be founded. Such sermonizing discourse would draw on those matters within the prevailing meta-narrative that are seen as immanent, such as a declared urgency with which teachers need to be more broadly or technically informed. Thus, a sermonizing discourse would reflect two apparent opposites. To the extent that pedagogical evidence and practices are seen as strongly linked, textual redundancy would reflect this certainty. If, however, a disbelief in the link between practices and evidence grows as inconsistencies mount, a sermonizing discourse would be one strategy to minimize damaging implications while at the same time calling for alternative evidence and reformed practices.

THE *PERIODIZATION* OF INTELLIGENCE

The concept of intelligence, although controversial, has remained a central focus of the discipline of educational psychology throughout its history. In earlier work, we identified three periods corresponding to shifts in the conceptualizations of intelligence which directly relate to teaching practices (Richardson and Bradley, 2005). We have labelled the three time periods as the period of the *individual* (1903–39); the *person* (1940–1969); and the *self* (1970 to present). We examined educational psychology textbooks published between 1903 and 2006, evenly divided across the periods.[1] We coded the titles of chapters within these textbooks based on terms that we identified as corresponding to the conceptualizations of intelligence over time (see Richardson and Bradley 2005 for further information regarding coding strategy). Table 12.1 extends our original sample to 71 textbooks and the results are essentially the same. The conceptualisation of intelligence as emanating from original nature diminishes over time, while an emphasis on motivation emerges with force in Period II (1940–69) and persists until the present. This appears to correspond to a discovery of the notion of *personality* during this period, an issue to which we will return. The notion of the self as a creative thinker (rather than an efficient and accurate test-taker) builds over time with particular emphasis emerging in Period III (1970–2006).

Table 12.1 Distribution of chapter topics across texts, for all years and by time period

Topic	All Years 1903–2006	Period I 1903–39	Period II 1940–69	Period III 1970–2006
INTELLIGENCE	58	16	25	17
Individual				
Original Nature	23	16	6	1
Individual Differences	39	12	13	14
Person				
Motivation	51	5	24	22
Personality	35	6	22	7
Self				
Creative Thinking	31	4	11	16
Development of Self	19	0	3	16
No. of Texts	71	20	27	24

META-NARRATIVES, PEDAGOGIC DISCOURSE AND PEDAGOGIC PRACTICE

The three strategies are best seen as mechanisms that function, as it were, to translate the meta-narrative into both the pedagogic discourse and the pedagogic practices of schooling. Thus, the vocabularies of motive denote both theories of learning as well as the instructional practices recommended to teachers in light of prevailing theories. Yet, both theories of learning and instructional practices are informed by the prevailing meta-narrative generally, and specifically by the tensions that inhere in the binary oppositions that compose the narrative. Examples of binary oppositions that constitute the prevailing meta-narrative for the three periods, and the corresponding 'discursive structures' for educational psychology and for management/labor, are given in Table 12.2.

We turn now to a more detailed inquiry into the structure and dynamics of pedagogic discourse generally, and of educational psychology in particular. Our discussion is guided by the theoretical framework outlined above. The discussion centers on three components of pedagogic discourse. The first and most defining is the central referent of schooling, namely the *individual* for Period I, the *person* for Period II, and the *self* for Period III. These terms are essentially indicators of more abstract referents. For Period I the central referent was intelligence, conceived as a real and measurable property that defined individual differences. For Period II, the central referent was personality, conceived as an outcome of evolving processes. For Period III the referent is the self, the most abstract and processual of the three. The progression from intelligence, to personality to the self reflects a genealogical career of intelligence itself, for the idea of intelligence never takes leave of either personality or the self.

The second focus is the structure for the classification of students, akin to Bernstein's hierarchical rules. Three levels of this structure are conceptualized. At the most external level are societal categories, such as idiot, moron, feebleminded, gifted. At the intermediary or meso level are the classificatory structures within schools and classrooms, such as ability grouping and tracking. At the most micro level is the 'instructional sequence' that structures the interaction between teacher and student (Mehan 1979). This elementary structure will reflect, in varying ways, how tightly framed classroom groupings are, as well as how societal categories can reach into instructional interactions (see Cazden 2001; Wortham 2006).

The third is pedagogic practice, the prevailing theory of teaching and the defined role of the teacher. Like the classificatory structure, the pedagogic practice of a time period will be informed by the central referent, and this will be informed by the prevailing binary oppositions that constitute the broader meta-narrative of the time.

We examine these elements within each time period, and explore their correspondence to the central ideas and terms of management/work in relation to the meta-narrative that prevailed at the time. For each period, the nexus between the

Table 12.2: Binary oppositions and the discursive structures of educational psychology, and management/labor, by time period

EDUCATIONAL PSYCHOLOGY *Pedagogic Discourse*	META-NARRATIVE *Binary Oppositions*	INDUSTRY/WORK *Management/Labor*
Period I **Intelligence**: Moral correlates Future achievement Abstract thinking Personal adjustment Physical superiority **Classification** ➤ Ability: Hierarchical **Pedagogic Practice** Teaching as Diagnosis: ➤ Test/measuring ➤ Ability grouping	 Citizen/Immigrant Civilization/Abnormality Progress/Subnormality Efficiency/Inefficiency Native-born/Foreign-born Manual/Non-manual	 'maximum prosperity' 'soldiering' 'piece-rate' 'task management' 'retention-fatigue' 'direct supervision'
Period II **Personality**: Basic Needs Affection/Belonging/ Independence/Social approval **Classification** ➤ Ability: Hierarchical ➤ Personality Types: Non-hierarchical **Pedagogic Practice** Teaching as Motivation/Guidance ➤ Individual instruction/ability grouping ➤ Vocational Guidance ➤ Character development	 Democracy/Dictatorship Equality/Inequality Integration/Segregation White/Nonwhite Person/Race	 'morale' 'wage incentive'
Period III **Self**: Attributes Self-concept: esteem; efficacy Self-efficacy; self-regulation **Classification** ➤ Ability: Hierarchical/Separate ➤ Attitude/Behavioral Types: Non-hierarchical **Pedagogic Practice** Teaching as Indirect Modeling ➤ Self-directed/cooperative learning ➤ Deferred gratification	 Developed/Underdeveloped Equality/Liberty Inclusion/Exclusion Public/Private	 'corporate culture' 'constant' improvement' 'quality' 'feedback' 'goals'—'aims'

pedagogic discourse of schooling and the workplace centers on the fundamental problem of each, how to extract and promote labor and maintain discipline (cf. Burawoy 1979; Witten 1993b). Whether it be the magnitude or quality of effort given to school subjects or the commitment of labor on the shop floor or the bureaucratic office, such organizational affinities between schools and workplaces are further strengthened by their temporal juxtaposition: students leave schools to enter work. Thus, shifts in the conceptualization of intelligence, and in the practice of teaching, are not internal to schools or to educational psychology. On the contrary, we view such shifts as reflections of the ever-present but ever-changing nexus linking schools and work.

With this temporal outline as background, we discuss in more specific terms some of the mechanisms that effect a *recontextualization* of the social division of labour, generating the 'modalities of pedagogic practice' (Bernstein 1990, p. 67). Finally, we present some empirical illustrations of these modalities from a sample of texts across the three periods. Our focus is on affinities between conceptions of intelligence, the hierarchical classification of pupils, and the instructional principles that define teaching and regulate the practices of teachers.

Period I: Individual Differences and the Narrative of Citizenship (1903–1939)

During the inaugural period of educational psychology, American society was experiencing dramatic social and economic transformation as shifts to large-scale industrial modes of production sparked the growth of large cities. For the early decades of the twentieth century, the binary oppositions of citizen/immigrant and civilization/abnormality described a prevailing tension about the direction and future of American society. For this period, these oppositions were reinforced by the tension between native-born/foreign-born. This opposition denoted a more specific content, a subset within civilization/abnormality. The conflicts between English speaking and southern and eastern European groups were symbolic of such broader themes as the potential of American society to be a civilization. These two binary oppositions, in turn, infused the tension between images of efficiency and inefficiency, be it in schooling or the workplace. The role of grade retardation became a symbol of inefficiency (Ayers 1909), and insofar as native-born students were behind in their grade, reforms designed to enhance school efficiency become linked to the broader oppositions between native and foreign-born, and between civilization and abnormality (Tyack 1974).

In their cumulative weight, these oppositions infused the division between the manual and non-manual. For pedagogical discourse and instructional practice, this opposition informed theories of learning and recommendations for the ability grouping of students. For this more proximate link, theories of learning that centered on the inheritance of intelligence and its complex of original nature represented the vocabularies of motive that rendered consistent the practice of grouping students by presumed ability level to the broader, external environment that was, in turn, rendered real.

The impact on education of the efficiency/inefficiency and manual/non-manual binary oppositions was especially strong through the prominence of Frederick Taylor's 'principles of scientific management' (Taylor 1911). Here pedagogical discourse paralleled the discourse of management (Callahan 1962, pp. 23–34). Taylor's principles were intended to provide standardized practices to sort job seekers and workers into two discrete categories: those with mental capabilities and those with physical capabilities, with little movement between these categories. In other words, those with physical strength had little future in intellectual endeavors. Individual capabilities were to be discovered and then assigned to duties. The few who were capable of mental, rather than physical labor, would direct the work of those less capable (see Haber 1964). They would be free of the burden of physical labor and use their intellectual talents to advance the profits of the company, and the economic progress of the nation. These aims were coupled with efforts to control an ever-growing workforce, increasingly characterized by racial and ethnic diversity among long-term American citizens as well as immigrants.

Concerns in the polity paralleled those of the economic sector. The massive influx of immigrants to urban and industrial centers raised concerns about identification of capabilities associated with increased racial and ethnic diversity within the schools, albeit loosely disguised as based on individual differences. That is, each individual possessed an intellectual capability that could be measured and quantified, operationalized as IQ. Scientific data in the form of standardized test scores provided the evidentiary base for sorting individuals into groups of capable and incapable students. The economic and socio-political spheres thus described did not merely provide context for schooling, but these changes and perceived needs of society acted as vocabularies of motive for pedagogic practices. Textbooks dwelled on the needs of this new society in a fairly repetitious fashion, or in a sermonizing manner. Societal progress *and* social harmony were at stake (see Judd 1918, 1934).

The pedagogic discourse of intelligence, student classification and the practice of teaching were communicated in the textbooks in a prominently neutral fashion. Beginning with E. L. Thorndike's foundation text in 1903, extending to the late 1930s, the central topics addressed in educational psychology textbooks were ones rooted in the statistical distribution of individual differences. The normal distribution of intelligence was the central objective fact from which the classification of students from dull to gifted was derived.

The sermonizing character of educational psychology texts for this period is especially evident in the 'moral correlates' attributed to its central concept: intelligence. There were a number of moral correlates associated with intelligence, particularly those with a superior level (see Appendix B). Such correlates as 'abstract thinking,' 'soundness of judgment' and 'keen perception' are consistent with the meta-narrative of this period: citizenship embodied the native-born, who in turn symbolized soundness of judgment and correction of perception, and all taken together were the essential keys to progress and to the preservation of civilization. Moreover, the moral correlates associated with gifted students mirrored the correlates for intelligence. Routinely juxtaposed to the dull student, the gifted pupil was the symbol of leadership and success, indeed the agent of progress and civilization. For this period, giftedness was a direct extension of intelligence; those endowed with superior amounts of intelligence were in effect stewards of the future progress of American society itself.

In addition to the neurological advantages of retention, memory and perception, there were moral implications of superior intelligence that accounted for the school success of some and the failure of others. Superior students were seen as more adept and skilled in a variety of social spheres, from extra-curricular activities to a greater number of friends. The moral dimensions of intelligence were central underpinnings to the classification structure. If capacity is fixed by heredity and original nature, students are naturally divisible in accordance with detectable levels of intelligence. More intelligence implied superior school achievement, which in turn implied a greater time horizon of accomplishments beyond school.

The practice of teaching mirrored the conception of intelligence and the classification structure of students. The role of the teacher was largely determined by the fixed capacities of students. More than anything teachers would be diagnosticians; their task was to test and examine individual students to determine their potential, and thus their location in a classification structure (McCall and Bixler 1928, pp. 6–11). Within this model, students bring to the classroom intelligence derived from original nature that establishes thresholds and ceilings for academic performance. The emphasis is on productivity and efficiency, in a manner analogous to concurrent emphases within the economic sectors of society. Tests of intelligence are characterized by the correct identification of the one correct answer. The moral student is one who provides evidence by way of test results that she has reached her (known) potential.

Sorting students by ability had dual aims: (a) To enable teachers to efficiently target appropriate teaching materials (books, exercises, tests) to students identified to have the same intellectual capacity and (b) to reduce discipline problems in the classrooms. Boredom in the classroom was portrayed as a potential hazard, calling for specific classroom management strategies. Students who were bored due their inability to understand the material presented in class were depicted as potentially disruptive, and likely to inhibit the learning of more intellectually capable learners. Likewise, students whose intellectual abilities were not sufficiently challenged were also likely to become bored and present distractions. In addition, material that was insufficiently challenging would not enable them to fulfill their capacity for learning. Sorting students by ability provided a straightforward remedy to both problems.

Within this period, teachers were advised to provide motivation by way of test results to prod students to academically achieve at a level consistent with their capability. Test results, plotted over time, were the appropriate instruments to provide external motivation to the able student, similar to the productivity quotas established for the factory worker. The bridge from the period of the *individual* to the period of the *person* is the concept of motivation. Evidence began to reveal that not all students responded positively to test data. This puzzle required explanation, or an account: students were discovered to have personality differences that require different forms of motivational practices. As students became identified as having more complex personalities, new pedagogic practices were called for.

Period II: Personality and the Narrative of Equal Opportunity (1940–1969)

While the pedagogic discourse and practice of schooling will 'strain toward consistency' with the prevailing meta-narrative, change weakens once prevailing binary oppositions and prompts oppositions now fashioned after new demographic, socioeconomic and legal tensions. As once prevailing oppositions weaken, vocabularies of motive give way to accounts, for once oppositions no longer delimit and define, they are out of step with ascending discourses and practices. This is particularly evident in the receding meaning of linguistic terms and expressions. With the advent of Period II, the tension between native and foreign-born appeared anachronistic, yet became its own version of the same content: the binary opposition became more narrowly sectarian, denoted by the division between 'white and non-white.' As the racial content of the wider society was reduced to this simple division, reinforced by census practices between 1950 and 1970, this opposition redefined the meaning of its previous opposition, converting citizen/immigrant into more immediate tensions, those between nation/race and person/race. Thus, new vocabularies of motive arise.

The successful passage of *Brown v. Board of Education,* resting as it did on the broader equality and authenticity of 'personhood,' gave empirical reality to these new oppositions. The economy and the polity were in turbulent times: another world war, the Korean and Vietnam wars, student protests, racial riots and a Civil Rights movement of international scope. Much that seemed known was upended. Democratic principles were at stake in the face of external threat and internal division. Questions of morality and the defense of democratic principles took center stage in the pedagogical sermons. Such new tensions reached into the pedagogic discourse of schooling, casting doubts on extant theories of learning that were anchored so firmly to the intractable reality of heredity. Sharply divided groupings based on ability levels presumed to derive from objective testing fell under suspicion.

The immediate post-war decades were ones of expanding opportunities, a general condition that promoted a broad-based movement for expanded rights to education, employment and housing. The broader discourse of rights cast into visible relief those policies and practices that sustained economic and social inequalities. As American secondary education began its 'second transformation' (Trow 1973), increasing numbers of students would complete high school and enter the work place or go on to higher education. The legalization of integration, diffused by the impact of *Brown*, amplified the ideal of equal educational opportunity. The opposition of citizen/immigrant that so defined previous decades could be dissolved through organizational reform.

The resolution of previous oppositions would be effected through the comprehensive high school. The publication in 1959 of *The American High School* by James Conant, former president of Harvard, proposed the combination of a common core of classes for all with a differentiated curriculum that would be tailored to meet particular vocational pursuits. Conant's proposal reflected earlier statements on general education that rested on claims that 20 per cent of the high school population was oriented towards vocational studies, another 20 per cent were preparing for college, but fully 60 per cent was filling the courses of general education with little specific direction. While the figure of 60 per cent was disputed, the presence of some proportion of students whose abilities and potential might go undetected was not. As a silent form of inequality, the central mission of education was not fulfilled by testing and ability grouping alone; rather, student potential needed to be detected through more intrinsic methods.

Against an imagery of intelligence as a hereditary defined capacity, individuals now presented variable degrees of potential. During the period of the *person*, educational psychologists identified more motivationally complex students. The earlier deterministic image of intelligence contrasted with the more flexible, and egalitarian image of personality, defined by as a 'phenomenon of personal individuality' (Allport 1960, p. 5). And to the strictly hierarchical classification structure based on ability grouping was joined the less strictly grouping of students according to basic needs and their personality correlates. Advice to teachers involved manipulation of student attitudes and the discovery of personality differences among children to appropriately match motivational technique with personality profile. The construction of appropriate attitudes becomes an important intervening variable between personality differences and academic achievement. Not all students were presumed to possess the same desirable attitudes toward achievement, nor the same motivation to work hard. Thus, teachers were increasingly called upon to motivate students to achieve, as well as provide instruction and assessment.

These efforts paralleled the (supposed) discoveries and applications of the Hawthorne experiments, which in turn give rise to the Human Relations Movement and applications of industrial psychology—how to motivate workers through inducements that include both material/extrinsic as well as psychological/intrinsic and social aspects (Roethlisberger 1950; Roethlisberger and Dickson 1950). The parallels between the role of the manager and the role of the teacher are striking, with the morale of the employee viewed in similar problematic terms as the morale of the student (cf. Roethlisberger 1950; Fenton 1949, chapter XIX). Like managers, teachers were now expected to be both diagnosticians and coaches. The testing industry expanded to include personality inventories and vocational guidance tests, as well as intelligence tests. Students became viewed as multi-faceted as their labor market counterparts. Indeed, identifying these multiple qualities in students would enable guidance towards realistic occupational aspirations for their futures. The moral correlates of intelligence during Period II (*person*) reflect the central imagery that we have described. The intelligent student exhibits curiosity as well as high test scores; they are open to guidance and maintain a future orientation.

The Hawthorne experiments and human relations movement also drew attention to the power of the group. Interpersonal relationships mattered, and teams exhibit social-psychological properties that could be harnessed to affect labor power. In a similar fashion, as teachers continued to puzzle over the challenge of motivating students to achieve, and accelerate their progress toward their 'potential,' sorting students into groups involved more than just ability grouping. The group dynamic itself became an important asset to teaching.

With the discovery of motivationally complex students (and workers), creativity became linked with intelligence. One measure of intelligence was ascertained by the number of correct answers to a given set of questions. Another aspect of intelligence looked at the same problem sideways: how many ways can we arrive at the same answer? As creativity was joined to motivationally complex students, a new account was called for. The period of the *self* was ushered in.

Period III: The Self and the Narrative of the Common Good (1970 to present)

The current period is characterized by divergent conceptualizations of intelligence, perhaps best characterized by the 'multiple intelligence' movement (Gardner 1983;

Sternberg 1985; but see Guilford 1959 for an early discussion). Creativity is celebrated, but is now found to be only moderately correlated with intelligence. There is no right answer; rather divergent thinking is acknowledged to be the equal of convergent thinking, and intelligence had multiple indicators that were little understood and perhaps poorly inter-correlated. Conventional, scientific methods of measuring and appraising intelligence were challenged on grounds of validity (Mercer 1973), and often determined to be inadequate and used inappropriately (Elliott 1987).

Such challenges to the very core of intelligence testing fueled the discourse of multiculturalism, and helped the professional implementation of alternative practices that were already in motion. Cooperative learning as a pedagogical practice was promoted, especially as different 'learning styles' were linked to different sociocultural backgrounds. No one learning style would be promoted over another, for learning emanated from the student outward as students were to be increasingly responsible for their own achievement as 'self-directed learners.' The teacher's role was to identify learning styles and adapt teaching practices to these variable styles. The classroom became a locus of discovery as students and teachers functioned in teams, with the teacher as coach.

As the central referent, the *self* simultaneously embodied the concrete individual learner as well as abstract processes, principally those of 'esteem' and 'efficacy.' Such notions were far from an inherited original nature, and were not simple correlates of personality traits. Rather, they were ongoing states that resulted from reciprocal interactions between fellow students, family members, teachers. The key mechanism was an altered conception of motivation, for self-concept came from 'self-directedness' more than from [a teacher's] assistance. The implications for the classification structure were considerable, for the dynamics of self-directedness, like the basic needs of Period II, were universally present among all learners, regardless of intellectual capacity, aptitude, or background. The hierarchical classification of dull-gifted that was the prominent structure in Period I was now the structure of 'special education,' paralleling the majority deemed normal and inhabiting 'regular education.' However, unlike the basic needs of Period II, the dynamics of self-directedness were less visible and more removed from conventional diagnostic technologies. Evaluations of the self were now more diffuse because the pace of learning emanated from differences in *style*. The self is a grander version of *personhood* (Meyer 1986; Rose 1996), and 'self-directedness' cannot be reduced to the mechanics of retention, recall, attitude, or motivation. Both pedagogic discourse and practice are more than removed from such mechanics; they are at odds with functional requirements and specific role performances. Both reflect a 'modern cosmology' where education is more akin to religion than to the practical transmission of skills (Meyer 2000). As such, the textual knowledge of educational psychology would be more like sermons than vocabularies of motive.

Like earlier periods, this modern cosmology and approach to classroom practices paralleled work in industrial psychology. Team-based work structures with rotating leadership and multiple perspectives are central features, rooted in the movement for total quality management (Marinaccio and Marinaccio 1977; Deming 1986; Mouradian 2002). The egalitarian nature of careers composed of quality circles, work teams, and flexibility in roles (for example, matrix style organizational structures) can also be viewed as a mechanism of control (Kunda 1992). Cultures of cooperative labour, whether student- or employee-based, can utilize peer pressure for conformity to corporate or educational culture toward the ultimate objective: harnessing labor power. In this way, pedagogical practices of the period of the *self* can be thought of as 'old wine in new bottles.'

The Moral Career of Intelligence and Invisible Pedagogy

The sequence from individual, to person, to self is notable for its increasing abstraction. For Period I, the *individual* denoted a concrete and visible entity, albeit a point in a 'surface of distribution.' With the emergence of the *person*, and the personality as its central referent, qualities and features began to replace measurable and distributable traits. What is instructive, however, is how these qualities emerged from the Individual, or, in effect, were dislodged from being anchored to the concreteness of heredity. Two interrelated processes are discernible, the process of constancy, and the process of change. For Period I, a central tenet was the constancy of the IQ, its growth rate evident as an ascending arc from early years to age sixteen. Change was acknowledged, but it was the determined outcome of the 'constancy of IQ,' a fact rooted in heredity. With the emergence of the person, and of personality as its referent, the dual processes carry over: the constancy of personality traits emerges with striking affinities to its predecessor. Similarly, some of the moral correlates of personality exhibit affinities to those of intelligence, while others are novel to it as a new construct. The critical change is in the 'ratio' of variable to constant elements: personality, and in turn the self, gain more elements, or moral correlates, that are variable. Such a gain is made by an increasing remove from biological roots, or from the preoccupation in Period I with *original nature*. The progression from individual to self reflects a change in causal logic: once the antecedent cause, original nature concedes its prior causal status to a new construct, one that bears much of the content of its predecessor, but has more features that vary independent of biological determinants. Thus, the change in causal logic entails two dynamics:

a new construct replaces a prior one as a central referent, and the strength of factors previously conceived as prior and causal recede in deference to those once conceived as effects. Put more directly, the legitimation of *personality* was conceived and achieved based on particular moral correlates of intelligence. Similarly, the legitimation of the Self builds from a selective emphasis on particular moral correlates of *personality*, to the repudiation of others (see Table 12.3 for the moral correlates of each period).

Table 12.3 'Moral correlates' of intelligence, personality, and self: Illustrative examples from texts

PERIOD I Intelligence	PERIOD II Personality	PERIOD III Self
'Achievement in school subjects'	'Achievement motivation'	'Achievement motivation'
'Keen perception'/'discerns resemblances'	'Curiosity'	'Creativity'
'Responses are appropriate'	'Moral development'	'Moral judgment'
'Not subject to emotional disturbances'	'Adjusted-maladjusted'	'Self-control/directedness'
'Abstract thinking'	'Intelligence'	
'Physical health'	'Social success'	'Physical maturity'
'Soundness of judgment'	'Susceptibility to persuasion'	'Esteem'
'Success in recognizing intellectual pursuits'	'Speech mannerisms'	'Success/goal-seeking'
'Incisive powers of analysis'		'Altruism'
'Informed about tasks'/'Efficient methods of work'		'Cooperation/school adaptability'

This sequential evolution is especially revealed in the moral career of a specific agent: gifted students. This group, or site within the classification structure, reveals more about the purpose and direction of schooling than does any other. As shown in Table 12.4, the moral correlates of this group exhibit affinities to those for intelligence and for personality. Images of the gifted student have been resilient over time, yet have changed in ways that yield insights into the long-term sequential evolution from individual to self. The crucial change most evident for the period of the *self* is the addition of negative correlates to the list of positive attributes. Now gifted students are bored, potential isolates and at risk of maladjustment. Their moral career, more than any other group, displays all three mechanisms that link pedagogical discourse to pedagogical practice. The designation of gifted students by virtue of high IQ scores constituted the vocabularies of motive that established the moral superiority of gifted students over all others. With the decline of the causal priority of heredity and original nature, the gifted student was especially affected, unhinged as it were from the moorings of biology. The gifted were now endowed with curiosity, and were the embodiment of superior personalities. As curiosity and intelligence became decoupled, the gifted were the empirical manifestation of its consequences: now superior intelligence and personality traits posed risks of boredom and maladjustment. Like Max Weber's puritans, the gifted most of all exemplified the 'maximum tension' of the reification and celebration of the self. Such tensions are, nonetheless, the real content of Bernstein's *invisible pedagogy*.

Table 12.4 Bright/gifted: examples of "moral correlates" by time period

Period I: Direct relation to intelligence.	Period II: Direct relation to intelligence; Indirect relation to creativity.	Period III: Modest relationship between intelligence and creativity; creativity is fairly independent of both IQ and achievement.
High general intelligence Creative and imaginative	High general intelligence Creative potential	High general intelligence More creative/talented / Exhibit greater flexibility in ideas
Develop refined literary and poetic appreciations Prefer more abstract school subjects Become leaders Sociable Engage more in extracurricular activities Healthier Accelerated in school/read extensively Have larger number of hobbies High character Have lofty ambitions/definite plans for future	Superior use of language Ability to generalize Show signs of leadership; initiative/originality Expect others to be interested in their involvements Understand relationships	Engage in abstract thinking Greater task persistence / School and occupational achievement
	Negative Adjustment problems Frustrations	**Negative** Bored, lose interest Frustrated Underachieving

Conclusion

As we have argued, the moral career of intelligence within educational psychology can be understood as unfolding within cycles characterized by vocabularies of motive (Mills 1940), sermon (Witten 1992) and account (Scott and Lyman 1968), respectively.

Our analysis of texts relies upon an examination of language as meaning structures that both reflect understandings about intelligence and construct pedagogical practices (Bernstein 1990). We began with an inquiry as to the use of language and metaphor to motivate certain pedagogical practices. Educational psychology texts are intended as handbooks of teaching practice. They present an evidentiary basis for their prescriptives that are intended to motivate action. Not incidentally, these motivational aspects are linked to moral purposes—the construction of an educated and moral citizenry that would be the foundation of a smoothly functioning democratic republic.

Following the establishment of motive and consistent with the moral focus of education, educational psychology texts rely upon sermonizing language and metaphors that become more loosely attached to the evidentiary base and more tightly coupled to the moral framework for interpreting pedagogical practices.

As the evidentiary base is re-evaluated and as the societal context for pedagogical practices shifts, new accounts of intelligence emerge and provide the conceptual bridge that leads to the next stage in the trajectory. This cycle of vocabularies of motive, sermon and accounts describes the dynamic nature of the moral career of intelligence that is foundational to the discipline of educational psychology.

NOTE

1. We identified these textbooks through a search of three library catalogs with extensive holdings in the field beginning with the emergence of educational psychology as a discipline: Western Washington University; Teachers College, Columbia University; and the University of Washington.

REFERENCES

Alexander, Jeffrey C., and Philip Smith. 'The Discourse of American Civil Society: A New Proposal for Cultural Studies.' *Theory and Society* 22 (1993): 151–207.
Allport, Gordon W. *Personality and Social Encounter, Selected Essays.* Boston, MA: Beacon Press, 1960.
Ayers, Leonard. *Laggards in Our Schools.* New York: Charities Publication Committee, 1909.
Bernstein, Basil. *The Structuring of Pedagogic Discourse,* Vol. IV, Class, Codes and Control. London and New York: Routledge, 1990.
Bowles, Samuel and Herbert Gintis. *Schooling in Capitalist America.* New York: Basic Books, 1976.
Burawoy, Michael. *Manufacturing Consent: Changes in the Labor Process Under Monopoly Capitalism.* Chicago, IL: University of Chicago, 1979.
Callahan, Raymond. *Education and the Cult of Efficiency.* Chicago, IL: University of Chicago Press, 1962.
Cazden, Courtney. *Classroom Discourse: The Language of Teaching and Learning.* Portsmouth, NH: Heinemann, 2001.
Conant, James. *The American High School Today.* New York: McGraw Hill, 1959.
Cuban, Larry and Dorothy Shipps (eds.), *Reconstructing the Common Good in Education: Coping with Intractable American Dilemmas.* Stanford, CA: Stanford University Press, 2000.
Deming, W. Edwards. *Out of the Crisis.* Cambridge, MA: MIT Press, 1986.
Elliott, Rogers. *Litigating Intelligence: IQ Tests, Special Education, and Social Science in the Courtroom.* Dover, MA: Auburn House, 1987.
Fenton, Norman. *Mental Hygiene in School Practice.* Stanford, CA: Stanford University Press, 1949.
Fischer, Frank. 'Organizational Expertise and Bureaucratic Control: Behavioral Science as Managerial Ideology.' In *Critical Studies in Organization and Bureaucracy,* edited by Frank Fischer and Carmen Sirianni. Philadelphia, PA: Temple University Press, 1984.
Gardner, Howard. *Frames of Mind, The Theory of Multiple Intelligences.* New York: Basic Books, 1983.
Guilford, J. P. 'Three Faces of Intellect.' *American Psychologist* 14 (1959): 469–479.
Haber, Samuel. *Efficiency and Uplift, Scientific Management in the Progressive Era, 1890–1920.*

Chicago, IL: University of Chicago, 1964.
Hanus, Paul. *School Efficiency.* New York: World Book Company, 1913.
Judd, Charles. *The Evolution of a Democratic School System.* Boston and New York: Houghton Mifflin, 1918.
Judd, Charles. *Education and Social Progress.* New York: Harcourt, Brace, 1934.
Kaestle, Carl. *Pillars of the Republic, Common Schools and American Society, 1780–1860.* New York: Hill and Wang, 1983.
Kunda, Gideon. 1992. *Engineering Control.* Philadelphia: Temple University Press.
Marinaccio, Anthony, and Maxine R. Marinaccio. *Human Relations and Cooperative Planning in Education and Management.* Dubuque, IO: Kendall/Hunt, 1977.
Mayo, Elton. *The Human Problems of an Industrial Civilization.* New York: Viking Press, [1933] 1960.
McCall, William A., and Harold H. Bixler. *How to Classify Pupils.* New York: Teachers College, 1928.
Mehan, Hugh. *Learning Lessons: Social Organization in the Classroom.* Cambridge, MA: Harvard University Press, 1979.
Mercer, Jane R. *Labeling the Mentally Retarded.* Berkeley, CA: University of California, 1973.
Meyer, John W. 'Myths of Socialization and of Personality.' In *Reconstructing Individualism*, edited by Thomas C. Heller, Morton Sosna, and David E. Wellbery. Stanford, CA: Stanford University Press, 1986.
Mills, C. Wright. 'Situated Actions and Vocabularies of Motive.' *American Sociological Review* 6 (1940): 904–913.
Mouradian, George. *The Quality Revolution, A History of the Quality Movement.* New York: University Press of America, 2002.
Richardson, John G., and Karen Bradley. 'The Moral Career of Intelligence and the Development of Educational Psychology.' Unpublished manuscript, Department of Sociology, Western Washington University, Bellingham, WA. 2005.
Roethlisberger, F. J. *Management and Morale.* Cambridge, MA: Harvard University Press, 1950.
Roethlisberger, F. J., and William J. Dickson. *Management and The Worker.* Cambridge, MA: Harvard University Press, 1950.
Rose, Nikolas. *Inventing Our Selves, Psychology, Power, and Personhood.* Cambridge, UK: Cambridge University Press, 1996.
Scott, Marvin B., and Stanford M. Lyman. 'Accounts.' *American Sociological Review* 33 (1968): 46–62.
Somers, Margaret F. 'Narrating and Naturalizing Civil Society and Citizenship Theory: The Place of Political Culture and the Public Sphere.' *Sociological Theory* 13 (1995): 229–274.
Sternberg, Robert J. *Beyond IQ: A Triarchic Theory of Intelligence.* New York: Cambridge University Press, 1985.
Taylor, Frederick W. *The Principles of Scientific Management.* New York: Harper & Brothers, 1911.
Taylor, Frederick W. *Scientific Management.* New York: Harper & Row, [1911] 1947.
Trow, Martin. 'The Second Transformation of American Secondary Education.' In *The School in Society*, edited by Sam Sieber and David E. Wilder. New York: The Free Press, 1973.
Tyack, David. *The One Best System.* Cambridge, MA: Harvard University Press, 1974.
Tyack, David, and Larry Cuban. *Tinkering Toward Utopia.* Cambridge, MA: Harvard University Press, 1995.
Viteles, Morris S. *Industrial Psychology.* New York: W. W. Norton & Company, 1932.

Witten, Marsha G. 'The Restriction of Meaning in Religious Discourse: Centripetal Devices in a Fundamentalist Christian Sermon.' In *Vocabularies of Public Life, Empirical Essays in Symbolic Structure,* edited by Robert Wuthnow. London and New York: Routledge, 1992.

Witten, Marsha G. *All Is Forgiven, The Secular Message in American Protestantism.* Princeton, NJ: Princeton University Press, 1993a.

Witten, Marsha G. 'Narrative and the Culture of Obedience at the Workplace.' In *Narrative and Social Control: Critical Perspectives,* edited by Dennis K. Mumby. Newbury Park: SAGE, 1993b.

Wortham, Stanton. *Learning Identity.* Cambridge: Cambridge University Press, 2006.

CHAPTER THIRTEEN

School Development and Leadership in Norwegian Demonstration Schools

RITA RIKSAASEN

INTRODUCTION

Norwegian 15-year-olds score average or lower than average on knowledge tests when they are compared with students from other European countries (The Program for International Student Assessment [PISA], 2004). The Norwegian students describe more discipline problems and more waste of time in school than students in any other Organisation for Economic Cooperation and Development (OECD) country. However, when Norwegian students are invited to evaluate their well-being, self-confidence and safety in school, they score nearly the highest in the world (Mullis, 2007).

In 2002 National tests were introduced in both lower and upper secondary schools. The results of the tests were made public. At the same time, the Ministry of Education and Research started a pilot project by appointing 22 demonstration schools for 2002–2004. The schools, on both primary and secondary levels, were selected because they had positive learning environments for their students, excellent teaching of Norwegian, Mathematics or English and/or the architecture of the buildings was especially suitable for using various teaching methods. Some parents had the opportunity to compare schools and select the best school for their children.

Each demonstration school was allocated NOK 1 million. For two years, the schools were going to present their effective practices to visitors, act as role models for other schools, and share their experience with other schools. Since 2002 new demonstration schools are appointed yearly. This practice was initiated by the conservative minister of education and research, Kristin Clemet, and followed up by the new socialistic minister of education, Øystein Djupedal.

This chapter presents the results of a qualitative study of school development, leadership and culture in the first 22 demonstration schools (Riksaasen, 2005). School development may be replaced with, for example, educational change, reforms or evaluation. The demonstration schools had worked with different projects for several years, and 16 of the 22 schools had already presented their practices to visitors before they became demonstration schools.

The study shows how principals and teachers in the demonstration schools had worked to change the educational codes from collection modes to integrated modes (Bernstein, 1977). 'A "code" is a regulative principle, tacitly acquired, which selects and integrates relevant meanings, forms of their realisations and evoking contexts' (Bernstein, 1990). The characteristic of a code is that it contains principles of guidelines for interpreting the world around us or governing our behaviour.

The heads of the demonstration schools often invited volunteers (innovators) (Rogers, 1962) to initiate projects. Later on, the positive experiences of the innovators inspired colleagues to introduce new practices (late adopters). Finally, some conservative teachers resisted change (the laggers).

When the 'progressive' teachers collaborated to change their practices, they seemed to replace a restricted professionalism with an extended professionalism. If the cultures are dominated by restricted teacher professionalism, the teachers are likely to be conservative and stress individualism and the here-and-now-situation. When the teacher professionalism is extended, the teachers are likely to be progressive, they cooperate and are oriented towards the future (corresponding to an integrated code). According to Berg (1999), empirical studies of school cultures may be based on the teachers' professional norms and especially their stress on individualism in contrast to cooperation.

THEORETICAL FRAMEWORK

After the first days in the field , the theory of Bernstein about educational knowledge codes was selected as the most helpful theoretical perspective.

An educational knowledge code concerns legitimate and illegitimate communication in a pedagogic context. In a school, formal educational knowledge is realised through three message systems: curriculum, pedagogy and evaluation (Bernstein, 1990). The curriculum defines what counts as valid knowledge, pedagogy defines what counts as the valid transmission of this knowledge, and evaluation defines what counts as a valid realisation of the knowledge on the part of those taught. The form an educational code takes depends upon social principles that regulate the classification and framing of knowledge. Classification does not refer to what is classified, but to the relationship between categories (Bernstein, 1996). Classification can be strong (+C) or weak (–C), according to the degree of insulation. Where there is strong insulation between categories, each category is sharply distinguished and has its own distinctive specialisation. If that insulation is broken, a category is in danger of losing its identity. Dominating voices within the category (subject teachers) risk the loss of influence and power. If there is weak insulation between categories, the categories are less specialised and their distinctiveness is reduced. The boundaries between categories are weak or blurred (subjects, teachers, students).

Framing is used to determine the structure of the message system, pedagogy. Framing can be strong or weak. Analytically, we can distinguish two systems of rules regulated by framing. They are the rules of the discursive order, the instructional discourse, (selection, sequencing, pacing and criteria) and the rules of the regulative discourse (control over the social base). The strength of classification and the strength of framing can vary independently of each other.

An organisation of educational knowledge which involves strong classification and strong framing is called a collection code. An organisation of knowledge which involves weak classification and weak framing is called an integration code (Bernstein, 1977). In a school dominated by a collection code, the subjects are clearly separated and stand in a closed relationship to each other. The teachers' identities are connected to single subjects and this contributes to a strong division of labour.

In a collection code, there will probably be visible pedagogy. With visible pedagogy, the teacher is concerned with transmitting specific skills. The existence of firm, explicit criteria makes evaluation rather easy to measure, there is a hierarchical organisation of knowledge and a key concept is discipline. Discipline means accepting a given selection, organisation, pacing and timing of knowledge realised in the pedagogical framing. The evaluation system places emphasis on attaining states of knowledge rather than ways of knowing. Knowledge of education is non-commonsense knowledge freed from the local level through various languages of the sciences or forms of reflectiveness.

In a school dominated by an integrated code, the various insulated subjects are subordinate to some relational idea, which blurs the boundaries between subjects. We can distinguish between a teacher-based integration in which the same teacher blurs boundaries between subjects, and a teacher-based integration, which involves relationships with other teachers. We can also distinguish between integration within a common subject, or an integration, which involves teachers of different subjects. In an integrated code, there is likely to be an invisible pedagogy (Bernstein, 1977). In an invisible pedagogy, the teacher's control over the student is implicit rather than explicit. In an arranged context, the student arranges his or her activities to enable shared competencies to develop (Bernstein, 1996). The idealism is to celebrate what we are in contrast to what we have become, and there is an inbuilt procedural democracy, an inbuilt creativity, an inbuilt virtuous self-regulation. The competence model of an invisible pedagogic practice is predicated on fundamental 'similar' to relations. The criteria for evaluating the invisible pedagogy are multiple and diffuse, and achievements are therefore not easy to measure.

Bernstein looked upon pedagogic communication as a relay for external power relationship: A relay for social class, gender or as a relay for skills of various kinds or ideological messages. Initially Bernstein considered conflicts between a visible and an invisible pedagogy as conflicts between fractions of the middle class. One fraction, which is employed in a direct relation to the economic field, arguing for a conservative (visible) pedagogy. The other fraction, which is employed in the symbolic field, arguing for a progressive (invisible) pedagogy at least at the primary stage. In his latest work, Bernstein states that 'which discourse is appropriated depends more and more today upon the dominant ideology in the official recontextualizing field (ORF)and upon the relative autonomy of the pedagogic recontextualizing field (PED)' (Bernstein, 1996:67).

In the study of demonstration schools the teachers and principals described in interviews how educational change was initiated because of the students' poor motivation for school work. When a school or a department introduced flexible school hours, private study periods, differentiated instructions or level-based teaching, the classification between subjects often became weak and the framing over instructional discourse became weak. The teachers did not direct how students worked with tasks at any time (flatter hierarchies). As the educational code changed, the interaction between teacher and students changed (an inbuilt procedural democracy (Bernstein, 1996).

The picture of the collection code school is consistent with the empirical literature about school as a bureaucracy (Tyler, 1988). The integrated code school, with flexible time scheduling and stress on collaboration, can be connected to the human relations movement and to the socio-technical theories that became especially popular in Norway, Sweden and Japan (Rossvær, 1985). According to the socio-technical theories, workers should be able to make their own decisions at the same time as they should be met with respect and individual support.

In the following discussion, we will observe how the principals in the demonstration schools often initiated educational change by inviting teachers to take part in project through voluntary participation,

Clegg (1990) interprets changes in organisational forms towards flatter hierarchies and more democratic forms of work organisations as a move towards postmodern organisations.

Methods

The Types of Selected Schools

The demonstration schools consisted of five primary schools, five 1–10 schools, six lower secondary schools and six upper secondary schools. Four of the schools were located in cities, 12 in small towns and six in the countryside. Schools from all the 19 Norwegian counties were represented. Even though this was not stated, I suspect location as well as good practices influenced the selection of the sample.

Selection of Informants and Observations

All the 22 heads (six women and 16 men) took part in individual interviews. The heads selected the sample of 87 teachers (55 women and 32 men) and the teaching they wanted to show. In a school with, for example, excellent teaching of mathematics, I always observed lessons in this subject. However, when I walked through the schools I often stopped and observed teaching in several subjects, even if this was not planned.

Usually I interviewed teachers who showed their effective practice. These teachers took part in projects, and thus were positive to school development. In three schools, the principal also invited teachers who resisted change to take part in interviews. In addition, I had several informal conversations with teachers who were sceptical to the present reforms.

The Fieldwork

The aim with the fieldwork was to explore the schools' effective practices and interview the heads and teachers about their leadership and educational change. In addition, it was possible to study schools in different local contexts. I spent 11 weeks travelling around the whole country. From October 2002 to March 2003, I visited each of the schools for two days. One day, I interviewed the head and groups of teachers; the other day, I observed in two or three classrooms. To give an overall review of the practices observed is a complex task. I shall only be able to mention a few examples.

The Interviews

Even though I used interview guides, the aim was to have natural conversations. Thus all the informants were not asked all the questions. The interviews were tape recorded and transcribed.

Often the questions were open-ended. For example: 'How do you work with educational change (processes, collaboration, common aims)?' To learn about leadership and school cultures the questions were indirect. For example, 'Can you describe an excellent principal? Which criteria do you use when appointing a new teacher?' In the lower and upper secondary schools, the informants were teaching different subjects, and the interviews might be interesting conversations between colleagues. For example, in two of the upper secondary schools, all the students had individual work plans. During the interview, with four subject teachers, we were warned of different consequences of this individually guided learning. When teaching car mechanics, the teacher spent more time on the high performers than on the low achievers because the students were working at separate tasks. The most competent students needed supervision to be able to use new machines. In contrast, the teachers in health and social studies could allocate more time to the low achievers when the students were working at separate tasks.

Observations

Generally, it was easy to be an observer in the demonstration schools. Teachers as well as students were used to visitors. I sat at the back of the classroom, taking notes for at least 45 minutes. Often I drew a map of the room and studied the interaction between teachers and students in the light of Bernstein's code theory. For example, if the students were not allowed to collaborate, they worked individually with the same task in the same subject, then the classification between subjects, tasks and students was strong and the framing over criteria for collaboration was strong (collection code). In contrast, if the students were allowed to work with different subjects and different tasks, they could select individual work or group collaboration, then the classification between subjects, tasks and students was weak and the framing criteria over collaboration was weak (integrated code). All the time, the focus was on the students' concentration.

The observations were designed to reveal answers to relevant questions about the present practices of teachers and heads, compare the practices of different schools and avoid studying of teaching ideologies instead of practices. For example, in one primary school, I observed special teaching of dyslectic students. The teacher taught with a commanding voice, and the students appeared not to be motivated. In an interview with two teachers in the same school, this teaching was put forward as an example of 'good practice.' Since I had observed an enthusiastic teacher in another school, teaching four dyslectic students at the same time as she tried to increase their self-confidence, I discussed the different practices with the two teachers, and we were able to reflect on good teaching of these types of students.

Data Analysis

The ethnographic descriptions from the classrooms were analysed by means of Bernstein's code theory and in the context of information from the interviews.

In the interviews, the questions were first categorised and grouped. These analyses were partly based on the code theory and partly on theories of leadership and organisation.

For example, the heads who were named 'facilitators' invited teachers to propose projects. Initially, they toned down their own viewpoints and prepared for the teachers learning. At the same time, they inspired the teachers to prepare for the students' learning. The positional principals, in contrast, explained how they talked 'to' teachers instead of with teachers, and they often left it to the individual teacher to select teaching methods (restricted teacher professionalism).

CHARACTERISTICS OF CHANGE AND RESULTS IN THE DEMONSTRATION SCHOOLS

Because the demonstration schools were selected using fixed criteria, they often appeared similar. Table 13.1 gives an overview over the similarities between the schools' developmental work.

Table 13.1 Similarities

	Primary level $N=5$	1–10-level $N=5$	Lower second. level $N=6$	Upper second. level $N=6$	Total $N=22$
Organising					
Alternative time tables	5	3		6	18
Flexible school hours	3	0	5	0	8
Subject integration	4	3	4	4	15
Teamwork	5	5	6	4	20
Mentors	1	1	5	2	8
Individually differentiated learning					
Level based teaching	1	0	4	2	7
Selection between Courses and themes	1	3	5	2	11
Mixed age groups	3	4	1	0	8
Individually work plans	4	4	6	5	19
Teachers' collaboration					
With students	2	3	6	6	17
With parents	2	2	4	1	9
With the after school centre	3	2	0	0	5
Evaluation					
Exploring different forms of assessment	3	4	6	5	18

Table 13.1 shows similarities among the organisation of the schooling, individually differentiated learning, cooperation and evaluation. The lower secondary schools seem to be the most 'progressive' ones. In the sections below, extracts from interviews and observations bring the analysis further.

Organisation of Schooling

The most recent national curriculum for primary and lower secondary schools and the last curriculum for upper secondary schools emphasise project work and teamwork. Several informants in this study perceived a fixed timetable as an obstacle to this scheme. For example, a headmaster of a lower secondary school changed the timetable when he 'lost' 22 of his ordinary lessons in social science before Christmas one year. The old timetable did not work any more, and the teachers and headmaster started to plan the teaching for only six weeks. The six weeks were divided into periods of 3 × 2 weeks. In other schools, the year was divided into thematic periods. The teachers selected parts of their subject that could be integrated during periods of three or four weeks. Eighteen of the 22 demonstration schools had introduced flexible timetables.

In 20 of the schools, the teachers worked in teams. Teamwork may be at different levels. That is, there may be common planning but individual teaching, or full cooperation on students and the teaching of subjects. For example, in one of the selected primary schools, a young female teacher was teaching initial reading and writing in the second form as did her young female colleague in the neighbouring classroom. Their teaching was almost identical. As an observer, I could see how closely the two teachers worked together when they planned their lessons. But one of them was calm and her students were quiet. The other was stressed and her students were restless. It is easy to argue that the students in the two classes might have behaved differently irrespective of the teachers and thus influenced the behaviour of the teachers. However, teachers who prefer full cooperation of students must discuss disciplining (the regulative discourse) as well as subject teaching (the instructional discourse). Members of a team should have similar perspectives on teaching and upbringing. An integrated code weakens specific subject identities and requires a high level of ideological consensus (Bernstein, 1977).

In all the primary schools, the students in the first three forms had weekly outdoor lessons. In one school, nearly 70% of the students were children of immigrants and there the oldest students also spent time outdoors one day a week, or went to museums or art exhibitions. The intention here was to stimulate the learning of Norwegian by using specific situations, teach the children to enjoy being out in the country (the school had a stock of skis and skates to lend) and integrate different groups of students. The outdoor lessons contributed to learning in a natural context. In Bernstein's terms, the students were close to the material base (concrets) when they for example learnt about plants.

In three of the primary schools and five of the lower secondary schools, the students had flexible working hours. The schools had different arrangements, but often the students could arrive at eight in the morning and leave at 3:30 in the afternoon. During the working hours, a teacher helped with the lessons, the students could work together or take part in voluntary courses which the teachers organised. When the students had 'saved up' time, they could take time off, for example every other Friday after 11 in the morning. It was an experience to observe young people doing their schoolwork at 8 in the morning when school really started at 9.

Two of the upper secondary schools had extended working hours, and 30–40% of the ordinary subject lessons were replaced with private study periods. The students had to learn by experience to take responsibility for their own work during these periods. When they had learnt this, they were sometimes allowed to work at home for a day if they wanted to. To the surprise of the teachers, the students often showed up in school because it was too boring to work at home.

In Bernstein's terms, the reorganisation of the teaching had helped to bring about weaker classification between lessons and subjects in study periods. The students had greater influence on the selection of subjects and tasks, and could also regulate pacing and sequencing more (weaker framing). A lower secondary school head pointed out that the students had become more mature. They made strategic selections and chose, for example, the lowest level in English for 2 weeks if they wanted to spend more time on mathematics.

In 15 of the demonstration schools, both the teachers and the heads spoke favourably of the integration of subjects. In primary and 1–10 schools, teachers and heads also pointed out the value of teaching mixed age groups. For example, a 1–10 school was working on a Minerva project, which focused on girls and mathematics. Girls from the 4th and 10th forms had joint lessons in the home economics classroom to learn fractional arithmetic by dividing bun dough in half and quarters. After this teaching, doubling and halving became easier for the youngest ones, and the 10th-form girls got an eye-opener when they taught the younger students. In addition, the girls bought food and learnt to keep an account.

In an upper secondary school, teachers in both mathematics and vocational training stressed the positive effect of teaching mathematics in the workshop. The use of specific examples increases the motivation of students who are tired of theory. If a student for example, study car mechanics and his main interest is cars, subject integration also contributes to weaker classification between everyday knowledge and educational knowledge. Especially for working class students this may be important. Studies show that working class students may have weaker classification between their home context and the school context than middle class students (Bernstein, 1990).

Individually Differentiated Learning

Individually differentiated learning means that the teacher takes into consideration both the functional level and the cultural background of the students. These teaching principles were stated in the curricula for Norwegian primary schools, lower and upper secondary schools and further education in 1993 (Anon, 1996). If the teaching does not correspond to the student's individual level, motivation is reduced and disciplinary problems may arise.

One primary school had organised a resource week for the second form. An interdisciplinary team observed in the classroom to find out whether anyone needed outside help. In addition to their ordinary subjects, the students in this school could select from a variety of courses. One course aimed at improving the self-confidence of timid students. The group consisted of five students, and the teacher used theatrical techniques. When a timid girl used masks and played the role of a princess in a fairy tale, her self-confidence increased and she started to talk in her class.

A teacher in a 1–10 school had begun systematic, initial training in reading and writing. Fifth-form students, who were still experiencing difficulty in reading and writing, were given the opportunity to take part in a course 15 hours a week for 12 weeks, which also aimed to develop their self-confidence. The parents had to cooperate and follow-up the lessons at home, and to accept reduced teaching in other subjects in this period. Three-quarters of the students needed minimal support after the course.

Four students were taking part when I observed this 'reading clinic.' One boy was using a computer to correct his spelling, but he pressed the OK key even when the spelling was wrong. When he showed the teacher his result, he said he had accidentally hit a key on the computer and removed the number of correctly spelt words. Without mentioning this deceit, the teacher asked how the boy evaluated his work. He said he should have spent more time on his homework.

This example is interesting because it demonstrated how the teacher used an indirect form of control. She did not focus on the cheating, but asked an open question. The teacher said she places emphasis on communication that creates inner motivation, but this is difficult. It is really hard for these students to learn to read and write. To make progress, they must reflect on their own learning. When I observed the dyslexic students, they seemed to be enjoying the work even though they were struggling with their reading and writing.

Four of the six lower secondary schools taught mathematics, Norwegian and English at several levels of difficulty. The number of levels varied between two and five. The students chose the level themselves, either by joining an established group or by selecting an individual work plan. The teachers argued that students who were poor in a subject felt more comfortable if they selected the lowest level of a course themselves, instead of leaving this decision to a teacher. A headmaster also described how students, who were under the supervision of the childcare department, ceased their truancy and changed their behaviour in the new system.

In two of the upper secondary schools, all the students had individual work plans, which meant that both the teachers and the students could make selections. For example, on a motor engineering course, the students were going to learn bodywork, commercial vehicle and car mechanics. When a student had learning problems, the teacher might allow him to specialise in bodywork, for example, and just manage a pass in commercial vehicle and car mechanics.

In an invisible pedagogy, the focus is both on equality as human beings (Bernstein, 1996) and on the uniqueness of every individual. Individually differentiated learning is a matter of course in this practice.

Cooperation among Teachers and Students

When a school introduces flexible working hours, private study periods and/or individually guided learning, the teachers spend more time with the students. Even though the school day became longer, the teachers felt less exhausted when they left school at half past three in the afternoon than at two o'clock. The interaction with the students became more positive when the teachers worked as supervisors. A headmaster described how the relationship between students and teachers changed:

> The old teacher role is left behind when you sit down among the students....Disorderly behaviour is reduced. Forgetfulness, arriving late, the many small things that led to difficult and negative interactions when we talked to parents are reduced. Students interact in a new way and teachers and students interact in new ways. We have no damage to property any more.

These experiences correspond with the results of a study by Metz (1986). In an open magnet school, the staff started cooperating with their students and noted that they had very few confrontations. In an invisible pedagogy, there is an in-built procedural democracy. The aim has been to produce emancipation from authoritarian modes of socialisation and to stress collaboration (Riksaasen, 1999).

Evaluation of Students' Learning

Since the students in the demonstration schools were often given full responsibility for their own learning, it was important for them to keep logbooks in which they wrote down their plans and aims for certain periods. They also evaluated their learning processes and performances together with their teachers. In some schools, the parents were expected to take part in the evaluation and sign the logbooks. This form of evaluation, based on cooperation with parents, may be far more wide-reaching than evaluating performances in tests.

Several of the demonstration schools used portfolios. Two of the primary schools were selected because of this, and students showed me their records. Even if the intention with portfolios was to emphasise the abilities of the students, it was easy to observe what was missing in the products when I compared the work of two students. When I read the record of a third-form student, I also gained an insight into the private life of the family. Even though students may perceive this indirect form of evaluation as more democratic than evaluation based on performance, more of their personalities are revealed and evaluated than in a visible pedagogic practice.

In the interviews, I often asked questions about the practices of the schools and the marks they received. To my surprise, many teachers and heads toned down the importance of positive or negative performances. They often argued that when students worked together in groups, marks showed neither their individual progress nor their social ability. Hence, they merely demonstrated a limited part of their performance. Some progressive teachers and heads even wished they had no examinations in the lower secondary schools. When the students' performances are evaluated by means of specific criteria, in for example, public examinations or national tests (based on a visible pedagogy), the results demonstrate differences between students. Then low achievers are likely to be more discouraged than when students are evaluated for progress in relation to their past performances.

In an invisible pedagogy, both equality as human beings (Bernstein, 1996) and the uniqueness of every individual are stressed. In this practice, the criteria for evaluation are diffuse, and teachers may give positive responses whatever the students perform (Riksaasen, 1999). Compared with, for example, American schools, Norwegian schools have restricted focus on credits and marks (Riksaasen, 2007). The Norwegian teachers do not emphasize learning aims and learning objectives or the criteria for evaluation like American teachers. The more diffuse the criteria for evaluation, the more invisible the pedagogy (Bernstein, 1977).

Leading Educational Change

An aim of the project was to explore how heads worked when they initiated educational change. The study shows that they selected different strategies, and it is possible to distinguish between four main groups of heads: the facilitators, the excellent teachers, the positional heads and the entrepreneurs. In addition, teachers were informal leaders.

The facilitators

The heads who were facilitators invited teachers to propose projects. Leadership was exercised by involving teachers as much as possible in decisions affecting them, but firm decisions were still taken in the light of objectives and values. In an interview, a lower secondary school headmaster described how he worked:

> At the beginning of January, we decided to start the next school year in a different way. We had no ideas about how we would work in the autumn. We started to consider the matter and looked at what other schools were doing. We collected ideas, and at Easter I suggested the teachers should start at 8 in the morning and work 35 hours a week. I also suggested we should introduce flexible lessons. The whole staff said they were not interested in this at present....I decided I would not give in. I said we would start with the 8th form this autumn. If anybody wanted to take part in the experiment, they should inform me....Eight teachers were interested. There is always someone who wants to take part....

Through voluntary participation, this lower secondary school introduced flexible lessons in the 8th form, optional courses and differentiated teaching. The parents supported the work of the progressive teachers in the first year. Colleagues became interested in the positive results, and the practices in this school changed in the course of three years.

A similar development could be observed in three other lower secondary schools. The most progressive teachers, the forerunners (Rogers, 1962), started working in a team at a specific level in the school. They became the supporters of the head. In some schools, the teams divided and the entrepreneurs became leaders of new teams. In other schools, the progressive teams continued their work while colleagues continued their conservative practices. Both heads and teachers stressed the importance of teachers taking part in the process of change on their own premises.

The excellent teachers

The facilitators invited teachers to propose projects. Even though some of these heads knew how they wanted to change the existing practice, they initially toned down their own viewpoints. In four schools, we met heads who were excellent teachers. They often invited teachers to discussions on education, but they initiated and defined projects or new teaching methods themselves. The excellent teachers were especially enthusiastic and interested in education and had been competent teachers and local educational consultants. They might help teachers to initiate new teaching methods in their classroom, or give talks on educational topics themselves. In other words, they were excellent teachers for their own staff. In an interview, one of these heads described how she talked when she wanted to motivate her teachers to introduce a new teaching method—'station teaching':

> I said: Will it be possible? Can someone consider? I had a long list of words. I am rather impatient. I had to make notes for myself and read them before I talked to the staff to avoid saying should, must, ought to, don't you agree, instead of will it be possible, could someone consider....all words that help people make a choice.

The headmistress said that three things are important when you are dealing with teachers who resist change. Firstly, you must speak like a colleague and not be hierarchical and you must use a loyal approach. Secondly, you have to make it clear that this is an important task for you: You believe in the project yourself and it is most interesting. Thirdly, you have to stress the positive effects you have observed earlier. When you work with non-conformists, they must be able to make choices all the time. Teachers dislike orders from a head. You may think of six new methods and ask if the teachers will try two of them for half a year.

This is an example of a headmistress who uses an indirect form of control (according to invisible pedagogy) when she initiates change. A group of teachers in the school said they experienced freedom because they always took part in discussions. They also felt secure and enjoyed learning all the time. Before the headmistress started a project, she followed majority decisions. A local study indicated that the school staff felt well suited for their job.

The positional heads

Three of the heads seemed to be more positional or hierarchical than their colleagues. In the interviews, they talked about institutional aims, their model of organisation and bureaucratic decision structures. In one of the schools, I heard the headmaster use commands when he talked to a group of teachers. I also observed three teachers in the same school cooperating in a third form. In the classroom, students could sit in an 'amphitheatre-like setting,' around tables working in groups, or work individually in a separate room. This was the most progressive classroom I have ever seen. The teachers nevertheless taught traditionally. The progressive set up thus became a backdrop for a conservative practice. In an interview, I asked about this observation. The teachers preferred an old-fashioned classroom with students seated at desks. When I asked whether the teachers had influenced the set up of their classroom, one replied:

> Yes, but when decisions have been taken, we have to do our best. It's all right and we are positive. When the system is like this, there's nothing to be done about it. It was more difficult at the beginning....

At the same time as these teachers said they had influence, they said decisions had been taken. During the interview, we learnt that a former head and a former chief education officer had decided to introduce a 'progressive' practice. The present head, who was young and a former teacher in the same school, followed up with a positional leadership style.

Lingard et al. (2003) uses habitus (Bourdieu, 1992) as a basis for analysing leadership. People internalise social structures so that the way they perceive the world—their unconscious schemes of perception—embody the historical structures that exist.

The three positional heads worked in schools in areas where most parents worked in industry or were farmers. In Bernstein's terms, the parents worked near the material base, and the students (and teachers) were probably socialised by means of a visible pedagogy. If so, it might be difficult to introduce an invisible pedagogy and thus change codes and habitus in the school. Educational codes as well as habitus are considered to be class-based.

The entrepreneurs

The three heads characterised as entrepreneurs worked in upper secondary schools. They had all been managers in trade and industry. They were all involved in local and private activities outside school, and stressed how trade and industry in the local community influenced the recruitment of students and teaching. In an interview, one of the headmasters described how he initiated a project where students worked in the workshop of a private company. During this period, they were able to consider what subjects they were interested in. Later on, the teachers used examples from the workshop in their teaching. The project was practicable because the headmaster knew the manager of the company.

In general, the entrepreneurs emphasised weak classification between school and society. In addition, they stressed the importance of subject integration, especially in technical college, and they initiated project work. Because these heads worked in large schools, they often had to delegate tasks to deputies. Several teachers criticised these deputies because changes seemed to be restricted to selected departments.

The four groups of heads mentioned above are not exclusive categories: Some heads worked more as teachers for their staff than others. We also met five heads who were more psychologically oriented than their colleagues. They often had their office door open and emphasised continual interaction with their teachers. Their focus was mainly on the informal part of the organisation. Four of the primary school heads were newly appointed. They were not a homogeneous group.

The informal leaders

In four schools, one teacher, or a group of teachers, had initiated projects. In a primary school, two teachers had initiated both outdoor teaching and workshop teaching. The headmaster was initially sceptical to these projects, but when he saw how they worked in practice, he became enthusiastic and supported the efforts.

In a lower secondary school, a group of teachers had introduced private study periods and flexible school time. In an interview, a teacher described how three different heads had supported this project. The first sanctioned it, but did not become involved in the work. The second was enthusiastic, and encouraged the teachers on their premises. The third and current headmaster laid emphasis on change, but was a positional leader. For example, his decision that all the teachers should use computers caused conflicts. However, when the teachers learnt to use e-mail, everyone was proud. There was tension between this headmaster and the teachers, but no serious conflicts.

In every school, we met informal leaders who initiated change. These were often competent teachers with relatively long experience. They cooperated with younger teachers. The informal leaders who resisted change were often older teachers. Trade union leaders seemed to have strong influence, and sometimes caused conflicts, especially if they resisted change.

Conflicts between Teachers

The premises for school development in the demonstration schools seem to be cooperation between teachers and time to plan things together. Teachers had to spend more time in school. Unless they were teaching, Norwegian teachers have had freedom to work at home. When heads invite volunteers to take part in projects, trade union leaders give their support even if a volunteer wants fixed working hours in school. However, if someone initiates a project and proposes that everyone should stay in school for 30 hours a week, conflicts is often experienced. In a lower secondary school, with fixed working hours, the head said it had been terrible to spend time discussing time. When I asked whether the discussion concerned firm opposition to extra work, the head confirmed this. Teachers, who have worked in the same way for 25 years, do not want new teaching methods. In this school, conflicts could be observed during lunch. The oldest teachers and laggers were sitting at their own table.

Several heads complained that some teachers had problems when they were expected to accept majority decisions. Teachers are used to taking matters up again. Especially in the upper secondary schools, teachers of traditional subjects had problems with subject integration and new teaching methods. One head told me:

> Most teachers have got used to the change, and have become better at their job. But I will not deny that some, especially science teachers, do not share our opinion....There is also a language teacher who is very popular among the students. We have to allow him to close the door of his classroom. He cannot understand what other teachers are going to do in his room....

According to the head, this language teacher is an excellent traditional teacher. He can spellbind the students for 45 minutes. The school really needs his competence, but every teacher is expected to use several teaching methods and show his colleagues how he works. An invisible pedagogic practice is often more visible to colleagues than a visible one. When the school stresses learning by cooperation, or the students use computers, the language teacher feels he has no contribution to make. Sitting there, listening, he considers himself a loser. Previously, he only received credit for his teaching. In the terms of Bernstein's theory, he has lost power and control.

Discussion—Learning and Teaching

In this chapter, we have outlined how the practices of invisible pedagogies and integrated codes have contributed to positive learning experiences for students as well as for the teachers. In 18 of the 22 demonstration schools, the heads and teachers had made efforts to change educational codes from collection codes in the direction of integrated codes. In schools dominated by an integrated code, the heads often seemed to use indirect forms of control to initiate educational change. Since educational codes are tacitly acquired (Bernstein, 1977, Riksaasen, 1999), heads should probably not use a hierarchical discourse to compel teachers to be more democratic. They can only help the teachers to learn by acting as models for their staff. Teachers will always have relative autonomy (Bernstein, 1977), and their classroom practices may differ from the 'dominating voice' in a school.

In the interviews, several teachers emphasised how they preferred subject integration, teamwork and collaboration. The teachers also described how they shared both positive and negative experiences with colleagues and the head. They were not worried about making mistakes. In 15 of the schools, the teachers, who took part in interviews, seemed to emphasise extended teacher professionalism.

Lieberman takes a professional learning perspective on school improvement. She examines the creation of 'a school culture of inquiry wherein professional learning is expected, sought after, and an ongoing part of teaching' (1995). This study shows that many demonstration schools may be called learning organisations. If schools are learning organisations, we must compare the learning of the students with the learning of the teachers (Karstens, 2000). Good heads work as teachers for their staff (Tiller, 1989).

A parallel to the individual selection of courses and tasks by students is the invitations made by heads to teachers to take part in projects. Voluntary participation is positive. However, both heads and teachers must take individual differences into consideration. In a lower secondary school, the head, who had been concerned with developing the school for 10 years, said that some teachers could not bear the initial chaos that often arises when new teaching methods are introduced.

McGregor (1960) distinguished between theory X: you look upon individuals as lazy; and theory Y: you consider individuals as initiators with loyalties. Some teachers use strict discipline and hierarchical leadership because they look upon students as lazy. Other teachers react negatively whatever is done. These laggers responded by withdrawal when they interacted with students.

Since I wanted to focus on good practices, I often observed the teaching of the 'forerunners' and the 'late adopters.' Sometimes the teaching of late adopters was difficult to evaluate. Positive feedback given to their progressive colleagues had inspired them to start changing, but some of them had not really learnt the indirect forms of control or the new teaching methods. The conservative practice of the laggers was easy to evaluate. In several demonstration schools, it was possible to see that school development was restricted to certain departments or levels.

During teacher training, students are often encouraged to teach according to a collection code and a visible pedagogy (Riksaasen, 1999). New teachers therefore have to learn an integrated code in school. Professionals continually learn on the job because their work entails involvement in a succession of cases, problems or projects that they have to learn about. However, the knowledge base of the professional may be relatively static or develop quite rapidly (Eraut, 1994).

Many teachers and heads in this study stressed the importance of subject integration for low achievers by, for example, introducing mathematics in the workshop. The teachers also underlined the importance of individually differentiated learning. Students, who are low achievers in a subject and/or are socially reticent, may have difficulty concentrating. In the old school, such students just sat at their desks with their heads more or less empty. Now they are more visible, walking around. A mentor must hang on their shoulders to help select tasks. Teachers, who change educational codes, learn that no practice gives priority to everyone. Some pupils simply need to be directed by means of fixed rules and hierarchical forms of control (visible pedagogy).

We have mentioned how Bernstein looked upon conflicts between visible and invisible pedagogies as conflicts between fractions of the middle class. The pedagogic practices of the working class parents, and especially the working class fathers, have probably been the visible pedagogy with an explicit form of control (Riksaasen, 1999). According to Bernstein (1996), a visible pedagogy is easier to 'read' for all groups of students.

However, educational codes may change in families and economic life. Then the educational code in school must change. Old forms of control and rituals do not work (Bernstein, 1976). In schools, it may be a shift from a social order resting upon domination to one resting upon co-operation, and this shift is related to a shift in the character of work relations in an advanced industrialised society (Bernstein, 1977).

In Norway today, bureaucratic institutions, outside school, are often replaced by flat network organisations. Workers should be able to make their own decisions at the same time as they should be met with respect and individual support. Sørhaug (1996) describes the typical Norwegian way of giving commands in the field of economics. Often we say: 'please,' 'when you have the opportunity to,' 'do you think?' These statements appeal to agreement, arguments and a horizontal reciprocity (corresponding to invisible pedagogy). A study by Dahlberg (1992) shows how parent–child interaction in the Nordic family has changed from obedience and subordination to a more reciprocal and empathetic relationship, especially in the new middle class.

When I walked through the schools while students were working individually or in groups, they reminded me more of office employees than of students in a traditional school. Teaching according to an integrated code seems to prepare students for work in both postmodern organisations and families.

The indirect form of control in an invisible pedagogy, based on relations rather than on principles, is an alternative form of control. When the teachers acted as supervisors and worked together with the students, the interactions between teachers and students became more positive. However, an invisible pedagogy is always mixed with visible pedagogy. For example, when heads invited teachers to participate voluntarily in projects, they paved the way for professional learning using invisible pedagogy. If someone refused to use the new methods after the voluntary period, the heads could be hierarchical when they asked the teachers to use the methods or get another job. They could also be very explicit when they referred to national curricula that emphasised new teaching methods, or to criteria for evaluation.

The appointment of demonstration schools combined with national tests may be a move towards a more market oriented pedagogy in Norway. But the political signals are ambiguous. Teachers and heads in the demonstration schools often toned down the importance of marks. Their main focuses were on development of positive learning environments and individually differentiated learning.

Since Norwegian students score low on PISA and 17% of the differences between students can be related to family background (Kjærnsli, 2007), school development and educational change have been in focus both in the official and pedagogic recontextualizing field. The social class differences can be observed in the same classroom or in the same school. Because nearly all students in Norway go to public schools with a common national curriculum, the differences between schools are small.

The conflicts between visible and invisible pedagogies are not only conflicts between teachers in the demonstration schools or fractions of the middle class, but conflicts between groups working with education in Norway. Kjærnsli (2005) argues that a democratic movement in society has contributed to that learning may be replaced by activities. The learning aims are not clear neither for teachers nor students.

Finnish students in contrast to Norwegian students score highest in the world on the PISA tests (Kjærnsli, 2007). In Finland, the correlation between the students' school results and their family background is weaker than in any other Nordic country. According to a recent study of a Finnish school (Riksaasen, 2009), the teaching is based on a visible pedagogy. The Finnish teachers stress the use of textbooks, the students work individually or in couples and the teaching is strictly directed by the teachers. The relationship between teacher and students is hierarchical, and subject integration or project work is difficult to observe. Several studies support these findings. Haug (2008) argues that the Finnish schools are like the Norwegian schools 30 years ago. However, the visible pedagogy and the high test scores on PISA in Finland are bought at a price. The Finnish students score low when they are invited to evaluate their well-being, self-confidence and safety in school.

Since the Finnish students are dissatisfied with their learning environment, several Norwegians professors of education and politicians, like the teachers in the demonstration schools, argue that there should not be too strong focus on marks and formal knowledge. For example, Ogden (2008) states that it should be a balance between the development of the students' social competencies and the stress on teaching of subjects. Nordahl (2008) proposes that the most important knowledge students acquire in school, is knowledge about themselves.

It is easy to see that the demonstration schools were appointed as effective schools in a typical Norwegian context.

Rustique-Forrester (2005) shows how increased testing and school ranking systems contributed to higher levels of students' exclusion in England. The testing pressures led to a narrowing of the curriculum and to the marginalization of low-performing students. A comparison of higher and lower excluding schools found that staff in the lower-excluding schools had extensive network of academic and social support structures for struggling students; they had a highly collaborative staff culture, and a school ethos aimed at valuing students as individuals. In Norway, the demonstration schools should be the schools that resist the testing pressures most.

Acknowledgement

Thanks due to the Norwegian Board of Education for financial support to this project.

References

Berg, G. (1999). *Skolekultur. Nøkkelen til skolens utvikling*. Oslo: AdNotam Gyldendal.

Bernstein, B. (1977). *Class Codes and Control Vol. III. Towards a Theory of Educational Transmissions.* London: Routledge.
Bernstein, B. (1990). *The Structuring of Pedagogic Discourse. Class, Codes and Control*, Vol. IV. London: Routledge.
Bernstein, B. (1996). *Pedagogy, Symbolic Control and Identity.* London: Taylor and Francis.
Bordieu, P. et al. (1992). *An Invitation to Reflexive Sociology.* Cambridge: Polity Press.
Clegg, S. R. (1990); Modern organizations. *Organization Studies in the Postmodern World.* London: Sage.
Dahlberg, G. (1992). Child–parent relationship and socialization in the context of modern childhood. Paper presented at the 5th European Conference on Developmental Psychology in Seville, 6–9 September 1992.
Det kongelige kirke- utdannings og forskningsdepartement (1996). Læreplan for grunnskole, videregående opplæring, voksenopplæring. Generell del.
Eraut, M. (1994). *Developing Professional Knowledge and Competence.* London: The Falmer Press.
Haug, P. (2008). Dagsavisen. Oslo 25.09.2008.
Karstens, S. (2000). Dutch primary schools and the concept of the learning organization. The Learning Organization, 7, no. 3/2000.
Kjærnsli, M. et al (2005). Hva forteller PISA undersøkelsen om norske skoler? Skolepolitikk. Oslo. Horisont no. 2, Næringspolitisk tidsskrift.
Kjærnsli, M. et al (2007): Tid for tunge løft. Norske elevers kompetanse i naturfag, lesing og matematikk i PISA 2006. Oslo: Universitetsforlaget.
Lieberman, A. (1995). Practices that support teacher development. Transforming conceptions of professional education. *Phi Delta Kappan* 76, 591–596.
Lingard, B et al. (2003). *Leading Learning.* Maidenheadmaster: Open University Press.
McGregor, D. (1960). *The Human Side of Enterprise.* New York: McGraw-Hill.
Metz, M.H. (1986) *Different by Design. The Context and Character of Three Magnet Schools.* New York and London: Routledge and Kaegan Paul.
Mullis, I.V.S. (2007). *IEA's Progress in International Reading Literacy Study in Primary School in 40 Countries.* Chestnut Hill, MA: TIMSS & PIRLS International Study Center, Boston College.
Nordahl, T. (2008). Dagsavisen, Oslo. 25.09.2008.
Ogden, T. (2008). Kvalitetsskolen. Oslo. Gyldendal akademisk.
PISA 2003: Problemløsing hovedrapport. OECD (2004): Problem Solving for Tomorrow's World—First Measures of Cross Curricular Competencies from PISA 2003 Paris: OECD Publications.
Riksaasen, R. (1999). Visible and invisible pedagogies in teacher education. A comparison of Norwegian primary and pre-school teacher education. Dr.polit. avhandling Trondheim: Inst. for Sosiologi og Statsvitenskap, NTNU Norges teknisk-naturvitenskapelige universitet.
Riksaasen, R.(2005). *Ny pedagogikk i praksis.* Trondheim: Tapir.
Riksaasen,R.(2007). En sammenligning av norsk og amerikansk lærerutdanning. I: *FoU i* Praksis 2007. Rapport fra konferanse om praksisrettet FoU i lærerutdanning. Trondheim 19. og 20. April 2007. Tapir Akademisk Forlag. pp. 293–306.
Riksaasen, R. (2009). A Comparison of pedagogic practices in Finnish and Norwegian school schools. Study in progress.
Rogers, E.M. (1962). *Diffusion of Innovations.* New York: The Free Press.
Rossvær, T.(1985): Organisasjonsteorier i sosiologisk belysning. Oslo: Juul Møller Forlag a/s.

Rustique-Forrester, E. (2005): Accountability and the Pressures To Exclude: A Cautionary Tale from England. Education Policy Analysis Archives vol. 13, no. 26, April 2005.
Sørhaug, T. (1996). *Om ledelse*. Oslo: Universitetsforlaget.
Tiller, T. (1989). *Ledelse i en skole i utvikling*. Oslo: Tano.
Tyler, W. (1988). *School Organisation. A Sociological Perspective*. London: Croom Helm.

CHAPTER FOURTEEN

Bernstein and Empirical Research

SALLY POWER

The focus of this chapter is the relationship between Basil Bernstein's theories and empirical research. It has often struck me as paradoxical that his theories are so little used within the sociology of education. As many of the chapters in this volume indicate, his work has enormous potential for addressing enduring debates and dilemmas within social science and education. And yet this potential remains largely unrealised.

In considering the relationship between his theories and empirical research, it would be easy to undertake an analysis based on Bernsteinian concepts. For example, one might ask questions about the strength of classification and framing within the research field; about the extent and processes of the recontextualisation of Bernstein's ideas; about their languages of description. However, it is possible that recasting the analysis in Bernsteinian language might perhaps be part of the problem and not the solution. Rather than attempt, therefore, a Bernsteinian analysis of Bernstein's legacy, the chapter asks much simpler questions:

What is the nature of the relationship between Bernstein's work and empirical research?

Why is Bernstein's work used in this way?

What, if anything, can be done about it?

Bernstein and Empirical Research

Bernstein himself was notoriously parsimonious in both his use of and reference to empirical research. Empirical reference was often of the following kind:

> Where the classification and frames were relatively strong, one would expect that if a pupil presented some work to the teacher which the teacher thought was unexpectedly good, he/she might say 'That's a very good piece of work. Did you do it by yourself?' Whereas if the classification, and especially the framing, was relatively weak in the same situation, the teacher might say, 'That was really exciting. Did you do it by yourself?' If the pupil said that he did, the teacher than might add, 'You might had got even more out of it if you had talked it over with some of the group? (1977: 9)
>
> Consider an infant school, fifty years ago...They may be drawing or painting figures, houses, etc. the teacher looks...and says 'That's a very good house, but *where* is the chimney.' . In some infant schools today...the teacher here is less likely to say 'What's that? (1977:119).
>
> Or the famous: 'Imagine four lavatories.' (1977: 153)

In these extracts, Bernstein generates fictional rooms and props and whole imagined conversations to illustrate the analytic distinctions. These references are genuinely illuminating and reveal the complexion of what he is trying to capture. However, they can hardly count as empirical support.

In his later writings (e.g. 1990, 1995, 1996), and perhaps in response to criticisms of the lack of empirical support (e.g. King 1983), Bernstein tries strongly to demonstrate the empirical applications of his work. However, there are a number of interesting aspects about this demonstration.

Firstly, it is very rarely research he has undertaken himself—certainly during the last 20 years. Secondly, and as indicated by Davies and Fitz in this volume, it tends to have been undertaken by a small cadre of PhD students. Thirdly, and relatedly, it has been undertaken under his supervision. For example, Bernstein (1995, 387–388) refers to the research conducted by the Sociological Research Unit *'under my direction'*; to Jenkins' research *'under my supervision'*; to that of Cox, *'who also worked under my supervision.'*

Although this partly reflects the close supervision which Bernstein's students enjoyed, it is quite an unusual way of developing a portfolio of evidence. For the last 30 years, sociological research has increasingly been based upon external project grants. The development of empirical support through doctoral theses also gives the impression of a campaign undertaken by a (small) army of empirical foot-soldiers under the direction of the theoretical general.[1] It also unintentionally contributes to a situation in which the development of a Bernsteinian research agenda appears to be more associated with testing the usefulness his theories rather than using them to address contemporary social problems.

The Use of Bernstein in Empirical Research

This form of empirical development of his ideas has hardly changed since he died in 2000. In order to explore how often and in what ways his research has been developed, I have undertaken an examination of Bernstein citations in the *British Journal of Sociology of Education* since 2000. Although this journal does not of course represent the field as a whole, it is one in which he himself published a number of papers and perhaps the outlet in which one might expect the greatest reference to his work.

With the exception of 2002, which saw the publication of a special issue devoted to Bernstein, the number of papers making reference to Bernstein is small, certainly when compared to the almost ubiquitous referencing of Bourdieu.

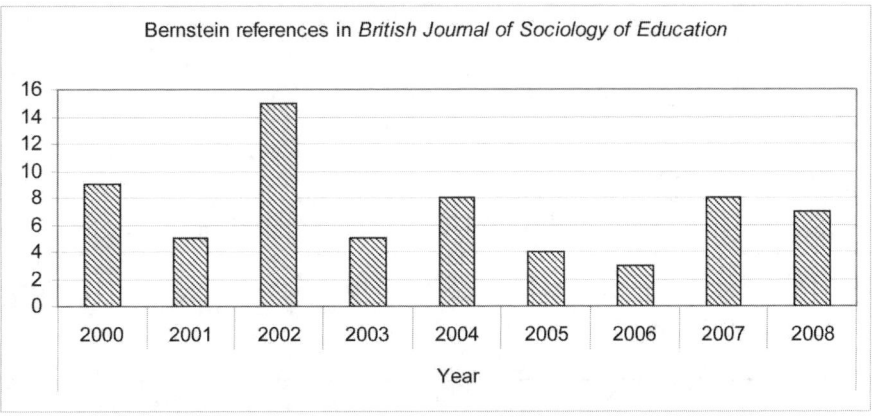

It is not only that there are relatively few references to Bernstein, it is also that he is often used in particular ways. Dowling (1999), who has undertaken a Bernsteinian-inspired analysis of those who use his ideas, identifies four 'modalities of relationship': disciples, vulgarisers, exploiters and heretics.

The voice dimension relates to the extent to which Bernstein's work is apparent in the analysis. The message dimension relates to the extent to which the author reproduces Bernstein's conceptual structures. Thus, vulgarisers reproduce but with only a weak (or superficial) grasp of his work. Disciples also reproduce, but they have a strong and deep grasp of his work. By contrast, heretics also have a strong grasp of his work, but use it to produce, rather than reproduce, new conceptual structures. Exploiters produce new conceptual structures, but with only a weak grasp of his work.

Dowling's framework points to some interesting differences, but the positioning of various authors depends largely on value-laden judgements about what is 'productive' (i.e. approved of) or 'reproductive' (i.e. implicitly disapproved of) and about what constitutes a strong (i.e. good) as opposed to a superficial (i.e. less good) grasp of Bernstein's voice. Rather than judge the uses of his work along such

	voice	
	strong	weak
message / reproduction	disciple	vulgariser
message / production	heretic	exploiter

The modality of relationship authors to Bernstein's work (from Dowling 1999: 2)

evaluative criteria, it is perhaps more useful to compare pieces of research in terms of the extent to which the underlying analysis is Bernstein-dependent or -independent. In other words, how essential is Bernstein to the analysis? Would anything be lost if the references were removed? If we were to construct a continuum, we might have work at one end of the spectrum work in which Bernstein's theories are scarcely present and are largely irrelevant to the analysis. At the other end of the spectrum is work which is so deeply embedded in Bernstein that it is impossible to grasp what is being said without a close familiarity with his theories:

Bernstein ⁻   ⁺Bernstein

Dependent 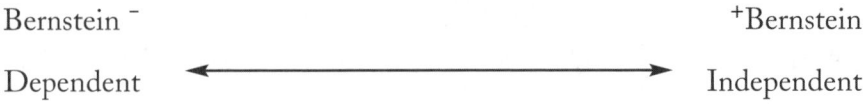 Independent

If we revisit those references to Bernstein in the *British Journal of Sociology of Education*, the largest number is Bernstein-independent. His ideas are 'mentioned in passing.' There would be no discernible difference to the analysis if the reference to his work were removed entirely. For example: Smith and Green (2004) mention Bernstein as a theorist of education. McCarthy and Dimitriadis (2000) make passing reference to Bernstein as someone who links education to reproduction. Shamai (2000) cites Bernstein as a key developer of the concept of cultural capital. Munns and MacFadden (2000) refer to the code theory paper in a footnote, but it is unclear how it relates to their analysis is any significant way. Indeed, sometimes the references are obscure or even misleading. Helland (2007) claims that Bernstein explains differences in achievement in terms of cultural deficiency in the working class, Findlow (2006) reminds us of Bernstein's claim that curriculum is a form of symbolic violence, and Swain (2003) refers to school as, according to Bernstein, 'essentially, a regulatory institution that attempts to control pupils and their bodies.' Two papers (Smith 2003; Nash 2005) make passing reference to the famous 'education cannot compensate for society' statement, but do not delve any deeper into Bernstein's position on this. Another two papers (Bird 2001, Shain and Ozga 2001) mention Bernstein when outlining a historical summary of the field.

After the Bernstein-independent work, the second largest group of papers drawing on his ideas are Bernstein-dependent. In these papers, his work provides the underpinning theoretical framework for their analysis. There are 22 of these—but it needs to be noted that ten were specially commissioned for the special issue and are, on the whole, different kinds of papers in that one of their main aims was to 'develop accessible accounts that could be used to teach his sociology of pedagogy at undergraduate and postgraduate levels' (Arnot et al., 2002: 525). One of the remaining papers is not really empirically informed. The main purpose of the remaining papers is the testing out and development of Bernstein's theories empirically in diverse settings with varied foci; from science syllabuses in Portuguese classrooms (Neves and Morais 2001), to 'Samoan' paraprofessionals in designated disadvantaged secondary schools in Australia (Singh 2001).

There are very few contributions which sit between the largely Bernstein-independent and the almost entirely Bernstein-dependent papers. These would include only a handful of those who draw on his ideas with more than a passing reference but who do not work *within* the framework. They take a more relaxed (or perhaps as Bernstein would have it 'profane') attitude towards his work. Again, the number that involve the interrogation of primary data are relatively few. But in these works, Bernstein provides one of several lenses through which data are viewed—sometimes as the researchers acknowledge (e.g. Gwimbi and Monk 2003, Nash 2005) with only limited success.

This brief analysis of the relationship between Bernstein and empirical research suggests that Bernstein is only rarely used to inform the interrogation of empirical data—except by those for whom he is the main informing theorist. In other words, you have to be 'inside' the Bernstein frame to use him. Of course, this may not in itself be a problem. However, there is not much to suggest that the number of those 'inside' the frame is growing—particularly as a significant number of the insiders were socialised into the frame through Bernstein himself. Those socialised by Bernstein himself may initiate new members through introducing doctoral students to his ideas, but this hardly represents a flourishing of Bernstein's ideas. To the outsider, the work of Bernstein may well look like some sort of exclusive club, where the gatekeeper has left and the door is locked.

The Difficulties of Applying Bernstein

One reason for the lack of empirical development of Bernstein's work can probably be laid at the door of Bernstein himself. During his life, Bernstein was often highly critical of those who used his ideas. He appeared to create a strong distinction between those who followed his work from within and those who selectively appropriated (or misappropriated) it from outside. The latter, he rather dismissively referred to as 'critics,' 'recyclers,' 'interpreters,' 'secondary servicers' and 'schizzers' (Bernstein 1990: 7–8).

Not surprisingly, those of us who used Bernstein had to exercise a high degree of caution while he was alive and acting as a guardian of his own ideas. One might have expected that after his death, there would be a renewed interest in his work, not only because death encourages one to reappraise an individual's contribution, but also because he could no longer disapprove of the (mis-)appropriation of his ideas. That this has not happened means that we must look beyond the man to the ideas.

Perhaps the most obvious problem with Bernstein's work is the difficulty of the language and the abstractness of the concepts. This is something which has been widely acknowledged—even by Bernstein himself. His language is not only opaque at times, but also his theories (and their subsequent elaboration and refinement) appear to have a life of their own. Despite his assertion that the purpose of sociology was 'to create news' (Bernstein 1977: 157), his own work became increasingly focused on itself. It displays 'a strong tendency to reside in the internal' (Dowling 1999: 15).

This makes it extraordinarily difficult for novices to get to grips with—as those of us who have taught sociology of education courses know only too well. It may well be that the complexity of Bernstein's concepts requires a lengthy induction that is difficult to realise in contemporary education and sociology courses. However, even for old hands, Bernstein is difficult. Of course the difficulty and abstract properties of the language reflect the complexity of the relations that are trying to be grasped and an attempt to provide precision. This is not therefore a criticism, but rather pointing to an obstacle.

However, the very demand for precision, particularly when dealing with the messiness of the social world, creates its own difficulties. As in many other ways, Bernstein's position on this is profoundly paradoxical. On the one hand, Bernstein (1977) is clear that, within sociology in general and sociology of education in particular, explanations will inevitably be weak. Indeed, in response to Michael Apple's assertion that empirical research can only be based on 'a coherent theory of class relations,' Bernstein points out that waiting for a coherent theory 'would rapidly bring all empirical research to an end. Empirical research would be replaced by the scholarly search for coherence and ideological correctness.' (Bernstein 1995: 386)

On the other hand, despite exhorting others to ignore theoretical gaps and inconsistencies, he was continually trying to refine his own ideas and concepts to the point where he could provide almost mathematical formulae. For example, the 'formulation for specifying specific code modalities' (1996: 194) is:

$$\frac{0^{E/R}}{\pm C^{ie} / \pm F^{ie}}$$

This search for perhaps spurious precision has arguably also led to particular limits within the analysis. For example, while the (usually) twofold oppositional distinctions he makes have a satisfying analytical clarity about them, they are difficult to spot in real life. Pring (1975: 71) has argued that his categories are 'empty' and claims that Bernstein fails to appreciate the process of using binary oppositions as a basis for comparison and contrast 'must assume that the differences within the types are less important than the differences between the two types.' As Pring points out, just because something called X isn't the same as Y, it doesn't mean that all non-Xs are Ys.

Of course, with all empirical research there is a danger of selectively using data to fit the theory, but perhaps this is particularly acute with Bernstein's theories. As Tyler (1988: 159) has argued, Bernstein's work

> generates its own methodological principles which make any 'objective' empirical test to some degree self-validating.

If you don't begin with the methodological principles, it's hard to get any kind of fit. The ongoing research that colleagues and I have been undertaking on the educational biographies of a cohort of young men and women (Power et al 2003) appears at first sight to lend itself well to a Bernsteinian analysis. However, a recent attempt (Power 2006) to locate our 300 respondents within Bernstein's typology of pedagogic identities proved extremely difficult. From the entire sample, I could only find five students to illustrate the different modes of identity, and even with these five, the connections were often somewhat tenuous.

The difficulty of matching data to the theory is recognised by Dowling (2005: 17) in relation to Bernstein's theory of vertical and horizontal discourses:

> The empirical is not absent in his theory building, but appears, shall we say, hazily. His description of vertical and horizontal discourses is illustrative…the difficulty arises when we try to assign empirical instances to locations in the network.

Dowling goes on to argue that the theoretical abstraction of the 'principles' divorces the phenomenon under investigation from the context in which it is produced. Empirical research is reduced to principle-spotting:

> The fetishising of knowledge—or indeed of discourse—as an entity or entities that have an existence that is in some sense independent of the actual practices with which it or they are being associated may be a helpful initial organising move in thinking about cultural regularity. It seems to me, however, to be a very unhelpful move if we have any interest in engaging with the empirical. Bernstein takes possession of the empirical only to enable him to ignore its voice. Bernstein's structure [of horizontal and vertical discourses] is anti-empirical pigeonholing. (17)

Of course, there are different ways in which theoretical engagement with the empirical can be realised. While some may privilege the integrity of the theory over the empirical, others (including myself) would rather privilege the integrity of the empirical over the theoretical.

Conclusion

The purpose of this chapter is not to try to prove whether Bernstein was 'right' or 'wrong'—this in itself would be to fall into the trap of the 'paradigms approach' of which he himself was so critical (Bernstein 1977). The purpose is rather to explore how we can develop a more productive relationship between Bernstein's work and empirical research. Indeed, this is something that he himself always wanted. As Atkinson (2001) has pointed out, Bernstein does not deserve the fate of most dead sociologists—reverence or amnesia. Bernstein's ideas have always been intended to drive a programme of original inquiry.

The potential of his ideas is clearly evident in this collection. For example, Daniels shows the potential of Bernstein's analytical tools for the empirical study of hybridity in multi-agency settings. Maton's exposition of the significance of knowledge structures for illuminating knowledge-building in the humanities is compelling, as is Gamble's illustration of the significance of classification and framing for analysing the distinctive nature of apprenticeship models. And yet, if the promise held out by papers such as these is to be realised beyond the relatively small circle of 'Bernsteinians,' something needs to shift within the field.

Rather than constantly refining his theories, we need to become more active 'critics,' 'recyclers,' 'interpreters,' 'secondary servicers' and 'schizzers' of his work. Perhaps his ideas need more vulgarisation and exploitation, as well as heresy. There is, after all, no clear and unambiguous dividing line between recontextualisation and misrecognition and the only way to avoid misrecognition is never to use Bernstein at all. As Dowling (1999) points out, Bernstein himself was a recontextualiser of ideas as he selectively incorporated elements from sociologists as diverse as Durkheim and Goffman.

Bernstein clearly disapproves of 'schizzing,' whereby 'the unity of an original corpus is split into at least two' and elements are subjected to 'discursive repression.' However, it may be the only way forward. Some of his corpus is better than others and some of it contradicts other bits (Dowling 1999; Power 2006). In Bernstein's own words, 'we need less an allegiance to an approach, and more a dedication to a problem' (1977:171).

Acknowledgements

I am grateful for the comments of Paul Dowling, Alan Sadovnik and the anonymous reviewer for commenting on this chapter and for their suggestions.

Note

1. The hierarchy of positioning is also evident in the texts themselves. As Dowling (2005) notes, the 'junior players' 'can only ever aspire to footnoted appearances' (22).

References

Arnot, M. et al (2002) 'Editorial,' 23 (4), 525–526.
Atkinson, P. (2001) 'The legacy of Basil Bernstein,' in Power et al (eds) *A Tribute to Basil Bernstein 1924–2000*, London: Institute of Education.
Bernstein, B. (1977) *Class, Codes and Control Vol 3: Towards a Theory of Cultural Transmissions* (Second Edition). London: Routledge and Kegan Paul.
Bernstein, S. (1990) *Class, Codes and Control Vol 4: The Structuring of Pedagogic Knowledge*. London: Routledge.
Bernstein, B. (1995) 'A response,' in A. Sadovnik (ed.), *Knowledge and Pedagogy: The sociology of Basil Bernstein*, Norwood, NJ: Ablex Publishing.

Bernstein, B. (1996) *Pedagogy, Symbolic Control and Identity: Theory, Research, Critique*. London: Taylor & Francis.
Bird, E. (2001) 'Disciplining the Interdisciplinary: radicalism and the academic curriculum, *British Journal of Sociology of Education* 22 (4) 463–478.
Dowling, P. (1999) 'Basil Bernstein in frame: 'Oh dear, is this a structuralist analysis.' http://homepage.mac.com/paulcdowling/ioe/publications/ . Accessed 4 April 2006.
Dowling, P. (2005) 'Treacherous departures,' http://homepage.mac.com/paulcdowling/ioe/publications/. Accessed 15 March 2006.
Findlow, S. (2006) 'Higher education and linguistic dualism in the Arab Gulf, *British Journal of Sociology of Education*, 27 (1) 19–36.
Gwimbi, E. and Monk, M. (2003) 'The reproduction of social stratification in Zimbabwe: a study of the attitudes and practices of A-level biology teachers in Harare.' *British Journal of Sociology of Education* 24 (1) 21–54.
Helland, H. (2007) 'How does social background affect the grands and grade careers of Norwegian economics students,' *British Journal of Sociology of Education* 28 (4) 489–504.
King, R. (1983) *The sociology of school organisation*, London: Methuen.
McCarthy, C. and Dimitriadis, G. (2000) 'Governmentality and the sociology of education: media, education policy and the politics of resentment' *British Journal of Sociology of Education* 21 (2) 169–185.
Munns G. and MacFadden, M (2000) 'First chance, second chance or last chance? Resistance and response to education' *British Journal of Sociology of Education* 21 (1) 59–75.
Nash, R. (2005) 'The cognitive *habitus*: its place in a realise account of inequality/difference,' *British Journal of Sociology of Education* 26 (5) 599–612.
Neves, I. P. and Morais, A. M. (2001) 'Knowledges and values in science syllabusis: a sociological study of educational reform,' *British Journal of Sociology of Education* 22 (4) 531–556.
Power, S., Edwards, T., Whitty, G. and Wigfall, V. (2003) *Education and the middle class*, Buckingham: Open University Press.
Power, S. (2006) 'Disembedded middle class pedagogic identities' in R. Moore, M. Arnot, J. Beck and H. Daniels (eds) *Knowledge, power and educational reform: applying the sociology of Basil Bernstein*, LondonL. London: Routledge.
Pring, R. (1975) 'Bernstein's classification and framing of knowledge,' *Scottish Educational Studies*, November 67–74.
Shamai, S. (2000) 'Cultural shift: the case of Jewish religious education in Israel,' *British Journal of Sociology of Education* 21 (3) 401–417.
Shain, F. and Ozga, J. (2001 'Identity crisis? problems and issues in the sociology of education,' *British Journal of Sociology of Education* 22 (1) 109–120.
Singh, P. (2001) 'Speaking about cultural difference and school disadvantage: an interview study of 'Samoan' paraprofessionals in designated disadvantaged secondary schools in Australia,' *British Journal of Sociology of Education*, 22 (3) 317–338.
Smith, A. and Green, K. (2004) 'Including pupils with special educational needs in secondary school physical education: a sociological analysis of teachers' views.' 25(5) 593–608.
Smith, E. (2003) 'Ethos, Habitus and Situation for Learning: an ecology.' *British Journal of Sociology of Education* 24 (4) 463–470.
Swain, J. (2003) 'How young schoolboys become somebody: the role of the body in the construction of masculinity.' *British Journal of Sociology of Education* 24 (3) 299–314.
Tyler, W. (1988) *School Organisation: A sociological perspective*. London, Croom Helm.

CHAPTER FIFTEEN

Pedagogic Translations

Dominant Pedagogic Modes and
Teacher Professional Identity

PARLO SINGH AND JESSICA HARRIS

INTRODUCTION

The issue of teacher professional identity under conditions of global knowledge capitalism has received extensive attention in recent times. Much of the literature has argued that there is a need for more teacher autonomy and advocated for an agenda variously described as 'informed professionalism' (Barber, 2002), 'democratic professionalism' (Whitty, 2006) and 'activist professionalism' (Avis, 2005, Sachs, 2000). At the same time, a number of educational researchers have proposed that the emergence of new forms of liquid global capitalism demand new modes of pedagogy, variously described as 'globalizing' (McCarthy and Dimitriades, 2000), 'productive' (Lingard and Mills, 2002) and 'reconciliation' (Hattam, 2004). In this chapter, we summarise Basil Bernstein's theories of the totally pedagogised society and pedagogic modalities and ask what these theoretical concepts have to offer the debates about teacher professional identity under conditions of liquid modernity (Bauman, 2004; Urry, 2003). In doing so, we challenge some of the assertions made in the previous chapter that Bernsteinian concepts have little empirical relevance (see Power, this volume).

Global Knowledge Society, Performativity and Uncertainty

A number of theorists have written about the knowledge or information society and economy (see for example, Uluorta and Quill, 2009). These theorists argue that we live in new historical times characterised by specific forms of social organisation 'in which information generation, processing, and transmission become the fundamental sources of productivity and power because of new technological conditions' (Castells, 2000: 21). The defining characteristics of the global knowledge economy have been described as the increased knowledge intensity of the processes of creation, production and distribution of all goods and services—with knowledge building on knowledge (Considine, Marginson, Sheehan and Kummick 2001). Bonal and Rambla (2003: 174) argued that:

> In flexible capitalism, rapid production and circulation of knowledge becomes a crucial input for economic performance. Knowledge becomes a raw material for the production process and earns tangibility. Although knowledge changes rapidly, it becomes an instrumental input for capital accumulation. The market shapes what is considered worthy or useless knowledge and also underlies the presence and the absence of its specific forms,

1. A number of researchers have highlighted the following characteristics of the global knowledge economy:
2. Sites for the production of new knowledge (research capacity and generation) are dispersed and include universities, the private-sector, non-government organisations and civic advocacy groups.
3. Sites of knowledge generation are globally connected via 'new forms of time-space 'distanciation' across the globe *and* the compression of time-space relations' (Urry, 2003: 3).
4. 'Performativity' is the new legitimating principle linking knowledge production, distribution and consumption (Lyotard, 1985).
5. Exponential growth (volume and complexity) of new knowledge increases the entry and acquisition costs to specialist knowledge.
6. Increased knowledge generation produces heightened social indeterminacy.
7. The risks and responsibilities associated with constructing individual life trajectories are increasingly individualised as the ties of tradition weaken (Ball, 2003; Hier, 2003).

Bernstein (2001) argued that the current era can be described as the second totally pedagogised society. According to Bernstein, the first totally pedagogised society was:

> that of the medieval period initiated by Religion. In the medieval period there was a seamless coordination of meanings, activities, and practices through the Catholic Church; a simple division of labour of symbolic control but all-pervasive in its functions, the realisation of a wholly coherent world and of place, position and function within it (Bernstein, 2001: 364).

In this second totally pedagogised society, symbolic control is via the social relations of pedagogy (Bernstein, 2001: 364). Thus pedagogy, the relation between teacher, learner and the knowledge they co-construct, takes on a central role in socialisation (Lusted, 1986). Moreover, it is through pedagogy that knowledge is selected, distributed and evaluated in the form of curriculum codes (Kallos and Lundgren, 1979).

Curriculum Codes and Pedagogic Modes

The term curriculum code refers to the underlying principles/rules, which shape the organisation of educational knowledge (Bernstein, 1975). According to Bernstein (1975: 85), curriculum types can be described firstly 'in terms of the principle by which units of time and their contents are brought into a special relationship with each other.' So curriculum types can be categorised in terms of the amount of time devoted to particular contents in the school timetable, and whether specific contents are deemed optional or otherwise by students. For example, in Australian primary schools the contents of mathematics, English language and literacy, science, social studies, arts, music and physical education curriculum are strongly bounded. Moreover, mathematics and English literacy curriculum are normally taught every day, early in the day, and with approximately two hours allocated to each of these contents. By contrast, art and music curriculum are likely to be taught for half an hour once a week. Secondly, curriculum types can be described by the strength of the boundary separating contents. Where contents are strongly bounded from each other, the relationship between contents is closed. By contrast, where 'there is reduced insulation between contents, the contents stand in an *open* relationship to each other' (Bernstein, 1975: 87). Using this descriptive language, Bernstein distinguished between types of collection curriculum codes (closed relationships between contents) and integrated curriculum codes (open relationships between contents) across different education systems in Europe, United Kingdom and the United States.

The curriculum organisation described in the example of the Australian primary school above is an illustration of a strong collection code. Although not always the case, collection code curriculum is often associated with visible pedagogic modes. By the term visible pedagogic mode, Bernstein refers to the relative visibility or explicitness of: (a) the rules of conduct between teacher and students; (b) control over sequencing and pacing of curriculum content; and (c) evaluation criteria in terms of recognising acquisition of curriculum content (Bernstein, 1975). According to Bernstein (2000), the 1960s and early 1970s witnessed the emergence of an invisible pedagogic mode in opposition to the visible pedagogic mode which was dominant in schooling systems in the 1950s and early 1960s.

> Invisible pedagogies...incorporated expressive and intangible forms of knowledge. Knowledge learned in educational institutions did not have to be necessarily linked to 'work and life' but to a specific habitus: that of the new middle class. Thus, in this pedagogic model the market can have only an indirect (and invisible) impact on what is learned at the school and how it is learned. The form of domination lies more in having access to a specific habitus than in possessing the necessary knowledge required by the market (Bonal and Rambla, 2003: 174).

In Australia, invisible pedagogies and integrated curriculum codes had some success in schools where teachers had a strong understanding of the syntactic structure of disciplines, and the time and resources to produce school-based curriculum. In the United States, Sadovnik and Semel (2000) described invisible pedagogic modes and integrated curriculum code practices in New York inner-city public elementary and secondary schools, suggesting that these made a significant difference to the educational attainment of students from low-income communities. Sadovnik and Semel (2000: 203) argued that within these schools:

> [C]urriculum is somewhat weakly classified, with for example, Central Park East Secondary School's day divided into two, three hour blocks, the first for humanities and social sciences and the second for mathematics and sciences. Framing is also somewhat weakly classified, with teacher as coach and facilitator an explicit part of the...philosophy. Classes are child-centered and democratic with...an advisory group, where a small number of students meet with a faculty advisor daily to discuss both personal and academic issues

However, as Whitty, Rowe and Aggleton (1994: 25) pointed out, the thematic approach to integrating curriculum contents was not taken up in British secondary schools. Rather cross-curricular themes related to 'the opportunities, responsibilities and experiences of adult life' were relegated to a 'separate programme of personal and social education' (Whitty, Rowe and Aggleton, 1994: 25).

As has been noted above, visible and invisible pedagogic modes and their associated collection and integrated curriculum codes demand different forms of teacher professional identity (pre-service and ongoing learning), investments in educational resources (textbooks, computer equipment, learning spaces and resources, teaching assistants), and subsidy from other educational sites (home, community, tutors). For example, Bernstein (1975: 108) argued that:

> The collection code is capable of working when staffed by mediocre teachers, whereas integrated codes call for much greater powers of synthesis, analogy and for more ability to both tolerate and enjoy ambiguity at the level of knowledge *and* social relationships.

Put differently, prescribed professionalism may be associated with visible pedagogic modes and collection code curriculum, while informed professionalism is associated with invisible pedagogic modes and integrated code curriculum.

Researchers such as Kallos and Lundgren (1979) elaborated on Bernstein's theory of curriculum codes by differentiating between official curriculum (prescribed by state authorities), planned curriculum (recontextualised at the level of the school, department and classroom), enacted curriculum (recontextualised in the everyday classroom interactions of teachers and students) and reflected curriculum (recontextualised in professional conversations of teachers). Kallos and Lundgren (1979) argued that while prescribed curriculum content was supposed to be the constant in classrooms, and pedagogy or teaching methods the variable, their studies of classroom lessons found that similar teaching strategies existed across classrooms, but curriculum content varied. This was a crucial finding, and helped to explain the unequal distribution of school knowledge to different groups of students. This has been the topic of continued research investigation over the last four decades, and evidenced in the work of many of the scholars writing in this volume.

Totally Pedagogised Society

Over two decades after publishing his seminal work on curriculum codes, Bernstein (2001: 368) urged educators to explore *the sociology for the transmission of knowledges*. He suggested that such a sociology 'would focus on the diverse sites, generating both claims for changes in knowledge forms and displacement of and replacement by new forms, creating a new field of knowledge positions, sponsors, designers, and transmitters.' Is Bernstein signifying a significant change to the time–content and space–content relationships described in his initial formulation of curriculum code theory? What impact does the compression of space–time under conditions of global cultural flows have on the theorisations of curriculum codes proposed by Bernstein in the mid 1970s? How are pedagogic modes, that is, the principles structuring teacher–student relations, control over the sequencing and pacing of curriculum content, and evaluation criteria of school knowledge affected by conditions of liquid capitalism? Bill Tyler (this volume) suggests that different international testing regimes (PISA and TIMMS) recognise different forms of school knowledge acquired via different types of curriculum codes.

Bonal and Rambla argue that within the knowledge society, 'the weak state of the global economy requires a strong state in the pedagogic field' (2003: 176). This means that the pedagogic recontextualising field increasingly requires regulation by the official recontextualising field of the state. In Australia, the symbolic boundaries insulating these fields (official and pedagogic recontextualising fields) are becoming increasingly blurred, as various levels of the state mandate national curriculum, national testing, and even preferred teaching methods. This situation contrasts sharply with the case of Australia in the 1960s and 1970s when the pedagogic recontextualising field (PRF) enjoyed considerable autonomy with respect to curriculum production and teacher education (Bernstein, 1996: 70).

Since 1979, in the Australian context, there have been regular reviews of initial teacher education. These reviews have made explicit connections between initial teacher preparation and student learning outcomes (see for example: Louden, Rohl, Gore, McIntosh, Greaves, Wright, Siemon, and House, 2005; Zammit, Sinclair, Cole, Singh, Costley, Brown, a'Court and Rushton 2007; Skilbeck and Connell, 2005; Standing Committee on Education and Vocational Training, House of Representatives, 2007). The importance of quality teaching to improving student learning outcomes is stressed in each of the reports, with varying definitions of what constitutes quality teaching. Clearly then, the Australian state views teachers as central to addressing the market needs of the global knowledge economy, and urges for a review of initial teacher preparation and ongoing professional development programs. The autonomy of the PRF in the preparation and ongoing professional development of teachers is clearly under question in each of these state commissioned reports. And yet many of these reports have been prepared by teacher educators, themselves located in the PRF, and engaged in struggles over what constitutes teacher professional identity and dominant pedagogic modalities in these new times.

PEDAGOIC MODES: STRUGGLES FOR CONTESTATION AND DOMINANCE

As has been mentioned above, a key feature of the totally pedagogised society is that it is 'state-driven and state-funded' (Bonal and Rambla, 2003: 175). The state attempts to regulate teacher professional identity by prescribing professional attributes and exit tests for teacher education institutions, and preferred modes of training for ongoing professional development. However, the speed at which new knowledge is produced and applied to economic production necessitates an adaptive professional orientation from teachers, not one that is prescribed and fixed by the states. According to Bonal and Rambla (2003: 174)

> Specialised discourses appear and disappear as fast as the market values them. At the same time, their content and form change because specialists themselves redefine them constantly and because the production of new knowledge and its access become crucial aspects for market access and competitiveness.

Bernstein proposed that the generic performance pedagogic (GPP) mode had gained prominence in the totally pedagogised society because it is based on a notion of short-term trainability. What is the notion of time and time—content relationships within new forms of curriculum codes under a GPP? What is the notion of spatial boundaries and open/closed boundary—content relations? Bernstein suggests that the relationship between contents is strongly bounded, and thus knowledge is packaged into segments with little explicit connection between the segments. The relationship of content to time is explicit, so that learners devote specified quantities of time to specific contents to display skills acquisition. For example, in Queensland Australia in order to maintain current teacher registration status, teachers are expected to show evidence of continuous professional learning. The quantity of time devoted to professional learning has been nominated in hours, the type of learning is stipulated in very general work-related terms, and the knowledge and skill outcomes are stated in very broad terms of evidence of continuous re-training. The implicit model of the learner within the generic performance mode is someone who has the inherent capacity to make oneself available to be trained, re-trained, formed and re-formed.

The generic performance pedagogic mode, together with the marked shifts associated with the emergence of the knowledge economy, has transformed the teaching profession. The rapid rate of knowledge production means that teachers are required to continuously update and upgrade both disciplinary and pedagogic knowledge. Bonal and Rambla indicate that 'the 'new' teacher must become a knowledge manager rather than a knowledge expert' (2003: 171). New understandings of the profession and the substantial influence that teachers have on student achievement have led to the finding that, in order to provide high quality education, teachers need to receive initial training and ongoing professional development to stay at the forefront of knowledge and skill (Caldwell and Harris, 2008).

Bernstein (2001) suggests that there are three aspects to teacher professional identity that need to be considered under conditions of liquid modernity, namely, pedagogic autonomy, ambiguity, and investments.

Pedagogic Autonomy

> Teachers are expected to be pedagogically autonomous, but this pedagogic autonomy does not have value in itself. It is a type of pedagogic autonomy that has to be knowledge oriented under the official scrutiny, since its validity eventually depends on its alleged utility for developing the necessary knowledge required by the market. Thus, it is an autonomy that nobody wants (Bonal and Rambla, 2003: 180)

The research and reforms that promote teachers drawing on their own professional knowledges in order to develop effective, contextualised approaches to meeting the needs of their students mean that it is no longer considered sufficient for teachers to simply enact prescribed pedagogies. Teachers cannot simply rely on 'routine expertise,' or the mastery of a single approach due to the rapid changes in knowledge and society. Rather, new approaches in education have placed significant value on the flexibility of teachers to acquire and apply new knowledge, concepts and approaches, referred to by Bransford and colleagues as 'adaptive expertise' (Bransford, Derry, Berliner, Hammerness and Beckett 2005: 48–49). Unlike routine experts, adaptive experts 'are much more likely to change their core competencies and continually expand the breadth and depth of their expertise' (Bransford et al. 2005: 48–49).

In the 1990s in Britain teacher professional identity was talked of in terms of informed prescription and informed professionalism (Barber, 2002; Whitty, 2006). Teachers were expected to utilise regulated curriculum materials and methods of disseminating particular content knowledge, which had been developed or identified by a central body but informed by research evidence. Educational researchers refer to this approach as 'informed prescription' as the prescription to teachers was based on research knowledge. Hopkins (2007) argued that informed prescription was a valuable method for generating new approaches within education systems. One weakness of this approach in many systems of education, particularly in England, is that the evidence-informed design of curriculum materials and new pedagogical practices were developed and subsequently mandated at the system level (Alexander, 2004).

Informed prescription in education, however, has not been limited to the field of education policy. Teacher education adopts a similar approach by constructing and privileging particular classroom practices as 'best practice.' There is an, often unspoken, expectation that pre-service teachers will replicate the 'best practice' approaches that they have learned in their own classrooms. Ensor argues that while specific practices may vary between teacher education institutions and teacher educators, each of the 'best practices' is 'derived from the past, [is] pedagogized in the present for application in the future' (Ensor 2004: 155). The major limitation of employing 'best practices,' either acquired during teacher education or externally prescribed, is that it may limit the flexibility of teachers in pedagogising knowledge, their adaptability in personalising knowledge and their autonomy to act on their own professional judgements. And flexibility, adaptability and professional autonomy within the context of knowledge performativity are key to teacher professional identity under conditions of liquid modernity.

The delivery of pre-packaged curriculum materials and prescription of 'best practice' can be seen to enable and encourage educators to develop, what is defined by Bransford and colleagues (2005) as 'routine' expertise. According to this definition, routine experts work towards developing a 'core set of competencies that they apply throughout their lives with greater and greater efficiency' (Bransford et al.

2005: 48). Teachers with routine expertise, therefore, can be expected to improve their performance in the delivery of a particular curriculum area or use of a 'best practice' approach to pedagogising knowledge throughout their career. While these approaches can result in teachers with high levels of skill in specific disciplinary areas or pedagogical practice, they may be challenged when pre-packaged curriculum materials, idealised classroom practices, externally created targets or schooling contexts change. The rapid changes associated with the knowledge society are eroding the viability of teachers being able to simply rely on routine expertise.

Pedagogic Ambiguity

Under generic performance-oriented modes of pedagogy, teachers are expected to be pedagogic translators who continually renew their specialised forms of knowledge and rapidly recontextualise or pedagogise this knowledge into curriculum for students. Research has both predicted and promoted the movement requiring teachers to become flexible experts who are able to adapt their core skills and competencies in order to effectively pedagogise knowledge. On the other hand, the expanded role of the state in the pedagogic recontextualising field and the advocacy of 'best practice' approaches in teacher education could be seen to limit teachers' autonomy in using innovative teaching methods.

Within the totally pedagogised society, the professional identity of the teacher is never prescribed or described.

> The requirements of flexible capitalism are translated into pedagogic ambiguity.... Official and pedagogic discourses identify the teaching profession as a key input for a successful socialisation for work and life. However, since work and life is shaped by intangibility, uncertainty and short-termism, a consequence of that is that the TPS carries the elimination of concrete definitions of teaching. This fact leads to a final paradox: the more important knowledge is for economic performance, the more pedagogy colonises life and the lower the content definition of that pedagogy. Of course, this basic contradiction produces risk-awareness, uncertainty and dislocation among teachers. Teachers are captured between the contradictory forces of the TPS and become a target group for the official and pedagogic discourses. It is therefore quite common to collect opinions of frustration and a sense of deterioration of their professional identities (Bonal and Rambla, 2003: 180).

Pedagogic Investments

In education circles, improving teachers' professional knowledge through ongoing professional learning and the use of reflective practices have become the mantra of the day. Current international research clearly demonstrates that the most effective teachers have received high quality pre-service training and actively participate in formal and informal continuing professional development activities (Barber and Mourshed 2007; Dinham, Ingvarson and Kleinhenz 2008). There is similarly strong support for the long-held argument that reflective thinking and evaluation plays a vital role in enhancing the quality of teachers' professional knowledge and skills (Schon 1987).

The research and reforms that encourage teachers to draw on their own repositories or funds of professional knowledge in order to develop effective, contextualised approaches to meeting the needs of learners suggest that it is no longer considered sufficient for teachers to simply enact prescribed pedagogies. These new approaches in education have placed significant value on the ability of teachers to be flexible, reflective and continuously focused on the acquisition of new knowledge, concepts and approaches. Teachers need adequate time, resources and support in order to become lifelong reflective learners, who are able to use their professional expertise to apply their expanding range of knowledge and skills effectively.

But how is the continuous education/training of teachers to be resourced? How is pedagogic renewal to be funded? Bernstein signals that the responsibility rests on the shoulders of individual teachers who need to make themselves available to be trained and re-trained, rather than on the state that is expected to provide time, resources and other support to facilitate pedagogic renewal.

Bernstein argued that these modes of socialisation into the totally pedagogised society erode commitment, dedications, and coherent time, and are, therefore, socially empty. Bernstein asks 'If the identity produced by trainability is socially empty, how does the individual recognise himself/ herself and others? Bernstein suggests that the products of the market relay the signifier whereby temporary stabilities, orientations, and evaluations are constructed.' However, this pedagogic inflation does not create autonomy for either the trainers or the trained, for both become subject to the fluidity and short-termism of the training and the targets set by the state (school league tables, literacy and numeracy test results). In other words, while able to organise and disseminate knowledge, generic performance oriented pedagogies offer prescribed approaches that may quickly become redundant.

The preceding discussion detailed Bernstein's theory of the second totally pedagogised society and the dominance of generic performance oriented pedagogic modes under conditions of liquid modernity. Bernstein's analysis of the social conditions that have generated particular modes of pedagogy and professional identities offer useful tools to reflect on sites for contestation, struggle and opposition.

In what follows, we outline a model of collaborative professionalism based on studies of education systems across a number of countries. We propose that this model of collaborative professionalism may take into account the positioning of teachers within the context of the global knowledge economy. Moreover, we suggest that the model of collaborative professionalism must account for pedagogic autonomy, ambiguity, and investments, particularly as this relates to ongoing professional learning and capacity to develop, implement and reflect on school/classroom curricula (Bernstein, 2000).

An Alternative: Collaborative Professionalism

While Bernstein indicates that under generic performance pedagogies the onus for teacher training and retraining lies with the individual teacher, current international education research suggests that a collaborative approach to continuous reflection and renewal may be more effective. International research into the practices used by thirty successful secondary schools from six countries, highlights the importance of a strong focus on teacher involvement in continuous professional learning and evaluation. Dedication to ongoing professional learning was a shared characteristic of the 30 case study schools from Australia, China, England, Finland, Wales and the United States involved in the International Project to Frame the Transformation of Schools (IPFTS) (Caldwell and Harris, 2008). Staff from all of these schools, which had achieved and sustained significant improvement in the academic performance of their students, demonstrated a strong commitment to constantly updating and improving their knowledge and skills to keep pace with the rapid rate of change in educational research and in the use of information communication technologies (ICTs) in the classroom. In the majority of these case studies, schools had gone to considerable effort to embed ongoing teacher professional development within the culture of their staff. James Campbell High School in Hawaii, for example, highlighted their commitment to teacher professional learning by changing their timetable to include four 80-minute classes in each school day. Every teacher was allocated one of these 80-minute periods per school day in which they are expected to focus on and extend their professional learning (Zhao, Ni, Yang, Chen and Zhang 2008). Many of the leaders of these effective secondary schools model behaviours associated with lifelong professional development, keeping abreast of educational research, regularly participating in professional learning seminars and activities and continuously evaluating their practice.

A culture of ongoing self-evaluation and reflection on professional practice was another shared characteristic of the 30 case study schools involved in the IPFTS (Caldwell and Harris, 2008). Teachers in these schools were expected to maintain their knowledge of current educational research, through professional reading and active involvement in professional development activities. Furthermore, many of these schools encouraged teachers to undertake their own action research projects to address areas of concern within their own classrooms and schools. All teachers at Wangaratta High School in Victoria, Australia, for example, were required to develop their own research projects as part of their individual professional learning plans (Douglas and Harris, 2008). These teachers were given access to a range of data, including student performance data, to monitor, reflect on and, ultimately, improve their own approaches to teaching and learning. These teachers were also required to work in pairs to observe and provide feedback on each others' classroom practices. In this way, these teachers were given the opportunity to participate in a collegial sharing of knowledge and reflective thinking about their teaching practices. The learning that took place in these in-school collaborative activities was highly valuable and these activities did not have the costs, in terms of time, facilities and resources, that are associated with externally provided professional development courses.

International education research clearly demonstrates that teacher reflection and the sharing of professional knowledge, with a strong focus on student learning outcomes, are highly effective in improving teacher knowledge and, consequently, student learning outcomes. The exchanges of professional knowledge, referred to in the literature as 'professional learning conversations,' provide teachers with access to a broad range of professional learning tools that can support them in changing their core competencies. These professional learning conversations may include knowledge brought from outside the educational context and enrich teachers' knowledge and result in the creation of 'new ideas, tools and practices' within the school environment (Earl and Timperley 2008: 2).

The theoretical model described by Earl and Timperley (2008) outlines a number of conditions for professional learning conversations to be successful. They found that the exchange of evidence-based knowledge or 'evidence-informed' (Fleisch, in Earl and Timperley, 2008) information was not necessarily sufficient for teachers to improve their professional practice. In order to achieve effective professional learning conversations, they argued that participants need to approach the evidence being examined with a mutual respect, which enables them to exchange knowledge, reflect on hypotheses and challenge ideas within a safe environment that focused on improving student learning. The second condition for an effective professional learning conversation is that participants adopt an 'inquiry habit of mind' (Earl and Timperley, 2008), an approach which enables them to critically assess and expand the 'breadth and depth of their expertise' (Bransford et al. 2005: 48–49).

Moreover, these conversations may support teachers with an 'inquiry habit of mind' to critically evaluate their own, often tacit knowledge. In other words, the sharing and critical reflection of knowledges may enable teachers to discover that their beliefs and perceptions about teaching and learning are 'only *one* frame of several possible frames' (Thomas and Pedersen, 2003: 327). Earl and Timperley (2008) indicate that these collaborative and collegial exchanges can enrich teachers' understandings of their own practices and those used by others and result in the creation of 'new ideas, tools and practices' within the school environment. In this way, effective and sustained inquiry-based conversations enable teachers who are open to critical reflection to become adaptive experts, with the ability to use their professional autonomy. The collaborative nature of this learning, however, seems to result in the expertise of the group to be greater than the sum of its parts.

Discussion

This chapter has drawn on Bernstein's theories of the totally pedagogised society and pedagogic modalities as a lens to examine issues of teacher professional identity within conditions of liquid modernity (Bauman, 2004; Urry, 2003). The new positioning of knowledge as a raw material in the global knowledge economy has caused seismic shifts in terms of increased state regulation of pedagogic recontextualising fields. Increasingly, the state regulates not only what is taught in schools, but how it is taught and evaluated. Teachers are expected to engage in continuous learning to keep abreast of rapid changes in disciplinary knowledge and ensure that the learning outcomes of students meet the needs of the global knowledge economy. Enter the totally pedagogised society—where teachers are expected to be active, autonomous pedagogises of new knowledge to meet the needs of human capital (knowledge workers) for the market. Enter a society where learning and training is dictated by the needs of the market, and although teachers are constantly criticised for not being 'informed' their professionalism is 'hollowed out' by the regulations of the state. Bernstein forewarns us of the dangers of the totally pedagogised society, and the impact of this society on the organisation of school knowledge (curriculum codes), pedagogic identities and relations (pedagogic modes).

In this chapter, we have argued that Bernstein's theory of curriculum codes, pedagogic modes and professional identity provides effective tools for analysing not only the troubling aspects of the totally pedagogised society, but also proposals for teacher professionalism (democratic, active) and new pedagogies (globalising, reconciliation) aimed at challenging/subverting these dangers. Tentatively, we explored changes in the temporal–spatial relations of curriculum organisation and pedagogic modes as a result of time-space compression under conditions of liquid capitalism. Following Bernstein, we proposed that generic performance pedagogies were the dominant pedagogic mode of global knowledge-based capitalism, replacing the invisible pedagogic modes of the late 1970s. Three aspects of dominant pedagogic modalities, including pedagogic autonomy, ambiguity and investments, were used to frame the debate and highlight inconsistencies and areas of concern.

We concluded the paper by providing an alternative to the generic performance pedagogic mode by arguing for a model of collaborative professionalism. We used cases studies from across the globe to explore what constitutes quality teaching and effective learning outcomes within a context of collaborative professionalism.

Acknowledgment

Funding for this study was provided by the Australian Research Council Linkages Scheme.

References

Alexander, R. (2004). 'Still no Pedagogy? Principle, Pragmatism and Compliance in Primary Education.' *Cambridge Journal of Education*. 34:1 7–33.

Avis, J. (2005). Beyond Performativity: Reflections on Activist Professionalism and the Labour Process in Further Education. *Journal of Education Policy*, 20(2), 209–222.

Ball, S. J. (2003). *Class Strategies and the Education Market. The Middle Classes and Social Advantage*. London, New York: RoutledgeFalmer.

Barber, M. (2002). *The Next Stage for Large Scale Educational Reform in England*. IARTV: Jolimont, Victoria.

Barber, M. and Mourshed, M. (2007). *How the World's Best-Performing School Systems Come Out on Top*. London; McKinsey & Company.

Bauman, Z. (2004). Zygmunt Bauman: Liquid Sociality. In N. Gane (Ed.), *The Future of Social Theory* (pp. 17–46). London, New York: Continuum.

Bernstein, B. (1975). *Towards a Theory of Educational Transmissions (Class, Codes and Control Vol. 3)*. London: Routledge & Kegan Paul.

Bernstein, B. (1990). *The Structuring of Pedagogic Discourse*. London: Routledge.

Bernstein, B. (1996). *Pedagogy, Symbolic Control and Identity. Theory, Research, Critique*. London and New York: Taylor and Francis.

Bernstein, B. (2000). Pedagogy, Symbolic Control and Identity (Revised ed.). Lanham, Boulder, New York, Oxford: Rowan & Littlefield Publishers, Inc.

Bernstein, B. (2001). From Pedagogies to Knowledges. In A. Morais, I. Neves, B. Davies and H. Daniels (Eds.), *Towards A Sociology of Pedagogy. The Contribution of Basil Bernstein to Research* (pp. 363–368). New York: Peter Lang.

Bonal, X. and Rambla, X. (2003). 'Captured by the Totally Pedagogised Society: teachers and teaching in the knowledge economy.' *Globalisation, Societies and Education*. 1:2, 169–184.

Bransford, J., Derry, S., Berliner, D., Hammerness, K with Beckett, K. L. (2005). 'Theories of Learning and Their Roles in Teaching.' In Darling-Hammond, L. and Bransford, J. (Eds) *Preparing Teachers for a Changing World: What Teachers Should Learn and Be Able to Do*. San Francisco, CA: Jossey Bass:

Caldwell, B. J. and Harris, J. (2008). *Why Not the Best Schools?* Camberwell, VIC, Australia: ACER Press.

Castells, M. (2000). *End of the Millennium. The Information Age. Economy, Society and Culture.* (Second ed., Vol. 111). Oxford: Blackwell Publishers.

Considine, M., Marginson, S., Sheehan, P. and Kummick, M. (2001). *The Comparative Performance of Australia as a Knowledge Nation. Report to the Chifley Research Centre.* Melbourne: Monash Centre for Research in International Education.

Dinham, S., Ingvarson, L. and Kleinhenz, E. (2008) *How Can we Raise the Quality of School Education So that Every Student Benefits? Teaching Talent: The Best Teachers for Australia's Classrooms.* Report for the Business Council of Australia.

Douglas, E. and Harris, J. (2008). *Why Not the Best Schools? The Australia Report.* ACER Press: Victoria.

Earl, L.M. and Timperley, H. (Eds.) (2008). *Professional Learning Conversations: Challenges in Using Evidence for Improvement.* Berlin: Springer.

Ensor, P. (2004). 'Towards a Sociology of Teacher Education.' In Muller, J., Davies, B. and Morais, A. (Eds.) (2004). *Reading Bernstein, Researching Bernstein.* London: Routledge Falmer.

Freifeld, L. (2008). 'The Knowledge Economy.' *Training.* 3 January 2008.

Fullan, M., Hill, P., and Crevola, C. (2006) *Breakthrough.* Thousand Oaks, CA: Corwin Press.

Hattam, R. (2004). *Buddhism as a Resource for Reconciliation Pedagogies.* Paper presented at the Australian Association for Research in Education. from http://www.aare.edu.au /04pap/hat04399.pdf (Accessed 9 August 2009).

Hattie, J (2005) 'What is the Nature of Evidence that Makes a Difference to Learning?' Paper presented at the Australian Council for Educational Research Conference 'Using Data to Support Learning' 7 Thousand Oaks CA 9 August 2005, Melbourne. Accessed at 2008.www.acer.edu.au/workshops/documents/Hattie.pdf. (Accessed 29 April 2008.)

Hattie, J. (2007). 'Developing Potentials for Learning: Evidence, Assessment and Progress.' Paper presented at the European Association for Research on Learning and Instruction 12th Biennial Conference. 28 August to 1 September 2007, Budapest. Accessed at http://www.education.auckland.ac.nz/uoa/hattie-conference Accessed 22 December 2009.

Hattie, J. and Timperley, H. (2007). 'The Power of Feedback.' *American Journal of Evaluation.* 28(4), 416–436.

Hier, S. P. (2003). Risk and panic in late modernity: implications of the converging sites of social anxiety. *British Journal of Sociology, 54*(1), 3–20.

Hopkins, D. (2007). *Every School a Great School.* Maidenhead, Berkshire: Open University Press.

Kallos, D. and Lundgren, U. (1979) *Curriculum as a Pedagogical Problem.* CWK Gleerup/ Liber Laromedel: Stockholm.

Liew, A. (2007). 'Understanding Data, Information, Knowledge and their Inter-relationships.' *Journal of Knowledge Management Practice,* 8, 2.

Lingard, R. L. and Mills, M. (2002). Teachers and school reform: Aligning the message systems. In: B. Webber, Teachers Make A Difference: What Is The Research Evidence?. NZCER 2002 Conference, Wellington, NZ, (63–82). October 2002.

Louden, W., Rohl, M., Gore, J., McIntosh, A., Greaves, D., Wright, R., et al. (2005). *Prepared to Teach. An Investigation into the Preparation of Teachers to Teach Literacy and Numeracy.* Retrieved. from. http://www.dest.gov.au/sectors/school_education/publications_resources/pro-files/prepared_to_teach.htm (Accessed 11 August 2009).

Lusted, D. (1986). Why Pedagogy? *Screen*, 27(5), 2–14.

Lyotard, J.-F. (1985). *The Postmodern Condition: A Report on Knowledge*. Minneapolis, MN: University of Minnesota Press.

Maton, K. and Muller, J. (2007). A Sociology for the Transmission of Knowledges. In F. Christie and J. Martin (Eds.), *Language, Knowledge and Pedagogy* (pp. 14–33). London: Continuum.

McCarthy, C. and Dimitriades, G. (2000). Globalizing Pedagogies: Power, Resentment and the Re-Narration of Difference. In N. Burbules and C. Torres (Eds.), *Globalization and Education. Critical Perspectives* (pp. 187–204). London, New York: Routledge.

McWilliam, E. and Singh, P. (2002). Towards a Research Training Curriculum: What, Why, How, Who? *Australian Educational Researcher*, 29(3), 3–18.

Moore, R. (2002, 17–19th July). *Between Covenant and Contract: Negotiating Academic Pedagogic Identities*. Paper presented at the Knowledges, Pedagogy and Society. The Second International Basil Bernstein Symposium, Breakwater Lodge, University of Cape Town, South Africa.

Sachs, J. (2000). 'The Activist Professional.' *Journal of Educational Change*, 1, 77–95.

Schon, D. (1987) *Educating for the Reflective Practitioner: Toward a new design for teaching and learning in the professions*. San Francisco, CA: Jossey-Bass.

Simkins, T. (2005), 'Leadership in education, what works or what makes sense?,' *Educational Management Administration and Leadership*, 33(1), 9–26.

Sadovnik, A. and Semel, S. (2000). Bernstein's theory of pedagogic practice: A sociological analysis of urban and suburban schools in the New York City metropolitan area. In A. Morais (Ed.), *Towards a sociology of pedagogy. The contribution of Basil Bernstein to research* (pp. 189–206). Lisbon: Department of Education and Centre for Educational Research, School of Science, University of Lisbon.

Skilbeck, M. and Connell, H. (2005). *Teachers for the Future. The Changing Nature of Society and Related Issues for the Teaching Workforce*. Canberra: Ministerial Council for Education, Employment Training and Youth Affairs.

Standing Committee on Education and Vocational Training, and House of Representatives. (2007). *Top of the Class: Report on the Inquiry into Teacher Education*. . Retrieved. from http://www.aph.gov.au/house/committee/evt/teachereduc/report/fullreport.pdf.

Thomas, J. A. and Pedersen, J. E. (2003). 'Reforming Elementary Science Teacher Preparation: What about Extant Teaching Beliefs?' *School Science and Mathematics*. 103(7), 319–330.

Tyler, W. (1999). Pedagogic Identities and educational reform in the 1990s: the cultural dynamics of national curricula. In F. Christie (Ed.), *Pedagogy and the Shaping of Consciousness*. London and New York: Continuum.

Uluorta, H. and Quill, L. (2009). In pursuit of the knowledge worker: educating for world risk society. *International Studies in Sociology of Education*, 19(1), 37–51.

Urry, J. (2003). *Global Complexity*. Cambridge: Polity Press.

Von Krogh, G., Ichijo, K. and Nonaka I. (2000). *Enabling Knowledge Creation—How to Unlock the Mystery of Tacit Knowledge and Release the Power of Innovation*. Oxford: Oxford University Press.

Whitty, G. (2006). *Teacher professionalism in a new era* Paper presented at the General Teaching Council for Northern Ireland Annual Lecture. from http://www.google.com/search?q=geoff+whitty+teacher+professionalism&rls=com.microsoft:en-au:IE-SearchBox&ie=UTF-8&oe=UTF-8&sourceid=ie7&rlz=1I7ADBF_en, (Accessed 7th August, 2009).

Whitty, G., Rowe, G. and Aggleton, P. (1994). Discourse in Cross-curricular Contexts: limits to empowerment. *International Studies in Sociology of Education,* 4(1), 25–42.

Zammit, K., Sinclair, C., Cole, B., Singh, M., Costley, D., Brown a'Court, L., et al. (2007). *Teaching and Leading for Quality Australian Schools: A Review and Synthesis of Research-Based Knowledge.* Canberra: Teaching Australia. Australian Institute for Teaching and School Leadership Ltd. Document Number).

Zhao, Y., Ni, R., Yang, W., Chen, Q. and Zhang, G. (2008). *Why Not the Best Schools? The US Report.* Camberwell, VIC, Australia: ACER Press.

Contributors

KAREN BRADLEY is Professor and Chair of the Department of Sociology at Western Washington University, USA. Dr. Bradley obtained her B.A. in English, along with a secondary teaching certification, from Providence College. She received her M.A. in Higher Education Administration from Boston College, and her M.A. and Ph.D. in sociology from Stanford University in 1994. Her research and her classes blend her interest in organizational processes, education, and gender. Much of Dr. Bradley's research has examined women's participation within higher education by field and by level of attainment within countries throughout the world. She is currently collaborating with Dr. John Richardson on a research project investigating the development of the field of educational psychology over time within the United States.

HARRY DANIELS is Professor of Education, Culture and Pedagogy, Head of *'Learning as Cultural and Social Practice'* Research Programme, and Director of Centre for Sociocultural and Activity Theory Research at the University of Bath, England. His research interests include socio-cultural and activity theory, special needs and social exclusion, social emotional and behavioural difficulty including exclusion from school. His key publications include Daniels, H., Cole, M., and Wertsch, J. (Eds) (2007) *Cambridge Companion to Vygotsk;* Daniels, H., Leadbetter, J., Soares, A., and McNab, N. (2007) Learning in and for cross-school working,

Oxford Review of Education; and Moore, R., Arnot, M., Beck, J., and Daniels, H. (2006) *Knowledge, Power and Educational Reform: Applying the sociology of Basil Bernstein*. London: Routledge.

BRIAN DAVIES is Professor Emeritus of Social Sciences at Cardiff University, Wales. Among his publications are Jephcote, M. and Davies, B., School Subjects, Subject Communities and Curriculum Change: the Social Construction of Economics in the School Curriculum, *Cambridge Journal of Education* (2008); Davies, B., Fitz, J. and Evans, J., *Educational Policy and Social Reproduction: Class Inscription and Social Control*, Routledge, (2005); Davies, B., Evans, J., Rich, E. and Allwood, R., The Embodiment of Learning: What the Sociology of Education Doesn't Say About 'Risk' in Going to School, *International Studies in Sociology of Education*, (2005).

JOHN EVANS is Professor of Sociology of Education and Physical Education at Loughborough University, England. He teaches and writes on issues of equity, education policy, identity and processes of schooling. He is currently researching the relationships between formal education, policy, pedagogy and the embodiment of identity. He has authored and edited a number of papers and books in the Sociology of Education and Physical Education—his most recent, co-authored with Brian Davies, Emma Rich and Rachel Allwood (2009) *Education, Disordered Eating and Obesity Discourse*, Routledge.

JOHN FITZ is Professor and Deputy Director of Social Sciences at Cardiff University, Wales. His recent publications include Fitz, J., Davies, W.B. and Evans, J. (2005) Education Policy and Social Reproduction, Routledge; Taylor, C., Fitz, J. and Gorard, S. (2005) Diversity, specialisation and equity in education, *Oxford Review of Education*; and The politics of accountability: a perspective from England and Wales, *Peabody Journal of Education* (2003) Gorard, S., Fitz, J. and Taylor, C. (2003) *Markets, Schools and Stratification*, Routledge.

JESSICA HARRIS is a post-doctoral research fellow in the School of Education at the University of Queensland, Australia. Her research interests include international education policy and the building and alignment of social, intellectual, spiritual and financial capitals for the improvement of schools and school systems.

JEANNE GAMBLE is an Honorary Research Associate in the School of Education, Post-Graduate Faculty of Humanities at the University of Cape Town. Her research interests are in the relation between knowledge and practice in curriculum and pedagogy, particularly in relation to vocational and professional education. In her PhD studies she explored the apprenticing pedagogy of craft and its relation to tacit knowledge. She has published widely and has co-edited a volume with Prof. Michael Young of the Institute of Education, University of London, entitled *Knowledge, Curriculum and Qualifications for South African Further Education*, 2006, Cape Town: HSRC Press.

GABRIELLE IVINSON is Senior Lecturer in social and developmental psychology in the School of Social Sciences, Cardiff University, Wales. She is one of the co-directors of the university Regeneration Institute (RI). The RI is a joint venture between the School of City and Regional Planning and the School of Social Sciences and acts as a vehicle for research in area-based regeneration, embracing academic and policy-related research at both local and international levels. Her specialism within this is education and she is currently exploring skills and learning in the secondary school curriculum as the boundary between work and schooling becomes increasingly blurred. She is looking at how boys from low socio-economic locales recognise skills encountered in and out of classrooms in order to develop new conceptual tools for understanding learning in school-based vocational courses. Here she draws on her prior experience as a secondary school teacher to develop new pedagogic tools for teachers and policy makers. This research calls on two of her long standing research interests; Bernstein's sociology of pedagogy and neo-Vygotskian socio-cultural approaches to learning with an emphasis on gender. Her book with Patricia Murphy, called *Rethinking Single-Sex Teaching* was based on ethnographic work in co-educational secondary schools that had introduced single sex teaching as an ameliorative strategy to deal with boys' underachievement.

KARL MATON is Senior Lecturer in Sociology at the Faculty of Arts, University of Sydney, Australia. Karl is the principal author of *Legitimation Code Theory*, an approach that integrates and extends the insights of Pierre Bourdieu, Basil Bernstein and critical realism. This approach is increasingly being used by researchers in sociology, education, philosophy and linguistics to study a range of national contexts including Australia, France, South Africa, and the UK (see: http://www.karlmaton.com). He has worked at the University of Cambridge, the Open University (UK), Keele University and Wollongong University and published extensively in sociology, cultural studies, education, linguistics and philosophy. He has co-edited collections on *Social Realism, Knowledge and the Sociology of Education* (with Rob Moore, Continuum Press, 2010) and on *Disciplinarity* (with Frances Christie, Continuum Press, 2010). Karl's book, *Knowledge and Knowers: Towards a Realist Sociology of Education*, will be published in 2010 by Routledge.

ANA M. MORAIS is Emeritus Professor of Education in the School of Science, University of Lisbon, Portugal. She has published widely in journals and books. She is coordinator of the ESSA Research Group (Sociological Studies of the Classroom) of the University of Lisbon. She has published extensively on the application of Bernstein's theory to science education, curriculum development and teacher education.

JOHAN MULLER is Professor in the School of Education and Deputy Dean of Research and Director of the Graduate School in Humanities at the University of Cape Town, South Africa. His research interests include curriculum studies, sociology of knowledge, and education policy. His recent publications include *Time-on-Task, Technology and Mathematics Achievement; Evaluation and Program Planning 31* (2008,with Johann Louw and Colin Tredoux); *Truth and Truthfulness in the Sociology of Educational Knowledge; Theory and Research in Education* (2007, with Michael Young); *Modes of Governance and The Limits of Policy;* and in N. Cloete et al (eds) *Transformation in Higher Education: Global Pressures & Local Realities,* Springer, 2006 (with Peter Maassen & Nico Cloete).

ISABEL P. NEVES is Associate Professor of Education in the School of Science, University of Lisbon, Portugal. She is coordinator of the ESSA Research Group (Sociological Studies of the Classroom) of the University of Lisbon. She has published extensively on the application of Bernstein's theory to science education, curriculum development and teacher education.

URSULA HOADLEY is Senior Lecturer in the School of Education at the University of Cape Town, South Africa. Her research interests include curriculum, teachers work and the sociological study of pedagogy. She has published widely on the application of the work of Basil Bernstein.

SALLY POWER is Professor of Social Sciences at Cardiff University, Wales. Her publications include The Deployment of Social Capital Theory in Educational Policy and Provision: the Case of Education Action Zones in England, *British Educational Research Journal*, (2006, with Gewirtz S, Dickson M, Halpin D and Whitty G, (2005); Education and the Middle Class: a Complex but Crucial Case for the Sociology of Education, *Education, Globalization and Social Change* (Lauder, H., Brown, P., Dillabough, J. and Halsey, A.H. eds) Oxford University Press (2006 with Whitty G; Markets and Misogyny: Educational Research on Educational Choice, *British Journal of Educational Studies* (2006*)*; 'Disembedded middle class pedagogic identities' in R. Moore, M. Arnot, J. Beck & H. Daniels (eds) *Knowledge, Power and Educational Reform: Applying the Sociology of Basil Bernstein* (2006).

CONTRIBUTORS | 271

JOHN G. RICHARDSON is Professor of Sociology at Western Washington University, USA. Dr. Richardson received his PhD from the University of California, Davis. He did his doctoral work on the historical and organizational roots of the misclassification of black and Hispanic students in special education in California schools. After one year at the University of Alaska, where he explored similar issues facing native students, he came to Western in 1974. His research interests have been in the areas of education, historical sociology and sociological theory. His publications include the classic *Handbook of Theory and Research in the Sociology of Education*, Greenwood (1986).

RITA RIKSAASEN is Associate Professor at Programme for Teacher Education, Norwegian University of Science and Technology NTNU, Trondheim, Norway. She was a doctoral student of Basil Bernstein, and her thesis was: *Visible and invisible pedagogies in teacher education. A comparison of Norwegian Primary and Pre-school Teacher education*. She has co-edited two books: *Klasse, kode og identitet. Bernstein i norsk forskning and Basil Bernsteins kodeteori og nyere empiri*. She has published several papers on teacher education and school. Most of her research has been influenced by the thinking of Bernstein.

ALAN R. SADOVNIK is Professor of Education, Sociology and Public Affairs and co-director of the Institute on Education Law and Policy and Newark Schools Research Collaborative at Rutgers University, Newark, USA. His publications include *Equity and Excellence in Higher Education* (1995); *Knowledge and Pedagogy: The Sociology of Basil Bernstein* (1995); *Sociology of Education: A Critical Reader* (2007); *"Schools of Tomorrow," Schools of Today: What Happened to Progressive Education* (1999, with Susan F. Semel); *Founding Mothers and Others: Women Educational Leaders During the Progressive Era* (2002, with Susan F. Semel) and *No Child Left Behind and the Reduction of the Achievement Gap: Sociological Perspectives on Federal Educational Policy* (2008, with George Bornstedt, Jennifer O'Day and Kathryn Borman).

SUSAN F. SEMEL is Professor of Education at the City College of New York and the CUNY Graduate Center, USA. Her publications include *The Dalton School: The Transformation of a Progressive School* (1992), *Schools of Tomorrow, Schools of Today: What Happened to Progressive Education* (1999, with Alan R. Sadovnik) and *Founding Mothers and Others: Women Educational Leaders During the Progressive Era* (2002, with Alan R. Sadovnik). She is the co-editor (with Alan R. Sadovnik) of the History of Schools and Schooling Series at Peter Lang Publishing, the Urban Education Series at Palgrave Macmillan and The Global School House Series at Greenwood Press.

PARLO SINGH is Professor and Graduate Dean of Research at Griffith University, Australia. Her publications include Native-speaker TESOL Teachers' Talk: Examining the Unexamined. *English Teaching and Learning* (2008, with C. Doherty); A New Equity Deal for Schools: A Case Study of Policy Making in Queensland, Australia. *British Journal of Sociology of Education*, (2007, with S. Taylor); The Logic of Equity Practice in Education Queensland 2010. *Special Edition of Journal of Educational Policy*, (2005, with S. Taylor); Global Cultural Flows and Pedagogic Dilemmas: Teaching in the Global University Contact Zone, *TESOL Quarterly*, (2004, with C. Doherty); Globalization and Education. *Educational Theory*, 2004; and Pedagogising Knowledge: Bernstein's Theory of the Pedagogic Device. *British Journal of Sociology of Education*, (2002).

WILLIAM TYLER is Adjunct Principal Research Fellow in the School of Social and Policy Research at Charles Darwin University, having lectured in sociology and sociology of education at universities in Canada (Memorial), the United Kingdom (Keele, Kent) and Australia (Monash, Charles Darwin). His recent interests have included the evaluation of early intervention programs for Indigenous students (National Accelerated Literacy Program, Exploring Together, Let's Start), as well as socio-spatial studies of the impact of electronic gambling in the Northern Territory and Victoria. His theoretical work explores the relevance of Basil Bernstein's writings on pedagogic discourse to a sociological interpretation of the effects of neo-liberal reform in the field of social and cultural reproduction.

LEESA WHEELAHAN is Associate Professor at the L.H. Martin Institute for Higher Education Leadership and Management at the University of Melbourne, Australia. Her publications include *Why Knowledge Matters in Curriculum: A Social Realist Argument* (2010), Neither Fish nor Fowl: The Contradiction at the Heart of Australian Tertiary Education, *Journal of Access, Policy & Practice*, (2008); Blending Activity Theory and Critical Realism to Theorise the Relationship between the Individual and Society and the Implications for Pedagogy, *Studies in the Education of Adults*, (2007); How Competency-Based Training Locks the Working Class Out of Powerful Knowledge: A Modified Bernsteinian Analysis, *British Journal of Sociology of Education*, (2007); and How Not To Fund Teaching and Learning, *Australian Universities Review*, (2007).

Index

A
Abbott (2001), 124
abstractness
    of Bernstein's concepts, 244–45
    in human semiotic development, 136
abstract theoretical knowledge
    CBT excluding access to, 56–60, 63
    as precondition for democracy, 47–50
    as vertical discourse, 53
academic curriculum, 55
academic disciplines, 53–54
access
    to education, emphasis on, 51–52
    to knowledge, exclusion from, 56–60
accounts, for unanticipated behaviors, 199–200
active realization, 20
activity theory
    research of, 106–7
    social world and, 103–6
adaptive expertise, 256
Alexander (1982), 165–66
Alexander and Smith (1993), 199
Alfonso (2004), 18, 128
Al-Ramahi and Davies (2002), 37–38
ambiguity, pedagogic, 257

The American High School (Conant), 208
Apple, Michael, 245
art, sex education and, 94–95
Atkinson (2001)
    on empirical research using Bernstein, 246
    on sociological concerns, 105
autonomy, relations of, 132–33
Avis (2005), 249

B
Bakhtin, M., 107–8
Bakhtin, on space of authoring, 117
Barber (2002), 249
Bauman, Zygmunt, 130–31, 249
Bernstein-dependent/independent authors, 242–43
'best practices,' 256–57
binary oppositions. *See also* meta-narratives and pedagogic discourse/practice, 203–7
bodily self-regulation, 132–33
body image, 39
Bolton (2005)
    on education for economic productivity, 42
    on evaluative criteria, 171
    on social class, pedagogy and achievement, 128

Bonal and Rambla (2003)
  on global knowledge economy, 250, 253
  on knowledge managing, 255
born gazes, 184–85
Borudieu (1977), 108
Bradley, Karen
  on educational psychology, 8
  on meta-narratives. *See* meta-narratives and pedagogic discourse/practice
  on moral career of intelligence. *See* moral career of intelligence
  professional background of, 267
Bransford (2005)
  on adaptive expertise, 256
  on routine expertise, 256–57
Braverman (1974), 125
Breier (2004), 42
British educational system
  collaborative professionalism and, 259–61
  policy processes in, 38–39
British Journal of Sociology of Education, 241–43
Brown v. Board of Education, 207–8

C

canons
  cultivated gaze and, 186–89
  overview, 185–86
  social gaze and, 190–92
Castells (2000), 250
Cazden (1986), 66
CBT (competency-based training)
  access to knowledge as grounds for democracy, 48–50
  Bernsteinian framework for, 52–55, 60–61
  exclusion of access to knowledge, 56–60
  introduction, 47–48
  social stratification of education, 50–52
Centre for Contemporary Cultural Studies (CCCS), 189
citizenship, individual differences and, 204–7
classification
  of academic disciplines, 53–55
  changing patterns of, with MPT, 111–14
  defined, 109
  Dowling's theory of, 69
  hybridity and, 114–16

  in middle class context, 78
  in structuring pedagogy, 68–69
  theoretical framework of, 219
  in working class context, 72–74
classroom-based research
  explicit evaluation and, 170–71
  in Norwegian demonstration schools. *See* Norwegian demonstration schools
  in South Africa. *See* social class, and pedagogy
classroom organization, 74, 75
Clegg (1990), 220
closed questionnaires, 13, 14
The Closing of the American Mind (Bloom), 177
code(s)
  modalities. *See also* knower structures, 181
  pedagogic, 21–23
  relativist, 181
  school, 67
coding scheme
  classification and framing, 72–74, 78
  instructional form, 74, 75, 78
  instructional strategies, 74–76, 78–79
  transmission of meaning and, 67
collaborative intentionality, 116
collaborative professionalism, 259–61
collection codes
  features of, 219–20
  visible pedagogy and, 251–53
common-sense discourse, 86–89
common sense fields, 122–26
competence
  craft, 128–30
  pedagogy, 40–41
competency-based training. *See* CBT (competency-based training)
conceptual accounts category, 2, 5–9
conflicts
  between teachers, 232–33
  between visible and invisible pedagogies, 235–36
Considine, Marginson, Sheehan and Kummick (2001), 250
Constas (1998), 14–15
control
  educational policy and, 35–37, 42–43

INDEX | 275

framing and, 68–69
of pedagogic device, 149–51
regulative discourse and. *See* regulative discourse
relationship to power, 110
cooperation
in Norwegian demonstration schools, 227
phase, in transformation of labour process, 130
core subjects, 38–39
crafts
ambiguous positioning of, 122–26
regulative discourse in transmission of, 128–30
creativity, correlation to intelligence, 209
Critique of Judgement (Kant), 185
critiques
of canons. *See* gazes, canons and critiques
of PISA surveys, 152–53
cultivated gazes
critiques of canons based on, 186–87
defined, 184–85
progress and growth with, 187–89
Cultural Literacy (Hirsch), 177
cultural worlds, 107–8
culture wars, 177, 186, 188
curriculum codes, pedagogic modes and, 251–53
curriculum texts, 26–28

D

Dahlberg (1992), 235
Daniels, Harry
on empirical study of hybridity, 5, 246
professional background of, 267–68
on subject position and identity. *See* subject position and identity, in changing workplace
data analysis, of demonstration schools, 222–23
data collection, 13, 14
data modeling, 152–54
Davies, Brian
on educational policy and social reproduction. *See* educational policy and social reproduction
empirical testing of Bernstein's theories, 3, 240

professional background of, 268
on restricted codes, 138
Davis (2004, 2005)
on evaluative rule, 164
on South African pedagogic discourse, 40–41
democracy, 48–50
demonstration schools. *See* Norwegian demonstration schools
descriptors
in analysis of curriculum texts, 27–28
in analysis of teachers' performance, 25
for pedagogic practice analysis, 23
device
pedagogic, 149–50
translation, 2, 4–5
differentiated tasks, 74, 75, 78
difficulty, of Bernsteinian language, 244
disciple, of Bernstein's work, 241–42
disciplinary knowledge, 56–60
discretionary space, 198–99
discursive hybridity
formation of, 114–16
professional expertise and, 107
social position and, 111
distributive rules
of pedagogic device, 149–50
regulative discourse at level of, 165–68
Division of Labour (Durkheim), 165
domains and strategies, in pedagogic practice, 69
dominant pedagogic modes. *See* pedagogic modes, and teacher professional identity
Dowling (1998)
on difficulties of applying Bernstein, 246
on domains and strategies, 69
on modalities of relationship to Bernstein, 241–42
on recontextualization, 169
Durkheim (2002)
on common-sense discourses, 88
on regulative discourse as sacred order, 165–68
relation between instructional/moral orders in pedagogy, 126–28

E

Earl and Timperley (2008), 260–61
economic productivity
   competency-based training and. *See* CBT (competency-based training)
   pedagogic discourse and, 40–42
educational assessment, typology of, 152–56
educational change
   entrepreneurs, 231
   excellent teachers, 229–30
   facilitators, 228–29
   informal leaders, 231–32
   positional heads, 230–31
educational policy and social reproduction
   anatomising pedagogic discourse, 40–42
   Bernsteinian framework for, 33–34
   for control of pedagogic discourse, 35–36
   policy conception/implementation, 34–35
   recent research, 37–39
   social class control, 36–37
   summary, 42–43
Educational Policy and Social Reproduction (Fitz, Davies and Evans), 33
educational psychology. *See also* meta-narratives and pedagogic discourse/practice
   introduction, 197–98
   moral career of intelligence and invisible pedagogy, 211–14
   periodization of intelligence, 200–201
   structure/dynamics of pedagogic discourse, 198–200
educational research
   classroom-based. *See* social class, and pedagogy
   on educational policy making, 37–39
   in framework of research methodologies, 13–15
   knowledge production and, 15–17
   limitations exposed through, 106–7
   models and instruments in. *See* models and instruments in research
   quantitative and qualitative inquiry for, 12–13
elaborated and restricted orientation, of pedagogic code, 21–23
The Elementary Forms (Durkheim), 165, 168

Eliot, T.S., 188
elite code, 181
empirical research, Bernstein and
   difficulties of applying Bernstein, 244–46
   overview, 239–40
   summary, 246–47
   using Bernstein in empirical research, 241–44
employability skills, VET and, 56–60
Engeström (1999)
   on hybridity, 114
   on social transformation, 104–5, 106
   on stabilization knowledge, 116
English, sex education and, 93–94
enhancement, pedagogic right to, 49–50
Ensor (2004), 41, 256
entrepreneurs, leading educational change, 231
epistemic relation
   of knowledge, 17
   to knowledge structures, 181
epistemological positioning of research
   framework of research methodologies, 13–15
   quantitative and qualitative paradigms, 12–13
   research and knowledge production, 15–17
   validity and reliability criteria, 17–18
equal opportunity, 207–9
esoteric domain principles, 79–80
ESSA Group (Sociological Studies of the Classroom). *See also* methodological approaches, specific, 11
evaluation criteria
   in analysis of teachers' performance, 24–25
   centrality of, 170–71
   with collection code schools, 219
   with integration code schools, 220
   in middle class context, 78
   in modalities of pedagogic practice, 21–23
   in Norwegian demonstration schools, 227–28
   in working class context, 73–74
evaluative rules
   condensing pedagogic devices, 170–72
   of pedagogic device, 149–50
Evans, John
   on educational policy and social reproduc-

tion. *See* educational policy and social reproduction
empirical testing of Bernstein's theories, 3
professional background of, 268
The Evolution of Educational Thought (Durkheim), 165, 167
excellent teachers, educational change and, 229–30
expertise
   adaptive, 256
   routine, 256–57
exploiter, of Bernstein's work, 241–42
expressive order, 162–63

F
facilitators, educational change and, 228–29
fields
   gazes and knower-grammars, 183–85
   as knowledge-knower structures, 180–83
   of pedagogic device, 28
fieldwork, 221
figured worlds, 107–8, 117
Findlow (2006), 243
Finnish schools, visible pedagogy in, 236
Fitz, John
   on educational policy and social reproduction. *See* educational policy and social reproduction
   empirical testing of Bernstein's theories, 3, 240
   professional background of, 268
flexible school hours, 220, 225
Flyvbjerg (2001)
   epistemological considerations of knowledge, 17
   on quantitative and qualitative approaches, 12
framing
   changing patterns of, with MPT, 111–14
   defined, 54, 109
   evaluation as strong, 171
   hybridity and, 114–16
   in middle class context, 78
   as pedagogic discourse, 164, 168
   strong vs. weak, 55
   in structuring pedagogy, 68–69
   theoretical framework of, 219
   in working class context, 72–74

G
Gamble, Jeanne
   on apprenticeship models, 247
   case study on craft pedagogy, 128–30
   on evaluative criteria, 171
   model of general/particular forms of knowledge, 123–25
   on moral order of pedagogy, 5
   professional background of, 268–69
   on transmission of moral order. *See* moral order, as mediator of tacit knowledge
gazes, canons and critiques
   cultivated gazes for critiques of canons, 186–89
   overview, 185–86
   social gazes for critiques of canons, 189–92
gazes, knower-grammars and, 183–85
generalization, 136
generic performance pedagogic mode, 254–55
gifted students, 202, 206, 210, 212–13
globalisation, 151–52
global knowledge society
   pedagogy and, 250–51
   quality teaching for, 254
Goldstein (2004), 152–54
The Great Books (Denby), 177
Grosz (1995), 86

H
habituses
   for analysing leadership, 230–31
   description of, 108
   expansion through cultivated gaze, 187–88
   horizontal knowledge structures and, 183
Hakkarainen (2004), 107
Halliday, Michael
   on human semiotic development, 135–37, 138
   on socialising contexts, 163
Hall, Stuart, 186, 189
Harris, Jessica, 243
   on dominant pedagogic modes. *See* pedagogic modes, and teacher professional identity
   professional background of, 268

on teacher identity, 4, 9
Hasan, Ruqaiya
    on semiotic mediation, 135–37
    on social position, 108, 111
    on theory of language use, 105
Hattam (2004), 249
Hawthorne experiments, 209
Hegel (1995), 124
Helland (2007), 243
heretics, Bernstein's work and, 241–42
hierarchical knower structures
    cultivated gaze and, 187–89
    legitimation codes and, 180–82
hierarchical knowledge structures
    description of, 187
    science vs. humanities and, 178, 180–83
    in vertical discourses, 90–91
hierarchy, rules of, 131–32
high socio-economic class, 52
Hoadley (2005, 2007), 128, 171
Hoadley, Ursula
    on differential access, 3–4
    on pedagogy and moral order. *See* pedagogy, and moral order
    professional background of, 270
    on regulative discourse, 6–7, 128
    on social class. *See* social class, and pedagogy
    on teacher effectiveness, 41
Hoggart, Richard, 186–87
Holland (1998), 107–8, 109, 117
homogenous classroom organization, 74, 75
Hopkins (2007), 256
horizontal discourse
    craft's position in, 122–26
    mundane knowledge as, 53
    personal, social and health education as, 96–97
    in sex education, 89–91
    TIMSS and PISA positioning in, 147–49
horizontal knower structures
    legitimation codes and, 180–83
    social gaze and, 190–92
horizontal knowledge structures
    science vs. humanities and, 180–83
    in vertical discourses, 90–91
horizontal modality, 80–81

horizontal models of international testing regimes. *See* vertical/horizontal models of international testing regimes
humanities, progress and knowledge building in
    introduction, 177–78
    knower structures. *See* knower structures
    summary, 192–94
human semiotic development model, 136–37
hybridity
    formation of, 114–16
    professional expertise and, 107
    social position and, 111

I

identity
    approaches to theory of, 107–8
    in changing workplaces. *See* subject position and identity, in changing workplace
    teacher professional. *See* teacher professional identity
inclusion, pedagogic right to, 50
indicators
    in analysis of curriculum texts, 26–28
    in analysis of pedagogic practice, 23
    in analysis of teachers' performance, 25
individually differentiated learning, 226–27
'individual' time period (intelligence)
    conceptualisation of intelligence and, 201
    individual differences, 204–7
    meta-narratives and, 203
    moral correlates of, 212
industry/labour
    development by time period, 203
    'person' time period developments, 209
    'self' time period developments, 211
    similarities to educational psychology, 198–99
informal leaders, for educational change, 231–32
informed prescription, 256
inquiry
    mixed methodology for, 14–15
    neo-Marxist, 14–15
    post-positivist, 15
    quantitative and qualitative, 12–13
in-service teacher education, 23–25
instructional context, of socialising, 163

instructional discourse
  in craft pedagogy, 128–30
  genealogy of, 162–65
  moral order and, 171–72
  regulative discourse in, 166–67
  in school context, 21–22
  in working class context, 73–74
instructional form theory
  in middle class context, 78
  in pedagogic practice, 70
  in working class context, 74, 75
instrumental order, 162–63
instruments of analysis
  of curriculum texts, 26–28
  of pedagogic practice, 21–23
  of teachers' performance, 23–25
integrated classroom organization, 74, 75
integrated codes
  features of, 219–20
  invisible pedagogy and, 251–53
integration of subjects, 225
intelligence
  conceptualisation of, 201
  moral attributes of. *See* moral career of intelligence
intentionality, collaborative, 116
international education research, 259–61
International Project to Frame the Transformation of Schools (IPFTS), 259–61
international testing regimes, vertical/horizontal models
  evaluation, globalisation and 're-centred state,' 149–52
  first positionings of TIMSS and PISA, 147–49
  introduction, 143–44
  results/reactions to international testing regimes, 145–47
  socio-semiotics of performativity, 152–56
  summary, 156–57
interviews
  in analysis of teachers' performance, 24–25
  for data collection, 13, 14
  for Norwegian demonstration schools, 221–22
investments, pedagogic, 257–59

invisible pedagogy
  evaluation of learning in, 227–28
  features of, 219–20
  indirect control in, 235
  individually differentiated learning and, 226–27
  integrated codes and, 251–53
  moral career of intelligence and, 211–13
invisible semiotic mediation, of tacit knowledge. *See* mediator of tacit knowledge, moral order as
IPFTS. *See* International Project to Frame the Transformation of Schools (IPFTS)
IQ scoring, 205, 211
Ivinson, Gabrielle
  on application of Bernstein's theories, 4
  on pedagogy and sex education. *See* pedagogic discourse, and sex education
  professional background of, 269

J

James (2005), 38
Johnson, Richard, 190–91

K

Kallos and Lundgren (1979), 251, 253
Kehily (2002), 99
Kirk (1999), 96
knower-code fields, 182–83
knower-grammars, 183–85
knower structures
  fields as knowledge-knower structures, 180–83
  gazes and knower-grammars, 183–85
  gazes, canons and critiques. *See* gazes, canons and critiques
  overview, 179–80
knowledge
  acquisition of, 170
  research and production of, 15–17
knowledge-code fields, 181–82
knowledge-knower structures, 180–83
Koehler (1978), 66
Kvale (1997), 137

L

La Psychoanalyse son image et son publique

(Moscovici), 87
leadership, in demonstration schools. *See* school development/leadership
leading educational change
 entrepreneurs, 231
 excellent teachers, 229–30
 facilitators, 228–29
 informal leaders, 231–32
 positional heads, 230–31
learner-centred pedagogy, 41–42
learning for and in interagency working (LIW) project
 empirical work with MPT, 111–14
 research and limitations of, 106–8
legitimation codes, 180–83
Legitimation Code Theory (LCT), 180–81
Leont'ev (1978)
 on human activity, 106
 on reproduced figured worlds, 107–8
Lingard and Mills (2002), 249
Lives of the English Poets (Johnson), 188
LIW. *See* learning for and in interagency working (LIW) project
localizing strategies, 74–76
low socio-economic class
 classified and framed knowledge for, 55
 school achievement and, 52
Lubienski (2004), 171
Lusted (1986), 251
Lvy-Bruhl (1925/1926), 87
Lyotard (1984), 151, 152

M

machinofacture, 130
manufacture phase, of labour process, 130
Martin (2007), 122–26, 135, 137
Marx (1867/1976)
 on transformation of labour process, 130
 on unity of head and hand, 125
master-apprentice pedagogy
 case study, 128–30
 relations of autonomy in, 132–33
 rules of hierarchy, 131–32
The Material Word (Silverman and Torode), 110
mathematics, 40–42
Maton, Karl
 on knowledge-building in humanities. *See* humanities, progress and knowledge building in
 professional background of, 269
 on significance of knowledge structures, 7, 17, 246–47
Mauss (1950), 88
McCarthy and Dimitriadis (2000), 243, 249
mediation, semiotic
 Bernstein's concept of, 108–11
 of tacit knowledge. *See* mediator of tacit knowledge, moral order as
 Vygotsky's concept of, 103–6
mediator of tacit knowledge, moral order as
 ambiguous positioning of craft, 122–26
 introduction, 121–22
 regulative discourse in craft transmission, 128–30
 regulative order as mediator of semiotic meaning, 135–37
 relation between instructional/moral orders in pedagogy, 126–28
 summary, 137–38
 work ethic as regulative discourse, 130–34
meta-narratives and pedagogic discourse/practice
 individual differences (period I), 204–7
 overview, 201–4
 personality and equal opportunity (period II), 207–9
 self and common good (period III), 209–11
metaphor, in human semiotic development, 136
methodological approaches, specific
 to epistemological positioning of research. *See* epistemological positioning of research
 introduction, 11–12
 models and instruments. *See* models and instruments in research
 summary of, 28–30
methodological dimension, of inquiry, 14
methodological orientation, to research, 13–14
methodological procedures, 19–21
Metz (1986), 227
middle class context
 analyzing classroom data, 76–79
 classified and framed knowledge for, 55

influencing educational policy, 36–37
rules for combination and, 79–80
vertical modality and, 81–82
Miettinen (1999), 106
Mills (1940), 199
mixed methodology
introduction to, 11
specific approaches of. *See* methodological approaches, specific
toolkit category of, 2
two forms of inquiry for, 14–15
modalities, pedagogic
horizontal, 80–81
of problem-centred approach, 40–41
vertical, 81–82
models and instruments in research
analysis of curriculum texts, 26–28
analysis of teachers' performance, 23–25
of modality of pedagogic practice, 21–23
overview, 18–19
theoretical assumptions/methodological procedures, 19–21
Moore and Maton (2001), 17
Moore and Muller (2002), 124, 148
Morais, Ana M.
anatomising pedagogic discourse, 40, 41
on classroom communication relations, 128
empirical testing of Bernstein's theories, 243
on pedagogic practice for success, 66, 121
professional background of, 270
on research methodology, 2, 13, 15, 18
on specific methodological approaches. *See* methodological approaches, specific
moral career of intelligence. *See also* meta-narratives and pedagogic discourse/practice
introduction, 197–98
moral career of intelligence and invisible pedagogy, 211–13
periodization of intelligence, 200–201
structure/dynamics of pedagogic discourse, 198–200
summary, 213–14
moral correlates, attributed to intelligence, 206
Moral Education (Durkheim), 165, 166, 167
moral order, and pedagogy
empirical studies, 170–72

evaluative rules, 170
genealogy of regulative/instructional discourses, 162–65
overview, 161–62
regulative discourse at level of distributive rules, 165–68
regulative discourse at level of recontextualizing rules, 168–69
relation to subject discipline, 126–28
summary, 172–73
moral order, as mediator of tacit knowledge
ambiguous positioning of craft, 122–26
introduction, 121–22
regulative discourse in craft transmission, 128–30
regulative order as mediator of semiotic meaning, 135–37
relation between instructional/moral orders in pedagogy, 126–28
summary, 137–38
work ethic as regulative discourse, 130–34
moral self-regulation, 132–33
Moscovici (2001), 85, 87–89
motivation
in demonstration schools, 220, 225, 226
in person time period, 208–9
in self time period, 210
test results as, 207
Muller, Johan
on classification and framing, 54, 55
on new middle class, 37
on pedagogy and moral order. *See* pedagogy, and moral order
professional background of, 270
on regulative discourse, 6–7
on teacher effectiveness, 41
on verticality of knowledge, 178
multiprofessional team (MPT), 111–14
mundane knowledge
CBT promotion of, 56–60
as horizontal discourse, 53
theoretical knowledge vs., 48–50
Munns and MacFadden (2000), 243
myths, sex education and, 86–87

N

naturalistic approaches, 13, 14

neo-Marxist inquiry, 14–15
Neves, Isabel P.
  anatomising pedagogic discourse, 40
  on classroom communication relations, 128
  empirical testing of Bernstein's theories, 243
  on pedagogic practice for success, 66, 121
  professional background of, 270
  on research methodology, 2, 13, 18
  on specific methodological approaches. *See* methodological approaches, specific
Nordahl (2008), 236
Norwegian demonstration schools
  conflicts between teachers, 232–33
  cooperation among teachers and students, 227
  evaluation of learning, 227–28
  individually differentiated learning, 226–27
  introduction, 217–18
  leading educational change, 228–32
  methods, 221–23
  organisation of schooling, 224–25
  school similarities, 223–24
  summary, 233–36
  theoretical framework, 218–20

O

observations
  for data collection, 13, 14
  of demonstration schools, 222
Ogden (2008), 236
On the Classification and Framing of Educational Knowledge (Bernstein), 126–28
orientation to meaning, 67
original nature, 201, 204–7, 210–11

P

Palestinian educational system, 37–38
paradigms, research. *See also* research, educational, 12–13
Parsons, 162
participation, pedagogic right to, 50
passive realization, 20
Pawson and Tilley (1997), 153–54
pedagogic ambiguity, 257
pedagogic assemblies, 79–80
pedagogic autonomy, 255–57
pedagogic code, 21–23

pedagogic device, 149–50
pedagogic discourse
  socio-semiotic typology of, 152–56
  structure and dynamics of, 198–200
pedagogic discourse, and sex education
  art and, 94–95
  common-sense vs. scientific knowledge, 87–89
  English and, 93–94
  introduction, 85–86
  personal, social and health education and, 96–97
  physical education and, 95–96
  science and, 92–93
  science and myths, 86–87
  scientific discourses and, 91, 97
  summary, 98–100
  tipping points and slippage, 98
  vertical and horizontal discourses, 89–91
pedagogic discourse, as relay for power
  access to knowledge as grounds for democracy, 48–50
  Bernsteinian framework for, 52–55
  exclusion of access to knowledge, 56–60
  introduction to, 47–48
  social stratification of education, 50–52
  summary, 60–61
pedagogic investments, 257–59
pedagogic modalities
  horizontal, 80–81
  of problem-centred approach, 40–41
  vertical, 81–82
pedagogic modes, and teacher professional identity
  collaborative professionalism, 259–61
  curriculum codes, 251–53
  curriculum codes and pedagogic modes, 251–53
  global knowledge society, performativity and uncertainty, 250–51
  introduction, 249
  pedagogic ambiguity, 257
  pedagogic autonomy, 255–57
  pedagogic investments, 257–59
  pedagogic modes, struggles for contestation/dominance, 254–55

summary, 261–62
totally pedagogised society, 253–54
pedagogic outcome, 128–30
pedagogic practice
    analysis of, 19–23
    control of, 35–36
    educational psychology and. *See* moral career of intelligence
pedagogic recontextualising field (PRF), 28, 38, 254
pedagogic rights, 49–50
pedagogised society, 253–54
pedagogy
    invisible. *See* invisible pedagogy
    relation between instructional/moral orders in, 126–28
    visible. *See* visible pedagogy
pedagogy, and moral order
    empirical studies, 170–72
    evaluative rules, 170
    genealogy of regulative/instructional discourses, 162–65
    overview, 161–62
    regulative discourse at level of distributive rules, 165–68
    regulative discourse at level of recontextualizing rules, 168–69
    summary, 172–73
pedagogy, and social class
    analyzing data; middle class context, 76–79
    analyzing data; working class context, 71–76
    classification and framing, 68–69
    domains and strategies, 69
    instructional form, 70
    introduction, 65–66
    methodology, 71
    pedagogic assemblies, 79–80
    pedagogic modalities, 80–82
    summary, 82–83
    theoretical approach, 66–67
Pedagogy, Symbolic Control and Identity (Bernstein), 33
Pedro (1981), 70, 163
performance
    craft, 128–30
    of subjects, 19–21, 23–25

performativity
    international testing regimes and, 150–51
    linking knowledge production, 250
    socio-semiotics of, 152–56
periodization, 200–201
peripheral subjects, 38–39
personal, social and health education (PSHE), 96–97
'person' time period (personality)
    conceptualisation of intelligence and, 201
    equal opportunity and, 207–9
    meta-narratives and, 203
    moral correlates of, 212
physical education, 95–96
Pirkkalainen (2005)
    on division of labour, 106
    on hybridization of expertise, 107
PISA (Program for International Student Assessment)
    first positionings of, 147–49
    results and reactions to, 145–47
    socio-semiotic typology of assessment and, 152–56
political dimension
    of educational policy making, 35–36
    of inquiry, 14
positional heads, educational change and, 230–31
possibility knowledge vs. stabilization knowledge, 116
post-positivist inquiry, 15
power
    classification and, 68–69
    in classifying and framing knowledge, 59–60
    in modalities of pedagogic practice, 21–23
    pedagogic discourse as relay for. *See* pedagogic discourse, as relay for power
    relationship to control, 110–11
Power, Sally
    on Bernstein and empirical research. *See* empirical research, Bernstein and
    on empirical relevance, 8–9
    professional background of, 270–71
practices, instructional and regulative, 21–22
PRF (pedagogic recontextualising field), 28, 38, 254

principles of scientific management, 205
Pring (1975), 245
problem-centred approach, 40–41
process, research, 17
product, research, 16
professional development
    collaborative approach to, 259–61
    for teachers, 257–59
professional identity. *See also* teacher professional identity, 111–14
professional learning conversations, 260–61
Program for International Student Assessment. *See* PISA (Program for International Student Assessment)
progress. *See also* knower structures
    with cultivated gazes, 187–89
    and knowledge building in humanities, 177–78, 192–94
    with social gazes, 190–92
PSHE (personal, social and health education), 96–97
public domain principles, 79–80
punishment, 166–67
Pye (1978), 124–25

Q

qualitative approaches, 12–13, 17–18
quantitative approaches, 12–13

R

rationalistic approaches, 13, 14
Ratner (1997), 104
A Reader in Cultural Studies, shared library, 189
realization rules
    in analysis of teachers' performance, 23–25
    for instruments of analysis, 20
    modality of pedagogic practice and, 109
're-centred' state, 150
recognition rules
    in analysis of teachers' performance, 25
    developing of, 55
    for instruments of analysis, 20
    modality of pedagogic practice and, 109
recontextualization
    defined, 54
    of pedagogic discourse, 28
recontextualizing rules

evaluation criteria at the level of, 171
    of pedagogic device, 149–50
    regulative discourse at level of, 168–69
Reeves (2005), 41–42, 128, 171
regulation rules, 23–25
regulative context, of socialising, 163
regulative discourse
    in craft pedagogy, 128–30
    as dominant, 168–69
    genealogy of, 162–65
    instructional discourse in, 127
    as sacred order, 165–68
    in school context, 21–22
    sex education and, 99
    as work ethic, 130–34
    in working class context, 73–74
regulative order, 135–37
relations of autonomy, 132–33
relations of subordination, 133–34
relativist code, 181
relay
    in different social class school settings, 82–83
    features of, 68
reliability criteria, 17–18
representational dimension, of inquiry, 14
research, educational
    classroom-based. *See* social class, and pedagogy
    on educational policy making, 37–39
    exposing limitations, 106–7
    knowledge production and, 15–17
    models and instruments for. *See* models and instruments in research
    quantitative and qualitative inquiry for, 12–13
research methodologies, 13–15
Richardson, John G.
    on educational psychology, 8
    on meta-narratives. *See* meta-narratives and pedagogic discourse/practice
    on moral career of intelligence. *See* moral career of intelligence
    professional background of, 271
Riksaasen, Rita
    on changes in pedagogic practice, 8
    on Norwegian demonstration schools. *See*

Norwegian demonstration schools
professional background of, 271
routine expertise, 256–57
rules
for combination, 79–80
evaluative, 149–50, 170–72
of hierarchy, 131–32
realization. *See* realization rules
recognition. *See* recognition rules
recontextualization. *See* recontextualizing rules
regulation, 23–25
Rules (Durkheim), 165
Rustique-Forrester (2005), 236

S

Sachs (2000), 249
Sadovnik, Alan R.
introduction to essays, 1–9
on invisible pedagogy, 252
professional background of, 271
school code, 67
school development/leadership
demonstration schools. *See* Norwegian demonstration schools
introduction, 217–18
methods, 221–23
summary, 233–36
theoretical framework, 218–20
schooling, organisation of, 224–25
school mathematics, 40–42
science, sex education and, 92–93
scientific discourse, 86–89, 97
scientific management principles, 205
Scott and Lyman (1968), 199
selection of schools, 221
'self' time period
common good and, 209–11
conceptualisation of intelligence and, 201
meta-narratives and, 203
moral correlates of, 212
Semel, Susan F.
introduction to essays, 1–9
on invisible pedagogy, 252
professional background of, 271–72
semiotic mediation
Bernstein's concept of, 108–11

of tacit knowledge. *See* mediator of tacit knowledge, moral order as visible, 135
Vygotsky's concept of, 103–6
sermonizing discourse
features of, 200
in 'individual' time period, 205–6
sex education, and pedagogic discourse
art and, 94–95
common-sense vs. scientific knowledge, 87–89
English and, 93–94
introduction, 85–86
personal, social and health education and, 96–97
physical education and, 95–96
science and, 92–93
science and myths, 86–87
scientific discourses and, 91, 97
summary, 98–100
tipping points and slippage, 98
vertical and horizontal discourses, 89–91
SFL (systemic-functional linguistics), 122–26
Shaffer and Serlin (2004), 12
Shamai (2000), 243
Silverman and Torode (1980), 110
Singh, Parlo
on access to knowledge, 51
on dominant pedagogic modes. *See* pedagogic modes, and teacher professional identity
on empirical research, 243
introduction to essays, 1–9
professional background of, 272
on scientific discourse, 98
on teacher identity, 4, 9
on tipping points and slippage, 98
Skocpol, Theda, 36
Smith and Green (2004), 243
Smithers (2004), 146
social class, and pedagogy
analyzing data; middle class context, 76–79
analyzing data-working class context, 71–76
classification and framing, 68–69
domains and strategies, 69
instructional form, 70
introduction, 65–66

methodology, 71
pedagogic assemblies, 79–80
pedagogic modalities, 80–82
summary, 82–83
theoretical approach, 66–67
social control
  educational policy and, 35–37, 42–43
  framing and, 68–69
  relationship to power, 110
social fields. *See* fields
social gazes
  critiques of canons based on, 189–90
  defined, 184–85
  progress and growth with, 190–92
social position, 108–11
social realist model, 152–56
social relation
  of knowledge, 17
  to knowledge structures, 181
social reproduction, and educational policy
  anatomising pedagogic discourse, 40–42
  Bernsteinian framework for, 33–34
  for control of pedagogic discourse, 35–36
  policy conception/implementation, 34–35
  recent research, 37–39
  social class control, 36–37
  summary, 42–43
social stratification
  competency-based training and. *See* CBT (competency-based training)
  of education, 41–42, 50–52
  pedagogy and. *See* social class, and pedagogy
  VET qualifications and, 60–61
social world, 103–6
sociological dimension, knowledge construction, 16–17
sociology of knowledge, 143–44
socio-semiotics, 152–56
Sohn-Rethel (1978), 124
Somers (1995), 199
sorting, of students, 206–7
South African educational system
  classroom-based research. *See* social class, and pedagogy
  pedagogic discourse, 40–41
space of authoring, 108, 117

specialisation, legitimation codes of, 181
specialized classroom organization, 74, 75, 78
specializing strategies
  middle class context, 78
  working class context, 74–76
specific coding orientation, 23–25
specific methodological approaches. *See* methodological approaches, specific
stabilization knowledge vs. possibility knowledge, 116
strategies, instructional
  pedagogic practice, 69
  working class context, 74–76
subjectivist relativism, 192–94
subject position and identity, in changing workplace
  Basil Bernstein and, 108–11
  empirical work with MPT, 111–14
  hybridity, 111–14
  identity and agency in cultural worlds, 107–8
  limitations exposed through research, 106–7
  overview, 103
  summary, 116–17
  Vygotsky, activity theory, and social world, 103–6
subordination, relations of, 133–34
Swain (2003), 243
systemic-functional linguistics (SFL), 122–26

T

tacit horizontal knowledge structures, 122–26
tacit knowledge. *See* moral order, as mediator of tacit knowledge
Tashakkori and Teddlie (1998), 12
Taylor, Frederick, 205
teacher performance
  instruments of analysis of, 23–25
  in working class context, 72–74
teacher professional identity
  collaborative professionalism, 259–61
  curriculum codes and pedagogic modes, 251–53
  global knowledge society, performativity and uncertainty, 250–51
  introduction, 249
  pedagogic ambiguity, 257
  pedagogic autonomy, 255–57

pedagogic investments, 257–59
pedagogic modes, struggles for contestation/dominance, 254–55
summary, 261–62
totally pedagogised society, 253–54
teamwork, 224
testing regimes. *See* vertical/horizontal models of international testing regimes
test results, as motivating factors, 207
theoretical assumptions, 19–21
theoretical knowledge
   CBT excluding access to, 56–60, 63
   as precondition for democracy, 47–50
   as vertical discourse, 53
Thomas and Davies (2006), 38
Thompson, E.P, 186
Thorndike, E.L., 205
TIMSS (Trends in International Mathematics and Science Study)
   first positionings of, 147–49
   results and reactions to, 145–47
   socio-semiotic typology of assessment, 152–56
tipping points, sex education and, 98
toolkit category, 2–4
Totally Pedagogised Society (Bernstein), 150
trained gazes, 184–85
Training Package Development Handbook, 56–57
translation(s)
   device category, 2, 4–5
   pedagogic, 257–59
transmission of moral order. *See* moral order, as mediator of tacit knowledge
Trends in International Mathematics and Science Study. *See* TIMSS (Trends in International Mathematics and Science Study)
Tyler, William
   conceptual accounts of testing, 6, 8, 253
   on international testing regimes. *See* vertical/horizontal models of international testing regimes
   professional background of, 272
   on schools as bureaucracy, 220
   on self-validating empirical research, 245
typology, of educational assessment, 152–56

U

Uluorta and Quill (2009), 250
uncommon sense fields, 122–26
uniform tasks, 74, 75
units of competency, 56–60, 63
Urry (2003), 249

V

validity criteria, 17–18
vertical discourse
   art as, 94–95
   craft's position in, 122–26
   English as, 93–94
   physical education as, 95–96
   in sex education, 89–91
   theoretical knowledge as, 53
   TIMSS and PISA positioning in, 147–49
vertical/horizontal models of international testing regimes
   evaluation, globalisation and 're-centred state,' 149–52
   first positionings of TIMSS and PISA, 147–49
   introduction, 143–44
   results/reactions to international testing regimes, 145–47
   socio-semiotics of performativity, 152–56
   summary, 156–57
vertical modality, 81–82
VET (vocational education and training)
   economic productivity and, 47
   exclusion of access to knowledge, 56–60, 63
   social stratification and, 51–52
visible pedagogy
   collection codes and, 251–53
   conflict with invisible pedagogy, 235–36
   features of, 219–20
   in Finnish schools, 236
visible semiotic mediation, 135
vocabulary of motives, 199–200
vocational curriculum, 55
voice
   Bernstein's concept of, 55, 110
   of power, 59
   of society, 87–88
   specialization of, 67, 70, 76, 80, 82–83

vulgariser, of Bernstein's work, 241–42
Vygotsky's socio-genetic theory, 103–6

W

Welsh educational system, 38
Wertsch (1991), 105
The Western Canon (Bloom), 177
What Good are the Arts? (Carey), 177
Wheelahan, Leesa
  on competency-based training. *See* CBT (competency-based training)
  on pedagogic models of training packages, 3
  professional background of, 272
Whitty (2006), 249
Whitty, Rowe and Aggleton (1994), 252
Williams, Raymond, 186–87
Witten (1993), 200
work ethic, as regulative discourse
  intertwining of normative relations, 134
  overview, 130–31
  relations of autonomy, 132–33
  relations of subordination, 133–34
  rules of hierarchy, 131–32
working class context
  analyzing classroom data, 71–76
  classroom-based research, 71–76
  educational policy, 37
  horizontal modality and, 80–81
  rules for combination and, 79–80
workplaces, subject position and identity in
  Basil Bernstein and, 108–11
  empirical work with MPT, 111–14
  hybridity, 114–16
  identity and agency in cultural worlds, 107–8
  limitations exposed through research, 106–7
  overview, 103
  summary, 116–17
  Vygotsky, activity theory, and social world, 103–6

Y

Young (2008), 55

THIS SERIES EXPLORES THE HISTORY OF SCHOOLS AND SCHOOLING in the United States and other countries. Books in this series examine the historical development of schools and educational processes, with special emphasis on issues of educational policy, curriculum and pedagogy, as well as issues relating to race, class, gender, and ethnicity. Special emphasis will be placed on the lessons to be learned from the past for contemporary educational reform and policy. Although the series will publish books related to education in the broadest societal and cultural context, it especially seeks books on the history of specific schools and on the lives of educational leaders and school founders.

For additional information about this series or for the submission of manuscripts, please contact the general editors:

>
> Alan R. Sadovnik Susan F. Semel
> Rutgers University-Newark The City College of New York, CUNY
> Education Dept. 138th Street and Convent Avenue
> 155 Conklin Hall NAC 5/208
> 175 University Avenue New York, NY 10031
> Newark, NJ 07102

To order other books in this series, please contact our Customer Service Department:

> 800-770-LANG (within the U.S.)
> 212-647-7706 (outside the U.S.)
> 212-647-7707 FAX

Or browse online by series at:

> www.peterlang.com